The Insider Audio Bathroom Reader

Paul D. Lehrman

THOMSON

™

COURSE TECHNOLOGY

Professional ■ Technical ■ Reference

ISBN-10: 1-59863-208-6

ISBN-13: 978-1-59863-208-8

Library of Congress Catalog Card Number: 2005938719

Printed in the United States of America

07 08 09 10 11 PH 10 9 8 7 6 5 4 3 2 1

Publisher and General Manager, Thomson Course Technology PTR:
Stacy L. Hiquet

Associate Director of Marketing:
Sarah O'Donnell

Manager of Editorial Services:
Heather Talbot

Marketing Manager:
Mark Hughes

Executive Editor:
Mike Lawson

Marketing Coordinator:
Adena Flitt

Project and Copy Editor:
Marta Justak

PTR Editorial Services Coordinator:
Erin Johnson

Interior Layout Tech:
William Hartman

Cover Designers:
Kathleen Fivel
Mike Tanamachi

Proofreader:
Gene Redding

THOMSON

★

COURSE TECHNOLOGY ™
Professional ■ Technical ■ Reference

Thomson Course Technology PTR, a division of Thomson Learning Inc.
25 Thomson Place ■ Boston, MA 02210 ■ http://www.courseptr.com

Foreword...

Into the Past

Eleven years ago, the editors at *Mix* magazine hired a guy named Paul "D." Lehrman to "mix things up a bit" by writing a provocative monthly column not only about the movers and shakers and the nuts and bolts of the evolving audio industry, but also about the "nuts" and "dolts" who populate the business and the culture that drives it. Well, if you ask me, they hired the right guy.

Besides being a writer, Paul is a musician, a filmmaker, a music-technology freak, a Web guy, and a teacher. Far from being a passive but passionate observer, Lehrman has long been a participant: He designed one of the first MIDI sequencing programs on the Mac, wrote one of the first resynthesis programs for a personal computer, produced and recorded the first all-MIDI record album, was among the first to use samplers to build the sound effects for a major film, and found a way to use modern audio and music technology to revive a notorious 75-year-old composition that could never be played during its composer's lifetime.

He also is cursed with a highly evolved, wicked sense of humor and parody that prove, more than ever, that "Everything You Know Is Wrong." Where else, tell me, can one read about equipment you'll never see, totally bogus college course catalogs, and in-depth interviews with semi-fictional, clueless, white teenage rap producers?

"My columns piss off more readers than anything else the magazine has done in 30 years," Paul likes to brag, even though he swears the editors love it, and he gets a lot of "laudatory" (or is that "louditory"?) feedback as well.

In this collection of the best of his "Insider Audio" columns, you'll also read between the lines about politics, ethics, education, legal issues, history, and the naughty backroom boardroom dealings of rapacious record companies. And as an extra added bonus AT NO ADDITIONAL COST, you'll get a unique collection of industry-related rumors, anecdotes, and hilarious jokes, ABSOLUTELY FREE!

Paul's been writing about pro audio and music longer than just about anyone else in the field and has been hunkered down in the trenches as a forward observer watching the analog world evolve into the digital...and beyooonnnnddddd. I know he was there, because as a member of the notorious four-man satirical comedy troupe, "The Firesign Theatre"—now celebrating our 40th anniversary and still going strong—I was there, too, (I think) and I've had the pleasure of sharing some of my experiences in the wonderful "Land of Ear" hosting several TEC Awards ceremonies, where I first met our author. (You might even find one of my jokes in here, eh, Paul?)

You see, when our group started recording for Columbia (now Sony) Records back in the mid-'60s (yes, we started in the '60s and we're now all in our 60s), we worked in spaces converted from the original radio studios of the '30s and '40s, haunted by the ghosts of performers past like Bob Hope and Jack Benny. We recorded on 16-track tape, and as we developed our multi-tracked, overlaid mix of comedy and drama, sound effects, overdubs, and music, we often had to "ping-pong" one bunch of tracks onto another to make room for more hilarity, while "waiting for the electrician, or someone like him," to help us attain our vision.

As our fame grew along with the amazing "pop"-u-larity of the recording industry, the studios shrunk, as more and more A&R offices cluttered up the territory there on Gower and Sunset, and the tapes grew into imposing hundred-track ribbons on sexy four-inch-high reels. We felt like Alice in Wonderland! We were shrinking!

Eventually, as the original studios were all supplanted by the mighty CBS News organization, we were forced to go offsite—even to movie studios—to record our albums. And then, everything changed forever.

One of our most prolific producers, Fred Jones, walked into our lives with a studio in the palm of his hand: the first digital recorder. We were free, free at last! And we recorded "The Three Faces of Al, A Nick Danger Mystery" on Rhino Records, all throughout the inside and outside of Fred's studios in Hollywood. It was the world's first Comedy CD, and we were nominated for a second Grammy of the three we've received...so far. Firesign even appeared later on the cover of *Mix* when we worked with pioneer Stan Cornyn in developing a prototype for CD-R games.

But enough about us; besides, you'll actually read references to (and in some cases, actual appropriations from) our work and that of Tom Lehrer, Jean Shepherd, and the Marx Brothers in this enlightening tome, as I'm proud to say we helped to inspire (or ruin) Paul's career. And isn't it appropriate that this is a "Bathroom Reader," as so many aspiring musicians honed their talents singing in the shower?

So let me finish here by writing "a foreword in four-words" which I think pretty well sums up the lad in a nutshell, which is where he should be confined: "Lehrman is a genius!"

So, please read this book. You'll learn, you'll laugh, you'll be astonished, you'll be disgusted, you'll get mad, and you'll want to get even. And you'll know a lot more jokes than you used to. Or your money back! Well, not really...

—Phil Proctor, Beverly Hills 90210, September 2006

Acknowledgments

My heartfelt thanks to everyone who helped make this book possible:

- To the intrepid editors at *Mix*—Tom Kenny, Blair Jackson, George Petersen, and "Li'l" Sarah Benzuly—for encouraging me all these years and at the same time making sure I stayed within the bounds of sanity and (usually) taste;

- To the editors of many of the other publications I've written for over the years, who taught me what worked and what didn't: Clif Garboden, Richard Elen, Mel Lambert, Keith Spencer-Allen, Tim Tully, SteveO, Craig Anderton, Tim Pfaff, Paul Ireson, Matt Bell, Mike Fay, Ande Zellman, Martha Baer, and Jon Zilber;

- To Mike Lawson of ArtistPro who started this ball rolling, and to my editor, Marta Justak, and publisher, Stacy Hiquet, at Thomson Course Technology PTR, for picking it up and running like the wind;

- To my students at the University of Massachusetts Lowell and Tufts University for keeping me honest, current, and questioning;

- To all the readers of *Mix*, especially the ones who don't hesitate to tell me when I'm right on or when I'm way off;

- To Phil Proctor, for being who he is and being willing to share some of that with me;

- To my mother, Emily Rosenstein Lehrman, who didn't speak a word of English until the age of 12, and yet taught me more about grammar, sentence structure, and meaning than all of the English teachers I ever had; and to my father, Dr. Nathaniel S. Lehrman, who taught me that right and wrong really do exist, although sometimes even he can be wrong;

- To the greatest practitioners of the art of storytelling I could ever hope to learn from: the late Jean Shepherd and my wife, Sharon Kennedy;

- And to Stephen.

About the Author

Paul D. Lehrman is a composer, educator, filmmaker, music technologist, and writer.

His compositions include interactive computer-based performance works and scores for documentary films. He has performed at Carnegie Hall, Symphony Hall (Boston), Davies Hall (San Francisco), and the Royal Festival Hall (London), along with hundreds of smaller venues, including many dingy clubs and bars. His scores have aired on PBS, A&E, History Channel, and Discovery Networks, and his library music has shown up behind the *Mickey Mouse Club* in Australia. In 1986 he was the creator of the world's first all-MIDI album, *The Celtic Macintosh*. In 1999 he realized and produced the world premiere of the original orchestration of George Antheil's 1926 masterpiece *Ballet mécanique*, and in 2006 programmed and co-designed a robotic orchestra to perform the piece at the National Gallery of Art.

He created the computer-music curriculum at the University of Massachusetts Lowell, where he taught for 12 years, and built the first Digidesign-certified "Pro School" in New England. Since 2000 he has been on the faculty of Tufts University, where he teaches Music for Multimedia and Electronic Musical Instrument Design.

His documentary film, *Bad Boy Made Good*, about the *Ballet mécanique,* which he wrote and produced, has been shown nationally on PBS and won prizes at film festivals in the U.S. and Europe.

He wrote the first audio analysis/resynthesis program for a personal computer, and helped design the first graphic-oriented MIDI sequencer for the Apple Macintosh. He has served as a design and documentation consultant for a number of music and audio software and hardware companies including Yamaha, Roland, Kurzweil, Digidesign, Lexicon, Opcode, Mark of the Unicorn, JBL, and AKG.

He is the author of *Getting into Digital Recording* (Hal Leonard), *MIDI for the Professional* (with Tim Tully, Music Sales Corp.), and *The Andy M. Stewart Songbook* (Music Sales Corp.), and a contributor to several other books. He has written over 600 articles on professional audio, music, broadcasting, food, travel, cars, and assorted other topics for *Studio Sound, Recording Engineer/Producer, Sound on Sound, Wired, Electronic Musician, EQ, Pro Sound News*, the *Boston Globe Magazine, High Fidelity, High Technology, High Times, Piano & Keyboard, Oui, MacUser, Home Entertainment Marketing, Creative Computing*, and the *Boston Phoenix*.

Contents

Introduction   xi

Chapter 1   Truth and Consequences: What We Do Makes a Difference, Whether We Admit It or Not   1

Chapter 2   A Tale of Two Countries   7

Chapter 3   Vintage? You Don't Know Vintage!   13

Chapter 4   Short Cycles: How Fast Can We Make People Buy into New Technology?   19

Chapter 5   Careers from Hell   25

Chapter 6   Revisiting Tom Lehrer   31

Chapter 7   A New York Minute: Grumpmeier Goes to AES   47

Chapter 8   Course Catalog for the Real World   53

Chapter 9   I Had Nothing to Do with Titanic   65

Chapter 10   In Memoriam: Three Pioneers of Electronics and Information   73

Chapter 11   My Favorite Vintages   81

Chapter 12   The Last Word on Upgrades   87

Chapter 13 Recalling a Legendary Playpen   93

Chapter 14 04/01/Y2K   99

Chapter 15 George Martin   105

Chapter 16 Perils of the Free Market   111

Chapter 17 Making the Most of Audio 101   123

Chapter 18 It's a Large and Confusing World, After All   129

Chapter 19 A Couple of Audio Moments   135

Chapter 20 How Do You Get to Carnegie Hall?   143

Chapter 21 Doctor, It Hurts When I Do This   151

Chapter 22 Caught Napstering   161

Chapter 23 Who Will Fix Our Stuff?   169

Chapter 24 Ask Grump   175

Chapter 25 Morons, Oxymorons, and Technology Patents   187

Chapter 26 SMPTE-ed Off   195

Chapter 27 RIP, Douglas Adams   201

Chapter 28 Living on Borrowed Culture   203

Chapter 29 Hardware, Software, Wetware   211

Chapter 30 I Ought to Have My Head Examined   217

Chapter 31 Son of Grumpmeier   223

Chapter 32 The World Above 20kHz   231

Chapter 33 Like a Broken Record   237

Chapter 34 War Stories   243

Chapter 35 Hacking and Hijacking   251

Chapter 36 Posting and Beaming into the Future   257

Chapter 37 The Kids Are Alright   269

Chapter 38 The Shadows of Motown   279

Chapter 39 Audio Products Go Wild!   285

Chapter 40 Bungling in the Jungle   291

Chapter 41 In a Silent Way   297

Chapter 42 Alone Again, Virtually   303

Chapter 43 A Law unto Itself   309

Chapter 44 Out of the Garden   315

Chapter 45 Back to the Future   321

Chapter 46 A Talk with John Chowning   333

Chapter 47 On the Road with Kronos   343

Chapter 48 Do You Hear What I Hear?   351

Chapter 49 Bikes, Harps, and Yo-Yos   357

Chapter 50 More Than Mice   363

Chapter 51 To Preserve and Protect   375

Chapter 52 Marketing to Myself   383

Chapter 53 False Sense of Security   389

Chapter 54 Two Hearts   395

Chapter 55 For the Benefit of Mr. Harrison   401

Chapter 56 A Bradbury Moment   407

Chapter 57 Remembering Stephen St. Croix   413

Introduction

Frank Zappa once said, "Writing about music is like dancing about architecture." But writing about music and audio production is something else again. In a business like ours, which is so fluid, filled with so many interesting gadgets and characters, and so dependent on technology as well as fashion, there's plenty to write about. Which is a good thing for me.

I have to admit that I never expected to be a Writer. Writers were the guys with master's degrees from Midwestern universities who published in tiny journals and had huge double-spaced manuscripts of their novels filling up their desk drawers. I was a Musician, and my expectations for when I grew up and had to find my way in the world were that I would be a rock and roll star, or a record producer, or a musical-theater director, or a nightclub pianist. Writing for money was something I started doing pretty much by accident: I was out of college a couple of years, I had left a straight job (which I hated), and I found myself trying to live on what I could make from gigs and private music lessons. Thanks to a small weekly newspaper in Boston, I discovered that I could make a few extra bucks relatively painlessly, putting together articles about consumer electronics and musical instruments.

All those other things I thought I would do, I did (well, I never was a "star," exactly, but I did play a lot of rock and roll), and some of them I did pretty successfully, and continue to do. But somehow writing has always been the thread that held everything together.

I began to write about professional audio in 1979, when I returned from a brief but highly eventful stint as the chief engineer of a new studio on a Caribbean island, and felt that I somehow had to tell my stories. (The sordid details can be found in Chapter 40 of this book.) I wrote up a couple of them and sent them to *Studio Sound* magazine in the UK, and within a few months, I became a regular contributor to them, and also to *Recording Engineer/Producer* in the U.S. (which was being run by a former *Studio Sound* writer), for whom I eventually became a columnist.

It was a great way to get involved in the music recording and production world. If I wanted to investigate a new technology or a new type of music, I could do an article about it, and people would talk to me. If I wanted to poke around and get to know the players in a high-end recording or post facility, I'd call them up and tell them I wanted to do a profile of them, and they'd not only let me in, they'd be happy to see me. If I wanted to check out some new gear, I could call up the manufacturer and tell them I was going to do a magazine review, and then beat the crap out of it. And when I did a project of my own that I thought was really interesting, or that taught me something exciting or profound, I could report on it.

The learning aspect was always the best part of writing: there always were, and are, new technologies, new mediums, and new musical forms to absorb. And sometimes what I found out while researching an article made a huge impact on my life. Although I had worked with electronic music as far back as the '60s, I disdained keyboard synthesizers and personal computers until an editor assigned me a story about an affordable system for multitimbral synthesis and sequencing built around an Apple II—and from that moment on, I was hooked on computer-music tools.

In 1995, *Mix* approached me and asked if I would take over the "Insider Audio" monthly slot from Ken Pohlmann. Ken, who is one of the great technical explainers of our industry, had been doing a fine job, but the magazine wanted to change course, and have a columnist who could write on a broader range of subjects, with more of a "user-friendly" orientation. I told them I could probably come up with enough topics for maybe a year or so, but that I was afraid after that I might run out of steam. They didn't seem to be worried. Well, here we are 11 years later, and the boiler's still percolating and spitting.

Mix has been a wonderful opportunity for me to learn about all sorts of fascinating things I might otherwise have let pass by, and also to broaden my expressive horizons. Besides tracking the enormous technological changes the audio industry has undergone in the last ten years, I've also been able to observe, and comment on, the changes in the legal and political influences that surround our industry. As the first essay in this book says, media professionals do not exist in a vacuum, and we affect the world as much as it affects us.

We live in very interesting times, as the ancient Chinese curse says, when powerful technological and social forces are, paradoxically, making the production and distribution of creative material both much easier and much harder. A lot of those forces are, by design, hidden or are not what they purport to be. Part of what I try to do is to shed light on them, so that we can all understand what they do and what they mean, for better or worse.

And I've also had the opportunity to learn how to write funny. I've always been told I had a good sense of humor, but to maintain a funny, parodistic tone for 2,000 or so words, without straying too far from the subject, and without sounding dumb or bitter, turns out to be not so easy. *Mix*, and its readers, gave me the chance to figure out how to do that.

I still think, as I have since I was very young, that music is the most transcendent of arts, able to communicate thoughts and emotions, both simple and complex, better than just about any other medium (and for some interesting scientific research into this, take a look at Chapter 54). Today, more than ever, the technology we use enables (or impedes) that transcendence. Frank may have believed that writing about music was not particularly useful, but I believe that learning everything we can about how to create and convey music is pretty damn important.

So why, you may ask, is this a Bathroom Reader? It's not because I expect you to read it in the shower—if so, we would have printed it on waterproof paper—but because I hope you'll read it in small doses, when you're…relaxed. We've put the columns in chronological order, but you can read them in any order you like, as many as you like at a sitting.

Of course, this book doesn't *have* to live in the bathroom. Leave a copy in your control room or studio lounge, to keep your clients out of your hair during those long moments when they have nothing to do. Keep it in the bedroom, so that your significant other might better understand just what it is, exactly, you do for a living. If you're a student, take it to class, to show your instructor how sophisticated you are. Take it with you on the plane to your next session or conference—it's made entirely out of non-liquid matter, so there's little danger it will get confiscated at the gate.

And enjoy it. Please. My fervent hope is that it's nearly as much fun to read as it has been to write.

About the Jokes

In my experience, jokes are not only a way of making fun of the world, or of dealing with the difficulties of living in the world (which is especially true in the Jewish tradition), but also of learning about the world. I loved reading jokes when I was a kid, whether they were the collections by Bennett Cerf I got from my grandfather, the cartoons in the *New Yorker* or (a little later) *Playboy*, or the articles in *Mad* magazine, every issue of which I devoured from cover to cover. If I encountered a joke I didn't understand, which was often, I would try to find out what made it funny—and that education felt as valuable as anything I was learning in school. I managed to remember a great number of them, which gave me a ready audience on the playground, and tended to keep the bullies away (although not entirely), and I seem to have retained just about all of them into adulthood. Today, I am frequently accused of having a joke for every occasion, whether anyone wants to hear it or not.

There are hundreds of jokes about music and musicians. Learning them is a rite of passage for anyone who goes to music school or who gigs, since it brands them as a "member of the club," and also helps them not to take what they're doing too seriously. Sit two veteran musicians down and tell them to trade jokes, and they can (and will, unfortunately) go on for hours. Thus, the majority of the jokes in this book have to do with music.

Jokes about computers are, for obvious reasons, of more recent vintage, but there are plenty of them out there, and some of my favorites are in here. Audio engineering and production jokes, on the other hand, are relatively rare, but I have managed to ferret out a decent number of them and they are here as well. There are, to my knowledge, only two live-sound engineer jokes in existence, and you will find they are both included.

Where do jokes come from? The great science and science-fiction writer Isaac Asimov (whom I was a great fan of at an early age, and who, among his hundreds and hundreds of books, published several collections of jokes) wrote a story about a scientist who tried to find the answer to that question. He couldn't find anyone who actually *created* any jokes, only people who either heard them or just *knew* them. So he asked the question to a giant computer, which responded that the only possible answer was that jokes were actually being planted in our brains by an alien race, as an experiment in human psychology. And as soon as the computer said this, no one could think of anything funny anymore.

I don't believe the truth is quite that out-there, but tracing the origins of jokes can be almost impossible. Except for the few that I wrote myself, all of the jokes here have personally been told to me by someone, either in the oral tradition or in an e-mail message. Many of them can be found on the Internet, often in multiple versions, and some in various printed collections. I assume, however, since they've all been floating around for so long, that no one's intellectual property rights have been violated by publishing them here. If anyone feels differently, please get in touch with me, and we'll work something out.

About the "Author Bios"

Those little tags that appear at the end of many magazine articles are called "author bios" and usually serve to tell the reader who this person is—"Joe Bloggs is an award-winning producer, engineer, contrabass sarrusophone player, and member of the Arizona state curling team"—but when you're in front of readers *every* month, that can get really boring. In *Mix*, Stephen St. Croix started the practice of saying something in the bio to reflect back on the piece itself, and I continued that tradition, using it to tie up a loose end, put the topic of the piece in context with my own experience, or just make a final joke, as well as to acknowledge anyone who inspired or helped with researching or writing the piece. Many of the columns here have their original author bio tags intact; if you don't see one, it's because, in retrospect, it didn't seem particularly useful or funny any more.

Chapter 1

Truth *and* Consequences: What We Do Makes a Difference, Whether We Admit It or Not

Preface

For my first outing as the regular *Insider Audio* writer (after doing a "guest" column the previous September), I decided to take the column to an area that, as far as I knew, no one in *Mix* had ever covered before: personal ethics. As someone who grew up in the turbulent '60s, I believe in the power of music and the media to influence people, for better or for worse. In the mid-90s, things were definitely getting worse: Rupert Murdoch was establishing his expanding media empire as the voice of the political right wing, a witch-hunt fueled by gossip-mongers posing as journalists was threatening to unravel the Clinton administration, and radio, a medium I had loved since I was old enough to find rock and roll on the dial, was turning into a sewer of hot air and hate. A lot of people I knew in the industry were being asked to do work for clients whose message they found repugnant, but were taking the work to pay the bills. Since my mission for *Mix* was to get people thinking, I figured this would be a good way to start—if I didn't piss off so many readers that they cancelled my column.

January 1996

There's an ad that's been running in some of the trades lately that rubs me entirely the wrong way. No, it doesn't feature female body parts or underclothing, or close-ups of bodily secretions. We all have opinions on *those* ads, and my opinion is that they are silly, but hardly worth getting riled up over. The one that gets me says something like, to paraphrase broadly, "While the nation was engrossed in a dumb, sordid, real-life legal soap opera *[the O.J. Simpson trial, lest we forget]*, fascists sneaked in and took over your government. But it's not our fault, we just wrote the soundtrack."

The ad, not surprisingly, is for a music company. Their point is that whatever happens, they can write appropriate music for its presentation on television. In fact, it's their "responsibility" to do so. Now, I've done some business with this company, and they do terrific work, and I have a lot of respect for them. The message in the ad is completely honest—no matter what's going on, when it comes to reporting it, they want a piece of the action.

Do we, as engineers, producers, editors, and musicians, have any responsibility for the effect on society of the work that we do?

But what bothers me is its "We're just hired hands!" subtext. Strange things are happening in this society as we approach the millennium, and those of us who work in the entertainment and information fields (remember when they were separate?) aren't just observers—we have tremendous influence over the way people perceive what's going on. Whatever we do, whether it's records, commercials, soundtracks, broadcast, or video games, we don't work in a vacuum. Which leads to a very, very complicated question: Do we, as engineers, producers, editors, and musicians, have any responsibility for the effect on society of the work that we do?

When I was in high school, a history teacher taught us about "moral dilemmas": situations in which an individual is caught between two strong, opposing forces. His favorite example was a Southern farmer before the Civil War who hated slavery, but knew that without it, he and his family would face financial ruin. Today's audio professional often encounters the same kind of dilemma. I'm not just talking about putting up with clients you don't like, I mean dealing with people who you think are doing bad things with the services you are providing them. But with all of the pressures on us to be the best, the fastest, the coolest, and the most up to date, not to mention the fact that some of us would like to have personal lives, it's hard to turn down paying work, no matter how reviled by it we may be.

Want some examples of moral dilemmas we might face? Okay, Say you set up a production facility in an area of the country where there isn't much competition, as a friend of mine did. By being there, you've attracted talent and business to that area, raised standards for everyone, and built up an impressive staff. After a few years, you catch the attention of local hate-mongers with more money than brains who want to use your place to produce slick programs denouncing the international Zionist conspiracy and "proving" the genetic inferiority of non-white people. Do you tell them to go to hell? Or do you do your usual great job, but figure you can take advantage of them by charging full card rate and snicker all the way to the bank?

Say you believe, as many intelligent people do, that tabloid television news shows have brought the practice of journalism to new lows and that the resultant pressure on traditional news departments has made the nightly news so dependent on sensationalism and scandal that it's impossible to watch. Since "More Americans get their news from TV than any other source," as one network solemnly assures us, more Americans than ever are ignorant about issues of any real importance. You know this, and at parties you'll tell it to anyone who listens. So what happens when *Hard Copy* calls you up to do sound design on a segment about yet another Washington bimbo eruption?

Say you believe, as a fiercely independent radio station I know once did, that the military is an inherently anti-democratic institution and an ultimately destructive career choice for minority youth. Suddenly, the Army's budget for recruiting advertising goes up. Do you shun them when they come knocking, or do you say, "Well, better their money should come to us than to someone else"?

Say you're a composer whose parents fled persecution in Yugoslavia a generation ago and taught you all the songs of their childhood. A producer wants to use you to produce some stirring, heart-rending arrangements of those songs for an overseas client. What do you do when you find that the music you're making is being used to punctuate impassioned speeches on Serbian radio calling for the extermination of Moslems? Observers of the civil war in the Balkans say that "patriotic" music on the radio has been an important tool in getting the various sides to hate each other.

Say you've got a record label that you've been building for years, and some of your artists are finally catching on. But you're seeing new acts come along who are espousing violence, misogyny, and racism, who think that drive-by shootings are fun and that a murder indictment is a badge of manhood. You know that their more venomous creations will create quite a stir and maybe boost sales of all of your roster. But you're also disgusted by them. Do you sign them up, tell the media you're championing free speech, and just pray that no one takes them seriously enough to actually put some of their preaching into practice?

3

I'm sure that you've encountered something like this at least once in your career. I've been there, too. Some years ago, I was hired to score an in-house instructional film for a large defense contractor. At first I didn't like the idea, being a dyed-in-the-wool swords-into-ploughshares type, but the independent producer who hired me, a former network news producer with political leanings not far from my own, assured me the film would be strictly "civilian"—it was to promote integrity and responsibility within the ranks of the workers and would focus on products from non-defense-related divisions of the company. The company had just been caught by the government being a bit, shall we say, creative in their contract-procurement procedures, and this was one way they hoped to show that they were sincere in their efforts to reform. I took the gig.

Most of the film was innocuous enough, but when they sent me the final cut, the last minute or so had somehow become a glorious montage of military hardware, climaxing with a shot of a fighter jet roaring into a red-white-and-blue sunset. I finished the piece and later groused to the producer that I resented his misrepresenting the content to me. He shrugged his shoulders and promised the next assignment would be more to my liking. Despite my misgivings about the film, I enjoyed working with the producer and his team, and I was quite proud of the work I did. I even used that final minute, war technology and all, on my demo reel for a time.

Not long after, the producer called again. The client had conceived some major new hardware for the "Star Wars" initiative and wanted to promote it to the Pentagon. Could I score the video? I replied that I could not. His response was, "Boy, I wish we could turn down work like that!" and he found someone else. In fact, since that time, he has *always* found someone else, and although we have remained friendly, I've never worked for him again.

Did I lose a lot of potential work because of a moral stance? Maybe. Would I make the same decision again? I would. But for me it wasn't such a hard decision—I've got other ways to make a living, and I don't have a huge facility to maintain.

In the early '80s, I was doing sales and marketing for a startup music-technology company. We had a great product, and I loved selling it. But a lot of people were having trouble with it. In the best tradition (which actually wasn't a tradition yet) of high-tech customer support, I told everyone who called that *a)* it was their fault and *b)* it would be fixed real soon. But when customers' problems got worse, and it was obvious that they were *our* fault, and they were *not* getting fixed, I had to do something. Should I stick it out, continuing to draw a salary and increasing my stock position, and hope that I could influence the people responsible for the product to get their act together? Or should I bail, cutting myself off financially and pissing away many months of unpaid work? Was my responsibility to the company, to the customers, or to myself? And if I could figure that out, would I be more effective trying to change things from the inside or the outside?

Ultimately, I jumped. But again, it wasn't such a hard decision—I knew the big bucks I had originally thought would be mine just weren't going to come, and the company was headed for the toilet. And that's where it ended up, a victim of lawsuits brought on by its deceptive practices.

The choices are not always this clear-cut. One client of mine is a charitable organization that finances major building projects overseas. My more politically radical friends tell me they're displacing native populations, and I should not be working for them. My client tells me my friends are wrong. I choose to believe the client. I may be fooling myself, but on the other hand, I'm not losing any sleep over it.

For those of us who have mortgages/families/payrolls/loans/insurance (check all appropriate boxes), giving up a lucrative gig because you don't agree with the client or the product is very hard. Scruples, as a friend of mine likes to say, are expensive.

But what's the alternative? What happens if we don't exercise any judgment over what passes through our hands? Perhaps the people to whom we aim these messages are smart and are able to sort out helpful messages from harmful ones based on their content, disregarding the slickness of the delivery media. And if you believe that, I'll bet there's a bridge over the East River I could convince you to make a down payment on. The danger of having no moral compass anywhere in the creation of content is that as media get more pervasive and more persuasive, you can end up with an anarchic, valueless society where things are only prized for their glitz or shock value.

As a society, we face some momentous decisions, some of which we have been brought to by technology. As we have increased human life span, how are we going to take care of vast numbers of elderly people—who, not too long from now, will include all of us? In the wired age, when infinite perfect copies can be made of anything by anyone, how do we protect the rights of people who create things and thus keep rewarding them for creativity—and avoid jeopardizing our entire industry? As large portions of the world newly accept the precepts of the free-market economy, how do we keep them from degenerating into medieval fiefdoms, where organized-crime-style brutality and intimidation move in to replace the vacuum created by the lack of centralized government? We, as producers of the messages that persuade people, have a tremendous opportunity—and even a responsibility—to help the *right* messages get across. We can help promote tolerance, cooperation, knowledge, and respect and tell people whose messages are hate, ignorance, exploitation, and violence that we won't help them—or we can simply stick with the "it-don't-matter-what-happens-to-you-as-long-as-I-got-mine" attitude of the '80s.

For some of us, because we are more flexible or have fewer financial obligations, making business choices based on personal morality is easier than for others. But even if you feel that it's your right, or your "responsibility," to take on all clients and treat them equally, it's important to keep in mind that all of your actions *do* have consequences. The better you are at what you do, the more effect you may have. If you don't care, or think the consequences are trivial, you're entitled to that. If you figure, like the song says, "If I don't do it, somebody else will," that's your decision, too. But when it comes to doing something you know to be wrong by saying "I don't have a choice," you've just made one.

Afterword

This was a pretty radical departure for *Mix*, and I didn't want to scare loyal readers, so I put in a little disclaimer at the end of the column assuring them that I wasn't going to use *Insider Audio* to preach every month. And I guess it worked, since I didn't get a single letter objecting to either the tone or the subject of the column, and I did get a few thanking me for opening up the range of topics that get covered in *Mix*. So I was off and running—but I did wait a while before I did any more preaching.

Chapter 2

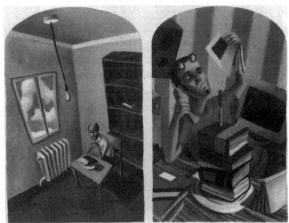
Kitty Meek

A Tale of Two Countries

Preface

I'd often heard other writers describe a piece of work—a story, an article, a screen-play—as something that "wrote itself." I wondered how I could get my column to do that, because obviously it would save me a lot of work. But it never happened—until this one.

August 1996

Sometimes it's a new song on the radio, sometimes it's a new piece of gear, sometimes it's the death of someone you know or admire. Once in a while, something crosses your awareness that makes you stop, really stop, and think. Last month, for me, it was two things: a letter and a phone call.

The letter was from a research associate in anthropology at a large Russian university. Written in excellent (although unmistakably Russian-accented) idiomatic English, laser printed, and addressed to me at the school where I teach, with 9-digit ZIP code, it contained a remarkable plea.

> *Once in a while, something crosses your awareness that makes you stop, really stop, and think.*

"As I do ethnomusicological research and often use a synthesizer for making demos and presentations," the gentleman wrote, "I have somehow been drawn into MIDI stuff. There is absolutely nothing published on MIDI in this country, so I learn it by myself, relying on what I can order through the West through interlibrary loan...I came across your book *MIDI for the Professional*, which I found most comprehensive and most helpful in all respects. I ordered it three times for the past year and wrote down for myself as much as I could. But, alas, I cannot do that any more, for they let you order any single book no more than three times. I could not copy it either, because the Xeroxing of the loaned books is not allowed for copyright purposes, and they also would not let me take it out of the library.

"For this reason, I decided to ask you, dear Dr. Lehrman [I'm not a "Dr.," but all of Eastern Europe doesn't have to know that], to send me, if possible, a copy of this outstanding book (of course, if you happen to have a spare copy).

"Please excuse me for such an impertinent request, but there is, frankly, no other way I could obtain the book. Unfortunately, I am not able to buy it from the publisher, since the price comes up to nearly half of my monthly salary (oh yes, Russian academy is surviving the worst days now).

"I hope you understand the complexity of my situation. I just cannot tell you how much I would like to have this book at hand. On the other hand, if you cannot send me a copy for any reason, I will understand, and I appreciate the knowledge I have managed to get from the book anyway. Thank you. With best regards, sincerely,"

I sent him a copy of my book. I figured that even if he's a scam artist, and he wants to sell it and make some money, I've got to admire his *chutzpah*. But I don't think he is.

When I showed the letter to the dean of my college, who has recently been to Russia and seen the state of the "academy" there firsthand, he threw in a couple of other books on music technology, took the package to the post office himself, and paid the airmail postage out of his own pocket. I hope the package is there by now, and I hope that it hasn't, as several colleagues warned me might happen, been stolen.

Meanwhile, I had been running an ad in a local newspaper offering some no-longer-needed equipment for sale. About a week after the letter from Russia came, I got a phone call from a fellow who said he "wanted to discuss the capabilities of the system." What he really wanted to do was pick my brain—he didn't know anything about me, but he figured that since I had some computers and studio gear for sale, I must know what I was talking about. The fellow writes music, he explained, and has an analog multitrack, which he is looking to replace with a digital equivalent, using a couple of thousand dollars he's expecting to get back from the IRS. He couldn't decide, however, between a stand-alone hard disk system, a computer-based system, or a modular digital multitrack tape deck. Our conversation went something like this:

Me: What kind of music do you do?

Him: You know, acoustic, guitar and voice, and maybe some synth and a drum machine.

Me: So you use MIDI?

Him: Yeah, I got a Korg module.

Me: And what SMPTE interface do you use?

Him: What's that?

Me: Well, how you get the tape to sync with the synthesizer?

Him: Oh, I just play in the parts to the tape.

Me: So you don't use a sequencer.

Him: No, everyone tells me that sounds bad.

Me: How did you decide on the Korg module?

Him: A friend of mine told me about it.

Me: What do you with the finished tapes?

Him: I make CDs.

Me: Oh, you have some records out?

Him: No, I send my masters to a guy in Texas, and he does them for me.

Me: So then you sell the CDs?

Him: No, he just makes one at a time. Charges me a dollar a minute.

Me: Why do you do that?

Him: I think it's more, like, impressive when I go to a record company to show them my CDs.

Me: But if you only have one of each, you can't give them any.

Him: Yeah, that's right.

Me: So what do you give them?

Him: Well, I haven't actually gone to any of them yet.

Me: Why do you want to get a digital system?

Him: I hear it sounds better than the [he names his analog tape deck].

Me: What don't you like about the sound of that deck?

Him: Uh, nothing. I just hear it's better to go digital. And I need more tracks.

Me: Do you know that the hard-disk system you're looking at has the same number of tracks as your analog deck?

Him: Yeah, but it's digital, so I can expand it, right?

Me: Actually, no, you can't.

Him: Gee.

Me: What else would you like to know about the computer I'm selling?

Him: Well, like how fast is it? Is it faster than [he names a low-cost hard-disk system]?

Me: I don't know what you mean by that. They'll both handle the same number of tracks.

Him: But does one work faster?

Me: As far as I know, they both play at the same speed. The hard-disk system has eight outputs, but the computer hardware has four.

Him: So the computer is only four tracks?

Me: No, four outputs. Actually, with the right software, it will handle 16 tracks.

Him: How do you get 16 tracks out of four outputs?

Me: Listen, do you have any literature on any of this stuff?

Him: I have a brochure on [he names a MIDI/audio sequencing program].

Me: Oh, so you do want to do MIDI sequencing at the same time.

Him: Gee, I don't know. This guy who gave it to me said it was a cool way to mix audio.

Me: Have you gone to a music store to look at any of this stuff?

Him: No, I just have some brochures. I called the company and asked them if their stuff will do what I want.

Me: Did they tell you that you could buy an audio editing program for one-third the price?

Him: I can?

Me: Tell me, what magazines do you get?

Him: Like what?

Me: You know, *Mix, Electronic Musician, EQ, Keyboard.* Do you read those?

Him: No. I think I've seen them, but I don't get them.

Me: Why not?

Him: Oh, I thought I could just figure it out by myself.

Obviously, he is wrong. I doubt I'm going to sell him anything, and in all good conscience, I wouldn't really want to. When I hung up, I couldn't help comparing him to my Russian correspondent. The American believes he is doing things his own way, but actually he is waiting for someone to come along and tell him what to do with his couple of thousand dollars. Unfortunately, all that is getting through to him is vague, incomprehensible hype. The companies he is talking to are doing their jobs, trying to sell him their products, but he refuses to look beyond what they're telling him, to find products that will really work for him. He is surrounded by information, in the form of books, magazines, dealers, and online services, but he refuses to make the effort to even look at it.

Over in Russia, on the other hand, is a system designed to *prevent* access to information. While the old autocracy at least saw to it that some few select scholars and scientists got the tools they needed, in the neo-capitalist chaos that is Russia today, it seems the only people who can afford to buy anything are those who have managed to attract investment from Western corporations or, in a tragically comic adaptation of one all-too-visible facet of Western civilization, to extort funds from their fellow citizens. Government support for education has been decimated. My correspondent gets no magazines, can go to no knowledgeable stores, has no access to a modem, a fax, or even a photocopier. And he certainly has no funds burning a hole in his pocket. Yet he is going to pursue his goal and figure out a way to continue his research, despite the fact that it will never make him rich, and even if it means begging someone he doesn't know, thousands of miles away, for scraps of information.

People I know who have been to Russia lately say he is very brave just to stay in his country. The old barriers to emigration are down, so it could be loyalty to his homeland, or personal concerns, or fear, or a combination of these that keep him there. Someday, as tens of thousands of Russians already have, he might decide it's not worth it any more and emigrate to a land of relative plenty. Perhaps he would show up at my door, looking for help or a job. And perhaps, at the same time, the fellow who can't be bothered to pick up a magazine or talk to a dealer, who's willing to let his artistic decisions be dictated by rumor and hype, who's perfectly happy abrogating all responsibility to himself and his muse to those who know far less than he about what is best for him, would show up as well. I know which one I would welcome into my house, and which one I would turn away.

Afterword

I never heard from my Russian correspondent again, so I have no idea whether the materials we sent were helpful, or if he even got them. These days most of the letters I get from overseas are e-mails from poor, pathetic widows of African bank managers offering me large sums of money if I will help them export their assets. I usually don't answer them.

Charles Stubbs

Chapter 3

Vintage? You Don't Know Vintage!

Preface

This was the first chance I had to write a column for *Mix* that was completely humorous. Of course I'd inserted jokes, puns, and snide remarks into other pieces, but I had never tried to be funny from beginning to end. For both the editors and me, it was an experiment.

A couple of the ideas came from my teaching colleague Dave Moulton, as I mention in the author's bio. To explain all of the jokes in this column would ruin the fun, but I will note that the first one is a bit of an homage to fellow *Mix* columnist Stephen St. Croix, inventor of the Marshall Time Modulator, whose real name wasn't "St. Croix" at all (it was, in fact, "Marshall"). Stephen, I knew, could be touchy about things like this, so I sent it to him before I submitted the final copy. He thought it was hysterical. More about Stephen in Chapter 57.

November 1996

Here is some "vintage gear" you may have missed.

Tortola Time AnTicipator
(Manufactured 1974-76)

This is a pre-delay unit that produces single or multiple iterations of a sound a specified period of time before it actually occurs. The design is based on research done by the late, discredited, Dr. I. Asimov into the endochronic properties of resublimated thiotimoline (USP), a substance that dissolves 1.12 seconds prior to it being put into water. Thiotimoline has been used (mostly unsuccessfully) in military, space travel, and communications applications, but the AnTicipator is its only known application in the creative arts.

Using "bucket brigade" devices made from real buckets—i.e., a tiny series of 16 water pails inside the unit attached to a small motorized cam, which continuously dumps the contents of each one into the next—pre-delays of up to 18 seconds can be produced. This makes it possible, for example, to move a laggard snare beat forwards, to compensate for a late entrance in the horn section, or perhaps to insert a chorus in front of a verse, before the singer has gotten around to actually singing it. The unit must be used in a horizontal position, as attempting to use it vertically would cause quite a mess.

The Time AnTicipator was very popular among unscrupulous producers who found they could stack several of them together and use them to record a session player's tracks before he or she showed up.

The Time AnTicipator was very popular among unscrupulous producers who found they could stack several of them together and use them to record a session player's tracks before he or she showed up. When the player did come around, the producer could say, "Oh, we already got that," and send him home without paying him. This shameful practice ended, however, after the players caught on and stopped coming to sessions they had contracted for, thus causing the pre-delayed tracks to come out blank. It is now primarily used by club DJs to do dance remixes of top-40 records before they are finished.

The AnTicipator was made in New Jersey, but the inventor named it after a tropical island that he thought sounded pretty cool, even though he had never been within a thousand miles of it. Original price: $2000; street price today: $400; water and thiotimoline refills extra.

Sputnik 1017 All-Glory-to-Marx-Lenin-Etc. Mikrofon
(Manufactured 1954-56)

This large diaphragm unit was the glory of the Soviet space effort and was used on newsreel soundtracks throughout the Cold War. Its 12-foot diaphragms were remanufactured from the hulls of decommissioned WWII icebreakers and weigh approximately 14 tons each. The 3-billion volt electret charge is provided by a Van de Graaf generator, which is cooled by a system containing pure alcohol derived from potatoes.

The 600-pound amplifier tube, the 3000000000DCX7GT, contains elements made from Uzbek yak hair and pure plutonium, smuggled in from the West inside pumpkins and Rosemary Clooney records. The power supply capacitors were manufactured from slightly used atomic bomb casings.

The 1017 has a dynamic range in excess of 200 dB, but its unique power supply creates a self-noise figure of nearly 92 dB, which has restricted its use to close miking of ICBM liftoffs, interplanetary visitations, bomb tests, and political conventions, but also makes it particularly suited today for radio talk-show hosts. All known units are currently in storage near a former power plant in Ukraine, making them very "hot" items.

Original price: 250,000 rubles; street price: $250 plus freight (FOB Chernobyl), and appropriate permits.

The John Dearie 704 Acoustical Compressor
(Manufactured 1907-09)

The Dearie company developed this device as part of a diversification effort to open up new markets for their best-selling Model 704 9,000-cubic inch, long-throw, two-cylinder agricultural and tractor motor, capable of developing 108 HP @ 725 rpm. Since the full dynamic range of a symphony orchestra could hardly be contained on the cylinders and wax discs used by the recording industry at the time (38 dB, max), acoustical compression was seen to be a practical technique for reducing that dynamic range. Although no record of complementary expansion has been found, this device could serve equally well as an expander, thereby permitting the development of companding noise reduction systems as early as 1908.

The technology of the Dearie 704 bears a striking resemblance to today's "active" noise-cancellation processors: The air pressure output of the double-acting pistons serves to cancel the detected pressure-fronts of the acoustical sound wave. Threshold is established by a pair of low-inertia, fast-acting mercury barometers (one inverted), which close and open relief valves for the pistons. While the signal level is below the threshold, the valves remain open throughout the engine cycle, so the sound passes unchanged, but when the threshold is reached, the valves partially or completely close (depending on the "ratio" setting), causing the 9,000 cubic inches of displacement to modulate the air in a kind of negative acoustic feedback, thus reducing the output level.

The threshold is adjustable from 8 to 25 microbars, or approximately 92 to 102 dB SPL—the high SPL numbers being necessitated by the incredible racket the device makes.

The motor speed is modulated by (and phase-locked to) the mechanical output of the two barometers. Eliminating the inertial flywheel of the motor allows it to accommodate rapid changes in frequency.

Attack and release times are a bit dicey, since the hysteresis of the barometer pairs is somewhat erratic. Use in an air-conditioned environment is mandatory, since high humidity can cause a change of state during loud positive excursions of the waveform, causing an intermittent spray of water and crankcase oil, modulating at the frequency of the signal, to get all over everything. Even with no flywheel, the motor has too much inertia to detect or compress signals greater than about 175 Hz (10,500 rpm), and so a steep low-pass filter must be used at the input, or the unit's attempts to process higher-pitched signals will quickly tear it to shreds.

The most serious problem of the 704, which eventually caused it to be pulled off the market, is its erratic pressure output, which occasionally lags in phase by as much as 150 degrees, causing expansion instead of expression. This, of course, would severely overtax the recording system. In one notorious incident, during an attempt to record the Boston Pops' Independence Day concert, seven gramophone diaphragms exploded simultaneously, injuring several Dearie engineers and catapulting most of the cello section into the Charles River. After this episode, the company went back to agricultural implements exclusively, closing the door on a most interesting, if idiotic, experiment in audio history.

Original price: $499.95; street price (a few remaining units can be found in abandoned equipment sheds and bomb shelters): $1500. Your mileage may vary.

Unterfunkengesellschaft USB1 Sub-Sub Woofer
(Manufactured 1908-14, remanufactured 1938-41)

This cylindrically shaped very, very, very low-frequency driver, affectionately known as "The Boot," represents the best in early 20th-century German metallurgical engineering. It was designed on orders from the Kaiser's public relations machine, which was desperately trying to convince England and France that all of the frantic activity in the Krupp shipyards was actually devoted to goods for peaceful, civilian use.

Capable of reproducing sound down to 1/10 Hz (later models can also, paradoxically enough, handle very short "ping"-like bursts in the 100 kHz range), The Boot can develop

180 dB SPL at 100 meters—sufficient to, so to speak, blow the competition out of the water. It is surprisingly portable over approximately 3/5ths of the world's surface area, as well as a few very large ponds.

The secret to its "oomph" is that it uses disposable, single-use charges known (depending on what city you are in) as "heroes," "hoagies," or sometimes "torpedoes." After performing a particularly taxing musical passage, like say Tchaikovsky's *1812 Overture*, or anything using a Roland drum machine, the unit must be "reloaded." At the same time, buildings in the immediate area should be checked for structural damage.

The superstructural material is steel, with special sound-absorbing black paint, for deadly silent, rust-free operation in even the saltiest of environments. It is best suited to residential studios with large, unused swimming pools, in neighborhoods zoned for military use. Of thousands built, very few remain, as they tended to self-destruct after a few months' use. Original cost: DM1,000,000; street price: $2,000 plus $200 per "hoagie," FOB Buenos Aires.

American Foods Gelaplex Reverberator
(Manufactured 1954)

American Foods (Amfoo) was not known for its professional audio products, and in fact, this was its only foray into the field. The Gelaplex was an attempt by the marketing department of the company's Gelatin Dessert division to go head-to-head with Jell-O® without resorting to the risky (as they saw it) medium of television advertising. Although it was a colossal failure, the Gelaplex presaged the acoustical modeling that became a crucial design element in the digital reverbs of the future.

The device is stunning in its simplicity. 1/114th-scale aluminum molds of desirable acoustical spaces are provided with the system, and purchasers can then create gelatin models of these spaces, using Amfoo's YummiGel® product. Sound is input into the YummiGel using transducers mounted in soft-drink straws (supplied with the original units). Other straws contain tiny microphones for picking up the reverberated sound. The vibrations from the transducers travel through the YummiGel to its boundaries and to the pickups in a manner equivalent to the way sound travels in a reverberant space. Since YummiGel transmits sound at a speed of 1/114-Mach, sound propagating through the model resembles a free-air reverberant field to a surprisingly realistic degree. Since any number of input or output straws can be inserted into the YummiGel, the user can simulate any number of feeds and pickups within the field, just like the multi-input, multi-tap digital devices of today.

Unfortunately, since stereo had yet to come into common usage (to say nothing of surround), the capabilities of the Gelaplex were not appreciated in its time. Further, Amfoo took a somewhat provincial approach in its choice of acoustical models to include with the system: the combination auditorium/gymnasium/cafeteria of the West Peedsville District Vocational and Technical High School, West Peedsville, IA; Bob's Lucky Strike Bowling Lanes and Billiards Emporium, Peeds River, IA; and Grain Elevator 17 at Amfoo's corporate headquarters in East Peed, IA. Requests from customers for more widely recognizable spaces, such as the Mormon Tabernacle, the Taj Mahal, Carnegie Hall, and Yankee Stadium, fell on deaf ears.

Gelaplexes, like many Amfoo products, sold like hot cakes, which is to say, in Aisle 6 of Amfoo stores. Few housewives, however, appreciated the incredible auditory qualities of these remarkable molds, and the company received many letters from irate purchasers along the order of "My pineapple-cherry mold won't set in this thing!" Of some 4,000 sold, approximately 20 remain, mostly in private collectors' hands (alas, no Bob's Lucky Strike Bowling Lanes survive), but they occasionally find their way into the vintage equipment market.

YummiGel itself was discontinued in 1956, and thus the supply is limited to aging desserts found in some Iowa refrigerators, all the way in the back behind the peach preserves, but many East Coast users report that rendered chicken fat makes an acceptable substitute.

Original price: $5.95; street price: $14,000, chicken fat extra.

Paul D. Lehrman usually finds truth much funnier than fiction, but occasionally makes exceptions. He profusely thanks Dave Moulton for his contribution of items from his priceless collection of fabulous equipment.

Afterword

Judging from the enthusiastic response we got from readers (and to this day I still get comments about the Gelaplex Reverberator), this column was a big success. It showed me that our audience had a great sense of humor and encouraged me, for better or worse, to write funny often.

Chapter 4

Short Cycles: How Fast Can We Make People Buy into New Technology?

Preface

Author Michael Crichton figures prominently in my personal mythology, as this column explains. Although his recent bloviations about the "bad science" behind the theory of global warming I find a bit bizarre, during his long career he's come up with many wonderful thought-provoking ideas about the role of science, for both good and evil, in modern society, and he continues to be a good read.

December 1996

Michael Crichton and I nearly share a birthday. We were born exactly 10 years and 6 days apart. On top of that, we grew up in the same town. I think I knew him. Though I'm not certain, I'm told it's likely that the tall, pleasant library aide at my elementary school, whose name was Michael, and who would get the Dr. Seuss books down from the top shelf for me during those afternoons in the first grade when I was so bored that my teacher threw me out of the classroom, was indeed the soon-to-be-famous novelist and Hollywood honcho.

In high school, he was a basketball star; I played the bassoon and rhythm guitar. We had the same senior English teacher, whom Crichton cites as one of his chief inspirations as a writer. I considered the guy a pompous jerk. But what did I know? Last year, Crichton's literary properties brought him an income of $22 million, according to *Forbes*. Mine didn't, according to anybody.

Crichton and I even lived on the same block in Cambridge, perhaps in the same building—he in the late '60s while he was attending Harvard Medical School and learning why he didn't want to be a doctor, but getting the inspiration for *ER* and I in the mid-'80s, when I was working in software development and learning that I would never be a great programmer, but getting inspired to write computerized Celtic folk music.

Why do I bring this up? Well, I've been thinking about Crichton a lot recently, as I find myself increasingly disquieted over the ever-accelerating march of technology. At the heart of a lot of Crichton's books is a warning that over-reliance on technology, especially that which is so new that we haven't had a chance to assimilate it and weigh its costs and benefits, is extremely dangerous. Would that I could say it as eloquently as he does—and make nearly as much money at it.

I am thinking particularly of an early book of his, *The Terminal Man*. A computer scientist who hates computers, by the name of Harry Benson, has a nasty (and utterly fictional) form of epilepsy, which causes him to kill people when he is in the throes of a seizure. A group of doctors implant under his skin a computerized device that reads his brain waves. It recognizes the pattern that precedes an attack and when it detects that pattern, it sends a little jolt of electricity to a pleasure-stimulating site in the brain, breaking the cycle and preventing the seizure.

The trouble starts when the computer that is monitoring the man/machine interface reports that the jolts of pleasure are starting to come closer and closer together. Crichton likens the process to someone's learning through biofeedback how to lower his blood pressure—the autonomic nervous system, responsible for things like respiration, heart rate, and body temperature, can be taught just the way the conscious mind can be. In this case. the patient's brain is learning to generate seizure patterns with increasing frequency so that it can get the resulting pleasure hits. The curve described by the events over time is a hyperbola, and its asymptote, the point at which the time between the events diminishes to zero, Crichton calls "tipover." When that occurs, as you can imagine, all hell breaks loose, and there are guns, women in peril, chases through dark airplane hangars, and death.

What does that have to do with audio? Well, the story popped into my consciousness recently during a conference I attended. The subject was DVD, the Digital Video (or is it Versatile?) Disc that promises to be the Next Big Thing ("NBT"?) in delivering audio, video, and data. Whether you know anything about it or not, there will be DVD hardware (if not software) in the stores by the time you read this. DVD is supposed to replace VHS videotape, audio CDs, and CD-ROMs with a medium that is trivially more expensive to produce than today's CDs but can hold about eight times as much data. There are dozens of issues surrounding DVD's launch: how movies are going to be compressed, how copyrights will be protected (not that again!), whether players will be backwards compatible with conventional CDs, and how multiple platforms will be supported on one disc, just to name a few. On the audio side, there are questions of how many channels will be delivered, what sampling rate(s) and word length(s) will be supported, and what kind of digital compression will be used, if any. These problems are doubly complex because they have to be decided both for audio-only discs and for audio accompanying pictures.

DVD seems to be designed from the git-go to be all things to all people, and history says that may not be such a great idea.

Now, understand that I'm not averse to the idea of DVD. Certainly, there's a lot to be said for a video delivery system superior to VHS (although we've had one for years—laserdiscs—but never mind that for now). The 600-megabyte limit on CD-ROM capacity, which seemed so generous not very long ago, is now looking pretty skimpy, so a 5-gigabyte medium would be welcome. As to whether the market will support 560-minute record albums, or people will pay premium prices for 6-channel surround versions of Steely Dan greatest-hits collections, that remains to be seen.

But I see trouble ahead. For one thing, DVD seems to be designed from the git-go to be all things to all people, and history says that may not be such a great idea. Look at any successful entertainment technology introduced in the last couple of decades, and you'll see that when it first came out, while it had a definite market niche and solved a specific problem, and it was easily understood by the buying public, as time went on, it grew and developed in ways unforeseen to its originators. Maybe that's not the ideal way to develop technology—if you don't at least try to predict all the uses of a new technology from the beginning, then you'll never see what limitations you'll bump up against down the road—but it has worked surprisingly well, especially in an industry as dependent on consumer acceptance as ours.

For example, when the first FM stations went on the air, no one dreamed of being able to broadcast in stereo. FM worked just fine as it was, and when stereo came along it was an added bonus, and it has kept the medium vital for over 50 years. When half-inch home video came out, its use as a high-fidelity video (S-VHS) or audio (VHS Hi-Fi, PCM-F1) medium was not on anybody's mind. Audio CDs gave birth to CD-ROM and Extended CDs, and it was that birth that triggered the explosion in CD manufacturing capacity that today makes the cost of making a CD less than that of making a cassette (now if only someone would tell this to the record companies). If the proponents of MIDI proclaimed in 1983 that this clever little scheme for hitting a key *here* and hearing a synth play over *there* would become a major factor in console automation, synchronization, and signal process- ing, they would have been laughed out of town. The Compact Cassette begat the portable multitracker; two-inch videotape transports were transmogrified into 16-track audio decks; and the personal computer—the accountant's best friend—somehow evolved into the pre- dominant tool for artists in every medium.

So is the rush to cover all the bases on DVD before it comes out really a wise move? Will those who would predetermine *everything* about DVD before it even exists kill the goose before it gets to lay the golden egg? And the corollary question that this begs is: Are all of the companies who want to make sure their patented technologies and existing markets are protected when the new medium appears going to make things so confusing and so closed- ended that consumers will never go for it?

But that's not even the most important question. What's really going to make or break this thing is the time factor: whether there's enough time for consumers to absorb yet another new technology. Has it been long enough since the last time we made them buy into some- thing altogether new that we can get away with convincing them to do it *again*? In an age when technology development is not only accelerating rapidly, but the pace of acceleration itself is accelerating, I wonder whether we're approaching a point where our next move is going to leave behind a whole lot of people—the very people whom we ultimately need to pay for it.

Already we're seeing races being run among competing technology companies that are approaching comic proportions. Generations of new products are blurring into each other. One major computer manufacturer who last summer announced screamingly fast machines is not only *not* delivering them yet, they aren't even delivering the line of hardware they announced *before* that. Meanwhile, their competition has announced similarly spec'ed products and is representing them to the public as being available imminently, when they know perfectly well that won't be in the pipeline until at least next summer. It isn't just our little segment of the market that is practicing "preventive" product introductions anymore. If we do it, it's annoying but sort of fun. When the big guys do it, there are some heavy stakes involved.

The last revolutionary audio technology we foisted on people, CDs, took a while to get off the ground. It was about seven years between the time that the medium began to be seriously discussed and the time real product appeared; then it was another seven years before it became firmly enough established to supersede its vinyl predecessor. Consumers had to be educated, cajoled, sympathized with, and in time won over with the promise of better quality, ease of use, and finally, a bigger catalog. The parallel to DVD is almost painfully obvious, and yet the DVD folks are not allowing time to work for them at all: They're trying to get their baby to market in about two years from inception and are expecting that it will be no more than three years before it becomes the medium of choice for video, audio, and data.

Can we absorb all this new technology so fast? Are people so ready to throw out their VHS VCRs (even if they bought them 10 years ago), their CD players (five years ago), and their CD-ROM drives (last Christmas)? Or are the little jolts of electricity, like in poor Harry Benson's brain, coming too close together? Are we in danger of a tipover, where the technological eras, the cycles of stimulus and response, are so short that they collapse into each other? If that happens, the host, that is, the buying public, will be paralyzed out of confusion and fright. Hopefully, unlike Crichton's character, they won't turn into homicidal psychopaths. But for them to turn off to what we have to offer—the music, the movies, and the multimedia of the future—because they can't deal with overwhelming and expensive new technology, whether it's being implanted under their skin or forced down their throats, would be just as deadly.

Afterword

Well, as in many of Crichton's novels, the warnings I made in this column were mostly unneeded. DVDs did take off like a shot and supplanted VHS even faster than most people had predicted. Although some technologies, like DVD-A, pretty much stalled at the starting gate, a lot of what DVDs were supposed to do but didn't were successfully taken on by TiVO and the iPod. Also, I see now I underestimated the hunger of consumers for new technology and their willingness to spend lots of money on the latest toys, whether they actually ever use them or not. But the dangers of adopting new technology too fast are still there, although the perception of those dangers has changed in the post-9/11 wired world: We're not so much worried about marketability as we are about security—which in fact means the stakes are much higher.

Chapter 5

Careers from Hell

Preface

You know what they say about revenge being a dish best served cold? Boy, did I enjoy this dish. I'd been annoying my friends with these stories for years, but I never got a chance to write them down or tell them to a wider audience. The only trick was how to disguise the identities of the people and companies I was talking about. I guess I did a good job, because I never heard from any of them—or their lawyers—after it appeared in print.

March 1997

Everybody who's been in this business more than two weeks has his own "Gig from Hell" stories. Singers drooling all over the microphones, record company execs with dubious hygiene abusing everyone in sight, guitar heroes who insist that louder is always better, advertising clients who *know* they can do your job better than you, producers using the console to lay out their nose candy—the list is endless. Some of my own favorite memories of the genre include the enraged, drunken mob of high-school reunioners who chased my little acoustic trio down a hill when they realized the punk band they thought they'd hired wasn't going to show up; the assistant engineer who filled a kick drum with sandbags but forgot to check that they were tied shut; the synth player who didn't know where the master tuning control was and so as the thing warmed up I had to keep changing the tape speed to match its pitch; and the day I was recording a 40-piece steel band outdoors with a dozen brand-new U87s and 414s, and a sudden monsoon came up. [I get to tell this story again, in more detail, in Chapter 40.]

But that's not what I want to talk about this month. However horrible an individual gig might be, if you love what you do, there's always another gig right around the corner that makes up for it—the incredible vocal track, the perfect drum sound, the ridiculously complex but successful remote, the miraculous edit, the mix that jumps out at you and screams, "This is platinum, baby!" But when you're in the wrong job, when you've made a really miserable career choice, the Gigs from Hell don't go away—you just get a new one every day. You begin to appreciate what Dante meant when he said: "Abandon hope, all ye who enter here." And that's what I want to talk about: the two worst, most onerous, utterly dead-end jobs I ever had.

> *But when you're in the wrong job, when you've made a really miserable career choice, the Gigs from Hell don't go away— you just get a new one every day.*

When I first got out of college with a degree in orchestral performance and a hankering to produce records, there were no clear career paths open. I interviewed at all the major classical labels and was told that staff producer jobs only become available when someone died—and the only slot that had opened up in the last ten years had been filled by someone just like me, just the year before. (He's still there, too.) I went around to most of the major studios in the city where I lived and was told they'd be happy to take me on, as long as I agreed to be a gofer at no pay, emptying wastebaskets and ashtrays and procuring sandwiches and occasionally drugs for the clients, with the hope that if I hung around long enough, I might someday be allowed to touch a button on a tape deck.

A friend of mine who had finished college the year before was working for one of the larger music stores and was constantly telling me how much fun it was. (I think he's now in the clothing business.) So I asked him to put in a good word for me, and I got a job there, too. It was long hours, at very close to minimum wage, and I was on my feet all day, but at least I could tell myself I was working in my chosen field.

I was hired as a "front counter" guy. That meant I handled things like guitar strings, clarinet reeds, sheet music, harmonicas, and the occasional student trumpet or saxophone. The folks at the "back counter" were selling guitars, amps, drums, and organs. They got to demonstrate all that cool stuff (and if I never hear the intro to "Stairway to Heaven" or the instrumental break from Stevie Wonder's "Living for the City" again, it will be too soon), hang out with the occasional famous rock musician (Mick Fleetwood, who was doing a gig at a nearby arena, came in one day to buy sticks), and not incidentally make a lot more money, because much of the merchandise carried "spiffs": $10 or $20 bonuses to the salesman who closed the deal.

You begin to appreciate what Dante meant when he said: "Abandon hope, all ye who enter here."

I asked to be transferred back there, but I got caught in a Catch-22: Because I was musically literate, I was "too valuable" up front. And so I stuck it out with the piano teachers and the kids in the junior-high bands and got more and more frustrated.

One day, the assistant manager announced that we could get a spiff on something, too: a student oboe had been gathering dust in the back room for years, and he wanted to get rid of it. He put a sign up advertising it at a bargain price, and offered $20 to the salesman who managed to pawn it off on somebody. It wasn't going to be an easy sale: for one thing, it was made of plastic. For another, it was missing the two lowest keys, because the manufacturer figured no beginning oboist would ever need to play those notes, and so they could save on the cost of the metal. I was a bassoon player, which wasn't *too* different, and so one weekend I took the instrument home, along with a plastic reed and a method book, and learned how to play a couple of tunes on it.

Lo and behold, about a week later a woman came in saying that her precocious 12-year-old son had just started to play the oboe, and rather than use the horrible one the school had, she wanted to buy him a "really nice" instrument. The other salespeople, knowing of my intensive preparation for this moment, called me over, and I proudly whipped out the plastic monstrosity and played the opening bars of Ravel's *Bolero*. Even after my brilliant demonstration, however, it was a hard sell convincing her this was an instrument that would "serve the boy well for years"—because, of course, it wasn't. It took two more visits (why she never brought the kid's teacher, I'll never know; no doubt he would have laughed himself silly over the thing), but finally she succumbed and wrote out the check. When she left, the whole store came over and congratulated me—I was a front counter hero, and my future in the business was assured. That night, after closing, I waved a cheery goodbye to everyone, walked out to the parking lot, and threw up.

One other incident in my short tenure as a music-store salesman stands out. We often stocked two types of accessories: brand-names and non-branded. The non-branded ones were referred to behind the counter as "GPS." Thus, we had Fender guitar picks and GPS picks; Selmer reed cases and GPS reed cases; Passantino music paper and GPS music paper. I didn't know what GPS stood for, but everybody said it, so I figured it was the name of a wholesaler who supplied the store or had some other official meaning.

One day a customer came in and asked for a guitar capo. I asked him if he wanted a brand name, and he said no, the cheapest one we had would be fine. The drawer in the counter where the non-branded capos lived was empty, so I got on the house PA, which was our way of communicating with the stock room, and announced: "Stock, send me up a box of GPS acoustic capos, please!"

From out of nowhere the manager of the store, the wife of the president of the company and a force to be reckoned with, stormed up to the counter and barked in my face, "Come with me!" She marched me away from the bewildered customer and into her tiny office in the basement and slammed the door. "Don't *ever* say that on the PA, and don't *ever* say that in front of a customer!" she screamed. "I never want to hear that again!"

I apologized weakly, assuring her it would never, ever happen again, and I dazedly climbed back upstairs, wondering what horrible thing I had done. It took a few hours, but finally the rest of the front-counter staff were able to stop giggling whenever they looked at me long enough to explain that "GPS" was an "unofficial" acronym, frowned upon by management, and not something to be said over the PA system. What it stood for was "Generic Piece of Shit."

My illustrious career in counter sales was followed by a somewhat longer stint in radio. I had done radio in college, and in fact had built the station at one brand-new school I attended. I was hoping for a gig doing production work, and maybe even be an on-air voice, but at the time the only jobs I could find were in engineering. I toiled miserably (although I learned a lot) for a while at a classical FM station in one city and then, to my great surprise, was hired as chief engineer for a similar station in another city. When I arrived there, however, I discovered they had brought me in over their assistant engineer, a slovenly-looking, Grateful Dead-loving, opera-hating, 21-year-old college dropout, whom they didn't want to give the chief's job to because they needed someone who projected a better "image." Trouble was, he was a far better engineer than I and was far more knowledgeable about the station's equipment (some of which was pretty ancient) than I could ever hope to be. Quite understandably, on the day I arrived he decided his primary mission was to make my life impossible.

Luckily, after a couple of months I learned that the station was selling off its AM arm, which played big-band music, and they needed a part-time production person. So I bowed out of my beleaguered chief-engineership and went with them. The new owners were building what appeared to be a state-of-the-art studio complex across town. Four gorgeous new Scully 14" tape decks were going into one room, with a brand-new broadcast board and a rack full of fancy equalizers, modulation monitors, and multi-band compressor/limiters.

I soon had a nice gig going. In addition to handling all the station's production—sign-ons, sign-offs, IDs, the DJs' personal jingles, and the occasional commercial—I also helped wire the new studios. One DJ never set foot in the station but sent his programs in on tape, and I took over the responsibility of putting them on the air, doing rip-and-read news and weather on the hour, and fielding the phone calls from his devoted (and mostly elderly) listeners, in which I'd explain patiently that "Bill is out of town tonight at an important charity event, and he prerecorded his show, and that's why he can't talk to you." Once a week I engineered a remote from a restaurant with the world's largest salad bar—the DJ and I got to pig out after the show was over. Other times I filled in for jocks on their days off, sometimes playing their song lists, and sometimes making my own. It was low rent, it wasn't my first choice for the type of music I wanted to play, and our audience was small and shrinking by attrition, but it was fun.

But one day when I showed up for work, the on-air studio was empty, the record library door was locked, and some kind of drippy background music was coming out of the monitors. The station manager called me into his office and told me that the new owner had that morning fired all the on-air staff. I was now going to be the morning man—full-time, six hours/five days a week, with even a small raise in pay.

The only catch was, the format was no longer big-band music. This very day the station was converting to "beautiful music," playing tapes from a programming service somewhere in the Midwest (this was before satellite links were cheap enough for the job). That's what the Scully decks were for. And it was going to be automated. However, the money ran out before the station could get the entire automation package installed, and that was why I was being offered a job: They needed warm bodies to run the tape decks.

The tapes were supposedly scientifically programmed to "create positive and productive mood cycles," whatever that meant, but only, of course, when they were played in precisely the right order. Here was the routine: On the hour, I was to announce the time and do a station ID and say one of five slogans, like "The sound of beautiful music." Then I was to start tape deck 1 and play one cut, exactly three minutes and forty seconds long. Then I was to play a cut from tape 2, then one from tape 3, then one from tape 4. At quarter past the hour: time, ID, and another slogan. Play tape 2, tape 1, tape 4, tape 3. At half past the hour: time, ID, and weather. Play tape 3, tape 2, tape 4, tape 1. At 45 past: time, ID, and slogan. For the last quarter hour, I could go hog wild and play the tapes in any order I darn well wanted.

I think if Jean-Paul Sartre had grown up in love with radio, this would have been his setting for "No Exit," that wonderful existential vision of purgatory. Picture it: Here I was, a conservatory-trained musician, a reasonably decent production engineer, and a fledgling deejay, in a studio with a brand-new board and four lovely tape decks, which were loaded with putrid, hateful, unidentifiable elevator music. I wasn't allowed to choose any of the music, I couldn't say anything about the music—heck, I wasn't even allowed to know what the tunes were!—and I couldn't even say my own name, even if I'd wanted to. In fact, I was barely able to go to the bathroom; if I did, I had to make sure I was in and out in less than 3'40", lest I wasn't there to switch tape decks when a tune ended and (God forbid!) two selections from the same tape played in a row.

I did my first air shift, and when it was over I went back to see the station manager. He had gone to lunch, so I took the card with my name on it out of his Rolodex and tore it into little pieces, leaving the pieces on his desk. Then I went home. I never even went back to pick up my check.

Paul D. Lehrman hasn't had a full-time job since 1979.

Afterword

The best part about doing this piece was hearing from the people who were there. At the AES show that fall, a guy who had worked the front counter of that music store with me and another guy who worked in the back, both of whom had gone on to successful careers in pro audio, found me on the show floor and told me they had fallen down laughing when they read the piece. "I remember that 'GPS' episode really well," said one of them. "I will never forget the look on ****'s face when she dragged you away!"

Then a couple of years later I ran into the young engineer at that radio station who pushed me out so successfully, who was still in the field, although not so young, and in fact was now the chief engineer at the top station in the city. I'm sure he had not read the piece. We eyed each other suspiciously but cordially, and I thought about how it was probably a good thing I hadn't written anything nastier about him.

Chapter 6

Revisiting Tom Lehrer

Preface

Being a journalist is a fantastic excuse to call up famous people who don't know who I am and get them to talk to me. I try not to abuse this privilege, but when the opportunity comes up for me to interview one of my personal heroes, like satirical songwriter Tom Lehrer, it is not to be ignored. Besides being a brilliant parodist, Lehrer also was a pioneer (although he didn't see himself that way) in the world of self-produced records, which makes him a particularly appropriate subject for *Mix*.

This piece was actually my second interview with Lehrer. The first took place in 1983, when a musical show based on his songs was about to open in Boston. I actually auditioned for the show to be the musical director, but I didn't get the gig. I did find out, though, that at the time, the usually very private Lehrer was in a rare period when he was not averse to giving interviews, since he considered that breaking his silence was worth it to help promote the show. I managed to convince the editor of the *Boston Globe Magazine* to assign me the interview, and it was very successful in all regards, except one: Lehrer never contacted me after it came out to let me know what he thought.

When I got to talk to him again, 13 years later (once again, he was promoting something, this time the reissue of his early albums on CD), I found out that he hated the picture of him that appeared with the article so much, he was embarrassed to contact me. The story behind that picture, and much more, is in the second part of this chapter: an edited transcript of our conversation, which has never appeared in print before.

December 1997

I'm going to depart from my usual format here (i.e., ranting and raving) because I want to tell you about meeting a legend. Deep in the bowels of my consciousness echoes a nasal, lilting, wonderfully cynical voice belonging to a former graduate student in mathematics at Harvard named Tom Lehrer. Lehrer is a legend for many reasons, one of which is that it could be argued he invented the self-produced hit record. Like many legends, he has a new record out. Unlike many legends with new records out, however, Tom Lehrer is not dead. Which is one of the reasons why I got to meet him and have a conversation with that voice, right there in the same room.

For the benefit of those to whom the name is unfamiliar, Lehrer hit a nerve in the '50s by writing, performing, and recording ditties and parodies like "Poisoning Pigeons in the Park" and "The Old Dope Peddler."

For the benefit of those to whom the name is unfamiliar, Lehrer hit a nerve in the '50s by writing, performing, and recording ditties and parodies like "Poisoning Pigeons in the Park" and "The Old Dope Peddler." His songs were clever, literate, and just naughty enough that those who heard them knew they were in on something special. I first heard his records when my older brother, who was all of 10, brought them home one day.

I didn't understand a lot of the lyrics: "Don't solicit for your sister, that's not nice/unless you get a good percentage of her price" (from "Be Prepared," his lampoon of the Boy Scouts) remained beyond my comprehension for quite a few years. But I listened, and I memorized. As apparently did many others: With just three albums in his catalog, Lehrer has sold something like a million-and-a-half records in the U.S. alone and thousands more overseas. A quick search for his name on the Internet reveals more than 600 sites *[this number has, of course, increased hugely since 1997]*, most of which are personal home pages from people (almost all of whom were born after he stopped recording) who list Lehrer as one of their primary influences.

Lehrer stopped writing songs for public consumption 30 years ago, but he is still very much alive and well, migrating with the seasons between Cambridge, Massachusetts, where he just "hangs out, puttering and frittering," and Santa Cruz, California, where he teaches a few college courses. He is a private person, who surfaces rarely for interviews (print and radio only–he won't do television because "I don't want to be recognized walking down the street,") and then only "when I've got something to sell." The last time was some 14 years ago, when British theatrical producer Cameron Mackintosh (*Miss Saigon*) put together a revue of Lehrer's songs called *Tomfoolery*, which eventually played all over the world. "I thought it would be easy to get the rights to perform Lehrer's songs," Mackintosh said at the time. "I figured he was dead."

This year Lehrer has once again invited the press into his life, thanks to Rhino Records, which has reissued his first two self-produced albums on CD. The CD also includes some "bonus" tracks and even a brand-new recording. So I got to talk to him about his recording experiences.

Jump back to January 1953, the same month Eisenhower began his first term. Lehrer had been performing his material, accompanying himself on the piano, at various functions around Harvard. Inspired by folk singers of the time, like Richard Dyer-Bennet, who put stuff out on their own labels, he wandered into a recording studio and laid down a dozen of his tunes. "There were two studios in the Boston Yellow Pages at the time," he recalls. "I went into one of them, and they were rude–like when you go into a restaurant and you're a nobody, and they treat you like they don't even see you." The other one, Trans Radio, was more receptive, and there Lehrer recorded the 12 tracks for his album in an hour.

"We did it with one mic for the voice and the piano. I did a song, and if I didn't like it, we backed up the tape and recorded over it. The tape cost extra, and this way there was no splicing or slipping. At the end of the hour, we had the whole album on tape. The recording budget was $15. I still have the receipt."

The studio had an arrangement with RCA Custom Pressings in New Jersey, so that's where Lehrer sent his tape to be pressed on 10-inch vinyl. He convinced the wife of a colleague to do the cover. "She did it for nothing. It had to be cheap to print, and no overlapping colors, so if the printing was off by an eighth of an inch it wouldn't matter." The record, *Songs of Tom Lehrer*, was released on the Lehrer label, catalog number TL 1.

"I asked people, relatives and friends and stuff, if I put out a record how many they would buy, and I figured I could sell 300. So I ordered 400. We sold 91 records the first week, and by the end of the month I sold them out. I made enough profit to press some more. There was never any risk, never any capital investment. The Harvard houses [residence halls] had newsstands, and there were three record stores in Cambridge who carried them as a service to the community, supporting local artists. The record was $3.50, and they paid me $3 each. Eventually I raised the price to $3.95.

"I actually owe my career to technology. The LP had come in around 1948, '49, and now it was feasible to do this. It would not have been possible with 78s; to make and ship all those multiple-disc albums would have been much too expensive."

Lehrer soon found himself being booked into nightclubs in and out of Boston, and his record started selling all over the country, mostly in college towns but also in San Francisco, after the *Chronicle* ran a major review of it. He considered recording for a major label but was told in no uncertain terms that his stuff was too controversial for a company that "sold refrigerators and other consumer items and wouldn't want any protests."

By 1959, he had enough material to do another album, *More of Tom Lehrer*, also on his own label. "The second record was a little bit longer. I went into RCA Studios in New York and booked some time. It was more professional. It took three hours, but we did it all in one evening. We did it in stereo–of course, I can't tell the difference. I suppose you can with earphones, but it's still just a piano and me. We put out mono and stereo versions and charged a dollar more for the stereo, hoping the market would determine which one people liked better. They were smart enough to realize the extra dollar wasn't getting them any-thing more, so the stereos have pretty much disappeared—I only sold 2,000 of them, ver-sus 72,000 of the mono."

At the same time, he recorded a live version of the same set of songs, which he called *An Evening Wasted with Tom Lehrer*, so that his between-songs banter could be preserved for the ages. It was taped at Harvard's Sanders Theater: "I wanted to make sure there was a friendly crowd. We did two nights, so I had a chance to make mistakes. A guy named Steve Fassett, who had a studio on Beacon Hill and did mostly classical music, recorded it. We edited it together. It was a change of pace for him, to put it mildly."

An Evening Wasted was nominated for a Grammy, in the "comedy with music" category. "That category only existed for two years. There aren't enough of those records any more to have a separate category from comedy with*out* music. In fact, there weren't even enough then. The winners were [piano/vocal duo] Jonathan and Darlene Edwards, who I think were worthy to beat me, but one of the other nominees was Alvin & The Chipmunks. I would have felt terrible if I had been beaten by Alvin & The Chipmunks."

After the second record came out, he re-released the first album as a 12-inch ("At 22 minutes, it was probably the shortest 12-inch in history") and toured New Zealand and Australia, where he also made some recordings. Some of those tapes ended up on *Tom Lehrer Revisited*, a concert recording of the songs from the first album. "I think the engineer was drunk–at least I was told that later–and it sounded terrible. It was pure self-indulgence on my part to use those tapes, just to prove I was popular in Australia. The rest of that album was recorded at MIT's Kresge Auditorium, where I played the same set. When Decca in England put out the record, they wouldn't use the Australian tapes, but instead they used the MIT tapes for the whole record."

Also during this period, two friends of Lehrer's in Boston who had a record label called Unicorn decided it would be fun to record him with an orchestra. They brought in Richard Hayman to arrange and conduct four tunes, which they hoped would make it as hit singles. "It was very strange for me, because what do you do with your hands? I had never stood still before to sing. My hands were always busy, so I never had to worry about what I was doing. Now I had to put them in my pocket, or something, and it didn't feel right. Like, do you sleep with your beard over the covers or under the covers?

"I will never forget the day when Hayman came in. It was 10 in the morning, a regular union group of players, and they put the music in front of them, with no title, no lyrics, no nothing. They ran through it a few times, figuring it was just this pretty waltz, and Hayman said 'Okay,' so I went into the booth to record. The engineer said, 'Poisoning Pigeons in the Park, take one,' and the piano player said 'Whaat?' and literally fell off the bench. I'd never seen that happen before.

"They put out a single of 'Poisoning Pigeons' and the 'Masochism Tango,' and it sold eight or nine copies in the United States, because of course we couldn't get airplay on it. Whereas in England, where they played it on the BBC, it sold quite well." Dr. Demento, who has gained many fans for Lehrer through his syndicated radio show, put one of the unreleased orchestral tracks on a 1995 collection, and all four appear on the new Rhino release (which has extensive liner notes by the good Doctor).

After his Down Under tour, Lehrer retired from performing ("I really don't consider myself a performer by temperament"), but a few years later he found himself writing topical songs for a satirical news show on NBC-TV called *That Was the Week That Was*, and when the show went off the air, he decided to cut another album. He booked himself into the hungry i nightclub in San Francisco for a few nights and played songs that had been on the show, like "Who's Next?" and "National Brotherhood Week," as well as some that weren't, like "The Vatican Rag." "I never even considered asking them to do that one," he says.

His recording of the gig ("We did it in stereo, in a more professional way with a guy up in the attic twiddling dials") was called *That Was the Year That Was* and came out on Warner Brothers' Reprise label. It sold 490,000 copies on LP, and it may represent another dubious record for Lehrer: It took 31 years to be certified Gold, which happened only after Reprise had issued the CD version. "Thirty-one years of hard work and discipline, and you, too, will get a Gold record," he cracks. "It's a fine example for our young people."

It was at this point that Lehrer decided it was a good time to get out of the record business himself. "I used *TWTYTW* as the bait–to get it, Warner Brothers had to take my earlier records, too. I was tired of all that nonsense. I didn't really have to do too much; it was all set up and flowing, but still it was a business."

"They wanted to re-release my first album, but they said the sound wasn't good enough and they wanted to re-record it, which, like an idiot, I did. First of all, I hadn't played those songs in five years, so I had to listen to the piano and say, 'What was I doing there?' and try to imitate it. Also I changed some of the lyrics to bring them up-to-date, which was wrong. I changed the order of the songs, which some people objected to because they were used to hearing one song after the other. So that was a big mistake." The new Rhino release uses his original tape from the first album, hiss and all. It sounds fine.

"They reissued the *Evening Wasted With* album, and I went back and re-edited it because there was too much applause, and it was too loud. I remember doing that in Los Angeles. Of course, you can't take out applause in the middle, you have to take it out at the peak, so I was cutting out all this wonderful stuff, and the engineer I was working with couldn't believe it. He said, 'Allan Sherman was here last week, and he made us put *in* applause.' So I said, 'He can have mine.'"

In 1990, Reprise put out the two live albums (one with bonus tracks of songs that Lehrer wrote for the children's TV show *The Electric Company*) and *That Was the Year That Was,* on CD. "Originally, they had released the *Evening Wasted With* album in mono and also in that fake stereo. The stereo one was what was on the CD. After it came out, Dr. Demento and NPR told me, 'We don't use that CD on the air because the sound isn't so good. We use the English version instead.' This was news to me, because I had never listened to the original stereo LP, and so I went back to it, and there was this tremendous echo. Twenty-four years this record had been out, and I had never listened to it. So they said they would remaster the CD. They sent me the remaster, and it sounded exactly the same, so I said try again. It took a long time, but eventually they sent me one that sounded fine. Apparently, what they did was take the mono and jazz it up with fake stereo, and when I complained they just went back to the mono, so now it sounds the way it used to sound."

But Lehrer's recording career was not quite over with. For this year's release, Rhino convinced him to go back into the studio one more time, to record "I Got It from Agnes," a breezy ditty about sexually transmitted disease that he had pulled out of his "trunk" and revised for the original production of *Tomfoolery*. "I was glad that *Tomfoolery* was all over by the time AIDS came in, because now you can't do the song. Most of the people who do *Tomfoolery* now leave it out, although I've heard that somebody does it as an AIDS awareness song–'Be careful, don't do this.'

"I had never recorded it, so they asked me if I would, and I said, 'Okay, I'll try.' They booked several hours at a studio"–Sound Techniques, near Boston's Fenway Park –"and I said, 'I'm not going to need several hours,' but I did, because there's 64 tracks of this and that, and I decided to do the piano track separately from the vocal because it would be easier, and I would have to practice too hard to do the piano and the voice simultaneously. But then I had to work to get them together on the different tracks, whereas before it was always automatic. They had to try different setups and different mixes, and it took forever, about three hours, to do this one lousy song." This from a man whose entire first LP took an hour.

Although Lehrer is now pushing 70, his voice retains that smug, sardonic grad-student quality of his earliest records. "I'm amazed it hasn't changed that much. Putting the new and old recordings side by side like that is pretty risky, but when I heard them, I thought, 'That's pretty good.'"

For me, the new release is a blast from my childhood, and the songs are still wondrously witty. But is the legend proud of his legacy? Besides the obvious material comforts his youthful endeavors brought him, is Lehrer still happy with them artistically? "The main thing I'm pleased about when I listen to the first album is not that these are the greatest songs ever written, but that I'm not embarrassed by them. I paid for the initial recordings, and I could have recorded anything I wanted. I had a whole lot of songs then that today I would be embarrassed by. So I am pleased with the fact that I picked those 12 songs. There are a few topical things, little things, that I would change, but I'm okay with it."

Me too. There's a real person connected with that voice in my head, now. The legend lives and is actually a very pleasant fellow.

Paul D. Lehrman (no relation) has been dreaming about poisoning small animals since the age of seven. Now he knows why.

Afterword

Unlike after my experience with the *Boston Globe*, Lehrer contacted me right after the article appeared in *Mix*. "I checked the website. Looks very good," he e-mailed me. "(Caught only two typos—I have the gene for proofreading.)" I fixed them. "I scored a *Mix* at Nini's," referring to a legendary magazine shop in Harvard Square. "It was even prominently displayed—they must have known a living legend was in it. Anyway, the article was excellent. Next to money I like adulation best. I know Rhino will be very happy. Thanks again."

A Conversation with Tom Lehrer

September 7, 1997, Cambridge, Massachusetts

Insider Audio: There are some other transcripts of conversations with you on the Internet, but they look a little weird.

Tom Lehrer: They [*Rhino*] sent me the disk of the Internet chats I did, so I could edit them. But what they did, apparently, was put the disk right in. I had some comments on previous questions, so I thought they'd go back and change the question, but no, they just put my comment in there. The guy who did the chat room isn't there any more. They call it "Rocky's" because that isn't his name. They can put a new Rocky in who's somebody else. In LA, I talked to Mr. KABC, who wouldn't say his name. Presumably that's the same kind of thing; if he gets fired, they can put somebody else in as Mr. KABC. But nobody cares. A guy leaves a soap opera, they put somebody else in.

I did a profile of you for the *Boston Globe* magazine about 13 years ago. The article came out well, but I understand you didn't like the picture that accompanied it.

I know that article was in the middle of winter because the photographer, whose name eludes me fortunately, wanted me to come to his studio so he could "get to know" me. He liked to "get to know" his subjects so he could really do justice to the photograph. I thought, "Oh God," but I didn't want to rock the boat. The *Globe* had put money in *Tomfoolery*, so I didn't want to make a thing of it, so I said okay, I'll go along with this. But fortunately my car broke down, and by the time I had it fixed, it was too late, so he came here and did all these weird pictures. So I learned my lesson then.

There was recently a piece on you in the *Globe* arts section, which had a picture.

That was fine, they just sent a staff photographer over. But the *New York Times Magazine* [*writer*] guy spent hours and hours and hours, starting in April, and finally in July they sent a photographer, and she was a real "photographer," and she wanted to get me holding something and posing, but I put some constraints on that. Then when I saw what they did to Andrew Weil and others, I said I hope that nothing gets published. The photographer didn't arrive till July, and this is September, and it hasn't appeared, and I haven't heard from the writer, Peter Tauber, a freelancer. I hope he can sell it somewhere else, because he spent so much on it. He would call me about last-minute corrections and stuff.

It didn't seem to be of any contemporary interest except when the record came out. That was the idea—he interviewed me in April so that in May it would be out, or even in June when there was some convention of *That Was the Week That Was* alumni in New York—I wasn't there, but they could time it for that. Past that, there was no point.

The hook was, isn't it amazing that after 40 years it's still selling, but without that there's nothing there. And now everybody else has covered it already. But I turned down the daily

Times because of that. I said I'll be glad to do it, but you should know the magazine is doing it, so he said, well I guess we can't. There goes New York. I got the Newark *Star-Ledger*, so that's close. And Long Island *Newsday*. [*The piece finally appeared in the Times in November.*]

You were one of the first to make a self-produced record album.

Young folks come up to me and say: "You made your own album. I want to do my own album. How do you do that?" And I have to explain to them that times have changed. I was doing stuff around Harvard, like dance intermissions, and it was basically the same people, and I really don't consider myself a performer by temperament, and technology reared its head: the LP had come in. A lot of people were doing this, including Dr. Shep Ginandes here in town, who had done a folk-song album, and Richard Dyer-Bennet, so I thought, let's look into this. So I called Shep, and he told me how he went about it, and I looked in the Boston Yellow Pages under recording studios, and there were only two—I looked the other day and there were four columns.

I was working at Baird Atomic, and I asked the wife of a business associate to do the cover. I told her what I wanted, with the flames. And I wrote the liner notes, and so it was all very cheap. She did it for nothing, but Rhino paid her a fee. She's in an old folks' home now. The jackets were printed at a local printer and then sent down to RCA in New Jersey for assembling and pasting. I had my home address on Kirkland Road in Cambridge on the back of the record.

[*At this point, he goes upstairs to retrieve his ledgers from 1953, which takes only a minute.*] So I made enough profit to press some more. There was never any risk. I invested the profits in another 300 records. Just a little fly-by-night operation, I was really keeping track of this stuff. When the second record came out, 10" records had just disappeared, so I redid the first one as a 12" cause it just seemed easier to. I didn't change the price. There's a nut out in Bloomington, Indiana, who collects all this trivia who keeps asking me, "When did you do this?" and "Why is this mono and this stereo?", and it's kind of interesting, and I go and look all this stuff up.

Because of the record, people heard of me outside of Cambridge, and I started performing, I got the Blue Angel in New York and Storyville here, nothing major, and then I went into the Army for two years, and that allowed the whole thing to spread by itself, without my having to do anything. When I got out of the Army in '57, a lot of people knew about it. There had been a songbook, a little hardcover which is out of print. It had the kind of piano accompaniment I play, which I find out now is called *stride piano, octave/chord*, and it's messy on the page, whereas now they just put one note in the bass, and you do the chords with your right hand.

So I got some offers to do concerts, as well as night clubs. At that time, there was no such thing as the pop concert circuit. If I had hung on a little longer, the college concert circuit was just breaking with the Kingston Trio and people like that. In my day there was Anna Russell and Victor Borge and me, and that was about it for comedians. Later on, of course, I could have called William Morris and said, "Book me for six months," but there wasn't anything like that. I did some of that, and then I got tired after a couple of years. So I figured I'll put out the rest of the material I had, and there was enough for the second record, and then I'd quit.

We recorded two nights at Sanders Theater [*at Harvard*], so I had a chance to make mistakes. The cover was taken at the Hanna Theater in Cleveland. It was taken from the back of the balcony, and it showed a lot of people there, and I was thinking maybe some guy was there with somebody other than his wife, and there he is on the cover, and I'd get sued, but nothing happened.

I wanted to do the record where there was a guaranteed friendly audience. We did it for the Harvard Liberal Union. In those days, the only way you could get Sanders Theater was to be sponsored by an undergraduate organization. Nowadays, it's big money. Steve Fassett recorded it. He liked the kind of stuff I did and had a bunch of comic records he had taped off the air. I'm sure he's dead. Everybody else I know is.

Would you ever want to re-record the old records?

I'm quite satisfied with the records. In 1960 I had done the concert version of the first set, *Tom Lehrer Revisited*, which was recorded at Kresge Auditorium at MIT. The picture for that was taken at Royal Festival Hall. I'm at the piano, and there are those two people sitting in the audience, alone. I like that idea. After the audience left, I had a photographer come in, and we took that picture. That was recorded in '59 but released in '60, after I had quit performing.

The re-release of *Songs of Tom Lehrer* had an orange cover, which was done by Eric Martin who did the *TWTYTW* cover. And it sold okay, and a whole generation of people think that's how it was. The CD [*on Reprise*] didn't come out until 1990, so for 25 years that was the only *Songs by Tom Lehrer* that was available.

So now we have three CDs out: *Tom Lehrer Revisited*, which is the complete MIT concert, plus two bonus tracks from *The Electric Company* which I got them to do, which I was quite pleased about because I wanted them to be preserved somewhere; *An Evening Wasted*, which is mono, but, of course, now it doesn't say on CDs whether they're mono or stereo—if it's digital, then *naturally* it's stereo; and *TYTYTW*. They were all put out on Reprise in 1990. So there was a 25-year interval between Reprise taking over the LPs and issuing the CDs. When Rhino called and asked if they could do the CDs, I said it's okay with me, but you have to get permission from Warner Bros., so I had my agent—I had an agent at that time—call Warner Bros., and they said "Oh, what a great idea, we should have thought of that!"

They had done it just in the nick of time, because LPs were fading fast. They did it in their usual way—I have a feeling these companies have a policy of not employing anybody over the age of 16 'cause it's very had to get anything done efficiently. I was very pleased with the whole thing; they eventually got it done. So this revives the old stuff, along with the orchestral versions.

How did the orchestral versions come about?

What happened was in 1960 Unicorn Records, which was Jimmy Stagliano, who played with the Boston Symphony and was also some kind of manager, and Bob Sylvester who ran Unicorn Records as a sideline, decided they could get some kind of single out of this. So I went to a studio in New York and recorded with an orchestra for the first time. We ended up with four songs.

They put out a single of "Poisoning Pigeons" and "The Masochism Tango." The other two were never released. I was going through my basement, as is my wont, and found the tape of the four of them, so I sent it to Dr. Demento and told him if he ever wanted to use them.... The others are "The Hunting Song" and "We Will All Go Together When We Go." Nothing much is added by the orchestra on those two, but the first two I thought were nice, especially the tango. So he played them, and he put two of them on his LPs and "The Hunting Song" on his "basement tapes," and when Rhino did this, they asked if they could do all four, and I said sure. I own all the rights to everything. When Dr. Demento did it, Stagliano was still alive, so I paid him a flat fee to make sure, in case there was any legal thing. I had no idea who owned what, but I assumed he owned the rights to something. So I paid him a flat fee, and we settled that.

The other song on the Rhino is "I Got It from Agnes." I never did it in concerts, because it was a "party" song. If you remember Ruth Wallis and Rusty Warren and those people had their own little bin in the record store for party songs, and I didn't want to be in that bin. The *Crepitation Contest*, that kind of stuff. So I never did it on record. But when Cameron Mackintosh was doing *Tomfoolery* in London in 1980, he asked if I had anything in the trunk he could use, and I dug that out and redid it and made it slightly more sophisticated. I'm quite pleased with it—it's much better than the original version, I think, it has a better verse and is more tightly packed.

I sent Rhino the whole [*multitrack*] tape [*with multiple takes on different tracks*], and I said, okay, you edit it, you decide. We did a mix in Boston that I was happy with, but we sent them the master just in case they changed their mind. But I was very happy with what they did. It's only 2-1/2 minutes, but it's stereo and all that. And it worked out fine. I kind of liked the idea that people know that I'm not only alive, but I can stand up, or sit down at least, and am ambulatory to that extent.

"I Got It from Sally" [*the original version of "Agnes"*]—if I had recorded it [*when he wrote it*], I would be embarrassed by it today, because it was so crude. I've made it very clear that "Sally" was written in 1952. "The Old Dope Peddler" obviously has a whole different resonance today. Nobody I knew took dope. Jazz musicians did dope. The reference in "Be Prepared" to reefers—reefers is kind of cute, kind of folksy, but on the Reprise release I changed it to grass, or pot, which was popular then, but it doesn't resonate as well, and it doesn't scan as well. I was delighted to find that "reefer" is on the live version. It was fun to hear the song in *Tomfoolery*, not here but in London. The audience would start to laugh when the guy would begin, and then the laugh would gradually die, cause it was a kind of chilly song. It was wonderful. He did it with absolutely no effect, not acting as though this is funny in any way, he's just thinking about this lovely old guy who used to be around the neighborhood, but without any kind of feeling about it. We had to go right to the next song without any applause, because the applause would have been kind of embarrassed. You're supposed to applaud because the song is over, but it's like the end of the first act of *Cabaret*—you don't know what to do, are you supposed to applaud the Nazis?

In the Boston production, Rob Fisher, who was the music director [*the job I auditioned for*], sang it from the piano, and it was the only time he ever sang on stage, and then it would go immediately to the next song. It was something surprising. He wasn't supposed to be an actor, and he did it marvelously, without affect at all, just straight, and as soon as he got through he went right into the intro for the "Vatican Rag," so there was no chance for applause. It was very nice.

So it just keeps going. Who knew? When I think about that—it's 44 years between the two recordings.

How come you shortened "We Will All Go Together When We Go" on the orchestral version?

The bridge of "We Will All Go Together" was taken out because the song is just too long. It's like 3-1/2 minutes long, and no disc jockey would play that. They wanted to put it on the CD, and I said, whatever, just as long as it's at the end so people don't have to listen to it if they don't want to. The "Hunting Song" had the second verse repeated to make it a little longer, and added the gunshots, to try to get a Spike Jones thing out of it.

The songs have raunch by 1950s standards, perhaps, but nowadays everything is so explicit. I was trying to be a little subtle, not like Redd Foxx or Rusty Warren and all that. Just a little suggestive here and there. I wouldn't have thought of it as raunchy, but I guess by '50s standards.... Some people did say, 'Oh, you can't play those naughty songs, or those dirty songs.' I remember playing Storyville on Cape Cod one summer. They had posters put in all the merchants' windows for who was coming each week, and there was one store that wouldn't put up the poster of me. They took all the others, but they thought my songs were dirty. I didn't think they were dirty, compared to all those party songs like "The Postman Has the Longest Route in Town" or "She's Got the Biggest Kanakas in Hawaii." I wrote songs like that, too, just for fun, but I would never record them or perform them. They were influences in the sense of what *not* to do. It was definitely just to be suggestive. There's that line in "My Home Town" about Parson Brown. *[Lehrer doesn't sing anything about the Parson after he mentions his name, he just says, "I think I'd better leave the next line out just to be on the safe side."]* There was nothing I could do there to be suggestive. I could come right out and say something, but that wouldn't be funny to me, but I couldn't find anything that was just suggestive enough, so I just left it out. And fortunately, since there were restrictions at that time, it made sense to say, "I got to leave this out," where today it wouldn't make any sense: "What could it possibly be that he can't say?" You have to know that it was 1953.

When I made the second record, I wanted to make sure that I would not be accused of raunchy songs. So there's almost no reference to anything sexual on the second record, unless you count "Oedipus Rex." "She's My Girl" has a little, maybe, and there's a couple of lines about the backseat of our roommate's Chevrolet *[in "Bright College Days"]*, but I didn't want to have any songs about sex, so people couldn't accuse me of writing dirty songs, the way they said I wrote those "sick" songs. On the first record, I'd say there were two I could call sick, and there were little parts of others. That was the identification: *Time* magazine had a thing about the sick comics, Lenny Bruce, me. Whereas now, it's really hard to be sick. You can be offensive, God knows.

Among the influences I hear in your music are the Marx Brothers.

I loved the Marx Brothers, still do, and certainly "Lydia the Tattooed Lady" was something I would admire as being a comparatively sophisticated song. Just slightly raunchy. I heard Groucho Marx talking about that, and at the end he's in command of the fleet, and he married Lydia, which made it all right. She can seduce him, but when the guy marries her, it's okay. That song particularly, but I wouldn't think so...who knows, maybe an unconscious influence.

What do you hear today that you like?

I don't keep up with things today. There are little bits of things. John Forster has several things, but there's no *whole* record that I wholeheartedly embrace. Forster's take on Paul Simon *["Fusion" on the album "Entering Marion"]* is so wonderful: "Remember who's the genius here." He has a whole sense of music, with the orchestrations and the sound effects, which I never aspired to. He has fun with music, too, which is very hard to do.

Every now and then I hear a song—Andy Breckman, Christine Lavin have a few good things. I try—any time I hear anybody say, "Oh, you gotta hear so and so." I rush out and get it. *[Pulls out "Funny Folk Songs" CD]* I saw this at Tower Records. It was some kind of concert with all these people doing one song, showing off. Some of them are quite funny. Lou and Peter Berryman have some funny songs. There are a lot of people who have some funny songs.

One of the distinctions, if I may toot my own horn, is that most of these songs are not interesting enough, in terms of craftsmanship. They're not shored up with rhymes and musical hooks, things to make it interesting, that you'd want to hear it more than twice.

That's the problem with a lot of these things. Whereas Flanders and Swann, people like that, I would listen to over and over again. Or Sondheim, or Sheldon Harnick, who write sophisticated songs. Some of these have funny *ideas*, and you laugh uproariously the first time, and a little the second time, but then they're not clever enough to quote the lines. You can see them in front of an audience who've never heard the songs; they think they're very funny, as I did when I first heard them, but a lot of them don't hold up. Sondheim does witty songs in his shows, and so do several others: Kander, and Ebb, and so on.

When I look back on the past 40 years and think of funny songwriters, I have a large collection of funny LPs of people who, right after me, were inspired to do the same thing, but all those people—Bob Peck, Ann Soulé, Paul Winter, Elliot Lee Hoffman, people nobody has ever heard of. There's this guy, Ronald Smith, who writes these books, *Who's Who in Comedy* and stuff, and he names all these people, and I wrote him, saying I can't believe that anybody else has these records except me. There were lots of them, but very few people I can think of, if any, with records of funny songs that got anywhere. There's Weird Al Yankovic, but that's parody. There are comedy records, God knows.

I mostly listen to show tunes and that kind of stuff, stuff with sophistication. Unfortunately, I don't really get the lyrics of most pop tunes. People tell me I should listen to, say, Steely Dan, so I really try, and then I have to read the lyrics, but then I say, "But I really don't understand what that means." So even the people that I like, like Paul Simon, I don't understand a lot of the lyrics, and I can't really get into it the way I can other things. I don't appreciate poetry. I don't mind admitting that now, I don't understand poetry. We studied it in high school and college, but they never told us why it was good. I got A's on all the exams. "Hail to thee blithe spirit, bird thou never wert"—what the hell does that mean? I have no idea. So I don't appreciate poetic lyrics. I'm not ashamed to admit it. I think that they may be great, and they're wonderful for those who can get it, but I don't. I appreciate Randy Newman, and people like that who are more accessible.

Comedy Central just put out a book about comedy, and they say that they're still making comedy records, but they're not selling and not as influential as videos, and the proof of this is that the Grammy Awards for comedy music are dominated by Peter Schickele. They still have comedy records, but Andrew Dice Clay and Dennis Miller certainly don't sell the way that Bob Newhart and Shelley Berman and people like that sold.

I love to talk. Barney Frank was quoted in the paper the other day, and someone asked him why he spoke so fast, and he said, I always find it more interesting when I'm speaking than when I'm listening. I don't mind a chance to spout off. Since it's professional, it's not just for myself, tooting my own horn is part of the deal. As long as I can get away with it, I'd rather talk about me than Princess Diana.

You're going to be 70 next year. *[Which was 1998, therefore he's 78 now.]*

Isn't that amazing? Nobody's more surprised than I am. Can't lie. Subtraction doesn't lie. I'm kind of looking forward to that, cause 69, 68 is so boring. If you say, "I'm 70," people say, "Wow!" It was like my mother would introduce me as her son; then she would wait for them to say, "I don't believe that you have a son this old," and if they didn't say that, she would be very disappointed. So if I say, "I'm 70," and they say, "Oh, really? I would have thought you were 75," then I'll know it's too late.

I'm cutting down [*teaching*] at [*University of California*] Santa Cruz over the years. This winter I'm just going to do a math course. I'm doing a three-unit, as opposed to five-unit, course on infinity, which I've never done before. I'm planning to study like crazy. It's for non-math majors. I'm trying to bring in the fact that infinity is when things get complicated. In calculus, algebra, probability, geometry, everything, so I'm trying to learn things like how perspective drawing uses infinity. So that'll take me three months. They won't appreciate it, but I will. I'll have fun with it. I've been teaching a course for non-mathematicians for years, and a lot of the stuff has already been covered there.

I don't do the musical theater course anymore. The interest in that seems to have declined. It became extracurricular, non-credit. Nowadays, there are so many course requirements, and people's eyes are on their careers, and they have jobs, so it's, "I can't come Saturday, or Thursday night." In the old days, people went to college to have fun. Especially Santa Cruz. So they were glad to do it. But now you have to give them course credit.

But I was also trying to introduce the undergraduate audience to some of this stuff, even at this primitive level of just readings [*of shows*]. But it turned out as the years went by, the old folks from downtown would come up, by the busload, and take all the good seats. They were a wonderful audience because they remembered all the shows and laughed at all the dated jokes, but it wasn't the audience that I had in mind, and the students didn't come in great numbers. So it was a combination of these two and the fact that it was a *lot* of work. So if there were a great groundswell, I might consider reviving it, but so far there hasn't been.

Thank God no one has gone from there to a Broadway career. I live in dread of that, although now actually it doesn't matter, but I wouldn't want someone to say they got their start with me, because they'd come out in droves. Actually, one of my students, Rona Figueroa, later became one of the Miss Saigons on Broadway for a couple of years. It had nothing to do with me. She was totally marvelous. One of the things I loved about it was when I asked her if she was a theater major, she said no, I wouldn't go over there; I don't believe in any of that stuff. I was *so* pleased because she was head and shoulders above all the theater majors in terms of natural talent. She sang in a rock band, and she was gorgeous. She could act, and she could sing, just because she could do it. And the stuff over there where they're doing these exercises, these really serious people—"now tell us your most embarrassing experience," "pretend you're a tiger"—oh God.

What question has nobody asked you that you want to have asked?

The answer is, "What question...?" No, those are too easy. If there is something I want to talk about, I can usually work it in. I learned that from being on the talk shows. Don't answer their questions, bring in your own.

I told Rhino *[I would give interviews for]* four months, until Labor Day, with an extension in your case. I figured that launches the record, and I don't think it's going to help to do any more. I wanted to support the record as much as possible. I did an hour on Chris Lydon *[NPR's "The Connection"]* about popular song. The idea wasn't just to plug the record—we plugged the record plenty, but the idea was to discuss comic lyrics and stuff like that. It went over so well that he asked me to do another hour sometime, but that won't be specifically for the record.

I don't do television. Absolutely. It's an invasion of privacy, for one thing. If you get your picture in the paper it doesn't matter—two days later nobody remembers—thank God. The other thing is, on television I'm not in control. On radio, I can have my notes in front of me, I don't have to shave, I don't have to worry if there's spinach on my teeth or which camera's on me, that kind of stuff. We can just talk. Also, there isn't the time restriction there is on television. There is time restriction, but usually it's taped, and then they edit it down, whereas on television it's *there*. I wouldn't want to perform on television—I don't really come across at all. I've seen myself enough times. A serendipitous thing is that the two times I was on Johnny Carson, the tape was erased and reused. In those days, they didn't keep it. This was confirmed when he had one of his anniversary shows, he said, "You notice there are no tapes, no examples from these years, and the reason is..." So I'm grateful. I was on Carson twice, I did all the talk shows: Merv Griffin, Mike Douglas, all the television that they wanted. I was on once with Carson and once with Bob Newhart as guest host. They never asked me back.

I said something that in retrospect, I'm glad I said it, but it didn't come out the way I meant it. It was during the Vietnam War. They asked me about the campus I was on, I was teaching at MIT at the time, and I said that the main difference from the old days was that for the male students, the thing uppermost in their minds was to dodge the draft. And I said, it wasn't true during World War II, but in those days we were on the right side. What I meant to convey was that there was *no* right side this time, but I was told that the audience reaction was kind of cold. The host didn't pick up on it. He didn't say anything. We went right on with the conversation. I was very pleased in retrospect that I had said that, even though it didn't quite come out the way I wanted. That may have been one of the reasons why they didn't ask me back.

I remember when Richard Pryor said something about how in South Africa, all the black people should pick up guns and kill all the white people, and they went right on with the interview, and nobody stopped him on that. "Oh good old Richard, what a card." As long as you're billed as a comedian, I guess you can say anything.

After-afterword

All I can say is thanks, Tom, for the pleasure you gave me years ago, and the great interviews you gave me in recent times.

Chapter 7

Jack Davis

A New York Minute: Grumpmeier Goes to AES

Preface

This was the first appearance in *Mix* of Phineas T. Grumpmeier, my obstreperous "alter ego" who ended up being featured in many of my favorite columns. Grumpmeier was actually the invention of my good friend (and former editor of *Electronic Musician*) Tim Tully, who asked me to do a satirical piece for his short-lived *Studio Software Report* newsletter. The piece I came up with (an expanded version of which ended up in *Mix* in April 1997 as "Next Year's Gear") was so inflammatory that Tim asked me, "Do you really want to put your name on this?" So we borrowed an idea from *The New Yorker* who, when they want to print a column without an author's name attached to it, start it off with "A friend writes:". Only Tim gave this imaginary friend a name, which he intended to reflect the personality of someone who could write such a piece: Grumpmeier. It was inspired, and I immediately appropriated it.

January 1998

I ran into my old buddy Grumpmeier at the AES show in New York, and he was not a happy puppy. "Look at this place!" he ranted, without even bothering to say hello. "It's got all the soul of an Erector set!" Somehow, the required "™" was missing from that sentence.

"Oh, it's not so bad," I countered. "There's plenty of exhibit space, all the booths are in one area, and it's easy to find things."

"Sure, if you don't mind walking three blocks to get to the demo rooms and conferences. Did you see how empty those corridors were? How few people bothered to make it to the sessions? I tell you, if you wanted to find the cleanest bathroom in New York, it was right there next to the meeting rooms."

"But," I gently reminded him, "don't you remember the days the convention was at the Hilton, when you could spend hours waiting for the elevators to get to the demo rooms? If you tried the stairs just to get from the fourth floor to the fifth, you always somehow found yourself on a locked stairway whose only exit was an alley off of 51st Street."

"Hey, so you'd duck into a deli, grab a knish and a coffee, and head back into the fray. You try the food here?"

I am constantly amazed at how fast he can change the subject. "It's not so bad," I sighed. "They have decent sandwiches and salads and fruit..."

"C'mon, your basic airport has all that now. This is New York! Food capital of the world! And those people who take ten minutes to find change for a fiver after you've spent two bucks on a cup of cold coffee—"

"Listen," I cut him off. "You want food? You've got to eat dinner every night, right? So make sure you go someplace wonderful and stop worrying about lunch!"

"Yeah, and by the time everyone's finished with their little after-show meetings and their cocktail hours and their press conferences, it's 10 o'clock, and you're so hungry and exhausted you'll be happy with Taco Bell," he bellows. "Not a great way to enjoy a meal, especially if you're blowing a hundred bucks per. Friend of mine and I stumbled into the Carnegie Deli one night around 11. He told me he hadn't eaten since breakfast, and he was so wasted he couldn't even open the menu—so he'd just have a hamburger. Can you imagine? At the Carnegie Deli?! I wrestled him to the ground and held him there while I told the waiter to bring him a bowl of chicken soup with an extra matzoh ball and a pastrami on light rye, and keep the pickle bowl full. He thanked me afterward.

"And another thing!" (There was no stopping him now.) "Where are you supposed to go after the show closes each day? You think people come to AES just to look at gear? No—

they come to see all these people they never get to see in person, the ones they talk to on the phone or, these days, e-mail. They want to get to know them, do the schmooze thing.

"Where are you supposed to go after the show closes each day? You think people come to AES just to look at gear?"

"You can't carry on any kind of conversation on the show floor. If you're working a booth, you have to pay attention to everyone who comes by, which sort of makes it hard to keep a train of thought on track. And if you're walking around and you do see somebody you know, it always turns out that at least one of you is in a terrible hurry because some meeting ran overtime, or 12th Avenue was blocked by some damn bike race and the taxi couldn't get through, so the only thing you can think of to say is, 'See anything cool?' To which the answer is invariably, 'Nah!' and you both shrug your shoulders and run off. And then two months later, you read in *Mix* that there really *were* some interesting things there, but somehow you missed them all.

"So at 6 o'clock, the Javits Center goes totally dead—empties out faster than Shea Stadium in September when the Mets are down by ten in the eighth inning. Everyone goes off to their hotels, but they're spread out over a 20-block radius. So maybe you get five minutes to talk to someone on the bus, and then you've lost them forever. Ever try to track someone down in their hotel room? When the hotel clerks can't spell anything more complicated than 'Jones'? Fageddabout it!"

He was turning into Joe Pesci before my eyes. "But," I countered, "there are all these parties every night. Surely you can meet people there."

He exploded: "What the hell makes all these companies doing the parties think that the people in *our* business want to spend their nights listening to bad music on bad sound systems at toxic SPLs?! We do that for a living—well, not the bad sound systems part, unless we're touring musicians—so why should we want to do that when we're *not* working? It's not like audio engineering types are known for being great dancers. You can't possibly hold an actual conversation at one of those parties. 'Hey, how you doin'?' 'Whaddyasay?' Maybe some people think this is fun, but either they're from another planet or they're kidding themselves. Nothing actually ever happens at any of these parties—unless someone from the company makes a speech, in which case you're definitely better off being somewhere else—but they figure if they keep the noise level high enough and the lights weird enough so no one can actually figure out what's going on, people will go home thinking they did something cool.

"Besides, if you don't smoke, you won't last ten minutes in there. So you're back out on the street, looking for someone to talk to. You take a cab over to the next party, but it's the same deal. You can keep it up all night, until you drop from exhaustion. And meanwhile, you haven't said more than three words to anyone."

49

"Well, you can always go back to one of the bars at the hotels," I suggested. "They're quiet, and usually pretty well-ventilated."

"Yeah, but where?" he retorts. "There isn't any one hotel that everyone goes to any more—there are 'official' hotels, but without the exhibits and demo rooms, there's no reason for anyone to hang around. So folks are spread out all over midtown and worse. I went one night to the Hilton bar, figuring that *someone* would be there. Turns out the only other person there was Alan Parsons."

"You really didn't know anybody else there?" I asked.

"No, dummy, there *was* nobody else there. Except for us and him and his friend—every other table was empty. Used to be on a Saturday night you couldn't find a waiter there for hours, you could die of thirst, but at least the conversation was hot and heavy, and if you hung around awhile, you could run into *everybody*. That night, the only people we *could* talk to were the waiters, who were hovering over us like a cloud of gnats. I never want to see a bowl of goldfish crackers again as long as I live. Hell, I even struck up a conversation with the piano player."

"Well, Alan's a very cool guy. Did you get to talk to him?"

"Sure did. Turns out the only reason *he* was there was that they were seeing *Riverdance* at Radio City Music Hall across the street. Being English, they wanted to get a drink during the intermission—the interval, he called it—and Radio City doesn't have a bar, so this was the closest one they could find!"

He stopped screaming and turned thoughtful. I even detected a hint of wistfulness. "Do you remember going away to summer camp?" he asked. "Sure," I said. "The latrine stank, the food was terrible, and I got beat up a lot." "Besides that!" he snapped and went nostalgic again. "You were with the same bunch of kids all the time. You did all these activities together during the day, and at night you sat around the campfire, or lay awake in your bunk, and tried to scare each other or gross each other out with stories. You talked about girls and the counselors and your mean teachers—all the things that mattered. Then you'd wake up in the morning and have those same people to deal with all over again.

"By the end of the summer, you *knew* these people, and whether you liked them or loathed them, you couldn't imagine life without them. When it came time to go home, you swore that you would see all of them every week all winter, and you'd all be back next year. Of course, you saw them maybe once, and the next year, half of them didn't show up. But the intensity of the experience, the—boy, do I hate this word—the 'bonding' that went on during those few weeks, imprinted itself on your psyche pretty deep. I'll bet you still remember those kids' names, faces and worst habits."

"I suppose I do," I said. "There was Jimmy, the son of a famous actor, who liked to expose himself in front of the girls coming back from the lake. And Dickie, who still sucked his thumb at age 12, although he tried really hard to hide it. And Bobby, who couldn't bring himself to use the latrine and so for two weeks—"

"Yeah, that's it!" he mercifully cut me off. "I'll bet you can't tell me stuff like that about your own kids!

"My point is,"—I figured he had one somewhere—"conventions are our generation's summer camps: You make connections with people you would otherwise never know. You find out that so-and-so was just as nuts about some obscure '70s band as you were, and maybe that's why the equipment he designs is so weirdly appealing. Or you find out that Joe Blow grew up in the next town and dated your sister, and that explains why you've always figured him to be a jerk. Or someone else is working on a project in his spare time that has nothing to do with what he does for a living, but that happens to be close to your heart, too, and maybe you can collaborate. Not to mention the folks who get romantically involved, either short-term or long.

"But to make that work, you've got to have an atmosphere where people can stop doing their arts and crafts and nature walks and swimming lessons—you know, stop writing orders and checking out the competition and doing nonstop sales pitches—and just sit down and be together. It works in Anaheim, where there just aren't very many places to go, but, of course, none of us will be going to Anaheim for the next couple of years, unless we're going to Disneyland. For some people it works in Las Vegas, and it used to work great in New York. But now, with everyone off to hell and gone after the 6 o'clock bell, there's no chance. And Los Angeles? Fageddabout it." Uh-oh, Joe again.

Jack Davis

I bought Grumps a drink and told him I had an important meeting to go to. Actually, I was off to the movies, by myself. I like to be around people, too, but anything was better than his complaining.

I didn't see Grumpmeier again until early morning on the last day of the show. Actually, I only caught a glimpse of him standing in Times Square in his underwear, unshaven, screaming and cursing. Poor guy, I thought. He really misses his summer camp, and now he's gone off the deep end. But I found out later he wasn't to blame—his beautiful, ultra-modern, world-unto-itself non-official-AES hotel was on fire, and he had to evacuate from the 26th floor. By the stairs.

Afterword

This column, in fact, was based entirely on real events. My English friend Richard Elen (at the time marketing director of Apogee Electronics) was the one who wanted to order a hamburger at the Carnegie Deli, and he thanked me later for interfering. And Jimmy, the kid who liked to expose himself, also existed—but I'm not telling you what his real name is.

Chapter 8

Will Terry

Course Catalog for the Real World
In This School, You'll Learn What Truly Matters

Preface

I started writing "April Fools" columns my second year on the job with *Mix*, and the response from readers was surprisingly good. I've always subscribed to the theory that any institution, like a magazine, that takes itself seriously all the time is not an institution I want to be part of. So for *Mix* to be willing to run columns like this—and for the readers to ask for more—I thought was a very healthy sign for our industry. And one of the great things about writing funny is that you can make points that might be hard to say in a serious piece: They'd come across too angry, or heavy-handed, or whiny. So the April issues provide a great opportunity to say all sorts of things about the audio business that we all know to be true but might otherwise never make it into print.

April 1998

There's never enough time to learn everything you need to know. That's true of life, and it's especially true of audio education. Whether it's a weekend course or a four-year undergraduate degree program, there's always more material that needs to be mastered than students have time to learn. And what with physics, math, acoustics, electronics, music theory, and all the other things that the student has to deal with, practical subjects often get short shrift. Many problems the student will have to deal with on a daily basis when he hits the workplace are barely touched on, if at all.

*In this curriculum, around which I am designing a whole new school—named for myself, of course— students will be able to ignore all that theoretical stuff and concentrate on what they **really** need to know to survive in the audio business.*

I'm going to take the opportunity this month, therefore, to propose a revolutionary new syllabus for training audio professionals. In this curriculum, around which I am designing a whole new school—named for myself, of course—students will be able to ignore all that theoretical stuff and concentrate on what they *really* need to know to survive in the audio business.

So here is the first List of Offerings ("LoOf") for the Lehrman Institute for the Real-world Practice of Audio (LIRPA):

Psychology 101a. *Understanding the Client, and Why He or She Hates Me.* How to deal with people who would much rather be doing what you do than what they do, and who resent you for it. How to deal with people who are sure they could do your job better than you, and resent you for it. How to deal with people who haven't got the faintest clue what it is you do, and resent paying you for it. Advanced seminar in turning the other cheek.

Psychology Net30. *Trying Not to Hate the Client.* Continuation of above. Understanding and overcoming your own feelings of hostility against people who use your console as a picnic table, your lobby as a day-care center, your mouse pad as an ashtray, your mixing sessions to make loud phone calls about their next gig, and your accounts receivable as a personal line of credit. Independent study in not taking it out on your domestic partner.

Live Sound I-90. *Surviving the Tour.* An intensive, eight-week traveling course starting with lower-digestive-tract conditioning, placing emphasis on tolerating day-old fried foods and week-old pies. Muscle-building techniques with concentration on avoiding hernia and back-sprain. The role of insulated footwear in avoiding electrocution when turning on the AC at outdoor venues. Defensive driving techniques for overloaded 18-wheelers and decommissioned Trailways buses with wild parties going on in the back. Secrets of mixing a 14-piece band on three hours of sleep. Laboratory fee covers trusses, knee pads, Pepto-Bismol, No-Doz, and Lysol. Prerequisite: Recreational Pharmacology 101.

Live Sound 007. *Self-Defense for FOH Engineers.* Units on pre-show crowd interactions, including the proper responses to stupid questions like: "Is that computer actually playing all the music?" "Can I plug this tape recorder into your board?" and, "Hey, got any blow in the truck?"; repelling mid-show heckling, kicking people off the riser and deflecting assorted missiles, organic and inorganic; minimizing post-show violence after the headliner shows up drunk and falls off the stage during the second tune. Advanced students learn how to use feedback judiciously to quell potential riots. Firearm permit required only if student plans to cross state lines.

Live Sound 00100. *Sign Language for Monitor Engineers.* How to interpret musicians' gestures, obscene and otherwise, and tell the difference between "More guitar," "More vocal," "More drums," "More everything," "Bring me a drink," "Get this cigarette out of my mouth," and "Which song are we supposed to be playing?" Preparing appropriate responses, particularly when you have no idea what's going on, with special attention to nodding, looking concerned, staring intelligently at the computer screen, and moving patch cords around.

Audio Production 35m. *Mixing for Cinema.* How to make mixes that sound wide, full, loud, and absolutely gorgeous on the soundstage for the studio execs, but also won't distort, crap out, create bizarre perspectives, and otherwise sound utterly atrocious over the 14 non-compatible systems found in the various local vest-pocket multiplexes where most of the paying customers will hear them. A multisemester course with no final exam, because it never really ends. Laboratory fee for popcorn (extra butter discouraged), but all students get a coupon for a free second drink. Advanced research seminars on "The Academy Curve: Annoyance or Bother?" and "What Does 'Formatted to Fit Your Screen' Mean, Anyway?"

Audio Production 2997df. *Mixing for Television.* Techniques for melding 128 discrete multichannel audio elements into something that sounds coherent coming out of a single two-inch speaker after being pumped through six randomly adjusted limiters. Lab fee of $3.95 per week to replace blown two-inch speakers. (Radio Shack gift certificates accepted.)

Audio Production 28.8k. *Mixing for the World Wide Web.* Compression, masking and bit-reduction techniques, concntrating on usng advncd algrthms to elmnat unncsry nd rdndt dta undtct..ndtct..dtct..tct..t..[error: broken pipe]..undetectably. Techniques for making MIDI-based Web music *not* sound the same all the time. MIDI Web music and how *not* to make it always sound the same. How to get Web music based on MIDI to *not* sound the same always. Sound MIDI music, and how Web time *not* to always it make constantly. Tricks for keeping listeners from falling asleep while they wait for "real-time" audio playback to start.

Audio Production 640cd. *Mixing for Computer Games*. Keeping. Files. And. Word. Lengths. Really. Short. Using. The. Same. Files. Over. And. Over. And. Over. And. Over. Again. Don't. Forget. To. Cmprs. &. Downsmpl.

Audio Production 5.1~b. *Hyping the Future*. Persuading clients to spend mucho extra bucks on alternative surround-sound mixes when no one has a clue as to how they're ever going to be delivered. Why surround systems designed for movie sound effects are great for music, especially if you really want to be sitting in the second clarinet chair in the Vienna Philharmonic. Convincing clients that they can hear images between the speakers when in fact there aren't any. Detailed technical explanations of how your mixes will sound wonderful at their homes, despite the fact that they are using five completely mismatched speakers, one of which is behind the couch and another facing the wall on top of the bookcase. Advanced students get to try to locate the sweet spot; microscopes are provided. Extra-credit seminar in how 96kHz sampling will solve everything.

Economics 2001q. *Planning Your Purchases*. How to determine whether the manufacturer of the proprietary platform you're about to invest $100,000 into is going to be around three years from now or whenever the gear is fully amortized, whichever comes first. Why whatever answer you come up with is probably wrong.

Economics 1984rip. *Waiting for Apple to Die*. An extremely long, painful course, taught mostly by business analysts and commentators who wouldn't know a decent operating system if it snuck up and bit them on the GUI. Analysis of how an endless string of CEOs can make incredibly stupid decisions and still maintain a huge base of diehard devotees. Course was scheduled to be discontinued (or moved to the Medieval History Department) several years ago but still manages to hang on, as students sign up out of either loyalty or morbid fascination.

Economics 4696tiger. *American Entrepreneurship*. Starting a high-tech company, attracting venture capital, designing products, hiring personnel, acquiring real estate, building manufacturing facilities, setting up marketing plans and advertising strategy, constructing a dealer network—and kissing the whole thing good-bye by selling out to any overseas company that shows interest at the first signs of slowdown. Advanced unit in tracking the yen for maximum leverage.

Legal Studies 1215b. *Copyright Law for Producers and Composers*. Answers important practical legal issues like: "How many notes do I have to change in a tune before I can claim it's original?" "How many seconds of a sample can I use without paying any royalties?" "How many times can I sell the same music to the cable networks before anyone notices?" "If it's on the Internet, it's public domain, right?" and "How do record companies get away with writing contracts that would make 18th-century slave traders blush?" Guest lecturers: former record company executives (who will address the class from behind an opaque, bulletproof screen), members of Negativland (assuming we can find any who aren't under a court order prohibiting them from speaking in public), and any L.A. gangsta rappers who aren't dead yet.

Communications T1. *Making Yourself Obnoxious on the Internet.* How to overwhelm audio-oriented Usenet groups and listserves with highly authoritative, definitive, and totally unsubstantiated claims about any subject anyone else brings up, making yourself look like the consummate authority on stuff you, in fact, know nothing about. How to spew venom at detractors and doubters so effectively that they never bother to post anything ever again. What to do when you find you're the only one left.

Materials Science 1555s. *Duct Tape Is Your Friend.* An ongoing seminar on the ever-expanding universe of this lowly but ubiquitous tool and its uses in equipment repair, musical instrument modification, telecommunications, studio design, plumbing, interior decorating, automotive engineering, marital counseling, child rearing, and client management. Unit on origin of its many names—"duck tape," "gaffer tape," and "gaffa tape" (UK classes only)—and when to use which so that people don't look at you funny. Second-semester students also get to work with bubble gum, old guitar strings, rubber cement, and blowtorches.

Meditation 777z. *Life on Hold.* How to use that time on the phone waiting for tech support to your advantage by deep breathing, stretching, yoga, tai chi, clipping your nails, brushing your teeth, and even going for a walk. Advanced laboratory seminar in simultaneously running a session and keeping the client happy and ignorant. Units cover silent Holds, periodically reassuring Holds, and obnoxious pitch-filled Holds.

English(?) 133x. *Jargon for Engineers.* Expanding your vocabulary to include the latest buzzwords that impress clients, ensure successful job interviews, and keep the people you meet at trade shows from deciding you're a complete moron. Learn how to drop terms like "jitter," "dither," "bit mapping," "sigma-delta-modulation," "thermal recalibration," "firewire," "throughput," and "streaming media" into your conversation, whether you know what they mean or not, as well as the true meanings (assuming there are any) of acronyms like SCSI, RAID, NTSC, CCIR, IDE, OMF, SMDI, VITC, NASDAQ, and, of course, WYSIWYG.

English(?) 386pdq. *Technical Writing for Audio.* Unit on how to distill three years of product research and development into an incomprehensible 42-page manual (with badly drawn pictures), followed by unit on how to write a 700-page, three-volume "user's guide" using nothing but the original engineering spec with no tutorials, practical information, or index. Advanced unit on writing reviews of obviously inferior products for trade journals and finding absolutely nothing wrong with them so as not to piss off the advertisers. Special unit (for visiting foreign students only) in how to convince employers that you should be in charge of user manuals for the North American market and then forgetting everything you've ever learned about the English language.

Information Management 8.0.1a. *In Search of the Lost File*. Learning how to keep cool while you look desperately for the last session file, which was undoubtedly inadvertently deleted when you thought you were cleaning all the dirty pictures you downloaded from the Internet off your hard disk. Students also focus on how to import "compatible" files from one platform to another in less time than it would take to re-record the whole damn thing.

Philosophy 666. *The Metaphysics of Audio*. Principles of crystal orientation in unidirectional audio frequency cables; choosing the right colored marker for stabilizing playback of Compact Discs; quantifying timing delays caused by inexpensive MIDI cables; and the role of gravitational orientation in vacuum-tube transconductance. Advanced unit on "Pin 2 or Pin 3 Hot?" Shovels provided.

Physics EMC2. *Comparative Studies in Chronological Science*. Time-determination methodologies of various segments of society and industry. How to tell the difference between a "Web year," a "Model year," a "Tax year," a "Fiscal year" and "Shipping in a year." How certain calendars manage to place the "first quarter" in August. The effect of Zeno's Paradox on product development: How time dilates as a product's release date approaches, eventually stretching out into infinity, so that the thing never really has to ship. Why Einstein didn't know the half of it.

Business Administration 999q. *Graduate Thesis in Resumé Writing*. See listing under "Fiction."

Paul Lehrman will be happy to reserve you a place in his institution if you send a deposit check made out to "Cash," in any amount, to his numbered bank account in the Cayman Islands.

Afterword

Except for some of the acronyms, not much has changed, has it? Thanks to my friends Coleman Rogers and (again) Richard Elen for some of the ideas.

Jokes: Part 1

In the middle of the night, in the middle of a field, a bunny rabbit and a snake bump into each other. Since it's so dark, neither one can figure out who the other is, so the rabbit suggests they try to identify each other by feel. "Okay," says the snake, "I'll go first. Let's see…you're furry and warm, have a twitchy nose, long floppy ears, and a fluffy tail. You must be a bunny rabbit!"

"Right! Now my turn," says the rabbit. "Hmmm…you're slimy, scaly, cold, crawl along the ground, and have no ears. You must be a record producer!"

■■■

How many…does it take to change a light bulb?

Q: …record producers…?

A: I dunno, what do you think?

Q: …drummers…?

A1: Oh, we have machines for that now.

A2: Seven: one to hold the bulb and six to drink until the room starts to spin.

A3: Just one, as long as the roadie gets the ladder, sets it up, and puts the bulb in the socket.

Q: ...bass players...?

A1: None—the keyboard guy does it with his left hand.

A2: One, but nobody notices. But if he doesn't change it, everybody wonders why it's dark.

Q: ...lead guitarists...?

A: Six: One to screw in the light bulb and the others to complain that they could have done it a lot better and faster.

Q: ...jazz pianists...?

A: Screw the changes, we'll fake it.

Q: ...singers...?

A: Just one: He stands there and lets the world revolve around him.

Q: ...folk musicians...?

A: At least 20: One to screw in the bulb and the rest to sit back look at it, shake their heads, and say, "Nope, no good, it's electric."

Q: ...boy bands...?

A: No one knows: light bulbs last longer than boy bands.

Q: ...Deadheads...?

A: 12,001: One to change it, 2,000 to record the event, and 10,000 to follow it around until it burns out.

Q: ...FOH engineers...?

A: Hey man, I just do sound, okay?

Q: ...Microsoft engineers...?

A: None—they declare darkness the standard and everyone else follows.

Q: ...high-paid convention-center technical staff ...?

A: Ten. You gotta problem with that, pal?

■ ■ ■

A man walks into a bar known as a musician's hangout and pulls a live octopus out of his pocket. "I'll bet any man in this place fifty bucks that this animal can play any instrument you give him!" he says loudly.

A clarinetist gets up and hands the octopus his instrument. The octopus twirls it around in two of its tentacles, sticks the mouthpiece in its beak, and plays the introduction to *Rhapsody in Blue*. The clarinetist, chagrined, gives the man $50 and goes back to his stool.

A banjo player comes over and gives the octopus his five-string. The octopus quickly tunes it up, slaps on a capo, and tears into the theme from *Deliverance*. The banjo player hands over his $50 and skulks back to his table.

A violinist comes up: The octopus grabs the bow in one tentacle and the fiddle in another and, using a third for the pizzicato, does a masterful version of Paganini's *24th Caprice*.

An accordion player drags his instrument over: Using all eight tentacles, the octopus rips off a breathtaking *Lady of Spain*.

Finally, a red-haired guy with a long beard comes over from his corner stool and carefully lays a set of Highland bagpipes on the bar. The octopus picks it up, looks at it carefully, turns it over a few times, examines each of the drones and the chanter, examines them again, and pokes gingerly at the bag a few times. After a while his owner starts to get worried. He leans over to the octopus and whispers, "Aren't you going to play it?"

"Play it!?" says the octopus. "As soon as I get its pajamas off I'm going to have sex with it!"

■ ■ ■

An anthropologist decides to investigate the natives of a far-flung tropical island. As he wades ashore from his boat, he hears many drums pounding in the distance. The drumming continues for many hours, the same patterns repeating over and over. His curiosity overcoming his fear, the anthropologist goes looking to see if he can find a native to explain what the drums mean. He soon encounters a chief and starts to ask him, "What do those drums...?" The chief interrupts him, and just shakes his head, saying, "Bad, very bad." The anthropologist pleads for more, but the chief is silent, and disappears back into the jungle.

The next day, the drums are still going. The anthropologist again goes to find the chief and asks, "Those drums! Those incessant drums! What do they mean?"

Again the chief just shakes his head sadly and says, "Bad! Very, very, bad!" and will say no more.

After three days the drums are still going, and if anything, getting louder and more intense. The anthropologist is getting desperate. He runs to the village and accosts the chief. "Chief! Please! You must tell me! What do the drums mean?! "

At that very moment, the drums suddenly stop. There's a deathly silence. The chief, turning pale, cries, "Ohhhhh nooo, even worse! Now come bass solo!!"

In a similar vein:

A group of missionaries in Africa climb up a mountain, and hear the sound of distant drums. They walk toward the sound, and as they get closer, the drums get louder and faster. One of the missionaries whispers, "I don't like the sound of those drums." From afar comes a distant cry: "It's not our regular drummer!"

■ ■ ■

To: Wedding Bands 'R Us
From: The happy couple-to-be

Dear Bandleader:

Thank you for agreeing to play at our wedding. If you don't mind, we have a few requests that we think you should be able to handle without any trouble. What we were thinking was:

• Any Keith Jarrett composition from his solo series. Please arrange for full ensemble and nothing in 4/4 please.

• Mahavishnu Orchestra, *Dance of the Maya*. Please have the guitar player play John McLaughlin's solo from the live performance November 16, 1972s, at the Nassau Coliseum. We were at that show and particularly liked his use of polyrhythms. If you find it too difficult you can leave out the feedback. Your choice.

• John Coltrane's duets with Pharaoh Sanders. I understand that their use of atonality is not everyone's cup of tea, but all of our guests really love high-register tenor saxes.

• We thought a little Stravinsky would be nice. We particularly like *The Rite of Spring*. If you want to use the sheet music, it's okay. We like it at about 93 bpm.

• For the candle-lighting ceremony, please learn Frank Zappa's *The Grand Wazoo*. If you want to play it in the original key of B-flat, that's fine. Cousin Jeannie would like to sing the baritone-sax solo. Please don't say no, it would really hurt her feelings.

• When John takes off the garter, could you play the opening of Varese's *Ionisation*? It's such a funny piece, we think it would go over much better than *The Stripper.*

• Finally, we have built our own musical instruments (it's kind of a hobby with us), and we would appreciate if you would use our instruments throughout the evening. None of them are based upon a 12-tone scale or on common harmonics, but our five-year-old tells us it's not really that hard to transpose once you understand the physics. Of course, we would be happy to pay each member an extra $25 for any inconvenience.

Thanks again, and don't be late!
John and Darlene

■ ■ ■

Q: How do you get a guitar player to turn down?

A: Put sheet music in front of him.

Q: How do you get a keyboard player to turn down?

A: Take away his sheet music.

Q: Why are sound reinforcement engineers always going "One-Two-One-Two"?

A: Because on "Three" you have to lift something.

Q: How can you tell when there's a singer at your door?

A: She can't find the key, and she doesn't know when to come in.

Q: Why is it important that drummers have a half-ounce more brains than horses?

A: So they don't disgrace themselves in parades.

Q: What's the best thing to play a banjo with?

A: A razor blade.

Chapter 9

I Had Nothing to Do with *Titanic*

But I've Had a Sync-ing Saga All My Own

Preface

Fighting with synchronization issues is a time-honored tradition in our world, especially among those who do audio for video, and the history of our business is filled with horror stories about people misunderstanding, misusing, and being miserable over sync. But I think this story, published right after a film about a certain doomed ship won several dozen Oscars, went beyond most.

June 1998

You know, with all the other things I do, like preaching, proselytizing, prognosticating, prevaricating, and prestidigitating, I don't spend as much time actually banging on my equipment as a lot of the people—maybe most of the people—who read this magazine. And yet somehow, I seem to find things going wrong with my equipment awfully quickly and awfully frequently. I am then forced, more by anger and curiosity than by duty, to isolate and report back said things going wrong to the manufacturers of said equipment. This is both a curse and a gift. It affords me a unique relationship with the companies ("Yes, he's a pain in the butt, but he's really good at breaking our stuff, so let's keep sending him updates!"), but it can make it hard to get anything *done.*

I discovered something that was very, very broken. Fortunately, the manufacturer already knew about it. Unfortunately, they never bothered to tell me, or anybody else.

On one recent post-production project, I had, for a change, few such problems. But after I was done with my part of the project, and the finished program was delivered to me, I almost had a heart attack. I discovered something that was very, very broken. Fortunately, the manufacturer already knew about it. Unfortunately, they never bothered to tell me or anybody else.

I was scoring a television program, an hour-long documentary with almost wall-to-wall music, which I wrote in my usual way with a MIDI sequencer and a room full of synths, samplers, and signal processors. The director/producer is a fellow I've done many projects with over a span of several years, and we know each other's working habits well. The fact that we're separated by 3,000 miles has little bearing on the efficiency of our working together, although when we're calculating budgets, we do have to take Federal Express's cut into account.

The bicoastal nature of our collaboration does cause some problems, the worst of which is how to get rough music cues to him for approval. Like most video producers today, he now uses an Avid for offline editing, but before he got it, I very often would send my music tracks over the phone. Not using ISDN lines, the way the fancy studios do, but the really, really cheap way—you know, using that technology that lets Candace Bergen hear a pin drop.

Fortunately, Candace wasn't around when we did this. The director/producer would roll video in his studio, shouting a count-off into his mouthpiece, and at zero I would start to play the music on the sequencer, holding my phone mouthpiece up to a speaker. Now, I would never recommend doing this with clients unless they *really* trust you, but in our case, it worked okay. When we needed better quality and a *little* tighter sync, I would send him an analog cassette of the rough cues, which he would then lay back onto 3/4-inch video, punching in at the start time I provided.

When it came time to deliver the finished score, our delivery medium of choice was standard DAT. To make sure my timing was dead-on, I would slave the sequencer to SMPTE being generated by a Mark of the Unicorn *Video Time Piece* (one of the most useful pieces of equipment in my studio, and one that has never, ever screwed up—so, naturally, the manufacturer has discontinued it), which, in turn, was genlocked to a local network-affiliate TV station. Thus, whatever was locking *All My Children* on ABC-TV was now locking my sequencer, and what's good enough for Disney is darn well good enough for me. At precisely two seconds and one second before the start of each cue, I would put in two short beeps, and of course, I would include a list of SMPTE start times for each cue with the tape. The DAT tracks would go to his post house, where they would be transferred to videotape, locked, and assembled with the rest of the program.

Timecode? We don't need no stinking timecode! Seriously, neither of us had a timecode DAT machine (cheap, remember?), and we never missed it. This method worked amazingly well—despite the lack of a SMPTE track, the audio cues consistently lined up perfectly. In the dozens of projects we have put together this way, the worst drift we ever encountered was something like three frames in five minutes—about 0.03%. As long as we kept the individual cues relatively short, this was more than acceptable. And the sound quality was much better than if I were to print to 3/4-inch videotape, which would have to be dubbed onto the master.

But now he has his Avid, and I've got *ProTools*, and we both have e-mail and *Jaz* drives, so for this last project, we figured it was time to get into the '90s and do the whole thing without any tape at all. For the rough mixes, I recorded my sequence directly onto a hard disk in mono, using one of the popular MIDI+audio sequencer programs (no, I'm not going to tell you who makes it, since I have not come to praise them) and my ProTools hardware, effectively recording the sequence into itself. I then took each audio track I'd recorded and, using the wonderful shareware program *ConvertMachine*, converted it to 8-bit, 22 kHz. I squashed the files even further using Stuffit and e-mailed them to the producer.

This was faster than FedEx, but as it turned out, not by much. Even squeezed down, some of the cues took up more than a megabyte, and so the upload and download would each take a half-hour or so. We found out that America Online, where he had his e-mail account, rejects mail messages larger than a megabyte—only it takes a couple of days to get around to telling you that it has done so. So he got an Internet account on another provider, and meanwhile I found some space on a local server where I could set up an FTP site, which he could then log into and download the file directly, avoiding the e-mail route entirely.

Another thing that slowed things down was that his modem wasn't on the Mac that was running his Avid—he had an older, slower Mac for his Internet access because, for understandable reasons, he was afraid to use his big machine for anything other than video editing. So he had to download my files on the older machine, convert them back up to 16/44.1 (the Avid won't accept any other format), and then "sneakernet" his Jaz drive over to the other Mac to load in.

Once we got the kinks out, this scheme worked pretty well. The sound quality was a hell of a lot better than doing it over the phone, and the start times always lined up correctly. If there was any drift, we didn't care because we were still dealing with rough picture at this stage.

And it got us good and psyched for using hard disk audio for the final product. Again, I used the *Video Time Piece* as a SMPTE reference, genlocked to a broadcast signal. I didn't have any way of locking the digital audio sample rate clock to the same SMPTE, but I figured it would be plenty close enough, as the *ProTools* audio card has a very accurate internal clock—much better than the clock in the Mac itself.

Once again, I recorded each MIDI sequence into itself and put the audio tracks (in stereo this time) onto a *Jaz* cartridge, which I sent off, with the usual list of start times, to the director, via our good friends at FedEx. There were ten cues altogether, ranging in length from about 30 seconds to a little under ten minutes. He laid them up into his Avid and aligned all the start times. Since his Avid isn't online quality, he brought all his "media" (that's Avid-speak for the digitized video and audio) to a post-production house, where they did the online assembly and mixed the audio, which consisted of my music, a narrator, some on-camera dialogue, and a bunch of flown-in sound effects. Everything locked very nicely, thank you.

When they were all done, however, the network didn't like it. So my overworked old friend went back into his Avid, brought in some new footage, re-recorded the narration (with a celebrity narrator, probably the biggest single item in the budget), and re-cut the show to accommodate the client's wishes. Then I went back into my sequencer and moved things around—tightening, lengthening, and otherwise reconforming the music to the new picture. Meanwhile, the sequencer manufacturer had sent me a new version of the program, with some new features I really could use, so I started to work with it. Once again, I recorded the tracks to a *Jaz* cartridge and sent it on its way.

Since we were now about a month behind on the project, the director didn't go through the step of putting my music tracks into his Avid but instead brought the *Jaz* cart with the music directly to the post house, where they laid the cues up into their online system on the day of the final layback. About halfway into the session, he called me to report that there seemed to be some sync issues—the music wasn't always matching the visual cues correctly—but he would slide things around and take care of it. Unfortunately, or perhaps fortunately, I wasn't home, and so my answering machine received this news with its usual equanimity.

A couple of days later, I got a copy of the finished video, and that's when I nearly dropped dead. Sometimes the music was exactly right, but a lot of the time it seemed to be horribly off. Many of the musical hits I had so carefully calculated were in the wrong places, the holes I had painstakingly left for the narration and sound effects now just sounded empty (since there was no narration or effects in them), and clashes between effects and music, which I had worked very hard to avoid, were rampant.

But the network loved the new version of the program. The director wasn't about to go back in and re-post it just because I didn't like my own music, and besides, he had a project overseas that was already behind schedule. So what was done was done. And I was left to solve this puzzle myself.

First, I decided to figure out exactly how far off the cues actually were and see if the numbers gave up some kind of clue. I compared the music on the video to my sequences and saw that all of the cues started at the correct times, so my SMPTE numbers were right, but they ran fast. At five minutes into one of the longer cues, the music was almost three seconds ahead of the picture, or about 1%.

The first possibility that had entered my mind was that the post house had screwed up and resampled my 44.1kHz files at 48 kHz, but that would have caused a discrepancy of about 9%, so they weren't to blame. Besides, if the sampling rate had changed, the pitch of the music would have been different from my original tracks, which, I was quite surprised to find out, it wasn't.

Another possible explanation would be a frame-rate problem, but the 1% figure also ruled this out. Had my SMPTE generator or my sequencer somehow been set to 30 fps instead of 29.97, or if I had used drop-frame instead of nondrop (or vice versa), the error would have been one-tenth as much, or 0.1%. Of course, this couldn't have been the case, since the whole setup was genlocked to a broadcast video signal. But it was worth considering because all too often I've seen this sort of thing happen to otherwise-competent engineers who get totally befuddled by the "30-fps" option on their "project studio" SMPTE equipment. They use that setting and thus totally screw up their tracks, unaware that, for all intents and purposes, _there ain't no such thing!_ So allow me to take this opportunity to propose that manufacturers who put that feature in their hardware (and don't even document why it's there) be _hung by their thumbs_ from the roof of the Anaheim Convention Center for the duration of the next NAMM show. Thank you.

Okay, back to our regularly scheduled program. So there had to be something else wrong. Was the timing on my _ProTools_ system that far off? Was my _Video Time Piece_ messing up in some horrible way? I went back into my sequencer and reloaded the audio files, placing them alongside the MIDI tracks. Immediately, I could see that something was not right: The audio tracks looked like they were recorded at a different tempo from the MIDI tracks and were consistently ahead. I had not compared the tracks like this before—I simply assumed that the sequencer would be in sync with itself. How silly of me.

I simply assumed that the sequencer would be in sync with itself. How silly of me.

So I devised a test: I sequenced a bunch of clicks, one second apart, recorded them on disk, and then played back the recorded audio against the sequence. I tried various combinations of SMPTE and digital sync, first making the Mac the master, then the *Pro Tools* card the master, then the *Video Time Piece*—both internally and externally clocked—and finally making another SMPTE generator the master. Not once, with any of the combinations I tried, could I get the MIDI and digital audio to match for more than a minute before they would audibly drift away from each other. Sometimes, in fact, it only took a few seconds. Obviously, the software was screwing up in a big, big way.

I went through the literature, both dead-tree and online, to see if there were any reports of this phenomenon in this sequencer or in any other MIDI+audio program on any platform. I found some vague references to timing issues in an obscure component of an ancient version of the software's operating system extensions, but they weren't relevant to my situation. So I called customer support. And I sent them an e-mail, to which an auto-responder replied: "We'll have an answer for you in one or two working days." And I sent e-mail to the product managers. Two weeks later, I got a response from someone in tech support: "I noticed you are using version ABC of the software and version XYZ of the operating system. There were sync problems that would show themselves in certain situations with these versions. I would recommend downloading new versions of both, which are available on our Web site."

In other words, the software was broken, and it would seriously mess up the timing of any digital audio that you record into it.

Now, you must understand, I am on this company's mailing lists. All of them. They know where I live, they know where I teach, they know where I write. I get their PR, I get their upgrade offers, I get their new-product announcements, I get their online mailings, I get invitations to their catered open-bar parties at trade shows. They spend lots of money on all of these things and on their packaging, their advertising, and their Web site. I don't seriously expect them to spend that kind of money on telling people what's *wrong* with their software. But I ask you: How much would it have cost them to send me something, either on paper or online, that said, "There is a serious timing problem with version so-and-so of this software, so if you are creating synchronized audio tracks, please use a different version."?

I would rather have received that, at a moment when I really needed it, than all the coffee mugs, key chains, hats, lapel pins, coconut-beer-battered shrimp, and free domestic champagne in the world.

Paul D. Lehrman is pretty sure he is operating in real time, but he's not sure about the rest of the world.

Afterword

Many readers wanted to know who the culprit in this story was, and a few them even tried to guess, but none of them were right. The company went out of business not long after this episode, although not because of technical issues (which were actually pretty rare in their case). But, if you think I'm going to spill the beans now, you're still wrong.

I'm still working with the same director, but thanks to broadband, QuickTime, and YouSendIt.com, we barely need FedEx any more. And synchronization problems are discovered much earlier and dealt with much more easily. But I'm happy to say the problems we've had since then have never been remotely like this.

Picture of Clara Rockmore courtesy of Moog Music.

Chapter 10

In Memoriam: Three Pioneers of Electronics and Information

Preface

Writing obituaries is never what you would call a "fun" task, but it can be deeply satisfying. The first memorial piece I ever wrote was in *Electronic Musician* magazine when one of my former teachers, Vladimir Ussachevsky, who was one of the true inventors of electronic music, died. It was one way I could thank him for all he had done to open my eyes, and in turn, the thanks I got from many far-flung former students and fans of Ussachevsky's, who felt my short piece had managed to do the man and his work justice, was genuinely heartwarming. When the three people in this column, not well-known but nonetheless important in the history of our industry, died within a few weeks of each other, I thought it would be worthwhile devoting a column to their memory.

September 1998

I want to pay tribute to three people who passed away recently—two after good long lives and one, sadly, in the prime of his career. You may never have heard of them—they were never on the cover of *Rolling Stone*, or *Mix* for that matter—but each of them, in his or her own highly individualistic and modest way, had a profound influence on the way I and, I would venture to say, many others make and think about music.

Clara Rockmore

Clara Rockmore, who died in May at the age of 88, was the first musical virtuosa of the electronic age. Her instrument was the Theremin, that eerie-sounding invention by the Russian physicist by the same name. It was the first musical instrument that could be played without touching it, and it found its way into dozens of science-fiction film soundtracks, started Bob Moog's career as an instrument designer, and captivated a new generation when Brian Wilson laid it on top of his masterpiece "Good Vibrations."

Rockmore, who was born in Russia, had been a child prodigy on the violin but developed hand problems that forced her to stop playing. She emigrated to New York in 1927, the same year Theremin first came to the U.S., and here the two of them struck up a close friendship and an intense professional collaboration. She played her first solo recital on the instrument in the early '30s and continued to be in demand as a performer for the next two decades.

By today's technological standards, the Theremin is a very simple instrument: two very high-frequency oscillators heterodyne ("beat," for those of you who missed Electronics 101) in the audible range, with the frequency of one of the oscillators controlled by hand capacitance. As can be seen in Steve Martin's wonderful 1994 film, *Theremin: An Electronic Odyssey*, Rockmore invented her own remarkable technique for the device, which transformed it from a curiosity into a true musical instrument. By using finger gestures that almost looked like sign language, she was able to play consistently in tune and produce a precise, repeatable vibrato.

She also demanded of the instrument that it be able to play staccato notes, and she had Theremin build her a special version with that capability. In his original design (the commercial version of which was marketed by RCA), moving the left hand controlled the volume by changing the temperature of the filament of the amplifier tube, a technique that invariably caused a distinct lag in the amplitude change. The instrument Theremin custom-made for Rockmore used grid control, which meant it could respond much faster. Using quick hand movements, she was able to make the instrument articulate in a totally unique way.

She was married to Robert Rockmore, a show-business attorney, whose clients included the great singer/actor Paul Robeson, with whom Rockmore toured before his career was destroyed by the House Un-American Activities Committee. Rockmore was not politically active, but she did count among her circle of friends many of New York's cultural and intellectual elite. Her sister, Nadia Riesenberg, was a celebrated pianist and teacher, and her nephew is the longtime program director of the city's only remaining commercial classical radio station.

Curiously, Rockmore never made any commercial recordings until 1976, when Bob Moog convinced her to go into the studio and record a large chunk of her repertoire, accompanied by her sister. That record is still available, now on CD, of course, on the Delos label, and Moog says enough material was recorded to make a second album, which he hopes to release in the near future. Moog (who is very happily and successfully making Theremins again) also recently produced a video of Rockmore, consisting mostly of footage shot in the mid-'70s, much of which was used on the CBS-TV arts magazine (remember those?) *Camera Three*. It's available through his company, Big Briar—on the Web at www.big-briar.com.

"She saw herself as a virtuosa, with all the responsibility that entails and all the respect that commands," says Moog. She was also a very private person. At the end of Martin's film, there is a fabulously touching scene in which Rockmore and Leon Theremin—who just before World War II was abducted from his New York apartment by the KGB and taken back to Russia to do military research—are reunited after 53 years. The film makes us wonder whether their relationship might have been more than just mentor/student, but as he enters her apartment, she looks straight at the camera, says tersely, "Cut," and shuts the door.

The movie, which I cannot recommend highly enough, is available on VHS through the usual outlets. It's a tribute to a great man and scientist (he died literally days before the movie was released) and a great woman and artist.

Ivan Tcherepnin

If you are familiar with the family name of Tcherepnin, it's because either you're a student of 20th-century classical music and know the work of Alexander (a composer who combined musical traditions of various cultures into charming and accessible music) or you're a student of early electronic music, and you know about the Serge Modular, one of the great toys of the analog synth age, developed by Alexander's son Serge. Serge Modulars are still being built and maintained by fanatical fans long after the age of ARP. But if you were lucky enough to be a student in the music department at Harvard University in the last three decades, or you hang around the contemporary music scene in Boston (which I am often guilty of), then you knew another Tcherepnin: Ivan.

The composer Ivan Tcherepnin (who, depending on his mood and whom he was with, sometimes pronounced his name the "American" way, EYE-van, and sometimes the Russian way, ee-VON) was one of a kind. He was an analog guy in a digital age and an individualistic voice at a time when many composers seemed to be emulating fashion, as well as each other. He was never afraid to mix many disparate elements in his music during a period when "pigeonholing," which makes it easy for record stores to know where to put things, is the rule. While many "serious" (or at least academic) composers still seem to judge their worth by how much they can intimidate their listeners, Tcherepnin's music was audience friendly, yet always challenging and demanding the attention of the listener; accessible, but never dumbed down. And every new piece of his that you heard sounded unlike anything you'd ever heard, from him or from anyone else.

As might be expected of Serge's brother, he was an early adapter of electronic techniques, and he was director of Harvard University's electronic music studio for some 25 years. But you would be hard-pressed to classify him as an "electronic" composer. His use of the technology never drew attention to itself, but instead his synthesizers and signal processors were always used to serve a more universal compositional purpose, and he frequently combined electronics with acoustic instruments in mutually complementary ways. In Ivan's hands, the synthesizer was never an end in itself; it was a processing tool as much as anything else, and the sounds emerging from his system were just as likely to be instrumental and *concrète* sounds as purely synthetic tones. As if to emphasize the "organic" orientation of his music, his studio was known for the abundance of green plants among the machinery.

His persona reflected a bit of the United Nations—his father was Russian, and his mother was a well-known Chinese pianist, and since he spent his early childhood in Paris, he spoke with a distinct French accent—and his music did, too. Besides combining widely varied sonic elements, he brought a diversity of cultural elements into his music, drawing from his own multicultural background and cheerfully adding other influences. For example, one of his best-known works is an opera based on the sounds he could get by processing a santur—a kind of lute he was given by an Iranian student—through racks of electronics.

In his music, the listener could count on a mixture of intelligence and humor, thoughtfulness and playfulness. His compositions were always surprising and often delightfully so—what came next was never what you expected, but it always seemed to make sense after you got there. He liked to use familiar themes, like folk tunes and references to other composers, not as samples but as compositional elements, which could reveal themselves over time, so that the listener felt not the instantaneous shock of recognition but the calm joy of having arrived at some place known and comfortable.

Ivan was constantly looking for new ways to add to his vocabulary, and he and I had a number of stimulating, sometimes near-shouting conversations over whether this or that new electronic gadget could do what he wanted it to. He never asked, "What's cool about this?" as if a new hardware or software tool could ever dictate to him what he would do. His question was always, "How can I get it to do what I need?" He was always getting the latest and greatest software toys for his students, but for his own work, intolerant as he was of buggy or unfinished software, he stuck with tried-and-true programs and, much to the chagrin of his wife and colleagues, used the same notation program for nearly 15 years.

Although he had a solid reputation among contemporary music cognoscenti, because he never engaged in the kind of self-promotion needed to become a "star" in even the "classical" composition business, his fame was always somewhat local. Nevertheless, in 1996 he won the prestigious (and remunerative) Grawemeyer Award from the University of Louisville for composition, in recognition of a Double Concerto he wrote for two of his former students, violinist Lynn Chang and cellist Yo-Yo Ma, and the Greater Boston Youth Symphony Orchestra.

But sadly, the award will not result in more music from Ivan. In the summer of 1995, he was diagnosed with liver cancer and told he had six months to live. He began a regimen of Chinese medicine, meditation, and herbs, and confounded his doctors by maintaining, as a friend says, "a high quality of life" for almost three years, which included a hiking trip to New Zealand, recording some of his works in Moscow, and a new marriage. This past April, however, at the age of 55, he succumbed. A unique musical voice, with something to teach everyone, has been stilled.

If you'd like to hear some of Ivan Tcherepnin's music, there's a collection of vocal and instrumental pieces, including selections from the "Santur Opera," available from CRI. The Double Concerto is on an Olympia (UK) CD, along with compositions of Ivan's father and his grandfather, Nikolai.

William Schwann

"Do you have this record?" "Has this piece ever been recorded?" "When did this album come out?" "Who's the soloist on this disc?" "Which one is this group's latest?" In the days when record-store personnel did more than inspect your shopping bags and serve lattes, if you asked any of these questions, or almost any question about a recording, you would invariably get the response, "Let me look it up in *Schwann*."

The *Schwann* catalog, also known over the years as The *Schwann Long Playing Record Guide*, *The Schwann Record & Tape Guide*, *Schwann Opus*, and a few other variations, has been the *ne plus ultra* of reference guides to American recorded music since it was started in 1949 by a Cambridge, Massachusetts, record store owner named William Schwann.

Schwann went to school in Kentucky, and when I met him in 1981, he still had a bit of the Kentucky Colonel about him. He was a large, friendly, soft-spoken man, with a bit of a patrician air, but nothing but kind words for those around him. He started his professional life as an organist, coming to Boston in the 1930s to study with the great E. Power Biggs, and was able to supplement his income by writing music criticism for local newspapers and setting up a small record shop—called, inventively enough, *The Record Shop*—across the street from MIT. "I was in a situation I always wanted to be in," he told me. "I was getting free tickets from the newspapers and free records from the store."

After World War II, in the face of shortages of the shellac used in 78 rpm records, he started a record dealers' association that allowed stores to share resources and trade inventory. In 1948, the LP was introduced, and by October 1949, there had been an explosion in recorded repertory (or so it appeared at the time): Eleven labels had issued some 650 classical and popular discs. "My memory was never all that good," he explained, "and I could never remember which records were on which labels, so I got the idea for a catalog that would combine all the labels." The first issue, released that month, contained 24 typewritten pages. Distributed through his dealer network. it quickly sold out its run of 11,000 copies.

With the second issue, the catalog went from bimonthly to monthly, and within a year it was being distributed nationally through record dealers, and Schwann was selling ads to record companies to generate revenue. In 1953, after 14 years in retail, he closed the store and devoted full time to the publication, which now had a staff and offices across the Charles River in Boston's Back Bay.

Accuracy and completeness were always the hallmarks of the *Schwann* catalog. Schwann was a stickler for detail and relied on his loyal readership to point out mistakes and suggest changes. Errors never lasted long in print, and soon the catalog gained a reputation for exactitude that made it as valued a reference work as the Grove or Grout musical encyclopedias. Classical listings included all of the soloists, conductors, and ensembles. Cross-listings let the reader easily find the other works on a disc. Jazz and pop listings, in the first month, gave song titles and, in later years, recording information; in subsequent issues, the date of the initial expanded listing was included for cross-referencing.

As the record industry grew, the amount of information *Schwann* encompassed became staggering, but the accuracy of that information, the consistency of the formatting, and the overall usefulness of the work maintained its amazingly high level. Records that were about to be deleted by the labels were highlighted, so you knew that if you wanted a copy, you'd better run out and get it before it disappeared.

And as new genres and technologies developed, the catalog adapted. When Wendy Carlos's *Switched-On Bach* came out, and there seemed to be no easy way to classify it (do you list it in the classical section under Bach, or under Carlos? Or is it pop?), Schwann created a new category: Electronic Music. When the size of the publication started to get unwieldy, he created a "supplementary" catalog, issued less frequently, with categories like spoken-word and international folk that didn't have to be updated quite as often. Stereo recordings appeared—Schwann responded by adopting new typefaces that allowed the reader to differentiate between stereo and mono versions. Then there were open-reel tapes, cassettes,

8-tracks, three competing quadraphonic formats, "audiophile" and dbx- and CX-encoded LPs, and finally CDs—all of which were handled cleverly and gracefully.

It was with the greatest of pleasure that I could point to a listing in the Schwann *catalog and say to the record-store clerk, "You really should get this."*

As a teenager, every couple of months I would go into my favorite big-city record store, take a new issue of *Schwann* off the huge stack by the front door, and drop a quarter in the box—the catalogs were the only items in the store sold on the honor system. I would immediately turn to the "New Listings" section, which let me know which experimental composers had just gotten their works recorded, and which of my favorite bands had new albums out. Often, stores would have new records in stock a month or two before they appeared in *Schwann*, but sometimes, when the record labels were able to release the information well enough in advance of the actual disc, the catalog got it first, and it was with the greatest of pleasure that I could point to a listing in the catalog and say to the clerk, "You really should get this."

Schwann sold the catalog to ABC Leisure publications (which also published the late, lamented *High Fidelity* and *Musical America*) in the mid-'70s, with the proviso that he stay on as publisher for ten years. ABC came close to killing the goose when they started selling ads in the catalog to record dealers, some of whom used the space to advertise cut-rate prices. Other dealers, naturally enough, were furious and stopped selling the publication. In response, ABC started making the catalog available by mail subscription, but they couldn't make up for the loss of dealer sales, and even after they stopped selling the offending ads, according to a source who worked for *Schwann* at the time, the catalog never fully recovered from the debacle.

Schwann's contributions to the music industry did not go unnoticed: He was twice commissioned by the RIAA to create and catalog a "White House Record Collection," with the express purpose of promoting the best American performers and composers in all genres.

He retired from the publication that bore his name in 1985. After that, the catalog was kicked around among several owners (one, the former publisher of *Soap Opera Digest*, flipped it after only three months), and in 1991 it was bought by *Stereophile* magazine. A couple of years later, the Boston office was shut down, and the catalog moved in with its parent company in Santa Fe, N.M. *Stereophile* put a lot of energy into the catalog, adding to the listings reviews and feature articles by its staff, and they divided it into two volumes: *Schwann Opus*, for classical records, and *Schwann Spectrum* for jazz and pop.

In 1996, the publication was bought by Valley Media in Woodlands, California, the largest independent CD distributor in the country. Since Valley took over, only the classical catalog has been published, although the non-classical catalog, according to a staff member, is due to return sometime in the next year. (The editorial offices are still in Santa Fe.)

Schwann Opus is now in a large 8×11 format, with over 1,000 pages, and comes out quarterly. The Artist issue, which lists records by performer as opposed to composer, and which in past years was issued at almost random intervals (the time between issues could range from 18 months to four years) is now promised to be an annual project.

As for Bill Schwann, he remained a well-known figure in the Boston classical music scene, serving as an adviser and board member for numerous musical organizations and schools. He was also an avid mountain climber, conquering most of the 4,000-foot peaks in New Hampshire's White Mountains, and an ardent supporter of environmental causes.

What always blew me away about the *Schwann* catalog was not just that it was an invaluable compendium of musical knowledge, but that this little book was the epitome of how information of the highest quality, dense and ever changing, could be organized and presented. Accuracy was paramount, but so was space—what today we would call *bandwidth*. Spend some time with the catalog, and you'll see what I mean. The amount of information presented is staggering, and the clarity and efficiency of the formatting are nothing short of brilliant. "Space was always a concern," Schwann told me. "Unlike a newspaper, when you run out of space, you can't just cut some copy. I'm always looking for new abbreviations, different ways to organize the listings. Sometimes, I'll go away on vacation and spend the whole time thinking about space problems."

There are many lessons to be learned by us today from a man who cared deeply not only about the information he was conveying, but also about how it was conveyed. Bill Schwann died on June 7, at the age of 85. All of us who work with music owe him our thanks.

Paul Lehrman played some pieces by Alexander Tcherepnin in his first piano recital at age 8. When he was 12, he built a Theremin, but it didn't work very well. Today, he owns several thousand LPs, tapes, and CDs, all very carefully organized.

Afterword

Sadly, the Schwann catalog didn't survive long in the age of the World Wide Web. In 2001, the last issue (without a date) was published, and in 2002 the company assets were sold at auction. In some ways, online resources like Arkivmusic.com and the All Music Guide provide more information and can serve up information faster than a printed catalog ever could, but as far as consistency and reliability are concerned, we may never see the likes of *Schwann* again.

Chapter 11

Jack Desrocher

My Favorite Vintages
Good Old Gear Doesn't Have to Cost a Fortune

Preface

Truth is often as entertaining as fiction. Two years after the November 1996 column (Chapter 3), in which I made up a bunch of "vintage" gear that no one ever heard of, I figured it was time to do a piece about *real* vintage gear that no one had ever heard of (with a couple of exceptions), but that I still had hanging around my studio. In the "Afterword," I'll tell you what has become of all of this stuff, now that the better part of a decade has passed.

November 1998

While the rest of the world is standing in line and on its collective head for the privilege of doling out a week's worth of billings for a matched pair of 12AU7s, made by slave labor in China out of parts from dead Soviet nuclear plants, I look around at my surroundings and think about what "vintage" means to me. Here's some of the stuff I've had for years that nobody makes any more and that I couldn't do without. And no, none of it's for sale.

JVC *XL-Z335* CD player. I didn't make that up, that's really its name. It's a pretty ordinary consumer model and doesn't even have multiple trays. It's eight or so years old, and I bought it from the Crutchfield catalog on a sell-off for about $250. It has the usual array of cueing options, remote control, fast play, etc., plus one amazing feature: an S/PDIF out. Now, I think the CD-audio-extraction routine built into Apple's QuickTime is incredibly cool, and there are some very slick audio CD-copying programs out there. But for speed and flexibility, when you are trying to find something on a CD to load into the computer, nothing beats an ordinary consumer CD player's transport controls. With this puppy, I can go right into my Pro Tools' digital input without skipping a bit. And with the remote control, I don't even have to move from my keyboard. I can't imagine getting sound effects or stealing licks off a CD any other way.

Rectilinear *XI* speakers. I bought these hulking things my first week of college, and I've never been without them. Built like trucks, they were considered very hip back when there was a controversy raging in hi-fi circles between the "New England" sound and the "California" sound, which was exemplified by JBLs. These were East Coast with a vengeance: Their sound is so reserved they make the original Advents sound harsh. Terrific for playing in the background while I'm trying to write, they also make great secondary (or in my case, tertiary) monitors: If I can get a mix to sparkle on these, it'll sound good on damn near anything.

TOA *280ME* speakers. The opposite side of the coin. No bottom to speak of, really beamy top, lots o' midrange. When a symphonic mix sounds smooth on these babies, I know I've got it. I mixed my first electronic album, *The Celtic Macintosh*, on them over a dozen years ago, and the mix still holds up. (The album's not bad, either.) One of the drivers went out last year, and guess what? TOA still makes parts! So maybe this doesn't quite qualify as vintage.

Auratone *5Cs*. I would never have bought these, but the company that made them called me up after they saw an article I had written in which I quoted a well-known remote engineer as saying that the only speakers he really needed for a certain high-visibility gig were Auratones. They offered me a pair of these little post-industrial suckers in exchange for permission to use the quote in an ad. Of course, they didn't really need my permission (it was just a sentence, and that's usually considered "fair use" under copyright law *[although* *these days it wouldn't be*]), but I appreciated the gesture and certainly didn't want to disappoint them, so I took the bribe. The ones I got are the "portable" version: plastic grilles that look like old drive-in-movie speakers, tough vinyl covers, a metal latch to lock them together, and a leather handle so you can tote the things around. The latch rattles, the grille buzzes, and the hardware makes it impossible for them to sit flat on a surface. Glorious. Today, most television speakers (and certainly most car stereos) sound better than these, but they're still great for that final check before you send off the master.

TOA *D4* and *D4E* mixers. Little rackmount mixers that I pull out of the closet for live gigs, extra tracks for mixdown when I'm using multitrack tape, or location recording, since they've got a couple of great mic preamps in them. Clean, straightforward, built like a Sherman tank, and just ridiculously useful.

AKG *ADR68K* reverb. When the old Ursa Major company was bought in the mid-'80s by AKG, this is what they were working on: a multi-effects unit way back before anyone else thought of the idea. Besides being a true double-stereo processor, sounding great (although a bit noisy), and having the best MIDI implementation of any studio processing gear before or since, it had a brilliant user interface—none of this "one-parameter-at-a-time-because-that's-all-there's-room-for-on-the-stupid-LCD" nonsense. You can see six parameters at once and quickly look at and adjust up to 40 more without going through menus, directories, or other horrors. This came at a cost—the original price tag on this baby would today get you three digital multitracks—but it was worth it, and it's still the most-used processor in both my home and school studios. (Disclosure department: I wrote the manual for the thing and helped develop the MIDI side. So shoot me if I really liked what we came out with!)

dbx *166* comp/limiter. Set for very light limiting and peak elimination at +10, with stereo channels linked. I just leave it there at the end of the signal chain and tweak it ever so slightly when the meters on my DAT deck object. Silent and totally deadly. Yes, I know the "Peakstop Level" isn't brick-wall, but that's what the "over" light is for. And right underneath it: a pair of the amazing dbx *163x* half-rack thingies. One easy-to-adjust slider, one hard-to-adjust level knob, and a stereo-linking jack in the back. Just nudge the thing back and forth until the bass and the kick sit in the mix right where you want them.

UREI *Platform*. (Disclosure again: I did the manual here, too. How do you think I end up with some of this stuff, anyway?) An ill-fated series of brilliant processors, developed in conjunction with a Danish company. Vertical half-rack modules including mic preamps, parametric EQs, mixers, compressors, limiters, and gates—sort of like the SCAMP or dbx *900* racks of old, all of which could be under MIDI control. The fastest, most versatile, and most downright astonishing dynamics processors I have ever come across. Control-voltage linking means that up to 11 units can be slaved in series with each other, making for ridiculously complex limiting/ducking/gating/de-essing/EQ-ing schemes. For cleaning up problem material, these babies are unparalleled.

Yamaha *TX7* synth modules. Remember these? The venerable *DX7* without a keyboard. Better functionality and quieter output than its older brother. Made to stack on each other in a weird but very cool way—I have three of them. FM is supposedly completely passé, but you'd never know it among the academic community, and they have a point. When it comes to real-time control over sound, nothing that's appeared since—with the exception of physical modeling and maybe granular synthesis, both of which make FM programming look like third-grade arithmetic—comes close. And nothing does clangs, bells, and nasty metallic noise better. Last year I had to do a cartoon for a bio-technology company, which featured the life and death of a red corpuscle, and I used the TX7s for 90% of the sounds. They wanted to know where I got all the cool samples.

Everything in my studio is locked to "Politically Incorrect."

Mark of the Unicorn *Video Time Piece*. I've already written about this a lot, but it's always worth mentioning. The new Digital Time Piece can do most of what this thing did, but it's a far more complex piece of gear, so therefore there's a lot more you can do to screw it up. The VTP does SMPTE-to-MIDI, VITC, jam synching, window burn, punches and streamers, graphic overlays onto video, and my favorite feature: It generates SMPTE and MTC locked to an external video source, which can be a black burst generator or, in the case of my cheap studio, the output of a VCR tuned to the local ABC affiliate. Think of it: Everything in my studio is locked to "Politically Incorrect."

Syquest 44MB removable drive. Laugh if you will, but this little sucker still works with all my samplers, is very forgiving of long and gnarly SCSI cables, and doesn't complain when I stick in a disk without first loading some special driver. And it can stay in place between my Mac and my samplers without crashing either one of them. Unfortunately, the cartridges have a failure rate of about 30%, which means that in another three years all of mine will have died, and the thing goes into the closet with the MO drive, the pre-ADB trackball, and the carcass of the Mac IIcx I blew up trying to upgrade the processor.

Mirror 19-inch black-and-white computer monitor. I bought it off the back of a truck for about $300 six years ago, before I blew up the IIcx. It requires its own NuBus slot, and the cards that go along with it have long since become scarcer than pre-war Telefunken tubes. But as long as it works, it makes a great second monitor for my Pro Tools system: all those faders visible at once!

Blue Sky Logic *MIXI*. You've probably never even heard of this one. A very clever product, a few years ahead of its time, that no one could figure out how to sell. They sent me one for review and then promptly went out of business. It's a MIDI fader box: 12 sliders, all configurable (if you know a little SysEx) as MIDI controller, pitch bend, or aftertouch, with loopback, bank switching, and a few other hidden goodies. It was pretty cheap: no readouts, no motors, just faders. I used to use it for Pro Tools before they disabled most of the MIDI input functions. Now it comes in very handy when I need a bank of real-time controllers for handling signal processors and complicated synthesizer functions.

Bogen *MX-6A* mixer. A classic, old-fashioned "P.A." mixer with four inputs feeding a pair of 12AX7As to a mono output. No EQ or pads, just four knobs. Do I use it for mics? Not a chance—I use it for guitar. With its high-gain, unbalanced, high-impedance inputs, when you crank it up all the way, it makes a fabulous distortion box, complete with the microphonics and compression that cause digital designers weeks of sleepless nights.

Yamaha *EM-130*. A signal processor? A synth module? A piano? No. Yamaha, on the identification plate, calls it an *amplifier*. But it is so much more. I had never heard of it when a friend who was working for a music store called me up frantically and said, "We just bought 500 of these, and they'll all be gone in two days! Get over here!" It's a six-channel mixer, with high and low tone controls (I hesitate to call them "EQ"), input pads and pan on each channel; a reverb send and a built-in spring reverb; line ins and outs; and a stereo 40-watt power amp with big, impressive meters at the outputs, where they do no good whatsoever. Oh, yes—and a beat box. You know, the kind that used to show up in home organs. It plays patterns like waltz, bossa nova, tango, march, ballad, and swing, using various kinds of filtered white noise, pitched to sound vaguely like drums. We're talking mid-'70s here. The rhythm section was in fact very "human" in a way its designers no doubt didn't predict: It sped up.

Originally made to sell for something like $1,200, this was a product that was obsolete before it even came out. My friend's store had bought all of Yamaha's stock and was blowing them out at $250. I bought three and immediately sold two of them for $400 each. Why do I love this thing? Not for the nostalgia factor, although it served as the P.A. mixer, and even on occasion as a recording mixer, for a lot of bar bands I served time with in the '70s. The sound? It's terrible. Honky, noisy, no headroom. The features? The tone controls would shame a transistor radio, the volume controls were scratchy as hell from the beginning and have definitely not improved with age, the input pads are intermittent, the rhythm section is good for testing out the P.A. and very little else, and the reverb sounds, well, like a cheap spring reverb. But for a quickie playing-out gig, when I don't want to pull a whole bunch of stuff out of my studio, I grab this thing and an old dual 15-inch bass cabinet I have wired in stereo, and I have an instant sound system. And it has never once, even if it's been sitting in a hot closet for five years and the hot sun for three hours, failed me. And that, friends, is for me the true meaning of vintage.

Paul Lehrman is from an early '50s vintage, and he just gets better with age.

Afterword

So where's all this stuff now? Okay, here goes…

The JVC CD player died. Fixing it would have cost more than I paid for it, and Apple's QuickTime extraction got so much better it didn't matter anymore.

The Rectilinear speakers live in my living room, with new tweeters.

The TOA speakers are my back channels when I work in four-channel (don't ask), and I also use them with the Yamaha mixer when I play out. The Auratones still do exactly what they always did.

The TOA mixers have been supplanted with a Mackie *1604*, which is bigger, but no heavier, and much more flexible. But now the Mackie qualifies as "vintage."

The AKG reverb, alas, gathers dust. Plug-in reverbs, with their infinite configurability, have taken its place. But I still get e-mails from people looking for copies of the manual.

The dbx *166* I no longer use, since the Waves plug-ins accomplish the same thing, with the advantage of digital look-ahead. The *163*, however, is still useful on live bass and guitar tracks.

The UREI *Platform* suffers the identical fate as the AKG reverb and also generates occasional inquiries.

The Yamaha *TX7*s are still amazingly useful.

The *Video Time Piece* isn't used much, since I now digitize any videotapes that come in and have the computer generate the timecode numbers, but it still serves to get me out of the occasional video-related bind.

The Syquest drive is somewhere in the basement. The Mirror monitor I had to pay my municipal trash department $25 to take away.

The *MIXI* is still handling secondary control functions in my studio, mostly balancing the insanely complex KDFX effects in my Kurzweil *K2500* module.

I bought a fancy Zoom guitar processor with overdrive, wah-wah, delay, and everything else and thought I'd never use the Bogen again, but I was wrong: When it comes to distortion, tubes is tubes.

Despite the funny looks I get from my fellow musicians, I still gig pretty often with the Yamaha mixer/amplifier.

Chapter 12

David Ball

The Last Word on Upgrades
A Personal Journey into the Heart of Darkness

Preface

Concerns about having to upgrade equipment, whether it's to accommodate new formats, improve our workflow, or as is all too common, not lose us business, are something everyone in the professional audio business has deal with constantly. It's particularly irksome when we've just gotten our current computer/software/console to work the way we want it, and now find we have to change it. Starting in December 1998, I did three columns in a row on the subject, with the last one—this one—bringing it all back home in the form of a personal story.

February, 1999

Y ou might be relieved to know that this is going to be my last column about dealing with upgrades—at least for a while. It's not a subject that's going to go away, but we need to pay attention to some other aspects of the recording and production life, not just how we're going to keep our tools working, even though that concern is taking up more and more time every year. In this installment, I'm going to relate a very recent— in fact, it's not over—horror story that illustrates so much of what I've been talking about. This is not Grumpmeier's story; it's mine.

For about three years, my main computer has been a Power Computing *PC100*, the very first Macintosh clone, a 100MHz Power PC 601 machine, equivalent to a Macintosh *8100*. I got it because in spite of my great affection for and loyalty to the Macintosh operating system, I've never been a fan of Apple's hardware. Even in the *Apple II* days, I owned a clone—a Franklin, *ACE* it was called—that was better built, easier to service, and performed better than anything Apple was making at the time. (Soon after I bought it, Apple, of course, shut the company down.) So when the first authorized Macintosh clones appeared, I jumped. Of all the computers I've owned, the *PC100* has been my favorite: It's reasonably quiet, well laid out, easy to get stuff like cards and RAM and hard drives in and out, built like a truck, and has never needed service.

But since Apple pulled the plug on its licensees, it's been an orphan. And by last year, it was beginning to feel like an old and feeble orphan. While it was still just fine for writing, MIDI composing, and most of the desktop publishing work I do, some newer applications, like Macromedia's *Dreamweaver*, which I use to create the pages on the Mix Online Web site [*which I was editor of at the time*], crawled like the Long Island Expressway at 5:30 on a Friday afternoon. And it was getting a little hairy reconfiguring it six times a day so I could work on Web stuff one hour and hard disk audio editing the next.

A dealer told me they'd have one for me in three days and then two days later went out of business.

So I decided it was high time I got a second computer. I have a heavy investment in NuBus-based audio hardware and didn't feel like replacing it all with PCI-based stuff, so I thought I'd dedicate the old machine to music, while I could use the new computer (an Apple G3) for writing, graphics, and the Web. At the same time, I thought, I could speed up that old machine and extend its productive lifespan by a year or two with one of the relatively inexpensive G3 upgrade cards that were now supposed to be available.

The first snag I ran into was the fact that said accelerator cards in fact *weren't* available. Between the time Newer Technology announced their G3 cards for 601-based Power Macs and the time I got mine installed, approximately nine months elapsed. These babies were so hot that most dealers weren't even taking orders—just names. One dealer said they'd put me on a "guaranteed" waiting list, but only if they could charge my credit card first. Another dealer put me in the queue, and then three months later lost my order. Another dealer told me they'd have one for me in three days and then two days later went out of business.

Meanwhile, I was learning from reports in print and on the Web that some of the G3 upgrade cards and some of the Power Computing machines didn't get along very well. Some reports said there were ROM conflicts. Others said, no, there were just conflicts over where to put the video card. You see, the accelerator card goes into the machine's PDS slot, where, ever since I bought the computer, there has lived a video card with four lovely megabytes of VRAM, enough to drive a 19-inch monitor at millions of colors. For people like me who don't want to sacrifice their video cards (and be forced to use the onboard video, which can only drive a 17-inch monitor at low resolution), the upgrade cards are available with a little piggyback system into which you can plug your video card. The problem was, I heard, that the Power Computing chassis was not laid out the same as the equivalent Mac that the card was designed for, and that in my machine there was physically no room for the video card.

"Exactly how much room did it need?" I asked Newer Technology, which was very good at answering the phone, even if they couldn't deliver any product. "Three-quarters of an inch clearance between the card slot and the chassis wall," was the reply. I measured my computer, and it was about 1/8-inch short. But I looked again and realized that on my particular computer (a tower configuration—apparently quite rare even by orphan standards!), you could actually remove one of the chassis walls, thereby creating essentially unlimited clearance for the card. I told this to a tech at Newer, and I could practically hear him shrug. "Might work," was all he'd volunteer. He had no access to a Power Computing machine for testing, so I was on my own.

Finally, the card came. And it was immediately obvious there was no way the video card was going to fit. The "piggyback" was connected to the G3 card with a thick copper strip, which bent over, but only one way—*into* the chassis. So no matter how much clearance I could make on the outside of the chassis, it wouldn't help.

Now I had a choice. I could use the processor card without a video card and rely on the *PC100*'s built-in video—which would mean my 19-inch monitor would become a doorstop—for sequencing and audio editing. Or I could forget the upgrade and hobble along with what I already had. Or I could unload the *PC100* and, in a desperate attempt to protect my investment in audio hardware, buy a used Apple *8100*. (By now I was getting dangerously close to spending enough to buy a brand-new machine.)

Or...I could sacrifice the video card and its lovely RAM, and instead find an old-style video card for the machine that fit into one of the NuBus slots. It would mean I couldn't expand my current *ProTools* system (which requires two slots, and the machine only has three) or put in SampleCell, but at least I could keep using my large monitor.

At this point, I realized that Newer Tech was hiding a nasty truth even from owners of Apple-brand NuBus Macs: When you use the video piggyback card, the video card has to go somewhere, and that somewhere is the middle NuBus slot. It's not actually connected to the slot, but instead hangs upside down in it, sort of like a three-toed sloth. But if you are familiar with *ProTools III* systems, you know that this arrangement cannot possibly work: Digidesign requires that the two *ProTools* cards reside in adjacent slots. So the computer-swapping scenario was out. Furthermore, anyone using *ProTools* on an *8100* (or *6100* or *7100*) was similarly hosed.

I started searching for an appropriate video card. If I couldn't find one, I decided, the accelerator was going back to the dealer—certainly there were hundreds more suckers waiting in line for it. I wasn't even going to test it—I was that scared of blowing something up and not being able to get my money back. At the school where I teach, our resourceful tech director found an old card made by Radius that had been bundled with some monitor we'd bought long ago and was no longer needed. I called Radius, and they said it would need a ROM upgrade to run with a Power Mac, but the resolution would be no better than what the computer provided from its built-in video. And the upgrade would be $100.

I scoured the back pages of the Mac magazines and the Internet, and I found a company called Radius Vintage (actually a division of some other company with no connection to Radius) that would sell me a high-resolution, Power Mac-compatible refurbished video card for $200. They wouldn't guarantee that it would work in my orphan machine, and oh yeah, all sales are final and no returns are allowed.

I found a Mac reseller, MacResQ, that had the exact same card for $100, and yes, they'd take it back if it didn't work, subject to a 15% restocking fee. I sighed; then I went ahead and ordered it. It didn't work at all—the computer wouldn't even boot. The ROM on it clearly said it was made in 1992, which led me to think that perhaps it might have problems with a computer made in 1995. I called MacResQ, and they told me, "The card works according to the specs when it was first released. If there have been subsequent upgrades, we are not responsible." Which meant if I wanted to use the sucker, I'd have to find a new ROM chip on my own.

Back to Radius Vintage. Yes, they had the ROM chip. It cost $100. No, still no guarantees or returns. And $17 for two-day shipping. So now, if this didn't work out, I was out $132, instead of $200. I decided it was worth a shot.

A week later, a very slim package arrived. Inside were eight pages of documentation: two on how to install the ROM chip, and six on how to use the enclosed antistatic wrist band while installing the ROM chip. There was also the antistatic wrist band, a folded square of paper with some copper foil wrapped around it. There was also an invoice, carefully explaining the no-return policy. What was noticeably absent, however, was a ROM chip.

I called up Radius Vintage and screamed. I got a very apologetic operator, who said they may not have any more in stock, and could she call me back later? I told her she could not, and I would hold while she checked. On my nickel, she searched her database and in 15 minutes found that there was indeed one more in stock. She promised to send it to me overnight.

A week later, after two more screaming phone calls and several e-mail messages demanding my money back and threatening them with everything from bad publicity to Ken Starr, another slim package arrived. This one had an actual chip in it, along with an invoice telling me my shipping charges would be refunded.

I vow never to go through anything like this again—but of course, in a year or two, I undoubtedly will.

I installed the chip onto the video card in less than a minute. Following some rather arcane boot-up instructions one thoughtful support person had given me, I got it to work. I installed the software drivers for the Newer Technology accelerator and then put the G3 card into the PDS slot. It worked, too. Most of my software is fine with the new processor, and my sequencer loves it—it's never felt so snappy. But *ProTools* has stopped working. I guess I'll have to check into that one of these days.

And now, as I sit typing on my new computer while my old one idles quietly in the next room, awaiting the next visitation of my muse, I vow never to go through anything like this again—but of course, in a year or two, I undoubtedly will.

Afterword

It took another month, but I did get *ProTools* working after a friend of mine who was a beta tester for Digidesign suggested I install the two PT cards in reverse order from what the manual said. Meanwhile, although the model numbers may have changed, the horror stories continue in your studio and in mine.

Photo of Laurie Spiegel at Bell Labs,
c. 1978, by Emmanuel Ghent

Chapter 13

Recalling a Legendary Playpen
A Revisit with Bell Labs

Preface

I can't think of too many companies or institutions that could hold a reunion of people who worked there 30 years ago, which would be of any interest to anyone outside the institution. But Bell Labs, as you will see, wasn't a typical place.

March 1999

Where does the spark of creativity come from when new tools and systems are designed? Is it from freedom or from pressure? Can an engineer working in an environment free of deadlines and milestones come up with anything useful? On the other hand, can that same engineer, working within the tight structure of a fast-moving, results-oriented corporation, bring a truly innovative perspective to a design? What would happen if an engineer were to strike out in an entirely new direction and work in an artistic field for a period of time? Conversely, what would happen if an artist were dropped into a laboratory and given carte blanche to tap the brains of the tech-heads and to play with the machines?

For those of us who consider ourselves artists, and who work with technology all the time, these might seem strange questions. After all, combining art and technology is what we do. Balancing freedom and structure is what we live with every day. We're constantly being called upon—or call upon ourselves—to do that left-brain/right-brain dance that requires being creative at the same time that we're mastering sophisticated technological tools.

Once upon a time, however, the worlds of the artist and the scientist were quite different. People wore different hats, and it was only under the rarest of circumstances that they trod on common ground and, if they dared, exchanged headgear.

In the companies where audio and music software and hardware are designed today, artists trained in technology and engineers with artistic hankerings work side by side. The artist who blithely goes through an entire career ignorant of the technological tools of his trade strikes us as a sad anachronism, and the technician who doesn't spend at least some down time fooling around with graphics, animation, or music seems to us terribly one sided.

But not too many years ago, engineers who admitted to having musical aspirations, or musicians who were willing to pick up a soldering iron, were rarities. When those people started to come together, a revolution began. And nowhere was that revolutionary fervor felt more than at Bell Laboratories.

Bell Labs, the research arm of AT&T, the erstwhile American local and long-distance telephone monopoly, was founded in 1925 in Murray Hill, New Jersey, about 20 miles from New York City. From the beginning, it was the site of some of the most important technological developments of the century—some having to do with telephones and some not. The transistor was invented there, and so was the laser. So were the digital computer, the fax machine, cellular phones, and UNIX. Bell Labs scientists discovered the background radiation left over from the Big Bang, and they were also the first to successfully synchronize film and audio. Manfred Schroeder, who developed the algorithms that are used in all of today's digital reverbs, was a researcher at Bell Labs, and Michael Noll developed at the Labs a three-dimensional force-feedback device, which is now a crucial part of what we call "virtual reality."

A rare look inside the Bell Labs of decades past was provided at a public meeting held a couple of months ago at Cooper Union, an art school in midtown Manhattan. Ten digital pioneers who worked at the facility in the '60s and '70s came together for a reunion. The meeting was presented by a small but ambitious outfit called Arts & Sciences Collaborations Inc. (ASCI), in conjunction with Bell Labs' present-day parent company, Lucent Technologies and several other sponsors. The participants talked about what they did at the Labs, demonstrating seminal projects and works from that era. Perhaps more importantly, they talked about how the philosophy and unique cast of characters that made up this protean think tank nourished their creativity. This atmosphere made it possible for them to conceive projects that, in a more conventional setting, an infinite number of engineers working on an infinite number of computer terminals would never have come up with.

It was during World War II that Bell Labs went from being the home of a dedicated bunch of communications engineers to a broader-based think tank. "The place exploded," explained Jerry Spivack, a pioneer in interactive graphics and the first of the alums to speak at the meeting. "Scientists were pulled from universities all over the country to work on radar. To attract them, AT&T needed to provide a fluid environment. Then, after the war, it stayed that fluid. We felt like we were in a period of unending growth, and in the next decade, the race to the moon gave us a lot of excitement and vision.

"People were studying everything that had anything to do with communications— frog mating calls, for example. We were told, 'Don't even think about money— this is research!'"

"AT&T considered us a national treasure," he continued. "People were studying everything that had anything to do with communications—frog mating calls, for example. We were told, 'Don't even think about money—this is research!'"

The facility was situated near a nature preserve, and scientists were encouraged to walk in the surrounding woods and think. But it was also very spread out and diverse, with different people working on entirely different problems right next to each other. "In order to go anywhere, you had to pass other people's offices," recalled Spivack, "and there was always something strange going on in there, so you'd poke your head in and see what it was."

Of course, not every project had totally positive consequences: "We did one exhibit with polyurethane," he laughed, "and when we were setting it up, we realized it would kill the audience with its fumes. Sort of gave new meaning to the phrase 'knocking 'em dead!'"

But there was more to Bell Labs than just a coming together of the best scientific brains. "The powers-that-be wanted to extend the capabilities of the technology," said Spivack, "and they felt the best way to do that was to bring in artists. We needed artists to think about what the technology *meant*." At the same time, those engineers who had artistic sides were encouraged to let them emerge. In another company, this never would have been allowed to interfere with their "real" work. Said composer Laurie Spiegel, "There were all these informal chamber-music reading sessions going on."

Max Mathews, today hailed as the father of computer music, held the title "Director of Acoustic and Behavioral Research" at the lab until 1985. In his comments at the meeting, he noted that Cooper Union was a particularly apt place to hold the event because the first public concert of computer music took place there in 1960. "There was a phalanx of New York police to protect the equipment," he recalled, "in case there was a riot."

At the first public concert of computer music "There was a phalanx of New York police to protect the equipment in case there was a riot."

Mathews created his first computer music in 1957: "Terrible bloops for 17 seconds," he recalled. In response to the difficulty he had organizing the sounds, he wrote the first dedicated musical computer language, MUSIC I. In 1960, he used physical modeling (!) to create the rendition of "Bicycle Built for Two," made famous in the movie *2001: A Space Odyssey*, as the last thing the HAL 9000 computer utters before it undergoes a lobotomy. Not long after that, he designed GROOVE, the first interactive computer music system, which used a computer to generate voltages, which in turn controlled analog synthesizer modules.

"By day, the computers were used for speech research, and by night, music research," Mathews explained. He could give passes to people who wanted to work overnight, and one of those was composer Emmanuel Ghent, who was also on the panel. "When Ghent's marriage broke up, and he remarried, I gave him the computer as a wedding present," said Mathews, "so he wouldn't have to come in and work all night."

Ghent talked about his work with the machines controlling both music and theatrical lighting dimmers, about developing a music-notation generator, and about how he used random number generators to create music, in the first experiments in computer-driven algorithmic composition. "Some random numbers sounded better than others," he recalled. "If I were a better programmer, I would simply have programmed things that I wanted to do. But because I wasn't very good, I had to simplify the programming. But then things came out that I never would have dreamed of by myself. So there's something to be said for not being a master of the technology."

Laurie Spiegel was another artist whose personal life was disrupted by Bell Labs. "I was going there all the time, and pretty soon a long-term relationship that I was in ended—he couldn't believe I was spending all those nights with a computer!" she said. A composer and instrument designer, Spiegel later developed the deceptively simple algorithmic program for personal computers, Music Mouse. Bell Labs gave Laurie her first exposure to computers. "I had always loved art and science and was working a lot with Buchla synths when I met Manny [*Ghent*] and Max at a concert at The Kitchen," she said, referring to a well-known downtown New York spot for experimental music. The scientists invited her to come down to the Labs and play at night. "I had no computer background at all, so I read a book on FORTRAN," she remembered. "I kept my sleeping bag in the lab's anechoic chamber—boy, was that a quiet place to sleep!"

Spiegel was intrigued by the real-time interactive aspects of the work. "You could hear interactively what you were doing for the first time and get feedback," she said. "Max coined a term for it in 1973: 'intelligent instrument.' It meant that the response you got was not in one-on-one correspondence with the physical gesture you made." She also saw the Labs as an opportunity to experiment with "automating my own decision-making processes as an artist."

The process of composing with computers, she emphasized, although it was interactive, was not fast. "The computers allowed storage, editing, and overdubbing of your performances, but all of these tasks were done in different rooms. The digital lab had a computer the size of four refrigerators, which had 32K of memory. The analog lab, where the synthesizer was, was 300 feet down the hall. There were 14 control lines, for pitch, amplitude, etc., and you constantly had to retune and calibrate the equipment. So we did a lot of running around—we were all in good shape. Meanwhile, in between the labs, you had to pass by this incredible window that was showing evolving visual images. Finally, I got up the guts to talk to the programmer, Ken Knowlton, who was doing them. We ended up collaborating on some projects." She was also inspired to write control programs for video synthesizers.

And speaking of refrigerators, "We often worked in parkas," Spiegel recalled with a laugh. "The computers had trouble if the room temperature was above 50 degrees. Someone would come every hour and take the temperature."

Spiegel referred to the work going on at Bell Labs at that time as "a Rosetta Stone for connecting between different sensory modalities"—in other words, multimedia. And there was a communal aspect to the work that one sees infrequently today: "We were proud of each other's accomplishments, not threatened by them."

As Spivack said, "Algorithmic technology is dangerous to the idea of a sole artist working in solitude. Works that come out are not necessarily products of ego. It allows a collaboration, which is rare in our culture but common in many others."

Although AT&T supported all of the strange goings-on, their attitude was somewhat ambivalent. Spiegel said, "What we were doing wasn't really a 'proper' business for a monopoly, so we had to keep a lot of it hush-hush." Ken Knowlton, among whose contributions were a graphic language to describe motion on a computer screen and the visualization of molecules and other sub-microscopic objects, recalled that "I did a computer-generated nude with artist Leon Harmon. The administration said that we shouldn't tell anyone where we did it—except when the New York *Times* published it, they told the *Times* to make sure the Labs got credit!"

After the breakup of AT&T in the early '80s, Bell Labs had to redefine itself more narrowly, and much of the "pure" research, and the open-ended collaborations with artists, ended. Bell Labs still exists (and, in fact, is probably larger than ever, comprising other research facilities all over the world) as part of Lucent Technologies, which before the breakup was essentially the Western Electric division of AT&T. It is still making contributions to the world of audio, most notably by developing codecs for squeezing high-quality audio into ever-smaller bandwidths. It's still a high-powered place: Recently, it announced that its scientists had achieved the first data transmission of 1 trillion bits per second.

And there are other research centers that still follow the Bell Labs model of putting artists and engineers in close quarters: IRCAM in Paris, MIT's Media Lab, CNMAT at Berkeley, and CCRMA at Stanford, to name a few. But, as Max Mathews said, "They no longer lead the technology. It's the companies that make the products that we use that are leading. I think that's good." But it follows a different model.

Lucent is very aware of its extraordinary heritage—the company was one of the sponsors of the meeting—and Dorée Seligmann, currently a researcher at the facility in multimedia communications, said she is doing what she can to recapture the spirit of those years by organizing collaborations between the Labs' researchers and artistic groups. "They told me when I came on board," she said wryly, "that I had missed the Golden Years. But I think there's a very important role for artists to play in development of technologies. They have to participate in the technical discussions. We have to always ask ourselves what technology is for, not just how to get the best bit or frame rate."

The answers, the methods, and the players are different from what they used to be, but the need for people who can ask those questions doesn't change.

Afterword

Emmanuel Ghent, composer, psychiatrist, and Bell Labs researcher, passed away on March 30, 2003, at the age of 77. His daughter Valerie, an accomplished musician, producer, and songwriter, produced an album of her father's previously unreleased children's songs, which is available on West Street Records.

The original Max Mathews rendition of "Bicycle Built for Two" can be found online at www.vortex.com/comphist. Laurie Spiegel has a lot of information about her work at Bell Labs at her site: www.retiary.org/ls/.

Chapter 14

Jack Desrocher

04/01/Y2K
What Really Happened

Preface

With all the silliness surrounding the "Y2K" problem, I couldn't let the April Before the End of the World pass without making fun of it, could I?

April 1999

Microsoft Corp. (NASDAQ=MSFT) announced today a change in the release schedule of its new operating system, Windows 2000, explaining that extra time was needed to bring it into full Y2K compliance. The release date is now expected to be second quarter 1901.

—an alleged Microsoft press release, circulating the Net

Date: April 1, 2000
From: Insider Audio Central
City: None of your business

Well, it's been quite the few months since the big year-o-metric tickover, hasn't it? Nothing happened as anyone predicted it would, at least not in the way they predicted, but a whole lot of things happened that no one expected. And our little industry wasn't unaffected, was it?

There were, of course, the great shortages and outages, as the doomsayers predicted. But the doomsayers got them right for all the wrong reasons. The technology didn't fail us: We managed to screw things up all by ourselves, just by expecting that the world was going to end.

Were you one of the millions who woke up the day after Christmas and decided you'd better fill your cars' fuel tanks, figuring all the pumps would stop working a week later? Actually, none of the pumps had clocks in them, but that didn't stop you from getting into one of those gas lines that made the '70s oil panic look like a picnic on a deserted beach. Prices soared, Exxon and Mobil called off their merger as their individual stock prices went through the roof, troops went on alert in the Persian Gulf, and Nigerian investment capital, of which there suddenly seemed to be a whole lot, bought out what was left of the Republican party. Three tanker ships, trying to make double-speed deliveries with crews forced into round-the-clock duty, went aground off Nova Scotia, causing spills that closed down the entire New England fishing industry once and for all, and suddenly scrod, which no one outside of Massachusetts had even heard of before, became a prized delicacy among the only folks who could now afford it: well-financed Silicon Valley Internet startups. While Boston fish markets were reduced to selling canned Japanese tuna, you could find all the scrod you wanted at Palo Alto sushi bars, at $600 per piece.

> *The technology didn't fail us: We managed to screw things up all by ourselves, just by expecting that the world was going to end.*

Or were you one of those who nearly precipitated an international banking crisis on December 30, when you decided you had to get all of your savings into a safe place, like under your mattress, and stormed your local ATM? When the cash supply dried up, an obscure piece of code in bank machines programmed by a certain Seattle-area company kicked in that caused the ATMs to actually print new currency. However, instead of Andrew Jackson's picture on the $20s, there was a holographic engraving of Bill Gates. Although most people didn't notice the difference (after all, they'd been dealing with weird-looking $20s for a while), there was enough of an outcry to cause deep concern at the Federal Reserve Board, and several Texas Savings and Loans teetered once again on the verge of extinction. But calm prevailed when it was announced that the bills (or "Willies," as we now call them) would be accepted at 100% of face value at all Starbucks stores.

Then there was the afternoon of December 31, when the "Super Bowl Halftime Effect," which until then had been considered an urban myth, became reality. But instead of all of America flushing their toilets at the same time, at 6:30 p.m. Eastern Standard Time, just as all three networks' nightly news led off reporting that unemployed persecutor Ken Starr had filed his 422nd sexual-harassment suit against Bill Clinton (this one involving an airline flight attendant who claimed he pinched her buttocks on a flight to England at the start of his Rhodes Scholarship in 1968), approximately 92 million households simultaneously decided this would be a good time to turn off their TVs and start filling every empty bucket, jug, bottle and bathtub in their house with water, in anticipation of the nation's water system breaking down. Of course, that precipitated the very event it was supposed to mitigate, and the resulting loss in pressure caused cooling failures and emergency shutdowns at several major nuclear-powered electric plants, thereby throwing large chunks of the North American power grid into blackness, and all three networks off the air.

The madness wasn't confined to our shores, of course. A couple of hours later, as midnight came to the Middle East, some 200 white-robed, blond-haired individuals appeared on hilltops overlooking the city of Jerusalem, each claiming to be the Messiah, come again to redeem humankind. Upon spotting each other, these individuals at first tossed insults, then began invoking divine wrath upon each other, and when that failed to have any effect, they resorted to hair-pulling, fisticuffs, and eventually stone-throwing. Local police, who fortunately were stationed close by collecting firearms and explosives from thousands of smiling pilgrims to the Holy Land, quickly quelled the altercations and arranged for the wackos to be deported back to the U.S. Today, of course, their talk shows fill Fox News's afternoon schedule, which those of us with battery-powered televisions can enjoy.

Finally, at midnight in New York, the 30 million who called the recorded telephone time lady to hear the year officially change not only got busy signals, they caused a voltage spike that erased James Earl Jones' voice from thousands of Bell Atlantic announcement chips, thus invoking a $100 billion severance clause buried deep in Jones' 214-page endorsement contract, immediately driving the not-so-Baby Bell into insolvency.

Those of us who still had electricity witnessed the spectacle of the Internet being brought to its knees, as a reported 65 million Web surfers tried to watch the AOL-exclusive live Webcast of Dick Clark riding the light ball down the TV transmitting tower atop the World Trade Center. Because of the overload, almost nobody saw Clark's panic attack, which climaxed in his screaming, "I don't care what century it is, I'm still a teenager!" and his subsequent rescue by a TV station helicopter.

Since that date, which has come to be known as "ECAWKI"—the End of Civilization As We Know It, pronounced "ee-kaw-kee"—the professional audio industry has been confronted with some of the biggest challenges in its short history.

Home and project studios—which because they typically couldn't afford floating floors and double-studding have always had to deal with the problems of ambient noise—were hit particularly hard by ECAWKI. The wood-powered electric generators they now have to rely on typically raise the noise floor in the control room/studio to 98 dB SPL. Many project studio owners are solving this problem by building "generator cellars," and a few, especially in the suburbs, are lucky enough to have old '50s bomb shelters in their yards, which proved perfect for this function. These cellars have the added bonus of protecting the unit from acquisitive and probably hungry neighbors.

Another problem faced by small-studio owners has been a sudden increase in competition from large numbers of new entrants into the field. These newbies, all former white-collar frustrated rock stars, found themselves with huge windfalls when the companies they worked for, all of whom used personnel-maintenance software designed in the '70s by Ross Perot, received computer-generated letters informing them they had due them 100 years' worth of back vacation pay. The letters offered them up to 30 years paid vacation or a one-time payment, which in many cases exceeded $8,000,000. Naturally, many chose the latter and cashed out before their payroll departments knew what hit them. After they bought the Lexus and the Ford Explorer, their attention turned to fulfilling their adolescent rock 'n' roll dreams, and digital consoles, multitracks, copies of vintage guitars, and over-powered monitors started flying out of dealers' warehouses. While this burgeoning market has been a boon to manufacturers and sellers of pro audio gear, ironically very few employees of those companies benefited from this particular Y2K bug, since almost no one in those industries ever sticks with a company long enough to accrue any vacation time.

A number of companies have managed to bring to market, remarkably quickly, new products that are well adapted to our post-ECAWKI world. Alesis Corporation, long known for providing useful new technology at rock-bottom prices, has had great success with its "true digital" 1-bit recording device, known as "Sucaba." It achieves economies by relying on finger power (hence, "true digital") and offline storage (when you get a number, write it down). Its continuously adjustable sample rate is not reliant on AC line frequency or voltage, which is particularly helpful in areas where there isn't any. Religious groups at first objected to the name and picketed Alesis's headquarters with signs saying "Stop the Spawn of the Devil" and "If God had wanted us to record digitally, he would have had our fingers coming out of our ears," but they quietly went away when it was pointed out to them that "Sucaba" was merely "abacus" spelled backwards.

A small company in the south of England has a hit with its model "Fred," a unique "power-independent" amplifier that is being snapped up by both studios and sound reinforcement companies as fast as the assembly line can turn them out. It features a massive cooling system with two large squirrel-cage fans, but no AC plug or even a battery pack. The secret is that the squirrel cages are indeed just that, and the unit ships with two healthy young squirrels, one male and one female, whose constant running, motivated by their reproductive imperatives and a supply of peanuts, provides a continuous, although somewhat erratic, source of current to the amp's power supply—enough to drive a pair of 4-ohm speakers to levels sufficient to drown out the noise of the unit itself. The company now plans to offer a slightly smaller, more portable version that uses hamsters, which will be called "Barney," as well as models for the domestic hi-fi market, "Wilma" and "Betty."

Casio has come back into the professional products arena with the first DAT machine that uses neither AC power nor batteries. The users' guide, produced entirely on an old Underwood manual typewriter, explains that an "angular motion storage and retrieval device" must be engaged prior to operating the unit, and users are then to "release the energy reserve drive mechanism" when they want to Record or Play—in other words, a wind-up crank and a spring. The only problem users have been complaining about is that the device can't be used indoors, since it needs bright sunlight to operate the D/A converters, but since no one has any indoor lighting anyway, this is not as much of a drawback as one might think.

One group that has made out exceptionally well in the last few months is exporters of pro audio gear to the Third World. Orders from China, the Arab nations, and Israel for computer-based DAWs soared in the final weeks of 1999 and have continued high since then. Companies in those countries that no one ever heard of suddenly had lines of credit worth millions, and they were snatching up Mac, Wintel, and stand-alone systems like it was, well, the end of the world. At the same time, major recording studios opened up or beefed up their overseas operations and started shipping large numbers of personnel to these outposts.

Only in this "advanced" civilization can the fears of the technology that we have created utterly negate all of the knowledge it has allowed us to accrue.

The reasoning behind these extraordinary moves became clear when a disgruntled employee of Seagram's (now owner of all 18 remaining major record labels) leaked an internal confidential memo: "How to set your computer's clock to local time." Prominent in the text were instructions for setting the year to conform with non-Christian calendars: In Moslem countries, it is 1421, which pushes the Y2K problem far off into the future, while in Israel and China, where the current years are, respectively, 5761 and 4698 (since February), the problem went away centuries ago.

So systems are working and people are living their lives as they always have, wherever they haven't gotten hung up on all of those zeroes and on a calendar that was four years off from the day it was created. It's only in our part of the world, where we boast of being rational, scientific, and technologically mature, that society has been brought to its knees by the power that, in our imaginations, numbers hold over us.

Only in this "advanced" civilization can the fears of the technology that we have created utterly negate all of the knowledge it has allowed us to accrue. Only here can the hucksters, screaming loudly that the end of the world is nigh, while they scurry about finding ways to cash in on the terror they create, actually bring it about themselves. As the immortal bard Pogo Possum might have said, had he lived into this last year of the 20th century, "We have met the Y2K problem, and he is us."

Paul D. Lehrman isn't hoarding batteries, canned tuna, or Sterno. But he isn't planning on being on top of any tall buildings next New Year's Eve, either.

Afterword

What no one noticed at all in the run-up to the end of the 1900s was how much the economy was being boosted by all the Y2K preparations, and thus no one predicted how far it would fall after the nonsense was all over. It all seems so dumb in retrospect, doesn't it? Especially considering the *real* disasters that followed in the years since the millennium began, which had nothing to do with calendars turning over.

Chapter 15

George Martin
Doing It on the Road

Preface

There has been so much written about George Martin that there is little left to say—other than he is the most important producer in the history of recorded music. Hearing him talk in person was a real privilege.

May 1999

In 1971, I wrote a college paper on the use of electronic music studio techniques in popular music. The paper, one of my favorite things I did in college (having to do with a course, that is), talked in detail about how Pink Floyd, Frank Zappa, and Jimi Hendrix used the tools——such as tape speed change, looping, echo, reversal, splicing, reverberation, and so on——developed by the pioneering composers of the electronic medium. These techniques opened up huge new vocabularies of sound to pop musicians and created a new type of rock music that could never (well, until the advent of samplers, which was quite a ways in the future) be performed on the stage.

In my introduction to the paper, I noted, "By far, the most important contributors to this new field were The Beatles, whose use of tape-manipulation techniques on such albums as *Sgt. Pepper's Lonely Hearts Club Band* and *Magical Mystery Tour* set the example for all of those to follow." My friend and fellow music fanatic Carl, when he read that paragraph, immediately opined, "That's an understatement." "Yes," I acknowledged, "but I don't know how to put it any more strongly."

Maybe today I do. How about this: What The Beatles were doing between 1966 and 1969 was so brilliant, so revolutionary, so liberating, so mind-blowing, so fall-on-the-floor-frothing-at-the-mouth amazing, that almost everything else, then or since, pales in comparison. And all of the toys and techniques that we use in the recording studio today, in fact, all of our careers, are a direct result of those projects.

Of course, when it came to the studio, the Fab Four were actually five, the fifth member being the classically trained George Martin, who redefined forever the role of the record producer. Known as Sir George Martin since 1996, he recently announced his retirement, sat for an in-depth interview with *Electronic Musician* magazine, and embarked on an eight-city public lecture tour, meeting fans and talking about his career, focusing especially on the creation of *Sgt. Pepper.*

The story of The Beatles and how they changed the recording industry has been told many times; they were perhaps the best-documented pop-culture phenomenon in history. A wealth of material can be found in Martin's still-available 1979 book, *All You Need Is Ears,* and there are countless others, both by people who knew what they were talking about and those who didn't. But in such a complex and inspiring story, there are always more things to hear—insights, off-the-cuff remarks, little interpersonal exchanges—that can cast new light on the era and the people in it. Martin's current lecture tour (which I caught at the second stop, the sold-out Berklee Performance Center in Boston) goes over much old ground, but he also offers enough new material to keep even the most jaded of pop music journalists, as another icon of the era put it, starry-eyed and laughing.

Martin is not a charismatic public speaker; his presentational style is more suited to small-group conversation. But he had the crowd in his pocket from the moment he appeared. In fact, he garnered a standing ovation before he even made it to the stage, and throughout his 75-minute lecture and ten-minute question-and-answer period, except for the laughter and applause, you could hear a pin drop. He initially had some trouble reading from his text and coordinating with the videos that accompanied his talk, but he got more comfortable as the lecture progressed, and it wasn't long before he had the whole crowd convinced they were in his living room.

"I was known as a comedian's producer," he said, "which stood me in good stead when I met The Beatles. I started doing comedy when I started with Parlophone, since nobody else was doing it. I thought if I fell flat on my face, no one would notice." Besides his success with such seminal assemblages as The Goons and Beyond the Fringe, he had a Number One record pre-Beatles with a group called The Temperance Seven: "They were called that because there were nine of them and they drank like fish."

As to how the legendary collaboration came about in the first place, Martin said, "The Beatles were rejected by every record company, including ours, and were regarded as something of a joke in the business. When Brian Epstein was told to come see me, he knew he'd hit rock bottom."

Quick jump to 1966, which, Martin reminded us, was not a good year for The Beatles. There had been death threats in Hamburg (which I had never heard about before), and an unfortunate, unwitting snub of the Philippines' most famous shoe fetishist, Imelda Marcos, resulted in the band being unceremoniously booted out of the country ("They made them carry their own bags at the airport and turned off the escalators when they got there"). And, of course, John's remarks about their audience being larger than Jesus' hit the teen press in the States and resulted in bannings, burnings, and other enlightened responses. Meanwhile, their concerts were becoming circuses. On one of the many videotapes Martin played, Ringo says, "The screaming was like a thousand jet planes. If I tried to play a fill, it would just disappear. I'd be watching the other guys' buns to see where the beat was."

So the decision was made that year to devote their time to making records, and the motivation was there to create music that couldn't be performed. The first experiment in that direction was "Strawberry Fields Forever," which got its name from a park Lennon loved as a child. McCartney, also appearing on video, explained that "Penny Lane" was his response to that: "It was a place John knew, because we'd go there when he came over to my place when we were kids."

Under pressure from EMI to get something on the charts, the two songs were released together as a single, something Martin called "one of the biggest mistakes I ever made. It meant the airplay was split between the two songs, so it only made it to Number 2. People were wondering if The Beatles were finished." Meanwhile, because they wanted record buyers to get "value for their money," the two songs couldn't appear on the next album, and what was to be *Sgt. Pepper* had to be started from scratch.

The album, cobbled together from bits and pieces, was not a "concept" album at the beginning. "The opening audience ambience came from a Beyond the Fringe recording I had done in Cambridge," Martin told us. The whole idea of *Sgt. Pepper*, which came about halfway through the process of making the album, was something that came to Paul after a trip to the United States—now that the band was done touring, they were free to travel on their own. "He started talking about the album being songs that Sgt. Pepper's band would write, not that The Beatles would write." Even the brilliant transitions between songs didn't emerge until after they were all recorded and they were assembling the final master: "Originally, the 'Sgt. Pepper Reprise' was supposed to come after 'A Day in the Life,' but we knew that nothing could follow that. So we put it before, and there was John's acoustic guitar coming up from under the applause. Then we found the way the guitar count-in at the beginning of the reprise sounded linked beautifully with the chicken squawking at the end of 'Good Morning.'"

"A Little Help From My Friends" was written by Paul, especially for Ringo, since he had a "limited range," using only five adjacent notes. "Except for the last note—and when he recorded that, all the others were out there in the studio with him, singing along, to give him confidence." On video, Ringo recalled, "The first line was originally, 'Would you stand up and throw tomatoes [pronounced to-mah-toes] at me?' Well, people were throwing all sorts of things at us, and I didn't want to give them any ideas, so I made them change it."

"Ringo was underemployed during the making of the record," recalled Martin, "because after he laid his tracks down, there wasn't much for him to do, except wait around in case we needed some extra percussion. He says his one memory of doing the album was that was when he learned to play chess." Ringo again: "I was lucky to be in a band with three frustrated drummers. They could all play drums, but each of them knew only one style."

On "Being for the Benefit of Mr. Kite," John wanted to bring in a real steam-driven calliope, but Martin found out that, besides the nightmare of having such a contraption in the studio, calliopes weren't played by hand but were programmed, like player pianos, using punched cards. "Just for us to make a card punch so that we could tell it what we wanted to play would have taken forever," he said. So instead, they built up the sound using a foot-powered harmonium, Lowrey and Hammond organs, with long-suffering roadie Mal Evans puffing away on a bass harmonica. Martin played the fast organ riffs with the tape running at half-speed. "As you all know," he told the crowd, most of whom did know, "it makes you sound bloody brilliant." And while Martin and engineer Geoff Emerick were pulling off the legendary cut-up-the-tape-throw-it-in-the-air-and-reassemble-it-at-random trick, "John was like a kid in a candy store."

At one point, "A Day in the Life" had 24 bars of empty space in the middle of it. "You can hear a little alarm clock at the end of the 24 bars, which let us know when to come in," he said. "I asked what they wanted to put in there, and they said, 'Let's have a symphony orchestra.' I said, 'Okay, what will they play?' and they said, 'Anything they like.' They didn't understand that symphony musicians can't play anything unless you put music in front of them." Martin sketched out the charts for the players, telling them, "'Don't listen to the chap next to you. If you're playing the same note he is, you're playing the wrong one.' All their lives, they'd been told to try to play as one man—in a few minutes, The Beatles changed all that."

After the "orchestral orgasm," the first idea was to have "a giant 'hummm,' like a Tibetan chant. I can't tell you how pathetic that sounded." The giant piano chord that they ended up with required three of them to play at the same time, and then to hold their breath. "At the end of it, the amplification was turned up so high," Martin said, "that if any one of us had coughed, it would have sounded like a bomb.

"I was a little worried we were taking people too far with this album," he told us. "But the head of Capitol Records in the U.S. came by, and I played him 'A Day in the Life,' and he was absolutely gobsmacked. 'I never heard anything like it,' he said. I knew if we had him, we'd got it."

And the multitude of faces on the album cover? They were a logistical nightmare—not just setting up the photo collage, but getting permission to use the likenesses of all the people on it. Remember, this was long before the Internet, and people still felt they had a right to their own images. "EMI insisted that we get clearances for all of them, but they wouldn't do it themselves. So Brian hired his old assistant to make the phone calls and letters. Leo Gorcey, an actor who had been in the Dead End Kids, wanted $500, so we painted him over. Mae West wrote back, 'What would I be doing in a Lonely Hearts Club?' So we got the four of them to write her a letter expressing their admiration for her, especially for her having spent ten days in jail for obscenity, and she relented. Think about how much that letter would be worth today—certainly a lot more than the $500 Gorcey wanted!"

By the time you read this, Sir George Martin's tour will be over, but some 10,000 people will have been privileged enough to experience it. We all owe more to this man than we can possibly express, and this tour was a reminder of that. But it was also his way of giving something back to the audience (or a very small segment thereof), who allowed him to pursue such a brilliant career. And my way of thanking him is to let him have the last word:

Music, I was told, was a nice thing to be able to do, but it wasn't something sensible people tried to make a living at.

"Music, I was told, was a nice thing to be able to do, but it wasn't something sensible people tried to make a living at. To me, it didn't seem any more hazardous than flying for the navy [which he did in World War II]. I always followed my gut feeling, whether it was whether I should go into music, or should I sign this band or do this film. And it's always worked. If you're a gambler, and you always bet the favorite, you end up losing money. If all you care about is statistics, you might as well be in the insurance business."

Afterword

A truly harrowing description of the incident in the Philippines is in Bob Spitz's recent, and highly recommended, *The Beatles: The Biography*. Spitz is a little weak on the music/tech side (he gets the origin of the word "flanging" all wrong and spells "VU" with a lower-case "u"), but his research on the people and incidents is astounding.

Chapter 16

Jack Davis

Perils of the Free Market
Grumpmeier Goes Looking for a Bargain

Preface

This didn't start out as a Grumpmeier piece. My original idea was to tell it in the first person, since I actually did what I accuse Grumpmeier of doing. I was going to begin with a line from the *Sylvia* comic: "Oh, like you've never thought of this…." But the editors at *Mix* objected, saying "You're advocating unethical behavior!"

Well, I think that's debatable, considering how much *really* unethical behavior is out there, but *rather than press* the point, I figured ol' Grump could take the blame instead. I think it came out funnier this way, anyway.

July 1999

I ran into my buddy Grumpmeier at the local 'Lectronics Land the other day, as I was mulling over a new microwave with more controls than my last mixing console. "That 50-year-old washing machine of yours finally give up the ghost?" I asked him. "Heck, no," he said. "I got that thing held together with fishing line and Silly Putty. It'll go another 30 years, I'm sure. I just came here to borrow some stuff for the weekend."

I laughed, "The library is across town, my friend."

"No really," he replied. "I do this all the time when I need something for just a couple of days. Come over here, and I'll tell you how it works."

We crouched in low behind a 64-inch TV set that was blaring out a trailer for *Terminator IX*. Arnold was climbing into a time machine that would take him back to early 18th-century Leipzig, while solemnly proclaiming to a crowd of awed onlookers, "I'll be Bach!"

"See, I'm in the middle of a TV project, and one of my video decks died yesterday," Grumps began. "It's pretty old, and it would cost more than it's worth to fix. Meanwhile, I just got this new cut from the producer, who wouldn't know what window burn was if it bit him on the behind. So I gotta have two decks so I can make a work print. I've got a new deck on order from a mail-order house—one of those industrial models, I push my decks pretty hard—but it's going to take a few days to get here. In the meantime, I don't want to fall behind on the project, so I'm going to borrow a deck from these guys to do the dub. Here, take a look at this thing."

He shoved a tiny camcorder into my face. "This has got more features on it, and the picture quality is better than the deck I'm throwing out. But it costs about a quarter of what I paid. Amazing, huh? Of course, the transport controls look like they'll break off if you look at them cross-eyed, and the case feels like it's made out of cardboard..."

"Borrow?" I interrupted him, as my eyebrows went up in tandem. "You mean you're going to try to steal it?"

"No, dummy!" he snapped. "I mean borrow. They have this 30-day, no-questions-asked return policy. I put the thing on a credit card, use it for a couple of days, put it back in the box with all the manuals and the other crap, and bring it back for a refund. No problemo!" he smiled, quite pleased with himself.

"But that's dishonest!" I cried, causing him to put his greasy hand over my mouth.

"Of course it is," he hissed. "But they're asking for it. Hey, I didn't tell them to make this policy. They do it to lure in customers, make them think they're not taking any risk when they spend their money here. Why can't I take advantage of that? Who does it hurt?"

"Well, for starters," I started, in urgent but hushed tones, "the store can't sell something that you've returned as 'new,' can they? So you're actually devaluing the merchandise when you do that."

"So they knock down the price a few bucks, so what?" he scorned. "They're still making money."

"But what if everyone did this?" I asked. "What if you had 300 customers come in to the store every Friday, strip the shelves of DVD players and cart out all the big-screen TVs, and then bring everything back Monday morning?"

"What if you had 300 customers come in to the store every Friday, strip the shelves of DVD players and cart out all the big-screen TVs, and then bring everything back Monday morning?"

"You don't think that happens some weekends?" he laughed. "The people who work here hate the Super Bowl. Not only do they get crazy busy in the days just before it, but all the time they're wondering how much of the stuff is going to come back the next week, and how many commissions they're going to lose. But you know what? A lot of stuff doesn't come back. People get these things set up in their living rooms, and then they decide, 'Hey, this is great, why don't I hold onto this thing?' If they hit the limit on their credit cards, they just apply for another one. You know how many credit card offers I get in the mail every week? Heck, even those radical left-wing political journals my wife subscribes to have their own Platinum VISA cards now."

"So I guess you don't own a computer, either, eh?" I challenged him. "You probably just come here and borrow one for a month and then return it and get the next model. That way you've always got the latest, and it doesn't cost you a dime, right?"

He took the bait. "Actually, they've got that figured out. With computer stuff, they charge you a 15 percent 'restocking' fee, which pretty much kills the deal. On the other hand, sometimes when I've needed extra storage space, I've been tempted to get a hard drive from them and write off the 15 percent as a rental fee."

"Do you pull this with everyone you do business with?" I wondered. "Do you order guitars from the music store chains and send them back when the album is finished? Do you tie up some poor dealer's ADAT inventory when you need a few more tracks?"

"Naw," he answered. "I just do it with stores I hate. And I hate these big chains that put all the locals out of business. Now they're trying to run the whole consumer electronics game themselves—like that chain that came out with that stupid 'Divx' thing. I mean, what's up with this 'disposable media' stuff? If anything's gonna kill DVD, that's going to be it. Can you imagine what would have happened to CDs if they'd come out ten years ago with disposable ones that only played twice? If they'd tried that, we'd all still be playing vinyl."

"So you do still support your local pro audio dealer and buy your high-end stuff there, right?"

"Naw," he replied without a trace of irony. "I do everything by mail order. It's cheaper, and everyone has a return policy. Pro audio dealers can't match that. And besides, they all hate me."

"Can't say I blame them," I laughed. "But you know, you should give them a chance."

"To do what?" he scoffed. "They gonna offer me price guarantees like Musician's Best Bud or Bert and Gert's World of Audio and Toaster Ovens?"

"You'd be surprised what they can do," I explained patiently, as a techno-grunge version of the *Toccata and Fugue in D minor* blasted away in the background. "The dealer I work with gives me great prices, and even if they can't always go as low as the big chains or the mail-order places, they can come close. I know if something doesn't work out, they'll take it back—they don't have to trumpet that as a marketing come-on; it's just their way of treating customers. And they've even lent me stuff for a couple days when I was in a real pinch, and I didn't have to pay freight charges. But they only do this because I've been doing business with them for years. I've only got my one personal studio, so it's not like I'm buying hundreds of thousands of dollars' worth of stuff, but they know that when I need something, I'll come to them, and when my school or one of my students or a client needs something, that's where I'll tell them to go.

"That's called loyalty." I emphasized the last word in case he had never heard it before. "And it works two ways. Maybe I end up spending a few more bucks than I would otherwise, but I know that when they sell me something, they've made sure it will be compatible with my setup and do what I need it to do, and it will work when I pull it out of the box. Try to get that kind of assurance from a mail-order place that makes more money on guitar strings and calculators than on pro audio gear. And if something doesn't work, they'll give me a lot more by way of assistance than just a Return Merchandise Authorization number.

"And there's another thing that a good relationship with a dealer can help you with." He was beginning to get fidgety, so I pushed harder. "If some manufacturer is doing a closeout on something, the only way you're going to find out about it is through a dealer. By the time it hits the magazines, you can bet all of the stock is gone. Last month a buddy of mine heard from his dealer that a manufacturer was blowing out a reverb that had only been out for a year at 60 percent off. He's a regular customer, so they let him be one of the first to know about it. He was smart enough to buy two—and he sold me one." I grinned triumphantly.

"Yeah, well thanks for the sermon," Grumps grumbled and signified our conversation was over with his usual subtle tactic of walking away. "I got a dub to make. Say, are you using all of your multitracks next week? I got a band coming in with a big horn section, and I don't know how I'm going to handle them all. You think I could borrow a deck?" I just smiled.

A couple of weeks later, I ran into Grumpmeier again, outside a coffee shop. "So how'd that TV project work out?" I asked. "Did you get any flack from the store about bringing that camcorder back?" "Oh, it went fine," he said, "and the store didn't give me any trouble, because I never took it back." He sighed. "My wife got one look at how good the picture was and demanded we keep it for our next vacation. And I'd already ordered the industrial deck for my studio, so now I gotta pay for both of them. And now she's screaming that we need a new TV set to match the quality of the camcorder. Guess I'll have to get another credit card." I was watching the utter defeat of a man whose sole purpose in life is to be cheap.

"But you know what's really bothering me?" he moaned. "My teenage daughter wants to have a big party next weekend, and she went down to that same store and came home with this enormous, ridiculously overpowered system with a subwoofer the size of a filing cabinet. I asked her how she could afford it, and she looked at me like I was a blithering idiot and said, 'But, Daddy, I'll bring it back next week!'"

Afterword

A good seven years later, this issue is still being kicked around. Many "big-box" stores have extended their restocking fees to a wider range of products, making it harder for folks like Grump to pull off this particular maneuver. But it came back with a vengeance in the spring of 2006 when the Beastie Boys put out their concert film, "Awesome; I F***in' Shot That."

The idea behind "Awesome" is cool: give video cameras to 50 members of the audience and have them shoot whatever they want, as long as they don't stop. Then the band edits it together: warts, out-of-focus shots of feet, bathroom visits, and all. Sounds like a great way to capture the feel of a concert, especially one in which the music itself is, well, not all that interesting.

The movie did quite well in theaters and is destined to make big bucks as a home video. So it's not exactly like these guys are hurting for cash.

In some of the many trade-magazine articles that appeared about the film, the writers asked the group what happened to all those video cameras after the shoot. And they responded—nay, bragged—that they took them back to the stores where they bought them and got their money back.

Now we're not talking about expensive professional HD cameras here; we're talking cheap. Let's be very generous and say that each of those cameras cost $1,000. So that's a budget item of $50k and another $1,000 or so for tape. The movie's grosses will easily be in the tens of millions.

I related this story to my young nieces, and they were horrified. "Why didn't they give them to a school? Did they really need the money?" the 12-year-old asked. I didn't have an answer, but I thought it would be a great question to ask the band. Anybody want to take them up on it?

Jokes: Part 2

If you're a musician or composer who's ever had any contact with academia, you'll love this first joke. If you're not, find someone who works in a college and have them explain it to you.

Found in the catacombs of a defunct college somewhere in Europe...

Dear Dean:

This is in response to your suggestion that we appoint Mr. Wolfgang Mozart to our music faculty. The music department appreciates your interest, but the faculty is sensitive about its prerogatives in the selection of new colleagues.

While the list of works and performances the candidate has submitted is very full, it reflects too much activity outside academia. Mr. Mozart does not have an earned doctorate and has very little formal education and teaching experience. There is also significant evidence of personal instability evidenced in his resume. Would he really settle down in a large state university like ours? Would he really be a team player?

I must voice a concern over the incidents with his former superior, the Archbishop of Salzburg. They hardly confirm his abilities to be a good team man and show a disturbing lack of respect for authority.

Franz Haydn's letter of recommendation is noted, but Mr. Haydn is writing from a very special situation. Esterhazy is a well-funded private institution quite dissimilar from us and abler than we to accommodate non-academics, like Mr. Haydn himself. Here we are concerned about everybody, not just the most gifted. Furthermore, we suspect cronyism on the part of Mr. Haydn.

After Mr. Mozart's interview with the musicology faculty, they found him sadly lacking in any real knowledge of music before Bach and Handel. If he were to teach only composition, this might not be a serious impediment. But would he be an effective teacher of music history?

The applied faculty were impressed with his pianism, although they thought it was somewhat old fashioned. That he also performed on violin and viola seemed to us to be stretching versatility dangerously thin. We suspect a large degree of dilettantism on his part.

The composition faculty was skeptical about his vast output. They correctly warn us from their own experience that to receive many commissions and performances is no guarantee of quality. The senior professor pointed out that Mr. Mozart promotes many of these performances himself. He has never won the support of a major foundation.

One of our faculty members were present a year ago at the premiere of, I believe, a violin sonata. He discovered afterwards that Mr. Mozart had not written out all the parts for the piano before he played it. This may be very well in that world, but it sets a poor example for our students. We expect deadlines to be met on time, and this includes all necessary paperwork.

It must be admitted that Mr. Mozart is an entertaining man at dinner. He spoke enthusiastically about his travels. It was perhaps significant, though, that he and the music faculty seem to have few acquaintances in common.

Furthermore, one of our female faculty members was deeply offended by his bluntness. She even had to leave the room after one of his endless parade of anecdotes. This propensity of his to excite the enmity of some is hardly conducive to the establishment of the comity that we aspire to maintain on our faculty, let alone the image that we wish to project to the community at large.

We are glad as a faculty to have had the chance to meet this visitor, but we cannot recommend his appointment. Even if he were appointed, there is almost no hope of his being granted tenure. The man simply showed no interest in going to school to collect his doctorate. This is egotism at its zenith.

Please give our regards to Mr. Mozart when you write him. We wish him our very best for a successful career. All are agreed, though, that he cannot fulfill the needs of this department.

We wish to recommend the appointment of Mr. Antonio Salieri, a musician of the highest ideals and probity, which accurately reflect the aims and values that we espouse. We would be eager to welcome such a musician and person to our faculty.

Sincerely yours,

The Chair and Faculty of the Department of Music

P.S. Some good news. Our senior professor of composition tells me there is now a very good chance that a movement of his concerto will have its premiere within two years. You will remember that his work was commissioned by a foundation and won first prize nine years ago.

■ ■ ■

Did you hear about the Microsoft programmer who died?

He found himself in front of a committee that decides whether you go to Heaven or Hell.

The committee told the programmer he could have some input into the matter and asked him if he would like to see both options before stating his preference.

"Sure," he said. So an angel took him to a place with a sunny beach, volleyball, open bar, and a great rock and roll band. Everyone he could see was having a great time.

"Wow!" he exclaimed. "Heaven is great!"

"Oh no," said the angel. "That was Hell. Want to see Heaven?"

"Well okay!" he replied enthusiastically.

So the angel took him to another place. Here a bunch of people were sitting in a park playing bingo and feeding dead pigeons. "This is Heaven?" asked the programmer.

"Yup," said the angel.

"Then I'll take Hell." Instantly he found himself plunged up to his neck in red-hot lava, with unearthly screaming, demonic laughter, and gnashing of teeth all around him. "Hey! Where's the beach? The music? The volleyball?" he screamed frantically to the angel.

"Oh, that was just the demo," she replied as she vanished.

■ ■ ■

One day in a pawn shop, a songwriter noticed an unusual statue of a golden rat. It was so phenomenally ugly, he just couldn't resist buying it.

Out on the street, as he was walking along with the statue under his arm, he heard odd noises behind him, and turning around, he found that he was being followed by a group of rats. And the group was nasty looking and hungry. He kept on walking, and more rats joined the parade. At one point he started to run, but the rats came on faster, and he realized they were gaining on him.

Now the herd of voracious rats was so big, it was beginning to stop traffic. People were screaming and running every which way. In his panic, he took a wrong turn, and the man found himself headed towards the waterfront. He was running onto a pier and knew he was about to be trapped. When he reached the end of the pier, frantic and breathing hard, somehow the golden rat slipped out of his arms, bounced off the end of the pier, and sank into the river. As he watched in amazement, all of the rats rushed headlong past him, dived into the water, and drowned.

Later that day, he went back to the pawn shop. The owner recognized and him said, "I hope you don't want to bring back that statue you bought," and pointed to a sign that said "All Sales Final."

"Oh no," said the songwriter. "It's fine. I was just wondering if you had any gold statues of record company executives?"

■ ■ ■

A salesman in a music store leans over the counter to a customer. "Hey, I just heard a great new drummer joke," he tells him. "It's a killer!"

The customer looks him straight in the eye and replies, "Hold on a minute. I happen to be a professional drummer, and I find drummer jokes offensive—you hear what I'm saying? And this guy next to me? He's six-foot-four, 225 pounds, and used to be a Green Beret. He's also a drummer. And the guy over there looking through the sheet music? Percussionist with the Cleveland Orchestra, and he's also a second-degree black belt. Now, do you still want to tell that drummer joke?"

"Nah, I guess not," replied the salesman. "I don't want to have to explain it three times."

■ ■ ■

Son: I want to be a musician when I grow up!

Father: Sorry, son, you can't do both.

■ ■ ■

These two bass players walk past a bar...

Well, it could happen!

■ ■ ■

What do you throw a drowning...

Q: ...guitar player?
A: His amp.

Q: ...lead singer?
A: Both his floor monitors.

■ ■ ■

Q: How does a band know when their manager is lying?
A: His lips move.

Q: How do you know when a violin is out of tune?
A: The bow's moving.

Q: How can you tell a trombone player's kid at the playground?
A: He bitches about the slide and refuses to swing.

■ ■ ■

A health insurance company executive was given a ticket for a performance of Schubert's unfinished symphony. Since he was unable to go, he gave the ticket to one of his managed-care reviewers. The next morning he asked the reviewer how he had enjoyed it. Expecting a few nice observations about the music, the orchestra, and the hall, the executive was instead handed a formal memorandum, which read as follows:

1. For a considerable period, the oboe players had nothing to do. Their number should be reduced, and their work spread over the whole orchestra, avoiding peaks of inactivity.

2. All 12 violins were playing identical notes. This seems an unneeded duplication, and the staff of this section should be cut. If a volume of sound is really required, this could be accomplished with the use of an amplifier.

3. Much effort was involved in playing the 16th notes. This appears to be an excessive refinement, and it is recommended that all notes be rounded up to the nearest 8th note. If this were done, it would be possible to use para-professionals instead of experienced musicians.

4. No useful purpose is served by repeating with horns the passage that has already been handled by the strings. If all such redundant passages were eliminated, then the concert could be reduced from two hours to 20 minutes.

5. The symphony had two movements. If Mr. Schubert didn't achieve his musical goals by the end of the first movement, then he should have stopped there. The second movement is unnecessary and should be cut.

In light of the above, one can only conclude that had Mr. Schubert given attention to these matters, he probably would have had time to finish the symphony.

Chapter 17

Making the Most of Audio 101

An Address to the Incoming Class of 2003

Preface

I started teaching music as soon as I got out of high school, first giving private lessons in piano, guitar, and saxophone, and then at community music schools, summer arts camps, and in weekend recording seminars. Though I had only a bachelor's degree, I was offered my first academic post in 1987, when the University of Lowell (now the University of Massachusetts Lowell) asked me to develop a computer-music curriculum for their up-and-coming Sound Recording Technology program. I stayed with the school for 12 years, building a couple of studios, designing several courses, and building up a lot of support from the industry, until Tufts University wooed me away in 2000 to work in their programs in Multimedia Arts and Musical Instrument Engineering.

Even though I've been doing this for almost 20 years, I still find I learn almost as much from my students as they do from me. Young people today are technologically and musically hipper than at any other time in history, and they can keep up with—and keep me informed about—trends that I know I should follow but haven't got the band-width or, frankly, the interest to do so.

But one advantage I have over them is that I know the industry they're trying to get into, and even though it's changing fast, I know a lot more than they do about what they should expect when they graduate and start forging their careers. My April 1998 column (in Chapter 8) put this in a humorous light—and was actually more about the industry itself than what students need to know—but this column, written for that "back-to-school" time of year, was more directly aimed at students, especially those just getting started. The first sentence refers to an alleged address by Kurt Vonnegut to the MIT graduating class of 1997, which turned out to be an urban legend (it was actually written by Chicago *Tribune* writer Mary Schmich) but was still a great start-ing point.

August 1999

First of all, don't worry about the sunscreen. For the next four years, where you're going to be spending all your time, you're not going to need it.

Worry instead about this: If you ever—well, more than once—ask yourself, "What am I doing here?" then you probably don't belong here. Pursuing a career in professional audio is no fun. It's not linear, it's not predictable, the hourly wage usually sucks, and the work-ing conditions are often less than ideal. You'll have to deal with all sorts of jerks, from marketing jackasses to egotistical clients, to wretched gui-tar heroes and worse. You'll be wrestling with user-hostile equipment, hopeless tech-support lines, and the constant threat of obsolescence of both you and your gear, while working the type of hours that make it impossible to even dream of having a personal life.

If you can't imagine yourself spending the rest of your life anywhere else except in front of or surrounded by a bunch of speakers...then you're in the wrong place.

So, if you don't love this, if you can't imagine yourself spending the rest of your life anywhere else except in front of or surrounded by a bunch of speakers, devoting all your energy and creativity to perfecting in one way or another the sounds you hear, then you're in the wrong place. This is not a business for the faint of heart or for those who just figure, "Hey, it's a cool way to get through college." If you can't say to yourself, at least most of the time, as you slog through classes, homework, exams, studio exercises, and term projects, "This is exactly what I want to do," then you should be doing something else.

Some of you will go out and do stuff that your teachers never heard of, because it didn't exist when we were teaching you. And we'll be very proud of you.

At the same time, realize this: You are not likely to come out of this program with the same goals and passions that you had when you started. Some of you today are completely convinced that you want to produce records or score films or mix live bands, and a few of you will indeed end up doing those things. But in the time you're here, both you and the industry will change. You'll discover that there are a lot more opportunities in audio than just the obvious ones, and many of you will fall in love with things you never knew existed before you came here. Some of you will end up wanting to be dialogue editors or sound designers for low-bandwidth video games or Web sites. Some will be interested in designing and installing sound systems for theaters or for air-ports. Some will get into radio or producing talking books or doing audio for educational CD-ROMs. Some of you will decide that you want to be on the manufacturing side and go for jobs with speaker designers, signal processing hardware makers, chip designers, or software publishers, finding your niche in product development or testing or marketing or customer support. And some of you will go out and do stuff that your teachers never heard of, because it didn't exist when we were teaching you. And we'll be very proud of you.

And speaking of change, get used to the idea that most of the equipment you'll be getting trained on here will be obsolete in five years. But that doesn't mean it's stupid to learn it. Being expert on a particular piece of gear is, by itself, not much use in an industry where product cycles can be counted in months. But learning *how* to become an expert is a skill that never goes out of date. And this is where you can learn that. This is where you'll develop the habits and attitudes that will let you learn things well—where you'll learn to learn. I spent two years of college getting really good at playing the bassoon, and after I graduated I barely touched it again. But I don't regret those years one iota: I learned how to focus, how to practice, how to set goals, how to break down a seemingly impossible task (the Alvin Etler sonata, for any bassoonists out there) into manageable chunks, and how to pace myself. On every new task I've been confronted with since, I have benefited from those skills.

Don't just learn what equipment does; learn *why* it does what it does. If you memorize every function on some piece of equipment by rote, when you are confronted with the next generation of hardware or software, what you know won't apply anymore, and you'll have to start from scratch. But if you know the principles behind the equipment, you can carry that knowledge over to every other system you encounter.

How do you do that? Well, besides getting a good theoretical grounding in electronics, acoustics, and digital logic, you should, if you have the choice, get as much training and hands-on time as you can with open-ended systems. They reflect the real world better than closed, self-contained systems. Don't just learn how to use a workstation—learn how to make it cooperate with and talk to other workstations and devices. Don't just learn one digital audio editor, learn several of them, so you get the broadest possible understanding of what digital audio editing is all about. When the next one comes along, you'll take what you know and be able to jump right on it. Don't just learn how to get SMPTE into your system—learn how it's generated, what the bits mean, what other purpose it has in the world besides linking your computer to a video deck, and why it's such a pain in the butt.

Don't forget to learn music. It's a language that's spoken by a lot of the people you'll be working with, no matter what you end up doing. Obviously, if you're working with musicians, you want to be able to understand what they're saying when they talk about taking it from the bridge, or putting in a key change, or doubling the voice at the octave in the middle eight. And you certainly don't want to embarrass yourself by telling a soprano sax player that his clarinet is too loud. But even if your gig is chopping up library music to make industrial video soundtracks, it's going to make your job go a lot faster if you know that splicing from the second beat of one bar in G major to the third beat of another in B-flat minor isn't going to work very well. Even if you're making speakers, you need to be able to talk to your customers and your marketing department not just about transient response, crossover slopes, and damping, but about how well the listener can pick the instruments out of an orchestra, and about how accurate the stereo field is—and that often means being able to tell the difference between a trumpet and an oboe and between a xylophone and a glockenspiel.

Don't be afraid to fail. Once you're in the real world, failure can be costly. But in school, no one's depending on you except you, so failure should be educational. If you suddenly realize that a project you have taken on is too much for you, don't just walk away from it—look hard at it and see where you've broken down. Learn from the experience so that next time you encounter a similar obstacle, you can get past (or at least around) it. And never be afraid to try new things, even though you think you might fail. School is an opportunity to go in many directions and to discover areas of the audio industry—and yourself—that you may not have thought of before. You may find yourself attracted to, and succeeding brilliantly at, something completely new. And having the experience of going into a new situation cold and being able to master it is going to stand you in good stead for the rest of your career—because it's going to happen to you a lot.

Now a little bit about basics. Two words: signal flow. No matter what you're doing—mixing, synchronizing, designing, or troubleshooting—understanding how signals move through and among components and systems is crucial to getting anything done. Learn to think about signal flow. The first time your studio goes down in the middle of an important project, if you can trace in your head how the analog and digital audio, MIDI, SMPTE, word clock, and other signals are supposed to route and distribute themselves, it will keep your efforts to put things right from degenerating into random switch-throwing and cable- (and hair-) pulling. Why isn't that sample being triggered? Why is that bass track so distorted? Why are the sound and picture drifting and hiccupping? You can't easily figure out why things have stopped moving if you don't know where they were supposed to go in the first place.

Along with that, learn how things break down and why. Because they do, constantly. Even if all the equipment in your school works all the time (fat chance), that's not the way things are in the real world. Inevitably, you'll be the only person in the studio at some crucial, down-to-the-wire session when all technical hell breaks loose, and you're going to have to take care of it.

If I can inject a personal note, my baptism of fire happened this way: I had been on my first job at a radio station for about six months, when my boss decided to take off to Europe for a couple of weeks, leaving me in charge. As I drove home one night after work with the radio on, I heard the station go off the air in the middle of a record, as if someone had literally just turned the transmitter off. I panicked, turned my car around, and discovered to my horror that all of New York City had gone completely dark. At least I knew it wasn't my fault. And I also knew there wasn't a heck of a lot I could do to fix it.

But I digress—hopefully, that's not the kind of problem you'll face on your first job. What you'll face will, of course, be blamed on you, even if it was caused by an act of God or the bad soldering technique of a maintenance tech who was fired three years ago. So learn what happens when an audio cable develops a short, when a hard drive loses its directory, when a motorized fader loses its motorvation. Learn the workarounds: how to patch around a bad cable or mixer channel, how to get a computer to boot from an emergency external disk, and how to salvage files from a munged drive.

And finally, do take care of yourselves. School can be fun, and for many of you it's the first time you're out of your parents' sphere of influence, and you're ready to do some serious partying. You're entitled to have a good time out of—and sometimes even in—class, but please, don't go nuts and do things that you'll kick yourself for in a few years. If you abuse yourself to excess, you will pay for it sooner or later. If you have personal habits that are going to get in the way of doing your work, now is a good time to break them—it's going to be much harder later. Same with personal issues: Believe it or not, it's easier to deal with those kinds of problems when you're in school than when you're out there hustling to pay the rent and pay off your loans. Do get out of the studio once in a while and get some exercise (and yes, I take it back, you may need sunscreen). Eat well: Late-night sessions are a great excuse to lay in mass quantities of junk food, but if that's all you're shoveling into your system, it's all too easy to get sick.

School is going to be hard. If it's easy, if there's no challenge, if you can breeze through everything based on what you learned on your own, then the program you're in is no good for you. Yes, there are some people with enormous amounts of native talent they can apply to an audio career, but even they won't be able to get by for very long without hard study of the basics and an understanding of how the industry works. On the other hand, school is a much more protective environment than you're going to find anywhere afterward, so it can be a good opportunity to ask yourself questions about who you are and what you want to do. Work things out. Talk to your peers and your teachers. Butt some heads. Stretch some minds. Enjoy the experience. And remember that your education won't really begin until after you leave here.

Afterword

The response to this column was very positive: A number of educators wrote me and asked if they could copy it for their classes to read. And as I read it today, it still makes a lot of sense.

Interestingly enough, when I wrote this column I myself was back in school, enrolled in a Master's degree program. My thesis, about George Antheil's *Ballet mécanique* (more on this in Chapters 19 and 20), was finished at the end of 2000. As *this* book is being written, I am enrolled in a Ph.D. program at Tufts University, doing a dissertation on the origins of multimedia, proving that your education indeed goes on, whether you're in school, out of school, or back again.

Tom Curry

Chapter 18

It's a Large and Confusing World, After All

Thoughts on Dealing with a Global Industry

Preface

In the summer of 1999, I spent a month in someone else's house in southern France. It was a wonderful experience, although not without its trials. It was the first time I had ever spent more than a week in a place where English was not the predominant language, and it opened my eyes in a lot of ways.

November 1999

No one speaks English, and everything's broken...

—**Tom Waits**, "Tom Traubert's Blues (Four Sheets to the Wind in Copenhagen)"

There is not a more self-centered country on Earth than the U.S.A. Thanks to the relentless blindering of our media and entertainment industries, our perception of foreign lands is predominantly of places with wars, floods, and earthquakes, where people talk funny and eat strange things, despite the fact that what they really want is McDonald's and Coca-Cola.

As a result of this, Americans have an odd—and, I used to think, unique—way of dealing with people who don't speak English. Since we can't conceive of a world where not everyone speaks our language, when we are confronted with someone who doesn't understand a thing we are saying, we simply repeat it, only louder. Of course, this doesn't work, and so everyone goes away from the meeting feeling that the other guy is stupid. It doesn't lend itself to a great deal of cross-cultural understanding, and it's one of the many reasons why Americans have a reputation the world over for being boorish.

> *When we are confronted with someone who doesn't understand a thing we are saying, we simply repeat it, only louder.*

I liked to think that I was above that. My mother arrived here from Russia at the age of 12, speaking not a word of English. My grandmother, who came with her, had lost much of her hearing before she left Russia, and so she never really learned English. I grew up thinking that Russian was a language that was always spoken at high SPLs, since that's how my mother and grandmother communicated with each other. But I also learned that when I am talking to someone who is not fluent in English, I need to speak slowly and clearly, and if they don't understand me, I should find other words that perhaps will be more familiar to them.

Nonetheless, a few years ago, I found myself characterized as an ugly American, thanks to an offhand comment I made in an online discussion group. A large Japanese company posted to the group a press release that was, to put it politely, somewhat awkwardly phrased. I expressed that I considered it dumb, if not arrogant, for a company with such formidable resources to issue an important press release without at least having it checked over by someone who spoke English well, just to make sure that English-speaking readers would be able to make heads or tails of it.

The group's reaction was fast and furious, mostly along the lines of "Lehrman, you ignorant/xenophobic/chauvinistic/racist/jingoistic slut/pig/Yank/(unprintable noun)! How dare you expect the rest of the world to speak your language! Don't you know there are billions of people who don't speak English? How would you feel if they criticized you every time you tried to write something in their language?"

The response was vehement enough (and from people whom I respected enough) that I uncharacteristically held my tongue and didn't pursue the matter. But this past summer I did something else equally uncharacteristic, and it brought that incident back to mind.

I am not much of a world traveler—I spent a brief time trying to work in Trinidad [*to be related in painful detail in Chapter 40*], and I have gone on short jaunts to Europe a couple of times on business—but this summer I let my wife talk me into spending a whole month in France on vacation. She had been wanting to do this for years, and I had run out of excuses, so through an agency we found a French couple who wanted to spend a month in New England, and we exchanged houses with them. Theirs was a lovely, modern house in Perpignan, a small city on the Mediterranean, very close to the border with Spain. We also exchanged cars, and so it worked out to be a relatively inexpensive way to have a fairly exotic vacation. At the end of the month, we spent a week in Paris, where I did some research for various projects and articles.

Now, we had been to France before. I had taken my wife to a computer-music conference in Paris when we first met, and a few years before that, she had done a tour of France and Italy. We didn't recall any major problems communicating with the locals, but this time, just to make sure we'd be okay, we hired a private tutor to help us brush up our high-school French before we got on the plane. He tried to warn us that we were about to enter *la France profonde*—the real France—as opposed to the more international areas of Paris and the Riviera.

And *profonde* it was. We found that literally no one in Perpignan or the surrounding area spoke English. We had been warned that, among Western European countries, France has the least number of bilingual citizens, and it was most definitely true in this region. We found a handful of English speakers, but they were either tourists or expatriates: Belgians, Dutch, Danes, and Germans, as well as English and Irish. But among the natives—the post-office workers, bank clerks, waiters, hotel clerks, even the government tourist-office staff—hardly anyone at all spoke English.

Furthermore, the thought that someone would be in their midst and not be fluent in French never occurred to them. When I would approach someone with a carefully thought-out sentence, in what I hoped was well-pronounced French, the response was either "Comment?" ("Huh?"), thus making me feel like an idiot, or, if I was successful at constructing a coherent sentence, and they actually understood what I said, I would be assaulted by a flood of idioms, contractions, and regional accents that were way too fast for me. I would then reply, "Pardon?" and they would act just like Americans: They'd say it again, louder, making me feel like an idiot.

I realized what my mother must have felt when she arrived in America as a child. In fact, I felt more like a Martian who had just landed in Dubuque. The lessons of that online discussion came back to me hard: We were now the strangers in a strange land. In fact, in French, the word for foreigners is just that: "*étrangers*." Here was a country that could be just as linguistically arrogant as the U.S., only this time we were the victims.

So I thought about those poor Japanese PR writers struggling to make themselves understood in a foreign tongue. Did I suddenly feel sorry for them? Did I now sympathize with people trying to do business in lands where the languages were different from their own? Did I achieve a new level of international tolerance and understanding?

Not on your life. What I realized was that if I ever wanted to do any serious business in France or any other country where they don't speak English, I had damn well better know the language a whole lot better than I already did or else hire somebody who did. No way I would try to do it myself, with the tools in my possession. And it made me even more resentful of companies that try to enter foreign markets without making a proper effort to know the language or the people they are trying to sell to.

The audio industry is more international than it's ever been. Our equipment comes from Germany, the Netherlands, Japan, Korea, England, Singapore, and even Russia, to name a few. Our studios are doing work for clients and audiences who speak dozens of languages, to be distributed on CD or DVD, over cable, satellite, or the Internet, to billions of people in hundreds of countries. If we make equipment, we're trying to sell it not just to Americans but to facilities in Israel, the Arab world, South Africa, India, and potentially the biggest market of all, China.

The globalization of the banking system, along with the Internet and cheap phone rates, has made it easier than ever to do business overseas. But the communications revolution hasn't had one particular effect that Americans seemed to expect—although English is more widespread than it's been since the heyday of the British Empire, it hasn't become the universal tongue. Language differences are surviving the age of the Internet and, in some ways, are thriving.

America itself, always a nation of immigrants, is perhaps today even more linguistically diverse than ever, as new waves of the economically or politically disadvantaged arrive. In spite of California's periodic efforts to outlaw them, Spanish speakers are increasing in number. In some areas of New York, you can walk for miles and never hear English spoken. And it's not just along the coasts—there are large enclaves of Haitians, Southeast Asians, Latinos, and Eastern Europeans to be found all over the U.S.

On the other side of the Big Ditch, the European Union's adoption of a single currency, the Euro—while it promises to make the arcane arithmetic of converting between francs, marks, and pesetas a thing of the past—doesn't mean that the language barriers are coming down. If anything, in the face of economic internationalism, cultural nationalism is being encouraged. In France, for example, regional dialects such as Catalan, Provençal, and Breton are being taught in the schools again as a way of maintaining or restoring a sense of cultural pride.

As more nations are joining the world economic and cultural community, awareness of language differences is more important, not less. And if we want to succeed in the international marketplace—whether we make or sell goods or run studios or work in them—we ignore these differences at our own peril.

What is the solution? One word: empathy. Think of yourself as the *étranger*. Make the first step so that your customers and clients feel comfortable with you and don't have to fight to make themselves understood. That means having people on staff who can speak the language of your clients or, if you are trying to run an overseas operation, having people on the ground who know the local culture and language well.

When manufacturers are not successful selling in other countries, it's these cultural and language issues that are very often to blame. Some companies don't trust their foreign reps and don't let them make their own business decisions, or don't give them the freedom and the budgets to let them create the support materials that will allow them to do their jobs. It's hard to convince customers to take seriously a company that prints its press releases and product brochures in pidgin English, or French, or Japanese. User manuals that are not translated (or even better, written) by native speakers are a great source of frustration—and sometimes hilarity. On my wall, I have a copy of a page from a manual for an electronic keyboard made in Asia. In it, the user is instructed to attach the legs to the bottom in a highly unusual and creative, not to say somewhat painful, manner. Some poor writer in the home office was apparently searching for the English equivalent of the word "screw"—and the verb he came up with is still considered unprintable in many English-language publications, including this one.

Companies that are penetrating (sorry!) foreign markets must have, besides good products, marketing organizations in place that understand the needs of local customers. And those organizations need to be headed up by people who are native speakers.

One fellow I spent some time with in France, Gérard, runs a medium-size audio hardware and software manufacturing company and recently decided it was time to take on the American market in a big way. His English is good (that is, it's a heck of a lot better than my French), but he knows that he could never handle the entire American operation with it. The way he sees it, his American office needs to be able to communicate with the customers first and the home office second. So he's staffing it with Americans who know the local market, talk the talk, and can learn the products. But he is also bringing his new American employees to France for several weeks at a time, not just to become familiar with the company, but to immerse themselves in the language so that they can communicate better with the home office. I applaud his sense of priorities, and I wish him well—and not just because of the absolutely amazing Catalan restaurant he took me to for lunch.

Studios that work extensively with non-English-speaking clients know the value of having someone on staff who can talk the client's language. And if you are dealing with dialogue or voice-overs in a language you don't know, running the finished product by someone who does know it can save a lot of trouble down the road—like when you find that a little edit you did trying to snip a half-second from the track radically changed the meaning of a sentence.

When you've been on planes and other forms of transit for 14 hours, and you find yourself in a supermarket dying for something to eat, but it takes you 20 minutes and four intensely frustrating conversations to figure out where and how to get a shopping cart—which was how our first day in Perpignan began—you get a certain helpless feeling. And let me tell you, it's something you don't ever want your customers or clients to feel.

Despite the initial difficulties, we really did have a wonderful trip, with many magic moments. One of the best happened when Gérard's six-year-old daughter met my wife, who entertains children professionally. They bonded instantly—even though the girl didn't speak a word of English. Their fascination with each other transcended the language barrier. After we came home, my wife was inspired to write a story for the girl, with her as the star, in the girl's own language. But before she sends it to her, my wife is going to be sure to run it past someone who really speaks French.

Paul D. Lehrman is glad to be home.

Jean Shepherd photo ©1966 Fred W. McDarrah

Photo courtesy of the estate of George Antheil

Chapter 19

A Couple of Audio Moments

Fidelity Isn't Always in the Specs

Preface

The *Ballet mécanique* project came knocking at my door in the spring of 1998 and has continued to engage and entertain me (and a whole lot of other people) ever since. In many ways it synthesized what my whole professional life has been about, making me call on everything I know about classical and avant-garde music, contemporary performance practice, piano and percussion techniques, conducting, sequencing, sampling, film scoring, synchronizing, MIDI system design, recording, mixing, mastering, and even tech writing. It's taken me into new areas of performing and producing that I don't think I would have been able to get into otherwise. Plus it has taught me lots of new skills, like film editing and production, DVD authoring, and the joys of dealing with record distributors and public television networks.

I've written about the *Ballet mécanique* extensively and used it as a central subject in a few of my *Mix* columns, like the one in the next chapter—not so much to brag about it, but to pass on some of the interesting things I've learned, and the novel ways I learned them.

This column, however, the first in which I discuss the project, is about a rather startling confluence of happenstances, resulting in an emotional—almost spiritual—experience, brought about with the help of audio technology.

March 2000

How do you define audio fidelity? Is it the signal-to-noise ratio, the frequency response, the distortion? Is it the number of channels, bits, or samples marching by per microsecond? Or do you perhaps take a different approach and define fidelity more subjectively, as the ability to re-create an aural experience—to stimulate thoughts and emotions that cause the listener to be transported, completely and "faithfully" (for such is the origin of the word) to another time and place?

In our business, we sometimes pay so much attention to the numbers and formulas of the former that we forget about the latter, figuring that if we do the tech stuff right, the emotional stuff will take care of itself. But, sometimes, one can have a transcendentally high-fidelity experience, despite a signal chain that is decidedly low tech.

Sometimes one can have a transcendentally high-fidelity experience, despite a signal chain that is decidedly low-tech.

In the past few months, as it happens, I've had two of these. They have brought together many of the things I have loved and worked with—radio, recording, avant-garde concert music, the Internet, writing, and story-telling—and that's a big reason why they were so meaningful. The technology and the delivery systems, while certainly useful, were decidedly minor players.

For the past two years, as I've been telling anyone who will listen, I've been doing a very exciting project with G. Schirmer, the music publisher. Schirmer recently acquired the rights to a historically significant piece of music that exemplifies the word "outrageous": the *Ballet mécanique*, by George Antheil. Although the piece was written in 1924, until recently it had never been performed in its original version. That's because the score calls for—besides seven percussionists, two pianists, seven electric bells, a siren, and three airplane propellers—16 synchronized player pianos. Antheil, who lived in Paris at the time but was actually from Trenton, New Jersey, thought he was composing something playable, but he was wrong: The technology for synching up two player pianos, to say nothing of 16, simply did not exist.

So he rewrote the piece several times, first in 1926, reducing the number of player pianos to one, and then in 1952, getting rid of that one and replacing it with multiple human pianists. The 1952 version is performed fairly frequently, and I first encountered it as a teenager when a percussion teacher at a music camp gave me a tape of it. Listening to it was a great thrill, especially the airplane propellers. From an early age, I loved uncategorizable modern music, the noisier the better, and for many years, I hoped that I would someday have the privilege of hearing this extravaganza performed live.

So you can imagine my delight when Schirmer asked me to take Antheil's original 1924 score—which I never knew existed—and translate it into a MIDI sequence. This could then control a stage full of modern MIDI-equipped player pianos, like Yamaha Disklaviers, which meant that this extraordinary piece, 75 years after its composition, could finally be performed as the composer originally intended. I jumped into the assignment with both feet, not only doing the sequencing but also obtaining samples of all the noisemakers, building a MIDI-controlled electric bell array, and even arranging last November for a performance of the piece at the school where I was teaching. The local NPR station, WGBH-FM, set up a live Webcast of the concert, and companies like Apogee, Tascam, Shure, Millennia, Redco, Kurzweil, EAW, and MIDI Solutions all pitched in with equipment donations so we could pull this off. Most importantly, Yamaha lent us 16 *Disklaviers*. The concert was a screaming, crashing success, and Yamaha is now trying to get the thing into the Guinness Book of World Records.

Working on the *Ballet mécanique* has been the most fun, over the longest period of time, I can ever remember having. One of the best aspects of the project has been the dozens of people who have discovered what I'm doing and have assailed me with questions, ideas, and contributions. Truman Rex Fisher, a retired music professor in Los Angeles, offered an incredible gift: Antheil's voice. Antheil died of a heart attack in 1959, and there are no films or videos of him available. But Fisher had recorded an interview with the composer just a year before his death for a radio station in Pasadena, and he was eager to send me a copy. So it was just a couple of weeks before the concert, after spending a year and a half studying this man and his work in microscopic detail, that I finally knew what George Antheil sounded like. Between the tape hiss, vinyl noise, dropouts, and random dips in level, there was magic in this recording, and I felt a delightful chill as I listened to the tape for the first time in my studio.

The magic was there for many others, too. Antheil was a great storyteller—his autobiography was called "Bad Boy of Music"—and this interview was no exception. I played a piece of it for the concert audience, in which he describes being, at age 3, so bitterly disappointed at receiving a toy piano for Christmas instead of a real one that he took it down to the basement and chopped it up with a hatchet. They fell out of their chairs laughing.

But there was more, even higher fidelity, yet to come. Flash once again back to the '60s: Not long after I became a *Ballet mécanique* fan, I found, in a totally unexpected place, another Antheil devotee: a writer and storyteller whom many credit with the invention of talk radio—Jean Shepherd.

Shepherd plied his trade late at night on WOR, a clear-channel AM station out of New York. For 45 minutes every weeknight (plus a 90-minute Saturday show live from a night-club in Greenwich Village, which I dragged my parents to twice), Shepherd would hold forth on the trials and tribulations of growing up in the Midwest during the Depression, regaling his invisible audience with tales of disastrous first dates, disillusioning visits to Santa Claus, renegade fireworks and drum majors taking their revenge on a small town on the Fourth of July, kids double-dog-daring each other to lick frozen light poles, and other milestones of "kid-hood."

Kid stories were not his only stock in trade; he also told stories of his Army days, and often he would spend a show expounding, usually with a great deal of irony and sarcasm, on some aspect of popular culture, whether it was a sneaky new advertising campaign, a dumb TV show, the fate of the Yankees, the rise of "slob art," or just some story in the newspaper that had caught his jaundiced eye. He was a master of the put-on, one night extolling his listeners to go out the next day and ask at their local bookstore for a racy Victorian memoir that didn't actually exist, causing booksellers all over the East Coast to frantically scramble for copies. Another night he told them to put their radios, cranked as loud as possible, in their windows and played the sound of a freight train guaranteed to wake the dead, or another night, he managed to convince them all to scream into the night, "Drop the tools, we've got you covered!," presaging by about 20 years the climactic scene in the movie *Network*.

Teenage boys, glued to the radios underneath their covers, knew that this disembodied voice in the night was delivering them The Truth.

But it was the stories—which occasionally appeared in *Playboy*, thereby increasing his coolness factor dramatically—that kept his loyal audiences, in large measure teenage boys, glued to the radios underneath their covers, knowing that this disembodied voice in the night was delivering them The Truth.

His lessons, as I learned them, basically boiled down to: 1. Other people have gone through what you're going through, so relax. 2. Whenever anyone says they know what's good for you, they have a hidden agenda and/or are trying to sell you something. 3. The secret to becoming an adult is coming to the realization that there is no secret to becoming an adult. Although he was hardly a political radical, it was important stuff for young people to be hearing in those turbulent times, and it shaped many minds of my generation to be wary of the world around them. And it was one of the most effective uses of the medium in its history.

Shep (as he was known to those who loved him) always sounded like he was winging it, improvising on the air, conversing one-on-one with an unseen presence in the studio, but he was, in fact, often working from carefully prepared notes, if not a script. While the beginning of his show often rambled, he always hit the punch line right on the dot at 11 o'clock, when his show (and his outro, the deservedly unknown "Bahnfrei Overture" by Eduard Strauss, the least-accomplished member of the famous Viennese musical family) ended. It was a masterful performance, night after night, and if he was known only to a select audience at the time, his influence was widespread and long lived: Garrison Keillor's stories from Lake Wobegon owe a huge debt to Shepherd, and the long-running TV series *The Wonder Years* literally stole his narrative format and watered it down for prime time.

After his radio career ended in the late '70s, he did several TV series for public television, both "video essays" and dramatizations of his stories, but he reached his biggest audience with the 1983 film, *A Christmas Story*, which spun together a half-dozen of his best seasonal tales around a young boy's wish for a Red Ryder BB gun for Christmas ("No, you'll shoot your eye out!"). Written and narrated by Shep, the film is now shown around the clock in December by various cable networks (which no doubt would not be the case had the studio agreed to keep his original title, "Santa's Revenge"). If you haven't seen this movie, go rent it right now—I don't care if it's the wrong time of year—and be prepared to laugh your butt off.

To further illustrate his stories, Shep kept on hand a highly eclectic library of music. There was '20s jazz (which he would play along with on kazoo or Jews, harp), sentimental "cheap" guitar music, dramatic film music, and some amazingly avant-garde stuff, including Stockhausen's electronic/concrète masterpiece *Gesang der Jünglinge* and, in the only extant recording at the time, Antheil's 1952 *Ballet mécanique*.

By the time I first encountered the Antheil work, I had been listening to Shepherd religiously for several years, so when I heard my teacher's recording for the first time, I thought there was something familiar about it. Sure enough, one night, while Shep was spinning one of his many tales about the hellfire of the blast furnaces in the steel mills of Indiana, this horrific industrial percussion music came up, and I almost fell out of bed. I knew what this piece was! I was probably one of the very few people in his audience who did, and I was certainly the only 14-year-old.

Flash forward to last year. As I began to put together the concert that would feature the Antheil premiere, the thought came to me that Jean Shepherd, wherever he was, would love this. Doing a Web search, I found several sites devoted to him, and one of them even gave a mailing address in Florida, taken from his amateur radio license registration (another reason why I loved him as a kid—I was a ham, too). So I wrote to him, telling him what we were doing, and invited him to come hear our revival of one of his favorite pieces. I never heard back from him, but I wasn't surprised. The Web sites all reported that he wasn't well and was keeping out of the public eye.

In the meantime, hidden in the back of an academic thesis on Antheil I had found gathering dust on a college library shelf, in an appendix entitled "Unpublished Recordings and Tapes," I noticed this item: "Jean Shepherd Show, February 14, 1959, program on Antheil. Tape. Antheil Estate." Antheil had died two days before that date—which meant Shep had eulogized him on the air! Since this was before my Shepherd days, I had no idea he had done anything like this. But now I had to hear this tape.

The executor of the Antheil estate is a San Francisco composer named Charles Amirkhanian, and when I asked him about the tape last summer, he confirmed its existence, but since he was not a New Yorker, its profound historical significance had escaped him. And unfortunately, since he was just about to leave for a year in Europe, he doubted he would be able to dig it out of the archives for me anytime soon.

And then, on October 18, exactly one month before my concert was scheduled, I woke up to see an obituary for Jean Shepherd, 78, in the morning paper. Immediately the Shep-zines on the Web started posting memories and testimonials from hundreds of men and women who grew up listening to him, and their stories all contained one common thread: In their formative years, Shep's voice was one of the few they could trust to tell them how the world really was, and they were forever grateful to him. The sense of loss, as I read these pages and pages of emotional outpourings, was palpable. I posted a memorial page on my Antheil site, too, relating how Shep was a fan of the composer's, and hoping that someday I would find a recording of that eulogy from 1959.

Several weeks later, I got an e-mail from one Richard Starr, who lived in Thetford Center, Vermont, a little town near the Connecticut River. Richard grew up in Brooklyn and was an audio tinkerer at an early age. He and his father put together a "hi-fi" tuner kit from Lafayette Radio (which, he recalls, didn't work and had to be sent back to the company to be finished), and they also had a Wollensak half-track mono tape recorder. In the late '50s, Shep was only on Sunday nights, and that being a school night, Richard's parents didn't allow him to listen to the program live. But through the magic of tape recording—and he was hip enough to connect the tuner and recorder electronically, not just sticking a mic in front of the speaker—Richard could listen to Shep the next day. Of all the shows he taped, he kept only one: the Antheil eulogy.

He is now a schoolteacher, but Richard still loves to fool around with audio, and he's done a lot of volunteer work for Vermont Public Radio. He doesn't have a reel-to-reel deck anymore, but a few years ago, when he did, he transferred the tape of that show to cassette.

Today he has a CD burner. The day before our concert, he heard a report on the Antheil project on National Public Radio's *Morning Edition*, and that night, lying awake at 3 a.m., he thought to himself, "Gee, I wonder if that guy would like a copy of this tape." So he found my Web site, saw that that was exactly what I was looking for, and contacted me. A few days later, I received in the mail a freshly minted CD containing Jean Shepherd's 1959 eulogy for George Antheil.

The track starts out with the *Ballet* underneath a typically warped retelling of the fable of the ant and the grasshopper (the grasshopper is rewarded for not doing any work), and as it ends, the music rises and there's a stifled cry from Shepherd as if he is being overwhelmed by it. A few seconds later, his voice returns, in an urgent whisper: "Isn't that great, this music? Do you know that I know the little guy who wrote this?" The music stops, and he bends down close to the microphone, telling how he met Antheil in the Horn & Hardart cafeteria on 57th Street in Manhattan. The composer invited Shepherd up to his hotel room to show his new friend that he had just accomplished a lifelong goal: He had bought a painting by Rembrandt. Shepherd goes on with more memories and stories, in a rush of images and snippets of conversation, and finally ends with, "And I never saw that little guy again."

Richard's CD sounds...well, just like an AM radio. There's a little background hiss, a little modulation noise, but Shepherd's voice comes across as clear as if I were listening to the trusty Lafayette Radio 4-band receiver (which didn't work all that well, either) of my youth.

But before I listened to it, I put that CD aside for a few days. When the concert and the subsequent recording sessions were all behind me, my wife and I escaped for a weekend to a little Maine seaside town normally overrun with tourists but gloriously abandoned in the off-season. And so we found ourselves all alone sitting in the car at a beautiful beach at sunset, watching the waves and the dimming light, listening to Jean Shepherd, just now gone, eulogize his friend George Antheil, now gone 40 years. But the crowning glory of Antheil's youth had just been heard by several thousand pairs of fresh ears, and so that part of him lives on. Shepherd, thanks to his writings, videotape, and the Web, also lives on. And I, hearing that voice, and that music, in all its lo-fi glory, found myself at once in the '60s of my youth, and in the '20s of Antheil's youth—all in the closing weeks of the '90s. And they were all, in that moment, equally real.

Now *that's* what I call fidelity.

Afterword

The Jean Shepherd eulogy for Antheil can be found on my *Ballet mécanique* website, www.antheil.org, along with several articles about the project I have written for *Electronic Musician*, *Wired*, and *Sound on Sound*, plus a whole lot more.

Ballet mécanique has now been performed over two dozen times in the U.S., Canada, and Europe (not to mention an automated installation of the piece at the National Gallery of Art, which played it over 100 times) and is available on CD. It's also on a DVD set called *Unseen Cinema*, where it's the soundtrack to a film of the same name by Dadaist artist Fernand Léger and cinematographer Dudley Murphy. The whole project is the subject of a documentary film I produced, *Bad Boy Made Good*, which has aired on public television stations around the country and is also available on DVD.

A terrific Jean Shepherd Web page, with memorabilia, forums, and links to downloadable program archives, is at www.flicklives.com. If you want to know more about this fascinating man, check out the 2005 book, *Excelsior, You Fathead: The Art and Enigma of Jean Shepherd*, by Eugene B. Bergmann.

Chapter 20

James Yang

How *Do* You Get to Carnegie Hall?
Adventures in One of the World's Great Concert Spaces

Preface

As I said in the last chapter, the *Ballet mécanique* project opened a lot of doors for me, and one of the first and most interesting was the stage door at Carnegie Hall. Interestingly enough, that particular venue looms large in the *Ballet mécanique* legend. After the young George Antheil had a resounding success with the piece in Paris in 1925, a New York promoter arranged to bring it to New York for its American premiere. But the Carnegie Hall audience, unimpressed by the enormous hype the promoter drummed up and unsympathetic with the technical problems that plagued the performance, just hooted and laughed. Overnight, Antheil's reputation as a composer took a nose dive from which it would never recover.

Conductor Maurice Peress revived the piece—in its one-player-piano incarnation—in 1989 and performed it very successfully in that very space, so it wasn't entirely up to me to make good on this particular aspect of poor George's fate. But performing the new realization of the piece, which I had worked on, in the hall was still a strong validation for the composer, and a thrill—and an education—for me.

July 2000

A couple of months ago, I got to take part in a concert in one of the great performing spaces on Earth, New York's Carnegie Hall. I wasn't exactly performing, but I wasn't exactly crew, either. Nor was I exactly conducting: The American Composers Orchestra, a group devoted to presenting large-scale works of 20th (and soon, presumably, 21st) century composers, had chosen to present the New York premiere of the multiple-player-piano version of George Antheil's *Ballet mécanique*, which I had helped prepare for publisher G. Schirmer. Although I had done my best to make the piece playable by any ambitious performing group, the ACO still wanted my help. So I had the distinct pleasure of sitting on the stage and overseeing a computer, a bunch of mechanical pianos, and an ensemble of amazing musicians raise the roof in one of the loudest "classical" pieces those walls had ever contained.

So I had the distinct pleasure of sitting on the stage and overseeing a computer, a bunch of mechanical pianos, and an ensemble of amazing musicians raise the roof in one of the loudest "classical" pieces those walls had ever contained.

The piece requires a computer running a MIDI sequencer to play the player pianos, and it also triggers siren, propeller, and bell samples and cues the conductor—who is leading a percussion orchestra of ten players—through a fiendishly complicated click track. After the initial "shakedown" performance by the student percussion ensemble at the University of Massachusetts Lowell, where I was teaching, the piece was ready to send out to the real world. The ACO was the first group to take up the challenge. The ensemble handled it beautifully—but letting my baby take its first steps, without me holding both its hands, turned out to have some interesting problems.

My job in New York was to supervise the MIDI and sound setups, answer any questions the conductor might have, and sit on a pre-concert panel discussing the piece. The orchestra hired Miles Green, a New York MIDI/audio expert who has worked with luminaries like Philip Glass and Laurie Anderson, to handle the hardware side of things. A couple of weeks before the performance, I sent Miles my *Performer* sequence files and the samples, which he loaded into his Powerbook G3 and his Kurzweil *K2000* rack unit. He hooked the computer up to a Mark of the Unicorn *Micro Express XT USB* interface and connected the interface to a bunch of synth modules so he could test everything out and hear what the player-piano parts sounded like.

Miles called immediately: There was trouble. The piano parts consist largely of huge, thick chords playing very fast, in precise rhythms. There are four parts, and in order to make them work at all, each part needs its own dedicated MIDI cable, or the note data would be way too thick—but this is no problem, one assumes, when you have a multiport interface.

But coming out of Miles' synths, the piano parts sounded alarmingly sloppy, and the click track was all over the place: sometimes early, sometimes late, sometimes disappearing entirely. It sounded as if he were trying to shove all of the parts down a single MIDI cable, and the dreaded "MIDI choke" was rearing its ugly head. The computer was certainly fast enough—heck, we had played the piece at school on a pokey, old 100MHz Macintosh *8100* with no problems at all, and in some rehearsals on an antique Quadra *650*—so that wasn't the issue. USB is supposed to be a much faster protocol than Apple's ancient serial driver, so that shouldn't have caused any problems. So what the heck was going on?

A few frantic calls and e-mails to Mark of the Unicorn revealed the cause. Most multiport MIDI interfaces that communicate with the host computer at a speed faster than MIDI itself have a "throttle-back" feature. This is necessary when you want to send a long string of data to a single device, something that commonly happens when you are bulk-dumping a synth's program banks to the synth using MIDI system exclusive. If the data coming out of the interface is too fast, the synth's input buffer will overflow, and the message may get garbled or lost. To prevent this, when the driver software controlling the interface detects this kind of rapid-fire MIDI stream, it throttles back the speed of the interface to the actual speed of MIDI and sometimes even slower. In the case of the MOTU interfaces, my huge, lumbering piano chords were being misinterpreted as a SysEx bulk dump, and the interface was deliberately slowing them down.

MOTU offered two solutions: We could use two interfaces, thereby lowering the data density through each and hopefully avoiding the throttle-back, or they could rewrite the drivers so that the throttle-back feature would kick in at a higher data rate. Miles opted for both solutions: MOTU sent him another interface *and* the updated drivers. There were no more problems.

But we weren't finished yet. A different kind of problem arose when I was told by the orchestra administration that the elaborate new sound system at Carnegie Hall was mono. Although none of the instruments need to be miked, the *Ballet mécanique* does require a sound system with as many as seven individual speakers; the exact number depends on how many of the sound effects in the piece are provided by a sampler and how many are played "live." The orchestra planned to use a live siren and bells, which left the three propeller sounds coming from Miles' Kurzweil. To keep the propellers from sounding like total mud and to give them a proper stage perspective, the sounds needed to be physically isolated from each other; a mono system wasn't going to allow that.

Fortunately, in the issue of *Mix* that had come out just one month before the concert, there happened to be a great article by Mark Frink about this very subject: the new Meyer Sound system in Carnegie Hall. The article described the system as consisting of two stacks on the sides and an impressive cluster that was flown above center stage—and although it didn't say so specifically, it seemed obvious to me that, yes, the whole thing was mono. But the article revealed something else that the orchestra hadn't told me: The hall also had a six-channel monitor system, with six Meyer Sound wedges. Since we weren't going for huge SPLs on the propellers, three of the wedges, pointed at the audience, would seem to do the job admirably. I posed this question to my New York colleagues, and their cautious reply was that if we could work it out with the hall sound crew, maybe we could use the monitors, instead.

Now, I had been warned about this crew. Union crews in New York are notorious for being difficult to work with. (Joke flying around the Javits Center whenever AES is in town: How many union guys does it take to screw in a light bulb? Ten! You gotta problem wid-dat?) And Carnegie Hall has a reputation in some circles for being one of the hardest venues of all. But when I arrived at the hall the morning of the performance (which was scheduled for 3 o'clock that afternoon), I found the absolute opposite to be true. The stage, sound, and electrical crews were cooperative, knowledgeable, professional, and eager to help with what they realized right away was going to be a fun gig. It didn't hurt that the sound crew were all avid *Mix* readers, especially when they realized that the piece I had just written about in my column the month before was the one that was about to be on their stage. And some were even Jean Shepherd fans.

It turned out my request that we use the monitor system had already been relayed to the crew, and so when we came in that morning, the wedges were in place and wired up. (Using the monitors also meant they wouldn't have to fly the center cluster, for which they were probably grateful.) It took us an amazingly short time to get everything in place and running. It simply couldn't have been handled better.

At the same time, the eight percussionists, two pianists, and the siren and bell players arrived and set up their hardware among the eight *Disklaviers* Yamaha supplied. A violist had been dragooned into the siren job, which she took on with great fervor—in concert, the sight of her formal black gown flying as she cranked furiously added immeasurably to the performance. A trombonist played the bells, which were connected to a MIDI-to-contact-closure converter using an old Yamaha keyboard synth.

Miles and I set up our MIDI paraphernalia on a table onstage, next to the door leading backstage, which the crew had supplied. We were originally told by one of the orchestra managers that we should set up offstage, so the audience wouldn't see the "machinery," but we convinced him that that was just too risky.

Before we got on the stage, the group had had only one rehearsal—the day before in a cav-
ernous rehearsal hall downtown—and this was going to be their only chance to run down
the piece with the Disklaviers and the full sound system. I have to admit I had trepidations.
At school, we had put four months of rehearsal into it, while these folks were going to do
it in two days. But I knew from the first downbeat that it was going to be fine.
Percussionists are a class of players I have always admired for their skill in navigating
seemingly impossible scores, and these cats were among the best New York had to offer.
They were *good*, and so was the conductor, Dennis Russell Davies, who threaded his way
through the more than 600 time-signature changes without hesitation.

The only glitch was that Davies couldn't hear the click track, which was the only way the
Disklaviers and the players were going to be able to stay together. I had specified a Shure
wireless in-ear monitor system (we used one at school, and it worked great), but the
orchestra had gotten something else—and it just wasn't loud enough. No matter how we
gain-staged the inputs and outputs, the thing would go into hard clipping whenever we got
anywhere near a usable level. So we got rid of it, and the crew quickly ran a cable from the
Mackie *1202* mixer handling the click (which itself was coming from an isolated output on
the Kurzweil), across the stage to a single headphone for Davies to wear. Now he had
plenty of volume.

Two run-throughs later, the ensemble had the piece up to the tempo they wanted, while I
spent the time jumping on and off the stage and running around the hall, checking the propeller levels, and signaling tweaks to the sound crew. It went like clockwork, and everyone
was happy.

And this is where the story should end, with a line like, "The performance was great, all
our preparation paid off, the audience loved it, and we got a rave review in the *New York
Times*." But it didn't quite turn out that way.

The pre-concert panel I was speaking on started at 1:30 p.m., 90 minutes before showtime.
A table with four mics was set up on stage, and the main house system (the side stacks)
was turned on. We panelists talked and answered questions for about 45 minutes, and then
final preparations for the concert began. Miles and I asked if we could do a sound check,
and the orchestra management said no. Since the house was open, too many people would
hear the noises, and they wanted to "surprise" them. So Miles walked around the stage
doing what he referred to as an "idiot check," making sure none of the MIDI cables were
pulled out or splitter switches inadvertently thrown, and I double-checked the MIDI-to-
bells hookup and listened to the click track.

The house lights went down, conductor Davies took the stage, put on his cans, nodded to
Miles, and we were off. After about 30 seconds, Miles and I looked at each other: Where
the hell were the propellers? We waited for another place where the propellers came in,

As nonchalantly as I could, I got up from my seat, left the stage, and announced to the crew that the propellers were not coming through the sound system. All hell broke loose backstage.

watching the score closely, and sure enough, no propellers. Fortunately, the table that had been set up for us was right near the exit door, and so, as nonchalantly as I could, I got up from my seat, left the stage, and announced to the crew that the propellers were not coming through the sound system. All hell broke loose backstage, so I, still nonchalantly, closed the door and walked back to my seat. After about a minute, the door opened a crack, so I got up again, and a sheepish crew member told me what had happened: During the pre-concert panel, one of the crew had powered down the monitor system and then forgot to bring it back up again.

Would it be okay, I was asked, if an electrician were to walk across the stage, while the performance was going on, to where the power amps were, and turn them on? No problem, I said. Cool as a cucumber, the electrician did exactly that, and at the next propeller cue, all was well. All the audience knew was that something had to be adjusted onstage. The piece finished in grand style, the audience did love it, and we did get a very positive review in the *Times*, which said, "This was probably the performance that Antheil had always wanted to hear."

At the reception after the concert, I asked Davies if he knew the propellers were missing at the beginning. No, he said, he was too busy conducting the live musicians. But toward the end of the piece, there are long sections in which the propellers sound by themselves, and had they remained turned off for the entire performance, there would have been huge inexplicable holes. Since I had the power to stop the performance by stopping the sequencer, I asked him if, in the event we couldn't fix the propellers right away and I had stopped the piece, whether he would have had me shot. He replied, "No, that would have been the right thing to do." He then told me a story of a piece he was conducting in Europe that starts with the entire orchestra playing an F major chord, except that one of the violinists played an F sharp. He stopped the piece, turned to the audience, and said, "We can do better than that." And they did. A class act, to be sure.

So there are a few lessons to be learned here. One, if you're doing a high-profile live performance, don't use the very latest technology or even Revision x.0 of anything. Go back a generation or two and use tried-and-true stuff. If you have to use brand-new tools, try to get some inside contacts with the company that makes them, so you can get problems fixed fast. Two, try everything out way ahead of time, in a situation as close to the real performance as possible, to give you room to maneuver in case things don't work the way they're supposed to. The interface problems that we were able to solve very nicely would have been fatal had we discovered them the day before the show. Three, even the best, most experienced people make mistakes. And four, which is a direct corollary to three, whenever you have the opportunity to check your equipment just before a gig, take it. And then check it again. Because even when you make it to Carnegie Hall, you still have to practice.

Afterword

After the New York performance, the piece was taken up by the San Francisco Symphony, conducted by Michael Tilson Thomas. The sound system worked great, but we had *other* technical problems—in fact, there have been technical problems of one kind or another just about every time the piece has been performed. It's that complicated, and its insane requirements are that unfamiliar to most musicians and technicians. One of these days I'll write a book about them. But despite the problems, it's safe to say that every one of the performances has been a great success and a real audience pleaser.

You can read about the project in detail at www.antheil.org and order a copy of the CD. Okay, no more plugs.

Chapter 21

Doctor, It Hurts When I Do This
Why You Should Be Worried About RSI

Preface

Every occupation has its hazards, and pro audio is no exception. But articles in trade publications about health issues are not very common—after all, what advertiser is going to want to have his ad run next to a headline like "Recording Studios: Dangerous to Your Health"? Being a columnist, however, has its privileges, and one of them is being able to not worry about the advertisers (well, not *too* much) and write about pretty much whatever I'm interested in at the moment. And when I wrote this, I was pretty alarmed at the number of people I knew who were waylaid by hand- and arm-related overuse injuries. So concerned, in fact, that I ran the column in two parts, which are combined here.

Awareness of these issues among media and computer professionals continues to improve, but it's still way too low, and too many people are still hurting themselves needlessly. At the end of the chapter is a list of online resources to check out so that you can avoid being one of them.

August/September 2000

A friend of mine who writes for one of the computer magazines, and who also happens to be a wonderful musician, gave me a shiver when he casually opened one recent column with, "When I trashed my wrists back in the '80s...." I got another shiver when I received this reply to an e-mail I had sent to another computer writer: "I am on a typing break right now to rest my wrists and cannot respond to any e-mail messages. I hope to return to my computer in about two weeks." Yet another friend, also a very talented writer and musician, had to give up both careers when his wrists gave out after just a few months working as a tech-support manager for a large company. Now he builds wooden boats and collects guitars, which he cannot play for more than a few minutes at a time. And just last month a student of mine showed up for his final exam with his arm in a brace so complicated that it looked like he must have fractured the thing in three places. "What happened?" I asked. "I've been working on my term project for my video course, and I've been editing at the computer for two days straight. I can't feel my fingers."

An occupational therapist I know puts the number of working musicians with job-related pain close to 75%.

Musicians' injuries are a well-discussed topic, and most of us are aware of the dangers of gigging and practicing too many hours for too many years. Two published surveys of working musicians back in the '80s concluded that about 50% of them had some kind of job-related pain, but an occupational therapist I know puts the number today closer to 75%. Composer and pianist Robert Schumann complained of overuse injuries more than 150 years ago. More recently, injuries derailed the careers of pianists Gary Graffman and Leon Fleisher. Max Weinberg, drummer for the E Street Band and bandleader on Conan O'Brien's TV show, once used to freeze his hands and tape his sticks to them to overcome the pain from tendinitis, just so he could get through a set. Now he says he's fine, and he continues to play five nights a week—but he's had no fewer than seven operations on his wrists and arms.

In the recording and live sound fields, when it comes to occupational hazards, the most popular topic among both engineers and performers has long been hearing loss. There is not a shred of doubt that exposure to high-decibel sound day after day leads to auditory degradation. Pete Townshend of The Who is the poster boy for what happens when you play too loud for too long—he surrounds himself with a plastic shell now whenever he's on stage. Thanks to groups like the House Ear Institute and OSHA, a lot of progress has been made, and awareness of the dangers is at an all-time high, as are sales of earplugs and in-ear monitors. Even classical musicians have raised their consciousness about the dangers of loud sound—symphony orchestras now routinely place transparent baffles behind the last rows of the string section to protect the players from the brass and percussion behind them, and the percussionists often wear earplugs.

Most of us who have worked long hours in the studio know about back and shoulder problems caused by sitting in the same spot while concentrating hard on the task at hand, paying no attention to those annoying little pains. Anyone who's felt that pain linger for more than a couple of days has gone out and invested in an ergonomic chair. We are also now paying more attention to those who insist we get out of the chair (no matter how good it is) and stretch periodically. Good console ergonomics can also contribute to back and shoulder health, and when they design their control surfaces, most console manufacturers take into account the amount and frequency of awkward stretches users might have to endure (although now, with the trend toward small-format, multifunction digital consoles, this is becoming less of an issue).

In the business world, however, there has been an alarming increase since the mid-'80s in repetitive strain injuries (RSI) and cumulative trauma disorders (CTD) caused by the huge increase in desktop computers in the workplace. Although it's true that the computer revolution has meant that fewer American workers are losing fingers in threshing machines or breathing asbestos fibers or coal dust, workplace RSI has reached epidemic proportions. According to CNN, in one recent year 60% of workplace-related injuries or illnesses were RSI related, costing the economy on the order of $120 billion in down time, lost productivity, and workers' compensation claims.

Today, we are all computer workers, subject to the same ergonomic dangers as the drones at temp agencies and telemarketing companies.

We in the audio business are not immune. Today, we are *all* computer workers, subject to the same ergonomic dangers as the drones at temp agencies and telemarketing companies. And the number of wrist and arm injuries from overuse among the professional audio and production community seems to be rising at an alarming rate.

"But I'm not an office slave," you insist. "I don't have to sit at a desk doing a boring job every day. I work for a great company doing cool things/I'm my own boss/I work out of my home/I can set my own schedule." Don't kid yourself. Any of these situations can actually make things worse. Large corporations are forced to pay attention to these issues, thanks to OSHA (and let's face it, the recent brouhaha about OSHA "invading" the home office was really just a smokescreen set up by big companies who despise any kind of government oversight), the threat of lawsuits and workers' comp claims, and those pesky unions who insist on a safe working environment. (Great bumper sticker I spotted recently: "Unions: The people who brought you the weekend!") But workers in most studios, especially small and home-based ones, don't have these kinds of protections.

If you're trying to grow your business, and you're the only one responsible for scheduling, updating the website, designing the brochure, writing contracts, and finishing that mix by deadline, the chances are high that you will spend far more too many hours than are good for you locked in front of your computer screen, manipulating words, numbers, slider-like objects, and pictures of waveforms with a mouse. Although it's not easy to pull yourself away from an intense work session, if you value your health, you'll learn how to do just that.

I've suffered from wrist/arm problems myself, but I'm one of the lucky ones. Some years ago, I jammed my right wrist sliding into third base in a hot and heavy softball game (I swear to this day that I was safe), and it swelled up like a balloon. Two weeks later, the swelling had gone down, but it still hurt like hell. I saw a doctor who gave me some anti-inflammatory drugs, which seemed to do the trick, but a couple of months after that I started working on the score for a film with a tight deadline, and after a week of ten-hour days playing my keyboards and manipulating my mouse, the pain in my wrist was back.

This time, the doctor wanted to operate. He didn't know what he was looking for—maybe a tear in the cartilage—so he told me it would be an "exploratory arthroscopy." The idea of someone poking around inside my dominant hand with a plastic tube appealed to me not at all, so I declined his offer and instead went to see an occupational therapist. She made me a custom wrist brace and gave me an ice pack, a squeeze ball to play with in free moments, and really good advice on how to take care of my hands. I still don't know exactly what is wrong with my wrist (the consensus is that I have a form of tendinitis), but I have managed to avoid significant problems. When I play tennis, ride a bike, or mow the lawn, I wear a simple Velcro strap that keeps my wrist from turning in certain directions. When I have serious pain, which happens once or twice a year, I take a lot of ibuprofen and immobilize my wrist for a few hours with the fancy brace. And when I feel the first pangs of discomfort after hours of typing or mousing around, I stop and do something else for a while.

There are actually a number of different types of hand and wrist injuries caused by overuse and repetitive tasks. Probably the best known (and scariest) is Carpal Tunnel Syndrome. This is common among pianists and typists, and it's what destroyed Leon Fleisher's career. The nerves that run through your wrist go through a relatively small conduit between some fibrous tissue and the wrist bone, called the Carpal Tunnel. If any of the tissues around the tunnel get swollen or change position, the result is a pinched median nerve—the nerve that controls the thumb and first two fingers. You feel tingling, burning, cramping, numbness, or "pins and needles," as if your hand has fallen asleep. In severe cases (like Fleisher's), surgery is necessary to remove some of the tissue pinching the nerve. Needless to say, it's very delicate surgery.

A related syndrome is Ulnar Tunnel Syndrome. The ulnar is the elbow, and the affected area is the "funnybone" nerve. This is often caused by over-reliance of armrests on office chairs; ironically, the armrests are supposed to relieve strain on the wrist and forearm, but actually they end up pinching the ulnar nerve.

A more common problem—since it has a wide variety of causes—is tendinitis. In tendinitis, one or more tendons—the cords that attach the muscles to the bones—get inflamed and cause pain, usually a dull ache over the wrist and forearm. This is a common problem among guitar players, drummers, and tennis players (most cases of "tennis elbow" are tendinitis), and it's one thing that Max Weinberg and I have in common.

Tenosynovitis is similar to tendinitis, but the inflammation is in the sheath surrounding the tendon, which lubricates it and keeps it moving smoothly. Other RSIs include adverse mechanical tension, or neural tension, which can be a reaction to muscle spasms in the shoulders where the pain travels down the arm, and Thoracic Outlet Syndrome, which is a compression of the nerves in the neck and shoulder. (It's what happens if you hold the phone between your neck and shoulder too long; it can also affect the arm.) There's also Myofascial Pain Syndrome, in which compression of the muscle tissue causes it to stiffen, creating painful "trigger points" that can move around and be very debilitating.

So what can you do to prevent or treat any of these conditions? I'm not a physician, and I've never even played one on TV, so I can't give you medical advice, but what I can do is relay some of the guidance that I've received on these issues and point you to various resources that might help you.

In general, you need to be aware of the need to rest your hands and arms. Ideally, you should cut down on the amount of time you spend at the computer. Of course, it's never easy to change your work schedule overnight, and Murphy's Law states that the worst problems will occur when you're on the most important project with the tightest deadline. But even just taking five minutes out of every hour and doing a few stretches (some good ones can be found on the Typing Injuries FAQ page at tifaq.org) will help. Checking out your posture and taking corrective measures if you see you're doing something wrong can help as well.

According to an article on the Typing Injuries FAQ page written by Jonathan Bailin, a physiologist at the University of Southern California, "microbreaks" are important to human physiology. "Computer word-processing now eliminates these 'microbreaks,'" he writes. "Computers have greatly simplified office activity, an advance that has at least one important disadvantage. The danger is found in the possibility for long-duration, continuous and relatively motion-free, precise, muscular activity called 'static exertion.' Humans were not well 'designed' for this."

In the recording studio, the equivalent to these "microbreaks" used to be tasks like changing reels on a tape deck, setting up mics and cables, adjusting outboard processing, reprogramming a patchbay, tweaking the parameters on a synthesizer, or even emptying ashtrays (remember ashtrays?). With the integration of all of these functions (except the last) into the digital audio workstation, this variety of motions and postures has been replaced with a much smaller set of tasks: sitting in a chair, moving a mouse, clicking the mouse, and pressing keys on a keyboard. In many studios, the engineer never even has to leave his seat to talk to the musicians, because they're all electronic or DI'd, everyone's in the same room, and the only mic that needs setting up is the lead singer's. So you need to consciously include these breaks in your daily routine. There are widgets and other freeware that can sound an alarm after you've been at the computer for a specified period of time, prompting you to get up and stretch, and some of the more aggressive ones will even disable the keyboard for a while.

In addition to rest, over-the-counter anti-inflammatory drugs, like aspirin or ibuprofen, can be useful; just don't take large quantities of these on an empty stomach or without plenty of water. Try applying ice packs during resting periods. If there's any swelling at all, this can calm it down. (Composer George Antheil, according to his extremely entertaining but somewhat dubious autobiography, claimed that in order to jump-start his performing career, he practiced the piano 16 to 20 hours a day. When his hands started to swell, he would place them in two fishbowls full of ice water until they were usable again. Maybe it worked for him, but I don't recommend it.)

If the pain or discomfort lasts for more than a few days, it's time to see a professional. Fortunately, the medical establishment has come a long way since the days when overuse injuries were diagnosed as being "all in your head," and even in the sorry mess that our current health insurance system has become, most plans cover treatment for RSIs.

Most primary care physicians these days have at least a rudimentary knowledge of RSIs and can offer a preliminary diagnosis. They can prescribe more powerful prescription anti-inflammatories, and sometimes a few days on those (combined with some new work habits) may be all you need. In some cases, cortisone injections may make sense for short-term relief from severe inflammation, particularly in the larger joints like the shoulder.

You also might get a recommendation for a simple over-the-counter wrist brace to help "enforce" rest, but unless you get specific advice otherwise, it's usually a bad idea to try to continue working while you're wearing a wrist brace. The motions you make to get around the restrictions of the brace may end up making your problems worse. Wear the brace only when you're resting or, if your health professional says you should, when you sleep.

If the problem is serious enough (and it often is, or else you wouldn't be there), the primary care physician will give you a referral to a specialist. In traditional medical practices and HMOs, this referral will often be to an orthopedist–another medical doctor who specializes in bones and joints–or a hand surgeon. There are some wonderful orthopedists and hand surgeons out there, but there are also those (like the one I described earlier) who seem to want to cut first and ask questions later. There are many, many other types of treatment you should investigate before you let anyone do any kind of surgery on your hands.

It might be worth your while to look outside the orthopedic community. Physiatrists (pronounced "FIZZ-e-AT-rists") are M.D.s who specialize in the diagnosis and treatment of musculoskeletal injuries and pain syndromes, mostly through nonsurgical methods, and many of them have practices that specialize in RSIs. They often work closely with other non-M.D. specialists. Other non-M.D. professionals you might consider consulting are osteopaths, chiropractors, kinesiologists (muscle specialists), and massage therapists.

A lot of your choices will depend, alas, on the kind of insurance you have: Some plans are more liberal than others at covering "alternative" therapies. One such therapy (or "modality," as health professionals like to say) that is gaining greater acceptance in Western medical circles is acupuncture. I went to see an acupuncturist for an unrelated pain problem, and although we didn't make much progress on my primary complaint, I found after a few sessions that my tendinitis, which had flared up earlier, completely disappeared. I also found it to be a thoroughly enjoyable form of treatment; all those endorphins floating around my system made for some of the most pleasant, relaxing "highs" I've ever had. Even better, my acupuncturist worked with a physiatrist, and the M.D. did all the billing, so when I sent Blue Cross the bills, they didn't even blink.

Some of the best treatment I've ever had from any medical provider has been at the hands (literally) of physical therapists and occupational therapists–the two are similar, but the latter are usually more specialized in their hand problem treatment. Help from PTs and OTs, in the form of teaching me exercises and stretches, simply heightens my awareness of when I'm doing something stupid to my body. Massage and ultrasound have significantly—and quickly—alleviated problems I've had with my knees, shoulders, back, and hands. The custom splint I resort to occasionally to rest my hand was made for me by an occupational therapist, under the direction of an orthopedist, and it works great.

As I see it, the philosophy of PTs and OTs (as well as many other noninvasive types of treatment) revolves around teaching the body how to cure itself. Although I'm hardly the eat-organic, take-only-natural-herbs, never-trust-the-medical-establishment type, I find this idea enormously attractive. Medical insurers are slowly coming to accept physical and occupational therapy, and now, if you play your paperwork right, many plans will cover a reasonable number of visits to a practitioner.

The relationship you have with the provider can be as important as the type of treatment you choose. There needs to be a high level of trust that they know what's wrong with you, and they know how to help you. They have to be able to listen to you and ask the right questions. You have to be able to listen to them and do what they tell you, whether it's exercises, rest, or adapting your work habits. If you think a professional is inattentive, incompetent, unknowledgeable, or doesn't take you seriously, find someone else. With RSIs, treatment is a two-way street. It's not like curing strep throat with antibiotics; you are as responsible for your getting better as the professional you seek out.

For some, direct treatment from a professional may not be as helpful as (or may be enhanced by) developing a new mind/body discipline. There are many who have suffered with RSIs who have achieved relief through yoga, Tai Chi, Alexander technique, or Feldenkreis method. Although the relationship is generally not as personal as with a medical professional, finding a good instructor who understands your problems and your goals is very important.

Given the number of people who have developed RSIs, it's no surprise that the market has of late been flooded with various gadgets that claim to prevent or even cure overuse injuries caused by computers. But given our current make-a-fast-buck-any-way-you-can-and-the-FTC-doesn't-care economic model, it's also no surprise that many of these products are useless and perhaps even harmful. Some devices are worthwhile if they are used correctly but dangerous if they are not. Wrist pads on computer keyboards, for example, according to most professionals, should be used only when the hand is actually resting. If you type while your wrist is on the pad, the position it forces you into can aggravate Carpal Tunnel and tendon problems.

New kinds of keyboards are often touted as RSI preventers. The lateral angle of the wrist can be an important factor in wrist problems. The forearms and the wrist should approach the keyboard in a straight line, not at an angle. Keyboards that are split down the middle, with the different sides at different angles, are supposed to promote proper placement of the wrists and are useful for some. The Dvorak keyboard is designed to minimize the number and complexity of finger movements while typing. Conventional keyboards are designed to slow down typists to prevent the mechanisms in the first typewriting machines from jamming. But in a studio situation, a Dvorak keyboard may not be much help, since much of what we do isn't straight typing, and the various key combinations used by DAWs aren't necessarily going to make any more ergonomic sense on a Dvorak keyboard than they do on a conventional one.

The mouse is a problem, especially when you're doing very fine adjustments, like editing waveforms. Make sure the mouse you're using fits in your hand naturally and doesn't require any uncomfortable stretches to operate the buttons. (The new Macintosh "puck" mouse deserves to be buried in a landfill—if you have one, replace it.) For studio work, a trackball (although my experiences with one led to cramping in my fingers) or one of the new dedicated control surfaces with large knobs can be helpful. A drawing pad with a stylus can help in some tasks.

Voice recognition software has improved by leaps and bounds in recent years, but it's still far more suitable for ordinary document creation than it is for studio work. (Can you say, "Open Insert 1 on channel 14, select Hall reverb, set diffusion to 80 percent and pre-delay to 40 msec, give me an LF boost of 1.6 dB at 500, goose the send level 3 dB, and route the return to aux 6"? I didn't think so...)

If you're on the phone a lot, get a hands-free headset so you don't find yourself scrunching the phone between your neck and shoulders. You'd be surprised how fast and seriously this can hurt you. If you play a lot of video games at your computer—stop. If you have a hand problem, you want to increase the variety of motions and reduce tension; video games do exactly the opposite.

Keep in mind that "No pain, no gain" may sometimes work for bodybuilders and linebackers, but for the rest of us, it's really lousy advice. Better to paraphrase the old hippie motto: "If it feels bad, don't do it."

At the end of *Return of the Jedi*, Luke Skywalker gets fitted with an artificial hand that's as good as his original. Technology has come a long way since that movie was made, but we still can't do that. So it's best to assume that the hands you have now are the only ones you're going to have. To quote Bob Dylan, "Take care of yourself and get plenty of rest."

Paul Lehrman still has the sound of 16 player pianos ringing in his ears, despite the use of earplugs.

Afterword

RSI Resources on the Net

A brief but very useful article by a physical therapist that covers all the important points is at **www.tifaq.org/articles/rsi_perspective-oct98-jackie_ross.html**.

A clear, cogent page with lots of good links put together by someone who is not a professional in the field but nonetheless knows what he's talking about is at **eeshop.unl.edu/rsi.html**.

An articulate and scary article by a non-professional, who herself went through RSI Hell, is at **www.amara.com/aboutme/rsi.html**.

The RSI Network, **www.ctdrn.org/rsinet.html**, features a monthly newsletter, a mailing list, searchable archives, and hundreds of articles from sources all over the world.

Another mailing list for people with job-related hand issues can be joined at **www.ucsf.edu/sorehand**.

Many other universities host excellent sites. Check out the Harvard RSI Action Home Page at **www.rsi.deas.harvard.edu** and MIT's RSI Information Page at **web.mit.edu/atic/www/disabilities/rsi/index.html**.

The typing injuries FAQ site is at **www.tifaq.org**.

A commercial site with solid information is **www.medicinenet.com**. Type "carpal tunnel" in the search window, and you'll be linked to several articles about the syndrome and its treatment.

Chapter 22

Caught Napstering
Why We're Missing the Real Problem with Digital Downloading

Preface

Internet delivery of recorded music is the most serious issue the record industry has faced in many years. How can record companies persuade people to pay for something that they can get (or at least think they can get) for free, and how can an industry—and all its subsidiary industries, like ours—survive without revenue? Millions of words have been written on the subject, and it has spawned hundreds of lawsuits and civil actions, several Supreme Court decisions, and a host of new enterprises trying to cash in on the new medium and on the confusion it has created.

Most of the noise, however, has been generated by the major players in the record industry through their lobbying organization, the RIAA, which has the money, the PR machinery, and the lawyers to make sure its voice drowns out all the others. But there are many sides to the issue, and this column, which generated one of the largest volumes of reader response in *Mix*'s history, attempted to join the chorus of smaller voices trying to articulate those other sides.

October 2000

"My experience in the music business began in 1960. Even though I've recorded over 25 records, I cannot support my family on record royalties alone. I recorded a CD that sold 500,000 copies worldwide. Except for a modest advance, I have received no royalties from that project. In 1977, I had a song that was a Top 40 hit, but the only money I received from the record company was in the form of a modest advance. The only benefit I got from releasing albums was that people would like them and come to my shows."

Are these the words of an old, uneducated Delta blues singer, forced by some greedy promoter in his youth to sign an exploitative contract that would haunt him all his life? Or are they the plaint of a jazz pioneer, driven by lack of airplay, record company support, and racism to live overseas? Or some innocent singer/songwriter from Brooklyn sucked into a lousy lifetime deal with an unscrupulous, midtown-Manhattan talent agency?

None of the above. That's Roger McGuinn, leader of The Byrds, arguably the most influential American rock group of the '60s, who, before his band sold millions of records for Columbia, was a backup musician and musical director for big-name artists like The Limeliters, the Chad Mitchell Trio, and Judy Collins.

Even more remarkably, these words were spoken not in a *Rolling Stone* interview, but in the chambers of the United States Senate Judiciary Committee, during a hearing on "The Future of Digital Music: Is There an Upside to Downloading?"

Later the same day, McGuinn told a newspaper reporter, "For years, the labels had all the power, and the artists were pawns. The artists were cattle." And when it comes to the major labels, little has changed. Although McGuinn worked out a new royalty arrangement some years ago with his old label (now part of the Sony empire), the bulk of his record income today comes from sales of new recordings through an organization that the large record labels view as a Jolly Roger-flying bastion of anarchy. It's one of the new companies and technologies that EMI/BMG/Warner, etc. would love to see be put out of business, either by litigation (well under way) or legislation (thus, the Senate hearings): the notorious MP3.com.

"They offered an unheard of, nonexclusive recording contract with a royalty rate of 50 percent of the gross sales," McGuinn continued. "I was delighted by this youthful and uncommonly fair approach to the recording industry. MP3.com not only allowed me to place these songs on their server, but also offered to make CDs of these songs for sale. They absorbed all the packaging and distribution costs. Not only is MP3.com an online record distributor, it is also becoming the new radio of the 21st century."

I know you've heard it all before—I've even written about it once or twice—and perhaps you've already taken sides on the issue, but things are moving very fast on the downloadable music front, so it's worth taking another look at what it all means. Like it or not, MP3, Napster, Gnutella, and whatever new file-swapping technology gets invented between the time that I write these words and the time you read them are changing the way that music is distributed in the industrialized world.

For anyone who isn't Britney Spears (or a member of the food chain that lives off her products), it's about time. New labels are cropping up all over the place, offering artists similar share-the-risk/share-the-profits deals to McGuinn (in fact, I just signed one myself), many of whom use MP3 files as come-ons: Download this song, maybe for free, maybe for a small charge, and if you like it, order the CD through our online shopping cart. They provide a glimmer of hope that as playlists of radio stations become increasingly tight and formulaic, radio (and the shrinking number of corporations who control the stations) will become decreasingly relevant. As the larger record companies continue their quest for risk-free, innovation-free, appeal-to-everyone, milla-vanilla "talent," they hopefully will—like the TV networks in the face of competition from cable, home video, and the Internet—steadily lose market share to independents and alternative delivery systems.

The record companies, naturally, are scared out of their pants about all this, but it's their own fault. They should have seen this coming and are only now scrambling to put the genie back in the bottle, trying to figure out how they can exercise some control over what may well be uncontrollable. And while they were screaming, "Theft!", they got caught recently with those pants down around their ankles. In May of this year, the Big Five labels settled an antitrust suit by the Federal Trade Commission that accused them of forcing retail stores to sell CDs at inflated prices, ripping consumers off for some $480 million. (By the way, if you look for this story in the normal media outlets, you may have trouble finding it: It ain't on the *New York Times'* site or *Wired* magazine's or Bloomberg News. It took me a half-hour of Web searching before I tracked it down at www.ftc.gov/opa/2000/05/cdpres.htm.)

The irony—pun unavoidable—of Metallica, who built their entire original fan base on metalheads swapping live concert tapes, screaming about Internet "piracy" is almost too absurd to be true. Almost.

This realignment of the record industry is good news. With the top-down orientation upended, a lot more artists and producers can participate and hopefully earn a decent, if not always spectacular, living. In the old structure, it normally took hundreds of thousands of sales before a record company could make a profit (or at least, that's what they tell the artist who's supposed to be receiving royalties), and an artist whose first record sells two million but whose second album sells "only" half a million is discharged like so much bilge water. The Britney Spears, 'Nsyncs, and Ricky Martins of the world would continue to multiply, while innovative groups would never have a chance. (And the irony—pun unavoidable—of Metallica, who built their entire original fan base on metalheads swapping live concert tapes, screaming about Internet "piracy" is almost too absurd to be true. Almost.)

But if an artist can spend a couple of thousand dollars producing a song in a studio, upload it to his site, and charge 50 cents to download it, even if he splits the royalties 50/50 with the site owner, it will take fewer than 10,000 people—the average drive-time audience for a second-rate radio station in a third-rate market—to listen to it before the artist breaks even and can go on to record another song. And maybe 5% of those people will buy CDs—there's another couple of thou in the bank. Maybe it's not going to buy him a villa on St. Barts, but there are a lot worse ways to make a living.

What college kid has so much spare time on his hands that he can download and burn so many custom CDs for his friends that it could possibly put a dent in record sales?

But what about the "death of intellectual property" that these file-sharing technologies threaten us with? Aren't they going to make it impossible for anyone to get paid? That's what the RIAA would have you think, and potentially it's possible, but I don't buy it. FM radio didn't kill record sales; it increased them. Same with home analog cassette decks. Probably the technology that most threatens the established order is the CD burner, but I don't see anyone trying to push through legislation that would ban them. *[By 2005, however, there was such legislation regarding video-copying-capable hardware, which so far, happily, has not gotten very far.]* Besides, when you think about it, what college kid (supposedly the typical MP3 fiend—although recent reliable surveys show that it's really the over-30s who are doing most of the downloading) has so much spare time on his hands that he can download and burn so many custom CDs for his friends that it could possibly put a dent in record sales?

There was a wonderful story written almost 50 years ago by the great science fiction writer Isaac Asimov that comes to mind. In "The Dead Past," a rogue scientist has discovered that the World Government had developed a "chronoscope," a machine that could view any event that ever happened, anywhere, in the past. But they kept it top-secret and never allowed anyone access to it, even going so far as to suppress any research into its engineering principles. So our hero decides to go ahead and make one himself. Only after he succeeds and publishes the plans for his machine does he realize that "the past" could mean 10 milliseconds ago, and "anywhere" could mean his neighbor's bedroom. In the story's last paragraph, the government agent sent to stop him, but now powerless to do so, proclaims, "Happy goldfish bowl to you, to me, to everyone."

But that's fiction. There is no World Government (although Bill Gates is certainly trying), and suppressing technology is almost impossible today (ditto). When the RIAA succeeded in getting a restraining order against Napster (which was overturned a couple of days later), people just went somewhere else: Gnutella, which represents an even greater threat to the RIAA since there's no central corporation behind it and therefore no one to sue. Gnutella reported its hit count went from 30,000 to 1.3 million the first day after the restraining order. When one technology is squashed, another will rise up instantly, like mushrooms during a wet summer.

Which doesn't bother me, because I think the RIAA is writing fiction, too. There simply is no objective data that supports its position that downloading hurts CD sales. The surveys it has commissioned have been deeply flawed (just like the one years ago that Warner/Elektra commissioned that tried to show how blank tape sales were killing LPs), and surveys from less-biased sources have shown quite different data: That in fact, in the few months right after Napster appeared, CD sales at major retail outlets actually increased.

When one technology is squashed, another will rise up instantly, like mushrooms during a wet summer.

Despite all their jabbering about artists losing control over their creations, the record companies—like the large book and newspaper publishers and broadcast/media networks—are not really concerned with that at all. They're concerned with their losing control over their artists' creations. As I write, the labels' lobbying organization, the RIAA, is pushing to get the words "work for hire" written into the part of copyright law that covers sound recordings, which means that even those piddling artist royalties that Roger McGuinn can't live on would disappear completely. *[This didn't fly either, at least not yet.]*

Also, witness the pickets at the *Boston Globe* protesting a new agreement that freelance writers are being forced to sign, which not only gives the newspaper the right to re-publish on the Web—or anywhere else—anything the writers create for that paper, but it instantly gives the paper the right to re-publish anything the writers have *ever* created for the paper. The *Globe* is now owned by the *New York Times*, which according to one source is using this as a testing ground before they try to force the same agreement on their own contributors.

For us as producers, studio owners, engineers, and artists, I'm optimistic that the net result of all this chaos will be positive. People who like music will continue to pay for it, if the music is what they want and the price is reasonable. Folk singers, rappers, garage bands, jazz players, world musicians, techno heads, and anyone else who wants to make a living in this business without turning their music into zillion-selling pabulum can't possibly be harmed by technologies that make it easier to get more music to more people, and we as professionals, helping them make their dreams into reality, will always be needed.

Maybe that sounds naive, but remember, despite dire predictions in our own industry, Fostex 1/4-inch, 8-tracks didn't kill the commercial recording studio and neither did ADATs or *Sound Forge*. Our business realigned itself to accommodate a larger number of players (albeit operating at smaller margins), and by most accounts, we're healthier than ever—as subscription figures for this magazine and hit counts on our website demonstrate. Even the giant studios who do lots of major-label work have known for years that they can't be dependent on that forever and have diversified into post-production, film scoring, multimedia, and other areas. I really think we in the recording business (as opposed to the "record" business—and we could all do the industry a favor by sending a little note to the editor every time we see a newspaper article that calls the RIAA "the recording industry") have a lot to gain by this little civil war.

Of course, it does need to be said that not everyone's hands are all that clean on the "pirates" side, either. The folks behind MP3.com stand to make a fortune on their piece of the downloading action, as well as advertising and promotion on the site, and the venture capital has been flowing into them. It's also been flowing into, amazingly enough, Napster, which since it doesn't charge for anything and has no e-commerce side, has no possible revenue source. Where's the investment money coming from? One could assume it's from people who hope to make a killing when some large corporation, like one of the Big Five labels or Microsoft, buys up the company, either just to put it out of business or to get exclusive rights to the technology.

And that, to me, is the greatest danger in all of this: not that the technologies exist, but that somehow they will be co-opted by the existing media conglomerates to serve their own ends. Already Microsoft (surprise!) has come up with an "alternative" to MP3 that can easily be controlled, metered, and watermarked and has entered into a distribution agreement with Sony Music. MP3.com, in an effort to settle some of the lawsuits that threaten it, has signed agreements with several of the major labels, allowing music in their catalogs to be downloaded for a price. That's all well and good for the larger labels, but what about the smaller ones? Do they have to sue to get a piece of the action as well? Or are they simply going to be shut out of this distribution channel?

There's one more side to all this that needs to be looked at. The cudgel that large companies are using against file sharing has another target, and that's the concept of "fair use." Fair use is the age-old tenet that allows anyone to comment, satirize, share for personal use, and create "derivative works" from copyrighted works. It's what lets me quote that newspaper story back in the fifth paragraph, or tape an episode of *The Simpsons* off the air, or write a research paper based around someone's autobiography, or take a CD out of my public library. The media companies are salivating at the idea of media being digitized and available from a centralized source, because then it can be controlled every step of the way. If they could somehow get those pesky fair use "loopholes" closed, they could get their gram of flesh every time a book is read, a movie is viewed, or a song is heard. And they're working on it—and they have lots of friends in Congress.

Island Records, some years ago, forced Negativland to bulldoze thousands of copies of a parodistic CD in a lawsuit that, if it had ever been brought to court, would have been thrown out on fair use grounds. But because the low-budget experimental band didn't have the legal muscle that the record company did, they couldn't afford to go that route. The idea that this practice might actually be legislated into existence is rather chilling.

As you listen to the RIAA and the MP3 community shriek at each other, keep in mind what the original purpose of the copyright law was. There was a very astute article on this subject recently in *The Nation,* which says it nicely: "Copyright allows users—that's citizens to you and me—to enjoy the benefits of cultural proliferation at relatively low cost through a limited state-granted monopoly." It doesn't say "no cost," nor does it say anything about an "unlimited" monopoly. It's there to protect the public, as well as the copyright holders. Let's hope that the current skirmish, which has tipped the balance at least temporarily one way, doesn't cause a backlash that will permanently skew it the other way. And in the meantime, just be grateful that you don't yet have to throw a nickel into the Disney-meter attached to your console the next time you complain that the guy who fixed your tape deck did a job that was strictly "Mickey Mouse."

Afterword

Of course, a lot has happened since this column appeared: Napster died and was reborn as a "legit" company, Sony and BMG merged so that now there are only the Big Four, and Apple stole everyone's thunder with the iTunes Music Store. "Digital Rights Management" is the hottest debate around, with media companies hoping to permanently lock up as much intellectual property as they can, while artists and consumer-rights advocates fight them tooth and nail.

Despite my optimism, there have been great changes in the pro audio industry since the downloading revolution began as well, not all of them good. There are still just as many, actually more, CDs being issued every year, but record labels have shrunk recording budgets, and many mid-sized and large studios that were dependent on record-company revenues have gone out of business. But is that a result of downloading, or of the growth of private and project studios, or of the accountants taking over companies that used to be at least partially run by creative people?

Some of the many responses from *Mix* readers, both agreeing and disagreeing with the column and with each other, can be found on www.insideraudio.com.

Chapter 23

David Ball

Who Will Fix Our Stuff?
The Future of Equipment Repair

Preface

While no one can argue that the falling cost of technology is a good thing, it has a downside: It becomes less cost effective to hold onto old gear. To make things worse, when old gear goes bad, it's hard to find someone who can fix it. And as this column explains, it's going to get harder.

March 2001

One of my computer monitors has been flaking out recently. At random intervals, one of the color circuits fails, and my screen turns a sickening pink. It's long past the warranty: It's one of those old, bright, Sony 19-inch jobs that weighs about 60 pounds and cost about $2,000 when it was made eight or nine years ago. (I don't know exactly when—I bought it used.) At first, it would respond to what my friend Coleman Rogers calls "the Fonzie technique," referring to the *Happy Days* character who could fix anything because he knew exactly where to whack it and how hard. But, as time went on, that became less reliable.

Fans of this column know how reluctant I am to part with old gear, and although I do like this monitor, it only displays at one resolution, and with all the different types of work that

I do, I came to realize it was time to retire it and replace it with a brand-new, modern, lighter, multisync model, which I was able to acquire for the piddling sum of $350. But I figured that if I could get my old monitor repaired, then it would be nice to have an extra 19-inch monitor lying around. So I went through the phone book looking for "Macintosh monitor service" and found a place, located some distance away but in an area I go to periodically, who promised to repair it for a fixed, payable-up-front fee of $165, assuming the tube was okay (which I knew it was). It would take two or three days, they said.

That was a month ago. I'm still waiting. They can't really tell me whether it's done. They tried it on a PC first because they said they didn't have the right cable to try it on a Mac, and it didn't work at all. So I gave them my cable, as well as the Griffin sync adapter that has served me well on many Macs and many monitors. They then told me that they had checked it out, soldered down everything they could see, didn't find any bad parts, but now it was working differently on different Macs, so they weren't sure if they had fixed anything. This week they asked me to bring in my own Mac so they can "synchronize" it properly. That means dismantling my whole SCSI-rat's-nest-infested, sound-deadened computer closet and letting them screw around with my main machine for a couple of days, while I am office-less and offline. Plus two special trips out there. They're being very nice about the whole thing, but as I write, we're at an impasse. And they do have the upper hand, because they have both my $165 and my monitor.

We're at an impasse. They have the upper hand, because they have both my $165 and my monitor.

If you've ever tried to get an older piece of equipment, or even a newer one, repaired, then chances are good that you've had a similar experience. Old schematics and parts are hard to come by. Newer, proprietary parts, like VLSIs, are expensive and often scarce. Component-level repair has become almost a lost art, as service manuals increasingly show how to disconnect and remove the different sub-assemblies in our gear and decreasingly tell us what's *on* them. With the price of technology constantly falling, manufacturers have taken the attitude that it's better to replace something—a logic board, a disk drive, an entire tape deck—than to fix it, and we, as consumers, are forced to agree. And the type of technical expertise that is capable of fixing our increasingly complex, planned-obsolescence-prone equipment is getting harder to find.

The pro audio service business is changing, as is in fact the meaning of the word "maintenance." Where once we strove to keep our equipment functioning at its original performance level for the longest possible time, today's economic and technological climate requires that our equipment constantly be updated with new firmware or software. The time to replace it is not when it no longer fulfills its function, but when its function no longer fulfills our changing needs.

"Things aren't built to be fixed the way they used to be," says Coleman Rogers, who is the head technician at Alactronics, one of New England's busiest pro audio service and installation shops. "We're no longer seeing consoles with ribbon-cable extenders that let you take a module out and lay it on its side, or tape machines where you hit two buttons and the whole panel falls off and you can get to everything. Mackie started the trend by putting all eight channels on a single board. I recently worked with one processing unit that was impossible to take apart. I spent much more time trying to figure out how to get it apart than fixing it. Designers aren't thinking about repair; they're thinking about how pretty something looks." They're also thinking about cost: The aforementioned Mackie consoles, of course, came out at a price point that was a fraction of what their immediate predecessors in the eight-bus field were charging.

Tom Courteau, owner of Aztech Electronics, another Boston-area repair shop who has been in business since 1977, agrees. "It's the new emphasis on computer-aided design and manufacture. It means that you can get terrific capabilities at affordable prices, but the stuff just isn't made to be repaired. Even to do something as simple as cleaning the controls, which is still as important as ever, you have to take off all the knobs and take the whole thing apart, since it's all built on one or two PC boards."

With the possible exception of power amplifiers and tube-based guitar amps, the days when you could put an oscilloscope onto a circuit and sort out the one component that had gone bad are also largely over. Especially in applications like high-end D/A converters, component values are much more critical, and small changes in values that may cause performance problems might not be obvious to a technician with a voltmeter. "Components interact with each other so much that a problem can be very hard to pin down," says Rogers. "Most of the time, it's not worth it to component-level troubleshoot, since the cost of replacing the whole board is comparable to the cost of the time that would be involved. When we replace the board, at least we know it's fixed, which makes it a confidence thing as much as a cost thing."

Courteau goes one step further. "When I see something that needs board-level repair or an entire new assembly," he says, "I'll send the whole piece to the factory. That way, there's usually a renewed warranty of some kind. It's worth it to me and the customer."

Many times a problem will be intermittent—like my monitor—and so the unit will have to sit on the bench a long time and be constantly monitored until it starts to exhibit whatever weirdness it's in for. In addition, technical documents may not be as comprehensive or as clear as they need to be. We all know (and I've written many words about) how bad user manuals can be, and service manuals, for better or worse, are often written by the same people. So if you think it's hard to find where the menu is for selecting the frame rate and word clock source on that digital disk recorder, then think about the poor bench tech who's trying to figure out what the waveform at pin 39 is supposed to look like.

Sometimes, products are just designed badly or without enough thought about how they will be used, and when they get out into the real world, they are simply bound to fail. Professional products that began life as consumer products are an obvious problem. The S-VHS transports that the original ADATs were based on, for example, were never designed to withstand the heavy high-speed use that professional studios put on them. But even the best professional gear can have problems from the beginning. Rogers cites a $3,000 box from one high-end manufacturer he's working on that's one-rackspace high and 15 inches deep. "That's never going to hold up in a rack," he says. "What were they thinking?" Courteau complains about potentiometers that are "getting cheaper, in every sense of the word. They're the key to controlling everything, but they wear out faster, and they can't take a hit. Unfortunately, people carry around the gear the same way they always did."

With the shift away from component-level repair, the most common hardware issues techs encounter is with interconnects, according to Rogers. "They will always be a problem," he says. "That's where the Fonzie technique comes in." Cables break, solder joints go bad, contacts oxidize. "On tape machines," he notes, "it's a particular problem because you have microprocessors connected to the mechanism, so you've got an interface where two things can go wrong. It's like a transducer, trying to go from a mechanical sensor to something electronic, with each one telling the other to do something."

Both shops are reluctant to take on musical instrument repairs. Rogers has a contract with Alesis (they work on literally hundreds of ADATs each year), so he will work on that company's synths, while Courteau says, "I avoid them. Occasionally, I'll be talked into taking some type of keyboard, especially if it's just a mechanical problem, but I'm not much of a computer guy, and that's what you need for those things." Rogers says, "The problem with MI gear is that no one wants to pay money to have it fixed. The average person who buys a keyboard is a mom who spent $100 for her 16-year-old, and when I tell them it costs $65 to fix, they say, 'Screw that.' An instrument is software based and mechanically interfaces with a keyboard, so there's that problem, and there are so many after-market software updates that it's impossible to keep up with them. It's just not a financially viable business for us to be in."

Courteau, in fact, does have one specialty, which Rogers won't touch: guitar amps. "I went to technical school in 1972, and I haven't learned anything since," Corteau laughs. "Tube amps have always had the same problems, either bad solder joints or thermal failures or the tubes themselves. The problem with working on this stuff was, by the late '70s and early '80s, we entered a long period in which the quality of the tubes declined. The manufacturing all moved offshore, and it became a major headache to get good tubes. I would cringe, because I'd be fixing some guy's Marshall head, and even if I bench-tested the tubes, I wouldn't know if they'd last the 90 days I was guaranteeing it. But in the last five years, they all started coming from Russia and China, and now you can get good ones without breaking the bank. We're the only industry still using tubes, but I don't think we'll ever get rid of them. But no one's learning about them anymore, so the fact that I know about them makes me a sought-after expert."

Except for specialties like Courteau's, Rogers sees the "repair" aspect of his field going away in the next few years. "In another four or five years, just about everyone will move away from analog and decide to go digital," he says. "The amount of time we're going to see a piece of equipment sitting in someone's rack will be much shorter. And the business is going to change. Training in system design and installation is going to be more important than component-level knowledge. Today, I'm on my way to a roller rink that had a guy come in and try to fix their system, but he couldn't. They called me, and I realized that they had a single graphic equalizer feeding three of the power amps, and it was fried. The owner wanted to know how much it would be to fix it, and I told him, so he asked how much is a new one, and it wasn't much more, so he went and bought a new one which is better than the one he had.

"I've had people scratching their head for two years over a problem, and I come in and find there's one piece of gear that's plugged in wrong."

"There's a lot of work to be had in installation," he continues. "People are changing over to 5.1, and that needs expertise. When people buy whole systems from a place like Guitar Center, most of them have no idea where the gazintas and gazoutas are and how grounds work. I've had people scratching their head for two years over a problem, and I come in and find there's one piece of gear that's plugged in wrong."

And where are the people who are going to be doing this work in the future going to come from? Electrical engineering programs in colleges are teaching computers, not how to build, fix, or install audio equipment. Another friend of mine teaches in a college with a highly respected electrical engineering department, where students are taught all of the elementals of electronics in class but never get a chance to use their basic electronics skills. When I asked my friend how many EE majors he thinks could breadboard a simple MIDI project, the reply was, "four or five."

Rogers, who has been teaching maintenance and repair at a college-based recording program for more than a decade, says, "There's a shortage of techs now. Given how busy I am, it's obvious people are having trouble finding somebody to do service. We have a one-semester repair and maintenance course, which is okay, but some students wish it were more. Syn-Aud-Con has one of the top programs, and it gives you both theoretical and hands-on work. But you always run into problems in the field, the exceptions that you'll never see in a classroom. There's only so much you can do watching somebody without doing it yourself. That's why we need internships and mentoring. Even the brightest student is initially going to make dumb mistakes until he gains real experience. It can be a slow process, doing the labor of soldering and grunt work of installation, while picking up the background material of why we're doing things this way.

"You have to have the hands of a surgeon and be good visually—read a schematic and know what you're supposed to be seeing by sticking an oscilloscope here or there. But you also have to know when to stop and maybe call somebody who might know more than you."

Being a good solder jockey, however, is only part of the gig. The similarities between the processes of becoming a good service tech and becoming a good recording engineer—a course that Rogers also teaches—are reflected in the similarities of the skill sets, he says. "There's just as much customer handling and public relations as in studio engineering. That's almost as important as being able to read a schematic and wield a soldering iron."

And computers, of course, are going to continue to gain importance, so that those already in the field, according to Rogers, are going to have to retrain: "Instead of a transistor gone bad, we're going to be looking for software conflicts," he says. Fortunately, for me, that's something I know how to do already, at least in my own studio. But I would be very happy if I could find an old-fashioned technician who could just give me my monitor back, with all the colors working, please.

Afterword

My monitor came back, all fixed, about a month after I wrote this column. It lasted five more years. Coleman has changed jobs a couple of times, but his services are still very much in demand.

Chapter 24

Will Terry

Ask Grump
Advice from the Dean of Curmudgeons

Preface

From 1997 to 2002 I was the editor for Mix's website, mixonline.com. For the most part, it was a fun, creative gig: I got to design the site's look, meet with the print editors by conference call every week to discuss what was going to be on the site, write and produce Web-only features, and moderate a number of reader forums. Some interesting issues came up in the forums, and the immediacy and interactivity they provided the participants—something a print magazine can't achieve—was novel and exciting. Of course, like any online enterprise run by "experts," we had to field a lot of practical questions, some of them pretty dumb, and some of which would come up over and over. So when it came time for another April column, I figured I'd call on Grumpmeier to field a few of them and put them to rest, once and for all.

April 2001

Every month, we at *Mix* and *Mix Online* get hundreds of e-mails and forum questions about how to do stuff: mike a drum kit, get into a school, get out of a school, get a record contract, get out of a record contract, achieve the sound that some well-known group has on their latest album, or handle an annoying client. We try diligently to answer these questions ourselves, and if we feel we can't, we refer the questioner to someone more qualified. This month, we are very pleased that my old buddy Phineas T. Grumpmeier, Lit.D., Pd.Q, L.S./MfT, now on the faculty of the Department of Misapplied Audio at the Southeast Hackensack Institute of Technology, has agreed to lend us his impressive expertise and respond to some of our typical questions. Over to you, Professor Grump…

What's the best computer for doing audio editing?

We all know the problems that both Macintosh and Windows machines have, and although things have gotten a bit more stable recently, I still don't trust either of them. I also don't think much of the fact that, because there's no way to move session files between them or even between most applications on the same platform, then whatever you get now you're going to be stuck with forever—unless, of course, whenever there's any kind of update, you're happy to convert everything you've ever done throughout your entire career into a new format. That's why I use a 1982 BBC Acorn for all my audio editing. I get 38 seconds of 8-bit, 6-kHz audio on each 5.5-inch floppy disk—but you know, what goes around, comes around. And, as it happens, it's just perfect for Web work. The disks are dirt cheap, if you can find them, which I sometimes can in flea markets and on eBay, although dumpsters behind office buildings are a more reliable source. But the best part is that I don't have to worry about those silly hardware or software updates, because I know darn well there aren't going to be any.

I'm building a studio in my parents' garage. I have a lot of experience doing live sound for solo acts at open-mic Mondays at a local club and hanging around with the DJs the rest of the week, and I work days at a video store where I get to watch a lot of TV. So I'm positive I'm ready to move up to the next step and record major label acts and score Hollywood feature films. I know that the gear isn't as important as how well you use it, and I think mine is good enough. I've got an 8-track cassette recorder in pretty good shape, a couple of microphones with the model and serial numbers scratched off (they're black and have a round ball at the end, if that helps), and some kind of mixer I found at a yard sale, which still has most of the knobs. I also have a pile of old 2x4s and some slightly used sheetrock behind the house and a couple of thousand empty egg cartons (my folks own a chicken farm), which I know will come in handy. What else do I need to buy, and where can I go on the Web to get free advice about design, acoustics, wiring, equipment, and recording and mixing techniques? I need to keep my total budget under $500.

The big studios' stuff may be flashier and more expensive, but that doesn't mean it works any better—if it did, why would they need to keep all that technical staff around?

It sounds to me like you've got all that you need to go head-to-head with the big studios. Their stuff may be flashier and more expensive, but that doesn't mean it works any better—if it did, why would they need to keep all that technical staff around? As for information about how to build your studio and how to produce records and film scores, there are dozens of acoustical consultants, designers, composers, producers, and recording and mixing engineers who have posted everything they know on the Web, and it's yours for the taking. After all, they've already made their money, so now they're happy to give their knowledge away to anyone who wants it. Just go to your favorite search engine, type in "How to make a hit record," and you'll be directed to thousands of great sites, some of which will also feature surefire ways of making $10,000 a week in only five minutes a day, while others will have grainy pictures of men, women, and animals (including chickens, you'll be happy to know) in truly remarkable poses. Best of luck to you. Just make sure those egg cartons are clean.

My favorite grunge-metal band is the P*gf*c*ers. They rule. Their lead singer, Nolo Vox, does this really cool thing on their tune "P*ss on Y*u B*t*h," in which it sounds like he's throwing up into a trash can. I want to get a similar effect on my band's next record. How did they pull off that amazing sound?

I checked with their producer, the London Conservatory-trained Trevor Trevor III. He told me, "We did most of the album at a studio in Hollywood, but for that one track, we rented a manor house in the Cotswolds for a week. We sent all the servants away except for the French cook and brought in three Sony digital 48-tracks, a 92-input Euphonix board, a trunk full of Neumann, AKG, Sennheiser, and B&K mics, and 16 channels of Millennia preamps, and we wired the banquet hall with big Tannoys in a 7.1 configuration.

"We tried recording Nolo in every one of the 52 rooms, putting him in different corners, on top of and underneath various pieces of the Louis XIV furniture, and setting the mics up in X-Y-, M-S-, ORTF-, and B-format Ambisonic. We filled about 20 reels of tape, but I wasn't happy with anything we had.

"Finally, at around midnight on the last night we were there, after a dinner of frog's legs, octopus, blood pudding, and trifle, Nolo suddenly said he wasn't feeling too well and ran out of the dining room. He didn't make it to the lavatory, but he did get as far as a large metal drum that was sitting in the hallway that had been filled with—um, uhh—sugar. As luck would have it, one of my assistants had accidentally dropped a Shure wireless mic into the drum earlier that day, and it was still on. So when Nolo blew his cookies into it, we had a clear signal right to tape. It was a wonderful moment, one that would be hard to reproduce, I'm sure."

I need to find a good audio engineering school. I'm not sure what I want to do, but I love music and want to make it my career. It's got to offer guaranteed job placement in a professional situation, a scholarship, free room and board, and not take longer than six weeks. And it shouldn't require a high school diploma. Also, it has to be near my home in Bemidji, Minn., so I can report to my parole officer every Friday. What's the best school that fits these criteria within a few hours' drive from me?

A quick look at the Mix Audio Education Directory shows that the Global Engineering and Technical Repository for Education and Audio Learning (GETREAL) has a brand-new campus—their 93rd, not far from you in Hibbing, above the hardware store. (The door's off the alley, knock twice.) They have six SSL rooms, four Mackie rooms, two Avid suites, and a soundstage large enough for a 70-piece orchestra. Their programs range from one week to three months—the longer programs also include everything there is to know about video and Web design. They will help you find a job, although you may have to accept an unbreakable lifetime contract as a washroom attendant at a theme park, with the possibility of promotion to assistant post-parade sweeper after five to eight years. Tuition is very reasonable, and room, board, and snowshoes are included. My sources tell me, however, that they are having a little difficulty attracting faculty.

I know that to make digital tracks sound "warmer" I need a good tube mic preamp. What's your favorite?

The best preamp I've come across is a totally discrete module taken from a 40-year-old RCA broadcast console, hand-remanufactured with oxygen-free silver wire and NASA-spec resistors by members of an animist motorcycle cult living on a Connecticut Indian reservation. It uses a matched pair of Nuvistor pentodes, whose numbers are still considered classified, and are today only made by Russian emigré monks in a small factory in Hokkaido on the second Thursday of alternate months. The waiting list for these units is about two years, while the tube makers are more like five years behind. Everything else out there sucks.

I have a Mac G4 running Pro Tools 5.1 *and* Cubase VST, *using dual* 888 *interfaces, a* MOTU *Digital Timepiece, Aardvark format converters, an* Opcode *Studio 5, and a Horita blackburst and timecode generator. My MIDI rig is a Kurzweil* K2600R, *a Roland S-760, and a Korg* Triton, *all with digital outputs. My microphones run through JoeMeek preamps and Apogee 24-bit convertors, and then everything goes into a Yamaha 02R, configured for 5.1, and out to an Event digital surround speaker system and a Tascam DA-98HR. I also have a Panasonic DVCAM deck feeding a 500-MHz Pentium 4 through FireWire, running* Edit DV *and* Vegas Pro *under* Windows 2000, *with a* Layla *card and a* SoundBlaster Live.

My problem is I can't get anything to sync to anything else. Whenever I turn on more than two devices, one of them starts flashing "Word Clock Error," and this horrible high-level burst of noise fills the room and sends me screaming out the door. It's very

The 119 dB of boost required at 45 Hz makes the speakers a little warm, but a couple of inches of asbestos underneath them keeps them from melting through the meter bridge.

tough to figure out what's going on under these conditions. I've already blown three midrange coils, and my doctor tells me I'll have to stop soon before I suffer from major hearing loss, a nervous breakdown, or both. Meanwhile, I'm working on a prime-time network production that goes on the air in 10 days, so I'm desperate for your help. Why does this have to be so darn complicated? I have no idea what should be the master, and what should slave to what, and how to get the clocks and sampling rates to agree with each other. None of the tech support people at the companies have a clue. Why can't manufacturers come up with some standard way of dealing with external sync? Or is it just me?

You're right—it's just you.

What's your favorite plug-in?

That would be "Speaker Maker" from a small company in Uzbekistan called "Grzsnykolpfbimt PLG," which, roughly translated, means, "Even lower than wholesale." It can make any speaker you've got sound like any speaker you could ever want. You can turn a pair of Genelecs into *NS-10*s or vice versa. I like to use it with the little Radio Shack mini-monitors sitting on my console, making them sound like Westlake *5*s with a sub-subwoofer. The effect is uncanny. The 119 dB of boost required at 45 Hz makes the things a little warm, but a couple of inches of asbestos underneath them keeps them from melting through the meter bridge.

What's the best microphone for vocals?

I like the Astrovox *466*, which we used to call "The Hackensack Hammer." That's because it was made right here in Hackensack, N.J., and you could bang nails into the floor with it and then sing into it, and it would sound just the same. It's also useful for pitch-correction. If your vocalist starts to go flat, then you can hit him upside the head with it and he'll straighten right out. It's got a huge proximity effect that's perfect for those "voice of death" goth-metal tracks. You can be sure that nobody will ever steal it, because it has a weirdo 7-pin connector that doesn't match anything else in the known universe. Best of all, the pop screen is electrically live, which discourages spitting and is useful for disciplining an egomaniacal guitar player: If you set up the polarity on his amp right, when he leans forward to sing, it'll fry his moustache right off. Of course, it sounds awful, but who cares about that?

What's the best way to equip my studio for surround?

It depends on what you're surrounded by. If you're planning on recording lots of rap and you are surrounded by hostile neighbors, then I would recommend a high-voltage electric fence. Make sure there are plenty of warning signs to keep lawsuits at a minimum. If your studio is out in the woods and you're worried about the birds and porcupines making too much noise around you, then a small-bore automatic pistol can be very useful. And if you're recording Christina Aguilera or Britney Spears and figure on being surrounded by screaming teenage girls, then a few cattle prods and cans of Mace are an excellent investment.

My PC-based DAW says that it handles 24-bit audio, but when I burn a CD, it's only 16-bits. What happens to the other eight bits?

The other eight bits are still on the CD, but they're in a special locked file that can only be opened by members of an exclusive record industry organization, the Society for Music Decoding and Interpolation, or "SMDI." Should your CD ever be acquired by a record label that is a member of this powerful but very secretive group, they will be able to recover the extra bits when they reissue it, after your copyright expires, as a 24-bit DVD-A. This ensures that their catalog will never go out of date, but of course, it does nothing for you.

i wanna be a audio engineer and do dejay stuf too. do you now any good books or soft-wears that can hep me lern!?

Start with *Travis Bratwurst Teaches Typing.* Then check out *Spell Checking for Blithering Idiots*, and when you feel you've mastered those, you'll be ready for *Where the Heck Is the Shift Key, Anyway?*

After 20 years in computer systems engineering, I want to get back to my first love, which is recording and playing music. But I feel like I've missed out on so much that I need to catch up on: digital recording, DSP, synchronization, MIDI, DAWs, automated mixing, Web streaming, and so on. Also, I'm very troubled by Napster and MP3 and what they mean for the music industry. If everything is available for free, then how is anyone ever going to make any money? I don't want to spend a lot of time learning all this new stuff and trying to make a career of it and then find out I'll never get paid. What would be your advice for the best place to go to study everything I need to know to get up to speed on all the important new issues in the recording field, and also to get the skills to be able to make a decent living in it?

Two words: law school.

Paul D. Lehrman apologizes for taking the month off. It won't happen again.

Jokes: Part 3

All-Purpose Musician Jokes

The following quickies can be applied to just about any unpopular instrument, including banjos, accordions, trombones, tubas, violas, or bagpipes. Feel free to replace the name of the instrument or player with your favorite...

Q: What do you call a trombonist with a beeper?

A: An optimist.

Q: What's a *real* optimist?

A: A trombonist with a mortgage.

Q: What's the difference between a dead skunk in the middle of the road and a dead tuba player in the middle of the road?

A: The skunk was more likely to be on his way to a gig.

Q: What kind of calendar does a viola player use to keep track of his gigs?

A: Decade-at-a-glance

Q: What do you call 500 bagpipers at the bottom of the ocean?

A: A good start. *(Also applicable to lawyers, producers, record company execs, etc.)*

Q: What's the difference between a viola player and a large pizza ?

A: The pizza can feed a family of four.

Q: What do you call a beautiful woman on a tuba player's arm?

A: A tattoo.

Q: What's the difference between a banjo player and a savings bond?

A: The savings bond eventually matures and makes money.

Q: What's the difference between a viola and a lawnmower?

A1: You can tune the lawnmower.

A2: Vibrato.

Q: What's the difference between a trombone and a chainsaw?

A: The chainsaw is easier to handle in a mix.

Q: What's the range of a bagpipe?

A: It depends on how strong your throwing arm is.

Q: What's the difference between an accordion and a trampoline?

A: You want to take your shoes off before you jump on a trampoline.

Q: What do you call a banjo player in a three-piece suit?

A: The defendant.

Q: A tuba player and a bagpipe player are trapped in a burning building and you can only save one. What ethical question do you have to ask yourself?

Q: Should I go to lunch or take in a movie?

Did you hear about the accordion player who parked his car one day on the street, leaving his instrument on the back seat? When he came back his window was broken and his worst nightmare had come true: There were now *two* accordions on the back seat.

■ ■ ■

The leader on a New Years' gig books a big band: bass, drums, guitar, piano, organ, horn section, lead singer, and two backup singers. But three days before the gig, every player bails on him! So he calls every musician he knows, but of course everyone's booked. Finally, in desperation, he starts going through the union directory, and finally manages to hire a banjo player and an accordionist.

Well, the gig is a smash. The club owner congratulates the band and immediately books them back for the next New Years' with a hefty raise. The banjo player turns to the accordionist and says, "Great! We can leave our gear!"

■ ■ ■

Radio disk jockeys are never supposed to leave the station unattended, but the late-night announcer at the classical station had to pick up his girlfriend at the airport. He knew that management never listened to him, so he thought of a great idea: he put on a CD of the first act of *Die Meistersinger*, that interminable Wagner opera, locked up the station, jumped in his car, and drove off. He got back just in time to change the disc—or so he thought. To his horror, he realized the CD was skipping and had been repeating the second two beats of the fourth measure of the overture over and over again for 58 minutes.

But he was a resourceful fellow, and he thought of a way out. Slowly, he faded down the volume, and then turned on his mic and announced solemnly, "That was a new recording of Symphony Number 7 by Philip Glass."

And while we're thinking about Philip Glass:

The Philip Glass Knock-Knock Joke:

Q: Knock-Knock! Knock-Knock! Knock-Knock!
Knocky-Knocky! Knocky-Knocky! Knocky-Knocky!

Knockiny-Knockiny! Knockiny-Knockiny! Knockiny-Knockiny!

Knockaninny-Knockaninny! Knockaninny-Knockaninny! Knockaninny-Knockaninny!

Knickanonny-Knickanonny! Knickanonny-Knickanonny! Knickanonny-Knickanonny!...

■ ■ ■

Four high-tech executives are in a car speeding to a meeting when they blow a tire. The software VP gets out, looks at it, and says, "I can't do anything—that's a hardware problem." The hardware VP looks at it and says, "There's nothing I can do here—we have to send it back to the factory." The tech-support manager says, "Try turning it off and then back on again and see if it fixes itself." The marketing VP says, "Hey, 75 percent of it is working fine—let's ship it!"

Here's a variation on the same theme:

An engineer, a project manager, and a tech-support specialist are in a limo traveling down a steep mountain road. All of a sudden, the brakes fail and the car careens down the road out of control. Fortunately, halfway down, the driver manages to stop the car by steering it into a grassy embankment, narrowly avoiding going over the side of the mountain.

Everyone gets out, shaken by their narrow escape from death, but otherwise unharmed.

The project manager is the first to speak. He says, "To fix this problem we need to organize a committee, have meetings, draw up a strategy, and through a process of continuous and careful improvement, develop a solution."

The engineer says, "That's dumb and will take way too long. Here—I have a penknife, a nail file, and ballpoint with me, so I'll just take apart the brake system, isolate the problem, correct it, and put it back together."

The tech-support specialist says, "You're both wrong. I think we should all push the car back up the hill and see if it happens again."

■ ■ ■

Q: What's the most common thing a college graduate says on his first job?

A: "You want fries with that?"

Q: What's the most common thing a graduate of an expensive, comprehensive, award-winning, four-year course in audio engineering technology says on his first job?"

A: "You want batteries with that?"

Q: How do you tell if a bass player is actually dead?

A: Hold out a check (but don't be fooled: a slight, residual spasmodic clutching action may occur even hours after death has occurred).

Q: How come computer programmers never get out of the shower?

A: "Rinse, lather, repeat."

Q: What do you call New Age music played backwards?

A: New Age music.

Q: Who are the players in a string quartet?

A: A good violinist, a bad violinist, someone who used to be a violinist, and someone who hates violinists.

Q: What do you call a guitar player who's broken up with his girlfriend?

A: Homeless.

Q: How can you tell when a stage is level?

A: The drummer is drooling out of both sides of his mouth.

■ ■ ■

What's the difference between …

Q: …a drummer and a drum machine?

A: With a drum machine you only have to punch the information in once.

Q: …a violin and a viola?

A: There is no difference. The violin just looks smaller because the violinist's head is so much bigger.

Q: …an opera singer and a pit bull?

A: Lipstick.

Q: …a bassist and a hippopotamus who's just eaten a can of baked beans?

A: One's a huge ugly useless thing that makes a deep farting noise and the other is a hippopotamus.

Q: …an oboe and a bassoon?

A1: The bassoon burns longer.

A2: You can hit a baseball further with a bassoon.

Q: …the first chair and last chair violinists in an orchestra?

A: About a half a beat.

Q: ...a drummer and a puppy?

A: The puppy will stop whining after a couple of months.

Q: ...a blues band and a moose?

A: On a moose, the horns are in front and the asshole's in the back.

Q: ...a cello and a coffin?

A: A coffin's got the dead guy on the inside. (*Which happens to be the title of a wonderful mystery novel by Keith Snyder. Check it out.*)

■ ■ ■

The touring orchestra was playing a grueling seven-day stand in one town, and the final program featured an especially long and difficult piece, Beethoven's 9th Symphony. The bass section was particularly exhausted and was not looking forward to the concert until one of their number reminded them that there is a 20-minute section in the last movement of the symphony in which the basses are "tacet"—they don't play anything—and if they were clever, they could all slip out and get a drink at the bar across the street from the concert hall during that interval. Just to be sure that they got back in time, the principal bassist attached a long piece of string to the conductor's score four pages before the basses had to come back in. The other end of the string he wrapped around his wrist, so that when the conductor turned that page, he would feel the string tugging.

The symphony started, and at the appropriate time the players gingerly laid their instruments down on the stage and tiptoed out the door. When they got to the bar, they were so relieved to be there that they all immediately ordered double Scotches. And then another round. And then a third. Just as they were about to start on the fourth round, the principal bassist felt a tug on his sleeve and was just awake enough to remember what it meant. He jumped up and announced to the group that they had to put down their glasses and get back to the hall, but two of them absolutely refused to stop drinking. The rest of the section lurched back across the street and in through the stage door, picked up their instruments and looked bleary-eyed at the conductor—who looked back at them, absolutely horrified.

After all, here it was the last of the Ninth, on the seventh day of the series, the score was tied, there were two men out, and the basses were loaded!

Chapter 25

Morons, Oxymorons, and Technology Patents

Strange Goings-on in the World of Streaming Audio

Preface

The combination of accelerating technological development, corporations that engage in outrageous behavior, the advent of greed as a political philosophy, and a government hell-bent on refusing to protect its citizenry from predatory business practices has created some bizarre distortions in the fabric of the universe. One such distortion, which grabbed my attention when I came across a story that was not only highly germane to our collective future but also involved someone I knew well as a featured player, is how the patent system is being abused in order to stifle progress and choke competition.

June 2001

If you want to see just how totally out of control the high-tech world is, then go to your favorite Internet search engine and type in the words "bogus patents." NorthernLight.com returns over 250 results—almost all having to do with companies and their lawyers fighting over the legitimacy of new technology patents. *[Google wasn't yet much of a presence when this column was written—today the number of results on Google is almost 12,000.]* Not over who did something first, but whether the patents should exist at all or not. In the old days, patent fights were about timing. The development of everything from the sewing machine to the television is littered with cases in which one inventor or company claimed he (it was almost always a "he") invented something before some other guy did and therefore was eligible for compensation.

The patent system was supposed to restrict and regulate competition, not shut it off.

And usually things were reasonably clear cut: Either someone could prove that they had come up with an idea and used it first or they couldn't. Patent officers and judges could determine, with a certain amount of confidence, when one invention bore too close a resemblance to another, or when someone expressed the main points of an idea—the concept known as "prior art"—before someone else did. The whole idea behind patents, like copyrights, was not just to ensure that an inventor could make money from a new idea but also to publish the details of the invention so that others could build on it—at the same time creating a reasonable monopoly for the original patent holder and requiring that others who wanted to use the idea would pay a license fee. The patent system was supposed to restrict and regulate competition, not shut it off. But it also had another role: to spread knowledge.

Today, however, many companies look at patents in a totally different light. A whole new industry has sprung up in "defensive" patents: Let's take out a patent on this idea, even if we're not using it and may never, just to make sure no one else can. It's become particularly nasty in the software world. Although software patents are illegal in Europe, in the USA thousands of patents are applied for every year for techniques such as handling e-commerce transactions, compressing images, or tracking Internet users' habits. To make matters worse, a lot of these concepts are far from original—they've just never been patented before. Companies are staking claims on ideas that have been floating around for years and used by many, but that doesn't deter them from demanding royalties on "their" intellectual property.

Let's take out a patent on this idea, even if we're not using it and may never, just to make sure no one else can.

For a patent to be valid, it has to be considered "non-obvious," that is, a genuine invention. A landmark Supreme Court ruling in 1882 read, "It was never the object of patent laws to grant a monopoly for every trifling device, every shadow of a shade of an idea, which would naturally and spontaneously occur to any skilled mechanic or operator in the ordinary progress of manufactures. Such an indiscriminate creation of exclusive privileges tends rather to obstruct than to stimulate invention." But the definition of what is "non-obvious," especially to those who smell money, seems to be rather fluid.

I have personally been involved in a couple of scrapes, within our own industry, over this issue. A few years ago, a musical instrument manufacturer tried to patent the idea of velocity-based sample switching; that is, how hard you hit a key on a musical keyboard determines which sample will play. Very early in the days of digital samplers, this might have been considered a patentable idea, but by the time this manufacturer got around to it, it was already in wide use throughout the industry. It was an obvious feature for any sampling keyboard that intended to reproduce the sound of a real musical instrument. The folks who objected to the patent being granted—another instrument maker—contacted me, and I was able to steer them to a user manual from an older instrument that clearly showed this concept being used to simulate a piano sound over a wide dynamic range. Having established prior art, the opponents were able to have the patent application thrown out.

More recently, I was a consultant for a law firm on the other side of the fence. A research institution was suing a commercial manufacturer for using a signal-distribution scheme the institution had patented, and I was asked for my "expert" opinion as to whether there was indeed infringement. My report said that, yes, the defendant was infringing on the patent, but I could name four other companies that were also infringing, because the idea was so obvious it should never have been patented. I was thanked (and paid) and told that my presence in court would not be necessary. As far as I know, the case is still pending.

One of the problems with the current patent situation is that many of the people who work at the U.S. Patent and Trademark Office don't seem to be the ideal candidates when it comes to making fair and well-considered decisions about the new concepts and ideas that are being constantly thrown at them. Given the ever-faster-spinning revolving door between business and government, it's not a stretch to think that many inspectors could be, as one critical report contends, "former lobbyists for the mega-corporations they're supposed to be overseeing." Other reports say that patent officers work on a quota system, and so they can't afford to spend more than the bare minimum of time and resources to investigate new filings. Whatever the reason, there is a new laxity in the Patent Office, and large high-tech companies are taking advantage of it, often to smaller companies' detriment.

"The patent bar has been lowered so far you can trip over it if you're not watching."

Computer writer Joseph T. Sinclair puts it this way: "For lack of trained personnel, the Patent Office in the last few years has approved thousands of patents regarding online business systems that will never hold up in court. Most of the patents have been filed defensively on the advice of attorneys. In other words, if a corporation sues your company for a patent infringement based on its bogus patent, your company can counterclaim for infringement on *its* bogus patent. The result is a wash and a moneyless settlement. But if you don't have a bogus online business systems patent *[and]* the money for an attorney, you're a victim in this Silicon Valley blood sport." Therefore, a lot of ideas—like that signal-distribution concept I looked at—receive patent protection when they shouldn't. Raph Levien, an inventor and programmer active in the open-source movement, says, "The examination process for software patents is a sham—probably half of the patents I've read are clearly invalid to anybody who knows the art." Perry Leopold, an Internet innovator, says, "The patent bar has been lowered so far you can trip over it if you're not watching."

Perhaps no more striking example of this can be found than patent number 6,004,596, "Sealed Crustless Sandwich," which is, literally, a patent issued in 1999 for a peanut butter and jelly sandwich. There's tremendous pressure from the high-tech community to shove through patents on "every shadow of a shade of an idea," just to make sure the competition doesn't do the same thing first. And it's led to some really interesting battles. Priceline, for example, the "name-your-price" airline ticketing service that William Shatner proclaimed was going to be "really big" (but which lost 98% of its value in the last year, not to mention Shatner), sued Microsoft over a name-your-price hotel room service on the software giant's Expedia.com travel site. Last year, on the other hand, Microsoft—which has been accused of being one of the worst offenders in this area—used its legal muscle to shut down an independent developer that had figured out how to decode their Active Stream Format (ASF). The developer maintains, quite logically, that it's ridiculous to patent a file format, but he hasn't got the money to battle Gates' legal minions.

Some government forces are trying to fight back. Congressman Rick Boucher, D-Va., co-sponsored a bill last session that would outlaw software patents by "creat*[ing]* the presumption that the computer-assisted implementation of an analog world business method is obvious and thus is not patentable." Given the current rabid pro-business atmosphere in Washington these days, it's hard to imagine this could pass, but stranger things have happened. (And, considering that Europeans have already done this, embarrassment can be a strong motivator.) *[It never got anywhere, alas.]*

So what does this have to do with our corner of the high-tech world? Well, one bogus patent that has the potential of screwing a large number of us pretty badly is currently floating around—and one of our number may have helped to stop it. Set the Wayback Machine to Philadelphia, 1981, Sherman, and we'll visit Perry Leopold, an itinerant singer/songwriter. Leopold had one well-received but minimally distributed self-produced record of "progressive folk," which he recorded in a single session in the basement of a shoe repair shop, to his credit, along with ten years of heavy touring. Taking a break from the road that year, Leopold set up a self-help organization for musicians, offering contacts and tips for dealing with various aspects of the music business, from self-promotion to copyright issues to record deals. It was called the Performing Artists Network, or PAN, and in 1983, it went online, using the services of Delphi (then a competitor to Compuserve and The Source, the two biggest online networks) and hooking up users around the country through the data networks Telenet, Sprintnet, and Tymenet.

"I always shared my contacts with friends and really anyone I met on the road," Leopold says today, "in the belief that it all came back to me somehow, and then some. PAN was an extension of that philosophy." The sign-up fee was a hefty $250, but Leopold waived the cost in many cases. There was no such thing as unlimited Internet access in those days, and for heavy users, it was not uncommon for online charges to exceed $100 a month. But musicians, engineers, programmers, and marketers in the burgeoning computer-music field signed up in droves, especially when Leopold started offering free memberships to customers of selected companies. I was working with a music software startup at the time, and we were one of the first to jump on the PAN bandwagon. We were the first, in fact, in the person of yours truly, to offer online technical support, both one-on-one and in open forum, and many, many manufacturers followed suit.

Leopold pioneered a lot of online features we take for granted today: He created the first online gateway between Japan and North America, his was the first service to market e-mail-to-fax and fax-to-e-mail conversion (as well as voice-annotated fax), PAN was one of the first private networks to get access to the Internet in 1992, and he even built, in 1992 (before it was strictly legal), what he claims was the world's first Internet-based shopping mall, in conjunction with a music dealer in the Southwest. PAN also had online areas for synth patches, MIDI files, and samples, and the service was the host for the MIDI Manufacturers Association discussion forums and files for many years.

At the 1987 meeting of the Audio Engineering Society, Leopold presented a paper on digital downloading of music, in its various forms. Significantly, he described a way to preview digital audio files: "At 2,400 baud," he recalls, "people weren't keen on spending 12 hours at $12 an hour to download a couple of megs of string sounds, so they previewed them by first downloading a small file from a collection of samples. Samples are digital audio, no matter how you look at it."

Jump forward to October 1996. A company in San Francisco called Intouch Group has applied for a patent on a "network apparatus and method for preview of music products and compilation of market data"—in other words, a way for folks to download snippets of music and for the hosts to keep track of who was doing it. The patent, number 5,963,916, was granted three years later. In the spring of 2000, Intouch Group decided to flex its muscle and sued Amazon.com, Liquid Audio, Listen.com, Entertaindom, and Discovermusic.com for patent infringement because they allow users to download and preview digital music and video. It would seem that as far as Intouch Group is concerned, anyone who sets up a system for downloading previews of any media file involving music is in violation of its patent.

Now it starts to get interesting. Amazon.com itself is embroiled in a patent suit against Barnes & Noble. Amazon has claimed that it owns the patent on "one-click" Internet shopping, and Barnes & Noble has been violating it. Amazon even managed to get an injunction against Barnes & Noble, forcing the company to take that feature off its website. Tim O'Reilly, one of the most respected publishers of books and newsletters about the Internet and an open-source advocate, wrote an open letter to Amazon CEO Jeff Bezos, criticizing the company for its action and calling on Bezos to relinquish rights to the patent. While Bezos didn't agree to that, he did something potentially more intriguing: He teamed up with O'Reilly and a Boston patent lawyer named Charles Cella to create a new Web-based company called *BountyQuest*, whose mission is "market-based patent reform." BountyQuest is looking for people—inventors, engineers, researchers, even graduate students—who might have information germane to a patent fight, but who otherwise might not think of getting involved.

How are they going to find these people? By offering "bounties" of up to $25,000 for information that helps to debunk any of the dubious patents and copyrights on their list. What goes on the list is determined by BountyQuest's corporate clients, who put up the bounty money (and BountyQuest takes a chunk). As of this writing, the list includes a patent on pre-paid cellular service, a patent on window shades that open and close automatically when the light changes, and a copyright on the design and image of a particular-style Japanese pagoda. The clients are usually anonymous, but sometimes it's pretty easy to guess who's looking for information.

Not surprisingly, one of the first bounties the site offered was for prior art that could damage Intouch Group's claim on previewing digital audio. Just nine days after the posting, Perry Leopold, alerted by his lawyer who read about the reward in the *New York Times*, sent a copy of his 1987 paper to BountyQuest. According to the latter's site, "It quickly became apparent that his submission precisely matched all the criteria necessary to make him a winner." And so Perry Leopold became one of the first four winners of a $10,000 prize for showing that he invented something—which he never claimed to own—that someone else was now trying to collect royalties on.

It's been many years since Leopold played his music on the streets and made records in basements. PAN, unlike many of the companies that used its services, was profitable from the word go and still is as a networking resource and Web hosting service. A lawsuit against Rupert Murdoch (who bought Delphi and ran it into the ground) won Leopold a hefty settlement a few years ago. But he could have conceivably made a lot more from the work that he did—with the help of some of the most important figures in the music technology industry in the '80s and early '90s. "Someone recently asked me what other things I might have patented, had I been of a mind to at the time," he says, "and if I had even realized such things were patentable." He then reels off some 18 ideas that most of us take for granted today, but for which he claims he could have "planted the flag."

"But I consider all of these things innovations rather than 'inventions,' *per se*, and thus, to my mind, are not worthy of a patent. It's not like inventing the transistor—now that is an invention!" And think of where we would be today if someone had taken out a defensive patent against the concept before Bell Labs came up with it.

Afterword

BountyQuest unfortunately didn't last very long. By the end of 2002 it was history, due to a number of factors. Tim O'Reilly wrote: "[It] could simply have been an execution issue, or market timing. But it could also have been the fact that the patent mess is a thorny thicket that doesn't lend itself well to penetration by amateurs." But Amazon and Barnes & Noble settled out of court, and since then Amazon hasn't sued anyone over the "1-click" idea.

I wrote more about abusing the legal system for fun and (mostly) profit in my August 2004 column, which you can read in Chapter 43.

Chapter 26

SMPTE-ed Off
Why We Can't Drop Drop-Frame

Preface

Ever since I started working with video in the early '80s, I've tried to figure out why the heck the frame rate we use is such a bizarre number. I attempted to write this piece a number of times since then for a number of magazines, but always gave up when my research hit a dead end. I recently found another writer who was working on the same issue and had a better handle on it than I did, so I asked him for his help. He was happy to do so (although when I first tried to reach him, one of his editors responded by telling me to "Do your own damn research," but he later apologized), and I was able to get the column done. There are still a few things I don't understand about what happened, but at least now I know enough to chalk it up to misinformation, laziness, and stupidity—the way a lot of things at high levels, which affect a great many people at lower levels, get done.

August 2001

Drop or Non-Drop? Pull-Up or Pull-Down? Thirty or 29? And what the heck is 23.976? All questions that strike terror into the hearts of post-production audio engineers, sound designers, and even composers all over this great land. And *only* this great land, if you also include Canada and Japan.

Anyone who works with sound for television has a nightmare story about dealing with this nonsense. I've been collecting them for years. One of my favorites, from the days when analog multitrack ruled the post-production world, involved a studio that striped 29.97 SMPTE on one track and 60Hz Nagra resolve tone on another and then told the synchronizer to lock to both. The hapless two-inch machine bucked like a clothes dryer with a bowling ball inside until the tape snapped.

Even now, in the age of digital, we still can't escape this insanity. I just went through yet another journey through sync hell with a score for a 15-minute film on Beta SP video that was being posted by an expensive transfer house in New York. I told them, "I can give you the music on audio CD, on CD-R as a Pro Tools session, on CD-R as .AIFF or .WAV, on ADAT or DA-88, or on timecode DAT. Which one would you prefer?" The response: "Ordinary DAT will be fine; just tell us at what frame of the film to start the audio." I thought this was great, since among other things, it saved me the cost of renting a timecode DAT machine (and can someone explain why they are still three times the price of a digital 8-track?). *[Yeah, because DAT got killed by the RIAA as a viable format. But let's not go into that here.]*

When I got the videotape back, the audio indeed started right on the money, but it ended about 40 frames after the picture did. For the next three days, the transfer house and I argued about mismatched frame rates. We used up my monthly allotment of cell phone air time and then some arguing about how to make the audio and the video come together. They tried different DAT machines, different video machines, and different operators. They tried transferring it from DAT to another videotape and pulled it up and down and probably in and out as well. Nothing worked. Finally I asked, "Is your DAT machine locked to house sync?" "How do you do that?" came the response. I knew all was lost.

I persuaded them to send back the tapes, and I took them over to a friend with lots of experience in this sort of thing, as well as access to a Beta deck. Everything locked up on our first try. All of the fretting about frame rates was totally unnecessary, and as long as everything in the house was running from the same master clock, there was no problem.

Our equipment certainly has gotten smarter, and for many of us, sync issues are routinely solved by having our computers do the required complex math on-the-fly, thus taking the worry out of it. But there's always that nasty little factor known as "pilot error": The equipment only works right if it's set up and operated correctly. At one point in the process of scoring this particular film, my synchronizer, unbeknownst to me, decided to change its default clock value to 30 fps instead of 29.97 non-drop, and suddenly all of my hits were in the wrong place, and the MIDI tracks weren't agreeing with the audio. That one took a couple of hours to find, not to mention a couple of years off my life. (And when we couldn't get the first transfer to work, I wondered whether or not it was my fault that they were having problems.)

In Europe and most of the rest of the world, of course, they laugh at us. Their video frame rates are nice whole numbers, and they don't understand how we could be so stupid as to make our video run 0.1% off, or why we spend so much time and energy trying to deal with it. (And, in point of fact, the real frame rate is 29.9700267/sec, but who's counting?)

> *In Europe and most of the rest of the world, of course, they laugh at us. Their video frame rates are nice whole numbers.*

Frankly, I don't fully get it either, although it's been explained to me numerous times. I'm not enough of a television engineer (despite my '70s-vintage First Class FCC license, which mostly proves I am good at taking multiple-choice tests, not that I actually know anything) to really understand what it's all about, but I think I get the gist of it. Most people, however, who think they know why the 29.97 frame rate was adopted have it wrong. And it's more than likely that those who do understand it correctly, but believe it was actually necessary, are also wrong. I was first alerted to this by a friend, who at the time was president of a synchronizer company. He pulled me aside at a demonstration of his wares at an NAB show and whispered, "You know, all of this B.S. really wasn't necessary." When I asked him to elaborate, he only said, enigmatically, "Take a look at the documents." That wasn't going to prove to be easy.

The version of the story that most people know is this: In the early days of television, when everything was shades of gray, the standard frame rate in the United States was 30 frames per second. Because each television frame consists of two "fields" of alternating lines, the field rate was 60Hz. When the color standard developed by RCA was adopted in 1953 by the NTSC (which stands for the "National Television Standard Committee," not, as some of our European friends insist, "Never The Same Colour"), it was discovered that the new color signals were susceptible to interference from 60-Hz AC fields, and if there was any difference between the line frequency and the scan rate of the received signal, then it would show up as a visual "beating." But if you altered the field rate enough, then the beating would speed up to the point that it was no longer visible.

A plausible scenario, but unfortunately it simply isn't true. Line-frequency beating never was the problem. And if it were, the cure is worse than the illness: At a field rate of 59.94 Hz, if there really was beating caused by AC-line leakage, then you'd see a bar roll across the screen about every 17 seconds. Not pretty.

The real reason is this: The lower frame/field rate is designed to prevent potential visual beating between the color ("chrominance") subcarrier in the broadcast signal and the audio subcarrier. Why is this a problem, and how does changing the frame rate help? Well, for various esoteric reasons, the color subcarrier frequency in the television signal needs to be modulated onto the picture carrier at 455/2 times the horizontal line frequency. At 30 frames per second, and with 525 horizontal scan lines per frame, this frequency is 15.750 kHz, which means that the color subcarrier would have to be at 3.583125 MHz. The sound sub-carrier (as established on the first monochrome TV systems) is at 4.5 MHz. If the two sub-carriers were to interfere and beat against each other, then the 916.875-kHz difference might be visible; and, in fact, according to one report presented to the NTSC, it was visible in *some* monochrome sets at the time, under *some* conditions. Because backward compatibility was a major consideration for the NTSC (and it was the major reason the CBS-developed system was abandoned in favor of the more finicky RCA system), this was a problem.

A close look at the technical documents and the committee proceedings around this point seem to show that the problem never really existed.

This report, written by an obscure General Electric engineer, went on to say that if the difference signal happened to be an odd multiple of one-half the scan rate, then this beating would be reduced. If the frame rate was dropped 0.10001%, then the scanning frequency would be 15.734264 kHz, the chrominance subcarrier would be 3.579545 MHz, and the beat product (if there was one) would be 920.455 kHz, which is very, very close to the 117th multiple of half the scan rate and therefore would-n't be visible. Did you get all that?

But a close look at the technical documents and the committee proceedings around this point seem to show that the problem never really existed. According to Mark Schubin, longtime technical editor and columnist for *Videography* magazine (to whom I am indebted for leading me to some excellent primary sources in dealing with this issue), there should not have been any cause for concern. "Remember, the sound carrier is FM," he told me recently. "The frequency swings and is never in its nominal position anyway, and so any beating wouldn't be steady, and therefore not visible."

Another video engineering expert, Tim Stoffel, says that a higher chrominance subcarrier frequency could have been used (495/2 times the scanning frequency) and the audio subcarrier also increased slightly to make the difference signal fall on the right multiple of the scan rate, and despite the change, he says, "most [black and white] sets would have tolerated it at the time." However, the TV set manufacturers' association "screamed bloody murder," and so the decision was made to leave the carriers where they were (or pretty close) and change the horizontal scanning frequency, and consequently the frame rate, instead. This didn't make the transmitter manufacturers or the stations very happy, says Stoffel, because, "It meant much expensive alterations to transmission equipment, as the AC line could no longer be used as a frequency reference for sync!"

An engineer who was there at the beginning, Rollie Zavada of Eastman Kodak, diplomatically calls the decision to change the frame rate "debatable." Other sources say that the very first generation of color sets, and also the black-and-white sets that were made by the time the color standard was adopted, had good enough filters on the audio section so that leakage between the subcarriers was simply not an issue.

The decision to lower the frame rate was probably, according to Schubin, a political one more than anything else. "I've talked to people who were there at the time," he says, "who also think it wasn't necessary, but it was several people's entrenched position [to change the frame rate], so others went along with it, because otherwise the standard might be blocked forever. RCA," who after all had invented the thing, "was apparently among those not in favor of 59.94."

"Thus," as he wrote in his April 1993 magazine column, "all of the problems of NTSC's 29.97 frame-per-second rate may have been caused because 'some' 1952 TV sets 'may' have had a problem sometimes," and changing the carrier frequencies "was said to reduce (not eliminate) the problem." In the same column, he points to another potential problem, which was thought to be serious at the time: interference between stations located some geographical distance apart but on the same channel. It might have been solved by a similar "interleaving" of frequencies, but it turned out not to be an issue at all.

While it's depressing and frustrating to realize that changing the frame rate to a near-irrational number probably wasn't necessary, what's sadder still is to realize that apparently we're never going to get away from it, although we recently had the opportunity to do so. We are, after all, on the cusp of a new age of television: Digital TV and HDTV (which are not to be confused with each other, although the second is a subset of the first) are already on the air. The original HDTV standards (and there are many) all specified a frame rate of 30 fps.

Progressive, interleaved, 1080, 720: Whatever variation you looked at, there was no mention of 29.97 anywhere in the proposals. But the HDTV programs now in production and going out over the air are running at—you guessed it—29.97 frames per second. The FCC mandate for HDTV is incredibly vague and has over the years been increasingly dictated by the broadcasters themselves, which means networks and stations have been free to do just about anything they want with it. And dropping the frame rate is something that came easily.

Mark Schubin puts it this way: "The colossal broadcast infrastructure is 59.94 Hz in all NTSC countries. Using 60 Hz would have meant dropping a field [from broadcast programs] every 16.67 seconds. Although devices were built that could deal with that, they were considered too cumbersome. So in the U.S., HD, like NTSC, is now 59.94 Hz based." And it is likely—nay, certain—to remain so. What's that line about the sins of the fathers?

Paul D. Lehrman is still operating at his original frame rate, more or less.

Chapter 27

RIP, Douglas Adams

August 2001/part II

Along with many others, I was saddened recently to hear of the death of Douglas Adams, author of *Hitchhiker's Guide to the Galaxy* and other brilliant books, essays, radio and television scripts, computer games, etc., not to mention the first human to realize that the answer to the meaning of life, the universe, and everything else was "42"—and now all we had to do was figure out what the question was.

I knew Adams slightly, having met him at a couple of conferences and book signings and having communicated with him in the early days of computer music on the PAN network, where his was an active (and very funny) voice. He was an avid amateur musician, and his use of MIDI sequencers and samplers found its way into his "Dirk Gently, Holistic Detective" books. He owned some 30 guitars (all left-handed), and on his 42nd birthday joined his good friend David Gilmour and the rest of Pink Floyd onstage to play "Dark Side of the Moon." He was a Macintosh fanatic from day one, and I was very proud that, for a while, I was listed on the masthead of one of the Mac magazines under the same "contributing editors" heading as he. But his true contribution to our industry and indeed the world was as a visionary and an augur, although he would never allow such serious labels to be applied to himself.

He envisioned how the technologies that we develop will soon be so ingrained into the culture that we won't even notice them, and he also saw how silly many of them might end up being. He wrote about computers trying to be "helpful" that end up putting their owners into life-threatening situations and created the character of a brilliant, super-strong robot with chronic depression (something Adams himself struggled with). Despite all of our advances, he wrote, human behavior is never going to change very much: There will still be plenty of greed, arrogance, selfishness, and just plain stupidity to go around. In both his fiction and his nonfiction, he provided a perspective that showed how destructively short-sighted so many of us are when it comes to the long-range survival of the planet and its life-forms (including us). And he inserted into that often deadly serious genre, science fiction, some of the wittiest and most memorable satirical writing since Jonathan Swift.

I love the primitive planet that is being colonized by marketing directors who can't invent the wheel until someone does research to find out what color it should be.

As the writings of Jack Kerouac limned the parameters of the Beat generation, and the writings of Abbie Hoffman and Paul Krassner codified the language of the Freak generation, so Adams' writings gave philosophy, vocabulary, and attitude to the high-tech generation of the '80s. If you haven't read the five books of the *Hitchhiker's* trilogy (yes, five) in a while, do go back and take a look at them. They're just as funny, and just as prescient, as ever. (I love the band that's so loud that the sound crew has to be 400 miles away in orbit, and the primitive planet that is being colonized by marketing directors who can't invent the wheel until someone does research to find out what color it should be.) And you'll find that a lot of the terms we use to talk about today's technology were in fact invented—although never without satirical purpose—by him.

Adams died the way one of his characters would, totally unexpectedly and with more than a little irony: He suffered a fatal heart attack while lifting weights at a gym in Santa Barbara. He was 49. So long, Douglas, and thanks for all—of everything.

Chapter 28

Living on Borrowed Culture
Things Ain't What They
Used to Be—Are They?

Preface

This is one of those columns that, once I got the inspiration for it, wrote itself. The lack of originality in today's pop music I find depressing, if not horrifying. Every generation deserves its own pop culture, but exactly what that is today, in terms of music, is very hard to define. I am constantly struck by how many students I encounter who are enamored of the music of *my* student years and have no use for their own generation's, while those students who *do* like current pop music have no idea why they like it, or what it's about, or where its origins lie.

September 2001

In one recent week, I could have seen the following shows within 10 miles of my home:

A Beatles tribute band at one of the hottest clubs in town, which sold out two nights in the first half-hour after tickets went on sale.

"Bob Dylan" nights starring the cream of local folk and rock performers at two different venues.

A band that plays nothing but the repertoire of John McLaughlin's early '70s Mahavishnu Orchestra.

A folk festival featuring the offspring of Arlo Guthrie, Harry Chapin, and Loudon Wainwright.

A group of sons and brothers of the original Parliament/Funkadelic who call themselves "Funk-Kin."

Stage musicals based on songs by Ellie Greenwich ("Leader of the Pack," etc.) and (God help us) ABBA.

And a sold-out concert by Robert Plant, who performed not only Led Zeppelin tunes but also songs by The Youngbloods, Donovan, Moby Grape, Tim Rose, and Arthur Lee & Love.

Not long ago, I walked into one of the funkiest little record stores in one of the hippest areas of Boston. You can't even get through the door of this shop unless you have at least five pieces of metal in your face (I passed because I'm old), and coming out of the speakers, I heard the Blues Project's 1966 "Flute Thing."

The latest Arbitron book shows that in my metropolitan broadcast market, three of the Top 10 radio stations are oldies or "classic hits" stations that differentiate themselves from each other by only the finest of hairs. One won't play anything recorded after 1972, another won't play anything post-1979, and the other won't play anything from before 1966. On a local public station, the most popular new show is called "Highway 61 Revisited," which features obscure and not-so-obscure folk-rock from the psychedelic era. The announcer barely has time to talk between all the phone requests.

What's going on here?

That "Flute Thing" I heard wasn't the Blues Project, it was the Beastie Boys sampling the Blues Project (and according to co-composer Al Kooper, making more money for him than the original ever did). It's one of thousands of old songs and riffs that are getting new life thanks to sampling, the Internet, and Napster, sometimes to the benefit of the original creator and more often not. The music of today doesn't just sound like the music of my youth, in an awful lot of cases, it *is* the music of my youth.

There are many possible explanations for why this is happening. One is, of course, the "baby-boom bulge." As that big bump on the population charts of people born in the 15 or so years after the end of World War II becomes firmly ensconced in middle age, we are taking our music with us, and—especially as cool new media come on the scene—we'll keep shelling out for reissues, new/old material, and compilations of our favorite artists from our formative years.

A university colleague of mine has a theory about this, which says that people most strongly identify with the music they hear between the ages of 13 and 19, and that identification stays with them forever. So it seems that the market for Jimi Hendrix, the Four Seasons, Three Dog Night, and other icons of the '60s and '70s won't die out until we all do.

Another explanation is that the '60s through the early '80s were the peak years for real "mass" media. After that, broadcasting became so fragmented that there were no longer any points of reference that everyone understood, no songs that everybody knew. A track from Radiohead, Ben Folds Five, or REM behind a commercial geared at a large general audience doesn't have nearly the recognition power—even among those who were born long after the songs came out—of tunes like "Everyday People" (Toyota), "Rocket Man" (AT&T), "Can't Explain" (Ford), "Our House" (Chase Bank Mortgage), "Brown Sugar" (Pepsi), and perhaps the most recognizable of all great sell-outs, The Beatles' "Revolution" in that series of Nike ads.

As media companies have become larger in size and fewer in number, the audience has become ever more Balkanized. Because so many radio stations within a given market are owned by the same corporate overlord, they are geared toward very specific demographics in terms of gender, age, race, and economic status, with each station delivering a particular section of the audience to the mothership. When I was growing up in New York, there were three stations that every kid listened to: the WMCA Good Guys, Bob Ingram and Cousin Brucie on WABC, and Murray the K on 1010-WINS. There were heated arguments in the schoolyard over which station was better, but the music they played was exactly the same. But today, if you listen to only one station, whether it's urban, new country, hot adult contemporary, alternative rock, or any of the 40 other categories in Arbitron's ratings book, you will never hear what anyone else is playing.

Television, too, is looking less at drawing huge numbers and more at targeting particular groups. Witness the rise of the WB and UPN networks, which are making plenty of money despite ratings that just a few years ago would have put their programming executives out on the street. Another indication of this is the fact that *All In the Family* had four times the audience of CBS's biggest hit today.

Yet another explanation lies in the fact that the '60s (which we all know actually lasted from JFK's assassination to Nixon's resignation) were—let's face it—a hard act to follow. A whole lot of new stuff happened then that we're still imitating and still trying to understand. Do you think obscene lyrics on major label releases are a recent phenomenon? Check out the MC5's "Kick Out the Jams, Motherfuckers!" on Elektra in 1969. When did angry urban blacks start making records warning white folks to watch their asses? At least as far back as 1970, when the Last Poets arrived on the scene. Is Marilyn Manson the original, misogynistic, death-obsessed, heavy-metal transvestite? No, that would be Alice Cooper.

Outrageous packaging? How about the cover of "Sticky Fingers" by the Rolling Stones, designed by Andy Warhol and featuring a real pants zipper, or Jefferson Airplane's "Bark," which came wrapped in a brown paper bag? Bands who only know three chords? The Ramones. Bands who only know how to make noise? The Stooges. Trance music? Kraftwerk. World music? The Incredible String Band. Bands with degenerate lifestyles? Too many to list.

Bands solely manufactured for television? The Monkees. Boy-toy bands? The Bay City Rollers. Navel-gazing chanteuses? Joni Mitchell and Laura Nyro. Navel-baring pubescent faux virgins simulating orgasms to slick, overproduced, cookie-cutter dance rock? Well, maybe there weren't any of those.

So, after a decade in which all these things were done for the first time, what do you do for an encore? A lot of the stuff was pretty awful, but a surprising amount of it was really good and still stands up after all these years, which is hard to say for more recent pop music. I can't imagine anybody caring much about Limp Bizkit or Blink-182 ten years down the road, any more than they care about Bananarama or Frankie Goes to Hollywood today.

One more thing that's contributing to the continuing barrage of "classic" hits on the airwaves—especially behind commercials—is the greed factor among aging rockers. Don't worry, I'm not about to slam Paul McCartney (one of the richest men in Britain) and his mates (also not too badly off) for selling their aforementioned ambivalent political anthem to one of the world's most notorious employers of sweatshop labor. That honor goes to Michael Jackson, who controls The Beatles' catalog, and who doesn't need the money either. *[Well, he does now, which is why he recently sold off The Beatles' songs.]*

When a reporter asked Bob Dylan about whether he saw anything wrong with licensing perhaps his best-known anti-establishment song to a large financial institution, he laughed and said, "I don't have any problem with that kind of thing." Mick Jagger made a big show of objecting to his manager's selling "Brown Sugar" to Pepsico but then turned right around and gave "Start Me Up" to Bill Gates for a mere $3 million. (And there's absolutely no truth to the rumor that when Windows 2000 came out, Microsoft tried to lock up the rights to "19th Nervous Breakdown.")

Surprisingly few artists have managed to resist the temptation of commercial bucks, among them Bruce Springsteen (who turned down $15 million from Chrysler), Tom Waits, and Neil Young, who has been very vocal in his opposition to the practice.

But the most significant reason why yesterday's music culture is so prevalent today lies in a full-page ad I saw in my local paper not long ago. It announced, "The most incredible music machine since the accordion!" Who was the advertiser? Gateway computers. For a thousand bucks and an Internet connection, you can have all the music you've ever wanted and do anything you want with it.

Technology has simply made it too easy and too tempting to steal from the past. And stealing is now considered an art form. Today's underground musical heroes are not singer/songwriters, or thrash-metal bands, or guitar heroes—they're remixers, rappers, and DJs, who build their fame by taking other people's creations, slicing and dicing them, ranting and chanting on top of them, or stringing them together. From the first sampled James Brown scream to the wholesale lifting of entire songs, many of today's "artists" are simply putting together musical jigsaw puzzles, rather than creating anything original. Yes, there is craft in this kind of composition, but it pales when compared to the true act of making music.

From the first sampled James Brown scream to the wholesale lifting of entire songs, many of today's "artists" are simply putting together musical jigsaw puzzles, rather than creating anything original.

Sample-based music is highly dependent on the fact that music from our collective past packs an emotional punch—even just a few seconds of a tune that once meant something to us is enough to trigger a response that instantly recalls the feelings we experienced when we first heard it. So in many ways, it's the emotional content of the individual pieces that we're responding to when we hear a remix, a rap, or a DJ's set, not what the person making the sound at that moment is doing. But what's even worse is that by ripping these musical moments out of their original context, we remove their original meaning for the next generation of listeners.

The result, it can be argued, is that today we live in a kind of cultural vacuum. Jaron Lanier, the technologist who is credited with inventing the term "virtual reality" and is himself an accomplished musician, wrote at the end of the 1990s: "Pop style stopped happening. This is the first period of the century without a distinctive new pop musical style....Artists of all kinds now work in digital tools. They cut and paste from the whole of human creation. In the distant future, when movies are made depicting the '90s, the only way filmmakers will be able to indicate the period is by putting vintage computers on the set."

Technological limitations have always had a lot to do with how styles and trends develop, and the lack of limitations can be stultifying.

Technological limitations have always had a lot to do with how styles and trends develop, he said, and the lack of limitations can be stultifying. "The sound of The Beatles was the sound of what you could do if you pushed a '60s-era recording studio absolutely as far as it could go. Artists long for limitations; excessive freedom casts us into a vacuum. We are vulnerable to becoming jittery and aimless, like children with nothing to do. That is why narrow simulations of 'vintage' music synthesizers are hotter right now than more flexible and powerful machines."

Now, I'm not saying that new artists have to throw out what they've heard over the past 40 years—on the contrary. All new art draws on the past: It gives us points of reference so that we can understand it. The Beatles could not have done what they did without Chuck Berry, Little Richard, Phil Spector, and Motown before them. Bruce Springsteen's music makes reference—sometimes overtly—to Roy Orbison, Woody Guthrie, and The Shirelles, to name but three. But Springsteen doesn't take an old Roy Orbison record and play it from the stage, layering breakbeats and vocals over it. Those records may play over and over in his mind, but it's how he assimilates, expands, and goes beyond his influences to create genuinely new art that makes him brilliant.

Technology has also removed the physicality of playing an instrument, as well as the joys and difficulties of working with a group, from the process of making music. Fingering a guitar, blowing into a flute, plucking a bass, the simple act of singing—these are all things that people who just work with computers and turntables never experience. Those who do more mainstream music but depend on sample CDs for every beat and lick are missing these things, too. Computers make music too easy: What's the point of putting a band together of real people, with all their egos, bad habits, and varying levels of musicianship, when you can "play" in your bedroom with virtual versions of Steve Vai, Will Lee, and Clyde Stubblefield?

So do I have an answer to this? I do: It's called music education. Music education puts the basic tools for creating musical art into the hands of children, who will be inspired by those tools and make them their own. By itself, a saxophone does nothing: It has to be played. And just that simple act of blowing into a tube and making a sound, and then another and another, and continuously expanding the vocabulary and quality of sounds that can be made, transforms a kid in a way that downloading the latest Britney Spears or Snoop Dogg can never approach.

Technology has also removed the physicality of playing an instrument, as well as the joys and difficulties of working with a group, from the process of making music.

Sadly, the state of music education in schools over the past couple of decades has become pretty miserable. Years of budget abuse in the name of tax-cutting, standardized testing, "back-to-basics," and other frauds have resulted in many school systems severely rolling back music programs, if not axing them completely. At the same time, there has been a tremendous emphasis on technology, giving students the message that computers can do everything. So, naturally, kids are drawn to computer-based music manipulation tools that make it easy. But they depend on other people's creativity for source material.

School bands, choruses, and orchestras are by far the best way to teach children about music history and repertoire that they'll never hear on the radio or even on Napster. And the feeling of participation in a joint creative effort that is dependent on hands, feet, lips, fingers, and tongues will internalize the music in a way that just listening to it or fooling around with it on a computer can't.

Parents have a role in this, too. If you play an instrument, even if you haven't pulled it out in a while, dust it off and share what you can do with it with your children. Teach them how to play an instrument, the same as yours or another, and then play together. Sing with them: teach them how to harmonize with you and with each other.

Children who experience first-hand the joy of making music through physical expression, without a computer as an intermediary, will learn how to develop their own ways of creating meaningful music. Ultimately, they'll have far less need for someone else to dictate to them what's good, and they'll have no need at all to steal. They will have the tools to become the real musicians—the innovators, not the imitators—of the next generation.

Afterword

I revisited the concept of making music without any knowledge, skill, or talent in my April 2002 column (see Chapter 31): an interview with my friend Grumpmeier's son, who had become a big star. And I think I got a little nasty.

Chapter 29

Hardware, Software, Wetware

Preface

In between the time I wrote the previous chapter and the time I wrote this one, a horrific event occurred. I wrote a column in response to the events of September 11, 2001 (actually, it was in response to the *response* to the attacks) that was published in December 2001 but I decided for various personal and practical reasons not to include it in this book. If you would like to see it, it's online at www.insideraudio.com.

The ramifications of 9/11 were felt in the music and audio industries immediately—for one thing, the AES convention scheduled for early October in New York was postponed, for the first time ever, because the Javits Center was still being used for emergency operations—and have, of course, continued to be felt ever since in many ways, some of which I wrote about, either directly or obliquely, in columns since then. One of the more immediate concerns was whether Americans, now apparently faced with the first collective physical threat they had experienced in over 50 years, were still interested in "entertainment" at all. Certainly the New York-based advertising community took an enormous hit in the wave of the attacks, and many agencies, producers, and studios never recovered. For many others in our business, there was an almost overwhelming fear of disruption, dislocation, and impending irrelevance.

This column, while acknowledging that fear, tried to look ahead and focus on more tangible issues. As it turned out, those fears eventually subsided, the industry realigned and (most) people went back to work, and the issues we had been dealing with prior to 9/11 became priorities once again.

January 2002

As we turn over the calendar to another New Year, we in the audio industry find ourselves asking the age-old question: Will we still have a job 12 months from now?

Actually, most of us *don't* usually ask ourselves that question, which is what makes this year so strange. But because we are living in the greatest era of uncertainty in about six decades, no one can really forecast what's going to happen. Let's try to hang on to a positive thought. Even hunkered down in bacteria-proof underground shelters, people are going to need to be entertained, and they will be, even if it means using car batteries to run their brand-new surround DVD systems.

So this month, let's not look at the gloomy side. With the Winter NAMM show right around the corner, let's instead ask ourselves that upbeat question that will be on the lips of everyone gathering in Anaheim: Is hardware dead?

Well, maybe that's not terribly upbeat for a lot of people—like the folks who make hardware—but it certainly seems to be getting a lot of attention. There are legions of people, the majority of them under 25, who think that using hardware for synthesizing, recording, processing, and mixing music is so, well, so '90s. They've never known a time when computers weren't fast and reliable enough to produce and manipulate untold numbers of tracks of super high-fidelity audio in real time. They're looking at us old fogies and our racks of processing gear and wondering why we need all that iron when they can do everything they can even conceive of on a $700 motherboard with a $200 sound card and $49.95 worth of software.

The other day, one of my students was describing his home studio to me, and when I asked him what kind of synths he had, he replied, "Oh, I don't have anything like that. It's all software. And I don't play the piano very well, so I never bothered to get a keyboard. Hardware's dead, anyway." A friend of mine, who also teaches college-level music courses, gave a lecture recently to a gathering of the local audio community on "Better Living Through Software Synthesis." "It's viable, it works," he says. "Do we need a box to do DSP or a special chip to do synthesis? Why bother?" Why indeed?

As much as in any field, computers have become "anything and everything machines" in the audio world. Do you want to do location recording? Get a laptop and a PCM interface card and put it in a corner of that road case with your mics, preamps, and headphones. Do you do film scoring or sound effects? Install a software sampler or two and a virtual rack of soft synths and plug-ins on your desktop machine, link them to timecode *[or even better, import the visuals as QuickTime movies, which was just becoming practical when I wrote this]*, and mix it all down right to your hard disk; when you're done, burn it onto a CD-ROM and send it to the Avid house. Is your specialty dance records or club mixes? All you need is a bunch of CDs of grooves and beats, looping software, and a vocal mic. How about processing, sweetening, mixing, and mastering other artists' recordings? All possible without ever turning away from your monitor.

In many ways, a software-based studio makes a lot of economic sense. After all, could you throw out an entire hardware studio that's only two years old and replace it with the next generation of faster, slicker gear—and end up spending less than $1,000? If everything's in software, that's not only easy, it's more or less mandatory. (Of course, the disadvantage is that you then have to reinstall all your software and spend a few sleepless nights fretting over whether or not your old programs will work on the new platform. Can you imagine having to do all *that* with a couple of racks full of hardware?)

But somehow, there are people out there who aren't getting the message—like the ones who send me those glossy 150-plus-page music and pro audio catalogs every month. Despite my student's pronouncement, lots of areas of the hardware business are still going quite strong, thank you very much.

Roland's disk-based, all-in-one studios have been that company's most successful new product line in years, and now the other usual suspects—Fostex, Yamaha, Tascam, Korg, and Alesis—have jumped on board. Despite the flood of software synths, the "knobs" craze on hardware synthesizers shows no sign of abating, as musicians rediscover the joys of real-time control and learn that there are better ways to design sounds than tweaking parameters on a crowded LCD, or even on a 20-inch monitor.

DJ gear is going like gangbusters: CD players that emulate vinyl turntables, groove boxes that emulate the crummy drum machines of the early '80s, and nasty high-Q filters you can operate by waving your hands around in the air are flying out dealers' doors. It's an interesting indicator of how the hardware world is evolving by considering that Alesis, which owned the project-studio multitrack tape-deck market for the better part of a decade, last year somehow managed to go bankrupt and had to be rescued by Numark, a company that has made its money in the vinyl-spinning scene over many years.

Guitars, basses, and amps are still big moneymakers, and the market for vintage and pseudo-vintage axes is as healthy as ever. There are so many different variations on Strats, Teles, Les Pauls, 335s, and Twin Reverbs that the mind boggles. (Although I still can't imagine that a $1,500 guitar with some rock god's signature on it actually plays twice as nicely as the $750 version from the same manufacturer.) On the other hand, the sounds of the guitars are becoming less distinguishable from each other, as more manufacturers pick up on the "modeling" idea, so that any combination of guitar and amp can sound like any other combination you want. (I have my doubts about this technology, though, especially for live performance. I was at a demo/concert of one manufacturer's electronic instruments recently, and the guitarist, trying to emulate a stack of Marshalls with a little stage amp, sounded as if he was miles away in a completely different hall from the rest of the band. Maybe it was the mix, or maybe it was a latency problem, but it wasn't in the least convincing.)

For those of us who want to use all of our fingers and other appendages to work with sound, hardware is still rather necessary. What all of the devices I just listed have in common is that they offer familiar physical interfaces: knobs, faders, strings, frets, turntables, and so on. As we all have discovered during the past few years, moving a mouse around is a lousy way to create music, or edit or mix audio. And so we've seen the rise of "control surfaces" that hook up to our computer-based workstations through serial or USB connectors and emulate the mixing and editing consoles we are used to.

For those of us who want to use all of our fingers and other appendages to work with sound, hardware is still rather necessary.

It's not just a gimmick that these devices present a familiar face. Despite our generally positive attitude toward new technologies, musicians and audio professionals tend to be a fairly entrenched lot, and old habits die hard. We learn to use certain types of systems—in the case of musicians, we spend years practicing them—and develop our working style and rhythm on them, and we aren't that interested in abandoning them overnight, even if there are new ways that are immediately and obviously superior. While we embrace new technology, we want it to work like the old, and manufacturers that try to force us out of old habits are taking a serious risk.

Examples of this are all over the place. In the film world, the widespread use of digital media at the dubbing stage took an amazingly long time to happen, even though the magnetic-dubbing technology they could replace should have been put out to pasture years before. It wasn't until digital dubbers were designed to closely emulate magnetic ones—to become their "analogues," as it were—that they were able to gain acceptance.

There's a similar situation in radio: Endless-loop cartridge machines, one of the worst-sounding and most finicky technologies I've ever had the displeasure of working with (I spent two years cleaning and aligning the suckers, so I know!), are still in use in many places—you can often hear the "ka-chunk" of the cart deck when the announcer forgets to mute his mic—despite the fact that digital audio systems and servers can do the job much better, not to mention that they don't need cleaning. *[Five years after this column appeared, thankfully, they're pretty much gone.]* Many digital systems, in fact, emulate the old cart machines and have front-panel slots for removable disks, even though with today's high-capacity hard disks and high-speed interconnects, they are hardly necessary.

But the role of hardware is not nearly the same as it has been traditionally. Perhaps the major change that computers have wrought, in terms of how hardware is used in the audio world, can be described as a kind of paradigm shift: Form no longer needs to follow function. Thanks to the explosion of computing power in cheap, mass-produced chips and motherboards and the almost total removal of analog electronics from the signal path, what a device looks like no longer needs to depend on what it does. Barriers between different functions—this box here is supposed to do one thing, while that box there does something else—are no longer necessary, or even desirable. Compressors and equalizers don't have to be in racks. Synthesizers don't have to have keyboards. Dubbers don't have to use tape. And guitars don't have to sound like themselves.

Instead, the physical form of a tool can be anything we want it to be. A tool's form may be defined as a result of its function—a hard-disk recorder can still look like a tape deck—or it may be completely independent. Alesis' new *airFX* and *airSynth* look like trackballs from the helm of the Starship Enterprise, but you don't touch them—they change their synthesis and DSP parameters based on the relative x-, y-, and z-coordinates of your hand. It's a far cry from knobs and keys. Yamaha's *WX* wind controllers resemble mutant soprano saxophones, but not only can you make any kind of sound you like with them, you can also play them polyphonically—which heretofore only Roland Kirk could do (and he needed two instruments). With new touch-sensitive fabrics such as those developed by Tactex, which are able to generate data in three dimensions, any kind of surface can be turned into any kind of controller.

Familiar tools can also be "extended"—given new tasks to do that are similar to their traditional tasks, but with a wider sonic or functional palette. One of the most interesting new concepts I've heard about involves, believe it or not, turntables. It's a kind of double-reverse: The turntables aren't doing what turntables normally do (in the post-analog era, that is), i.e., play records in weird ways. Instead, they are acting as controllers for a digital system that, well, plays records in weird ways.

You might have read about it in last month's issue of *Mix*'s sister publication, *Remix*. A couple of clever DJs have figured out a way to have access to hundreds of records without having to carry around heavy crates of vinyl. They show up with only two vinyl discs and a laptop. The discs have nothing but SMPTE timecode recorded on them. They feed the output of the turntables through a converter into the computer, which is loaded up with audio files (.WAV or MP3) and some custom software. They tell the software which files they want to play and start spinning the platters. The timecode on each turntable tells the computer where to start playing each file, how fast, and in which direction. The DJs can skip around, go faster and slower and backward and forward, just as if they were playing vinyl records—but when they want to change records, instead of having to swap vinyl discs, they simply call up a new file on the computer.

Right now, the system, which is being produced in limited numbers, has a pretty steep price tag: around $3,000. But by the time you read this, Stanton, the turntable and cartridge manufacturer, will have a production version that promises to cost a lot less. After that, who knows—maybe someone will come out with a "virtual" turntable and laser-equipped tone arm that doesn't need any records at all. And then they can put some touch sensors in them so that if you bang on them, they make a sound like a stylus skipping....

As the functions of our tools and the forms they take continue to disengage from each other, we can expect to see some radical new designs in human/machine interfaces. Some of these will be brilliant, some will be awful, and some no doubt will be both. With any luck, the present trend in software front-end design, in which every program resembles either the console of a spaceship or a nightmarish, oozing, primordial Salvador Dali landscape, will abate, and new design aesthetics that are more inspiring and less self-conscious will prevail.

But however technology develops, it's a safe bet that reports of the death of hardware will continue to be, as Mark Twain might have put it, premature. As long as we have hands, fingers, and feet, we will need to be able to hold, push, turn, press, squeeze, and stomp on our tools if they are going to feel like they're ours. Until, of course, purely synaptic-driven interfaces (with appropriate neural feedback) are perfected. At that point, all bets are off.

Paul D. Lehrman knows that next year's model will be different. Just don't ask him how.

> *As long as we have hands, fingers, and feet, we will need to be able to hold, push, turn, press, squeeze, and stomp on our tools if they are going to feel like they're ours.*

Afterword

Since this column appeared, user interfaces have become one of the hottest areas of research in music, in both the academic and the manufacturing worlds. A whole community has in fact grown up around them and since 2000 has even had its own annual conference. In 2005, I went to that conference, and my report appears in Chapter 50.

Chapter 30

I Ought to Have My Head Examined

Adventures in Otological Existentialism

Preface

My columns on Repetitive Strain Injuries (in Chapter 21, August/September 2000) were inspired by learning about other people's problems, but this one was about a bad thing that happened to me. For a musician or audio professional, the prospect of having something going wrong with your hearing is pretty frightening. And as music continues to get louder, hearing problems among our industry and our listeners are going to get worse. This story, at least, has a relatively happy ending.

March 2002

What do you call it when you hear noises that aren't really there? No, I'm not talking about what happens when you drink too much or when all that LSD you swallowed all those years ago flashes back at you. I'm talking about the whistles, rings, whooshing sounds, and other aural artifacts that are associated with a head injury, high blood pressure, taking certain medications (like aspirin), or hearing damage. It's the condition known as "tinnitus," which doctors like to pronounce "TIN-uh-tis," while the rest of the world says "tin-EYE-tis." With tinnitus, the ears seem to be picking up sounds that don't exist externally. It takes many forms and has many, many causes. About a year ago, all of a sudden I got very interested in it, because all of a sudden I got it. And I also got pretty scared.

For most of my post-adolescent life, I was quite sure I had escaped the fate of so many of my fellow '60s and '70s rock 'n' rollers, managing to avoid any damage to my hearing from years of playing in and listening to bands that were, let's face it, too damn loud. These days, at the levels I typically listen to music, both for pleasure and for business, it seems unlikely that I'm going to do anything further to screw up my ears. The bulk of my studio work is film scoring, and I usually work at relatively quiet levels because I figure that's the way it's going to end up anyway when the mixing guys are done with it.

But about a year ago, I had a chance to do a score for an old silent film, and a pretty raucous score it was. I spent several days on it, monitoring at uncharacteristically loud levels. One day, after a few hours of sitting in one position, my back started to hurt a bit, so I did what I always do under such circumstances: I got up, took a long stretch, and walked over to the bathroom to get a couple of ibuprofen. That night, before I went to bed, I popped a couple more of the pills, just to make sure I wouldn't have trouble sitting through the next day's session.

Imagine my surprise when I awoke in the morning and discovered my ears were ringing. Well, actually they weren't ringing, but something inside of them seemed to be. It sounded like a sine wave generator up at around 8 kHz or so, and it was in both ears and quite constant. Imagine my further surprise when the ringing lasted all day and into the next. Whenever this had happened to me before—usually because I was at a really long, loud concert without any ear protection, something I haven't done in years—it never lasted more than a few hours, and never overnight.

Was it the ibuprofen, which, like aspirin, can cause a ringing in the ears, or was it the unusually high levels that I'd been listening to? Or was it the combination of the two or some other medications I had been taking? But the real question, the one lurking underneath all the others, was: Had I done something to myself that had permanently damaged my hearing?

> *Had I done something to myself that had permanently damaged my hearing?*

Let's step back a minute. Like most folks past 30, especially men, my hearing is not as acute as it once was. When I was working in the electronic music lab in college, I would often test myself, seeing how high I could get the old Heathkit oscillator to go (without looking at the dial) before I couldn't hear it any longer. It was usually, I was proud to see when I turned around, up around 22 to 23 kHz. When I worked in radio a few years later, I was the only guy in the place who could hear the 20-kHz track on the Magnetic Reference Laboratory Reproducer Test Tape. And for a long time, I could walk into any room—heck, any house—and tell you if a television set was on, because I could hear the 15,750-Hz whistle that the flyback transformer made.

But as we get older, our high-frequency hearing drops off. It's normally an extremely gradual thing, so we don't notice it. One day in the '80s, during a period when I was reviewing a lot of high-end recordings for consumer magazines, I was checking out my system with a test CD and discovered, to my dismay, that I couldn't hear the 20kHz band. A few years later, I realized that the only way I could tell if a TV set in a room was on was to look at it. And for some reason, I can't hear my wife as well as I used to when she shouts from her office on one end of the house to my office on the other end. I don't think it's because our house is growing bigger.

Fortunately, I really haven't had too much trouble resigning myself to the fact that, like sliding head-first into home, diving from the 5-meter board, or hitchhiking up the East Coast, hearing 20 kHz was just one of those things I was never going to do again. My hearing *perception*, on the other hand, seems to have improved over the years, which makes sense. Although being able to hear high frequencies is certainly an important part of it, aural perception is very much a product of knowledge, smarts, and experience, which is why there are plenty of guys well into their '60s who are still great mixing engineers. Maybe I can't hear the sampling clock on a CD player, but I can still tell you who's playing the wrong note in a 20-piece big band, or at what bar the drummer is coming in just a hair late, or exactly where to set the mid-band EQ to bring the vocal up out of the mud. And I think I can do all of these things quite a bit better than when I was younger.

So you can see why I might be terrified when the sudden noise in my ears wouldn't go away. After the second day, I called my primary care doctor, and he said it was probably the fault of the ibuprofen and the noise would go away in a few days. After a week, when it was still going strong, I called another doctor, a pharmacologist. She said it probably wasn't the drugs but the result of all that loud music I'd been listening to, and if I was lucky, it would go away in a few more days.

But it didn't. After two weeks, I was beginning to get really nervous. I started stuffing my ears with cotton whenever we went to hear any amplified music, which made me feel worse, because the music sounded so awful and the ringing actually seemed louder. Then I started plugging my ears whenever I got into the car. A fire engine would go by, and I'd put my head down between my knees as if I were expecting a bomb to drop. After a month, my wife was ready to kick me out of the house.

I sent an e-mail to the Hearing Education and Awareness Foundation in Los Angeles, a group that specializes in treating musicians with hearing problems and also happens to be one of the organizations that benefit from the TEC Awards banquet and other Mix Foundation activities. It has a great website (hearnet.org) that lists affiliated hearing specialists all over the country. Unfortunately, there's no one on that list less than 100 miles from me. Fortunately, Kathy Peck, one of the two founders of the organization, e-mailed me back the same day and gave me the name of an audiologist at the Massachusetts Eye & Ear Infirmary, which (except in rush hour) is only about 15 minutes from my house.

I got an appointment right away and met Dr. Christopher Halpin, a pleasant fellow around my age who, as it turned out, was also an electronic music freak when he was in college. In between feeding me sine waves, recorded speech, and various other types of noises through a pair of heavy headphones, he and I had a grand time talking about the bad old days of drifting oscillators, finicky 16-step sequencers, lousy speakers, and roaring EMT plate reverbs.

Chris gave me a complete workup, and when it was over, he handed me a sheet of paper with the results. "Hearing is normal through 3 kHz," it read, with "a very mild symmetric sensory loss above that." "Typical for a man your age," he said. "You're right in the middle of the range."

The graph he plotted for me, with 1 kHz at zero, went down 15 dB at 4 kHz, 20 dB at 8 kHz, and 50 dB at 12.5 kHz. That seemed like quite a drop-off, and nobody I know would tolerate a microphone that did that, but he said it was perfectly normal for human ears.

> *"Tinnitus is not an ear thing at all—it's a phantom percept."*

"What about above 12.5k?" I asked him. "Oh, we don't measure that," he replied, "because there's no way for us to specify a sound pressure level as a reference point. At those frequencies, the waveforms get affected by the construction of the ear itself: You can get standing waves as small as the ear canal. Since everyone's ears are different, there's no way to tell objectively what's going on." This took me rather by surprise, but I had more important issues to deal with.

Like, what the heck was causing my tinnitus? Chris' reply was that, while he couldn't tell what was causing it, he was pretty certain that it was not caused by my recent studio sessions. "If you've been listening for years and years at loud levels, I'd say that could be a factor, but one loud mixdown session isn't going to do it. Something like that might cause a temporary threshold loss and maybe a ringing, which recovers in a couple of days." Decades worth of high SPLs, he explained, could damage the cilia, the frequency-sensitive, hair-like nerve endings that serve as our personal D/A converters; they literally break off. But that wasn't my problem. If I did have any hearing loss, and it wasn't at all clear if I did, it was more than likely due to genetic factors. My grandfather, after all, was stone deaf by the time he was 50. "But none of these factors are strongly related to tinnitus," Chris said as he shook his head. "Really, tinnitus is not an ear thing at all—it's a phantom percept."

After I gave him a hug, he suggested that if I wanted to learn more about tinnitus and maybe pin down the cause, I should make an appointment in the same hospital with Dr. Robert Levine, an otoneurologist ("oto" means "ear"), who is recognized as one of the world's tinnitus experts. Before I left the clinic, I bought a pair of musician's earplugs for $25 that he recommended. Now I didn't have to carry cotton balls around with me, and I could go into a club and still hear the music without worrying about frying my cilia.

Dr. Levine's office, to my dismay, told me he only saw patients one day a week, and he was booked solid for six months. I made an appointment anyway and told the secretary that if anything opened up (not during rush hour), she should call me. Three weeks later, after someone had canceled, I was sitting in Dr. Levine's office. And I found out why he was so hard to see: He ended up spending almost two hours with me.

Dr. Levine is a researcher as much as a practitioner, and his mission is to find out how tinnitus affects people. He asked me all about my ethnic background (which was almost identical to his, it turned out—we could be cousins), medications I was taking, past injuries and operations, family medical history, the nature of the sound I was hearing, and dozens of other questions. I noticed that his office seemed to be rather noisy, and I looked around for the source of the sound: There was an object on the floor, about the size and shape of a small birthday cake, which was emitting a sound like rushing water. It was a sound masker—an acoustic dither generator. He saw my glance and smiled. "I have it, too," he said.

He catalogued some of the many causes of tinnitus. Besides exposure to loud sound, there are ear infections, wax buildup, benign tumors, drugs (a common sedative, alprazolam, can, in different people, be either the cause or the cure for the condition), and stress: physical, biochemical, environmental, or emotional. He moved my head, arms, and hands into various odd positions and asked me whether the sound changed. He was delighted when I reported that sometimes the pitch of the sound changed and that sometimes the level changed. Apparently, very few of his patients can tell (or articulate) the difference between the two.

I was delighted when I discovered that if I locked my fingers together in front of me and tried to pull my hands apart, the intensity of the sound would diminish noticeably. Not that I could walk around all day like that, but it meant I could feel that I had at least a tiny bit of control over the thing.

So, after two hours, what did this leading scientific authority have to say about what was causing my problem? Dr. Levine shrugged and said that he really had no idea. The good news was, he agreed with Dr. Halpin that it didn't have anything to do with the sound levels I had been subjecting myself to. The bad news was that although he thought it might go away by itself, "I wouldn't want to bet on it." He suggested getting a noise-making machine like his or keeping music going in the background all the time. And he did have one optimistic thing to say: "In three months, you'll hardly notice it."

He was right. I still have the noise in my head a lot of the time, but I really only notice it occasionally, and it rarely bothers me. (Although, at the moment, because I'm thinking about it, it's pretty loud.) But the whole experience of learning about tinnitus and what audiologists know and don't know has actually brought to my mind a whole new set of questions. Is research in audiology so far behind what we in the audio profession consider to be current state-of-the-art that we know more about how frequencies in the top octave of our range are supposed to behave than audiologists do? What happens if you look at it the other way around? How important is it really that our signal chains be dead flat up to 20 kHz, because most of us can't hear anywhere near that high, and audiologists can't measure how we respond to those frequencies? And what about the world above 20k? What is its role in the way we perceive music and sound—if it has any?

In the meantime, keep your levels down and your ears protected.

I've started pursuing these questions, and I've been coming up with some surprising answers, which I'll tell you about in a future column *[May 2002, Chapter 32]*. In the meantime, keep your levels down and your ears protected.

Afterword

This one hit a nerve, so to speak: I got e-mails from literally dozens of readers after this column appeared, including a couple of old friends I hadn't heard from in a long time, telling me about their experiences with tinnitus, some of which were quite a bit scarier than mine. A lot of them were afraid to go to doctors because they feared being told they had brought it on themselves, so they were grateful for my conclusions. I hope if that's your situation, you won't hesitate to get yourself checked out.

As for my tinnitus, it hasn't changed. I generally listen to soft music first thing in the morning, to keep myself from being overly aware of it, and then I'm usually able to forget about it the rest of the day.

Chapter 31

Jack Davis

Son of Grumpmeier

Preface

This is one of my personal favorite columns. It manages to get in digs at just about every aspect of the record industry that I hate and packs more jokes per square inch than anything else I've ever written. And it apparently resonated with readers: One, a rather famous composer of my acquaintance, wrote, "Excellent! It has the tang of sarcasm and loathing of the topic at hand. I believe firmly that the best parody is not done from love but anger, and this one seethes beneath the surface. I like that in a take-off."

April 2002

Once in a great while, I get the chance to talk to and write about a rising young musical star like the one in this month's interview. He has stunned and thrilled the music industry with his revolutionary approach to making hit records. His five triple-Platinum CDs have dominated the HippityHop and Alternative Geek Dance charts on *Bullbored* magazine for the past year, and his award-winning videos have been in heavy rotation on all of the major cable music channels, including Groove24/7, Moshvision, and GaKk-TV. He has been profiled on public television's extremely serious *Great Pretensions*. And he's been nominated for 14 Grammy®©™ Awards, most recently Best Classical Producer, for his brilliant "original" composition *Beethoven Bytes*.

I have known this young man since he was merely a glint in his father's eye (which was immediately followed by a look of disgust in his mother's). His father is none other than my old friend and sometime nemesis, P.T. Grumpmeier, audio engineer, producer, raconteur, and world-class cheapskate, a gentleman whose rantings are well known to loyal readers of this column. Both of you.

P.T. Grumpmeier Jr., whom his father affectionately refers to as "Hey you," is only 19 yet erudite beyond his years. He started out in the business very young, when his crib was used by his father as a bass-drum weight in his father's studio, when his (the son's) mother wasn't watching. This early exposure to extreme SPLs of low-frequency sound no doubt helped mold his (the son's) later passion for extremely loud, beat-oriented music, with not much going on above 3k.

The young man's big break as a solo *artiste* came at his best friend's Bar Mitzvah, when the hired DJ fell (or perhaps was pushed) into the champagne fountain. Young Grumpmeier immediately took over the turntables and brought the entire crowd to its feet with a breathtaking journey through time, space, and the animal kingdom, starting with the "Bunny Hop" and "The Alley Cat," then "Muskrat Love" and "Rocky Raccoon," followed by "A Horse with No Name," "Piggies," and finally roaring into "Who Let the Dogs Out," all the while rapping spontaneously about the 12- and 13-year-old "ho's" and "bitches" on the dance floor. The father of one of those girls, a VP of A&R for mega-label Dreque Records (a subsidiary of Getouttamaway Communications, owner of more than 5,000 radio stations and several small former Soviet Republics), signed him on the spot to an eight-figure multi-album contract.

With the label's backing, the young man saw his albums, released under the name "DJ Grump Jr." on vinyl and 8-track tape only ("I consider the sound of the tape mechanism going 'clunk' every few minutes to be an integral part of my art," he told *Rolling Boulder* at the time), rocket to the top of the charts within minutes of their release and sometimes before. But the artist was unhappy about the label's treatment of him ("They tried to pay me in XFL stock," he later told *Money or Your Life* magazine), and so he hired famed litigator and family friend Johnnie Cochrane to get him out of his contract.

Free of his obligations to the corporate empire, the teenage superstar formed his own totally independent record label, ReGurge Records, which is distributed by AOL/Time/Warner/Reprise/Atlantic/Nonesuch/CNN/Headline News. He dropped the "DJ" moniker ("That's so, like, last year," he told *Behind the Music* last year) and—following the example of celebrated artists like Bush, Bjork, Beck, Jewel, Joe, Moby, moe., Charo, Cher, Sleepy, Dopey, Doc, Pink, and Floyd—adopted the single-word *nom d'artiste* "Grump."

Let's talk about **Beethoven Bytes.** *How did you come up with the inspiration for this incredible record?*

M'ol' man had this, like, pile of 78 plattahs down in the cella', ya seen 'em, right? Really heavy mutha*****s? So, like this one day I was flipping them out in the hood, like a fris-bee, numsayin'? And ma homey goes, "Yo, there's a ittle-bitty pitcher of a dawg on this one." So I'm like, "Whassup widdat?" And ma homey goes, "Hey, y'all down with ani-mals, let's hear what this sucka sounds like!"

You grew up in Scarsdale. Why do you talk like that?

Oh, I'm sorry. There was a guy here from *MTV News* this morning, and they really like it when you sound "street," especially if you're white. Guess I got into it.

So you played the 78s. Did you have trouble finding something to play them on?

My father never throws anything away, you know? And my mother hates that because we got a whole basement and two garages full of old electronic junk, but my dad says it'll all come back some day as "vintage" shit, and we can sell it for big bucks on eBay. But me and my friends used to play in it, climbing all around gettin' wires in our ears and stuff. And I remembered there was this Howdy Doody & Clarabelle record player in there, down on the bottom, and I dug it out, and it still worked, sort of. I mean, it sent off a few sparks, but the turntable moved. Anyway, it turns out that record we were flipping was a sym-phony by this guy Beethoven, conducted by this wild dude named Toscavetskakowski. Or something like that. And I just really dug it.

> *"All of the people on it are dead, and the composer's dead, and the producer's dead, and if there are any companies left that still own any of the rights, they've been bought up by AOL, so no problem."*

So, of course, you sampled it. Were there any legal issues involved?

Nah, Johnnie says that all of the people on it are dead, and the composer's dead, and the producer's dead, and if there are any companies left that still own any of the rights, they've been bought up by AOL, so no problem.

What else did you use for sources?

My dad also had these old Morse Code records, you know, lots of beeps? And I thought that was cool, 'cause I could use them to set up a kind of rhythm I could rap off of. 'Course, I had to chop them up into four-bar loops. The amazing thing about those records is that you can play them backward and forward, and they sound exactly the same!

Besides your own voice, there's a weird voice in the background that's just numbers, over and over again, but you can barely make it out. What's that voice doing?

My engineer hooked up an old harmonica contact mic to a telephone, and I punched in numbers on the phone at random, and we'd record the voice that says "this number is not in service" and the number we'd dialed. I figured out how to get non-working numbers all over the world, so we got samples in a bunch of different languages.

But the samples we got just weren't enough in-your-face. So we called the phone company and found the dude who could tell us who was the model for that voice. Turns out it was this housewife somewhere in Nebraska, so we flew her to Minneapolis to Prince's studio, stuck a pair of U47s in front of her, and got a 192-kHz stereo digital satellite line hooked up to here.

Then how did you process it?

Well, we wanted it to be really grungy, like it was coming through a cheap phone in a thunderstorm. So we needed an old analog filter. I read somewhere that to get the true sound of an analog filter cutting off at 3 kHz, you have to use a sampling frequency of 3 MegaHertz. So I hired this guy who had been laid off from Intel, and he hot-clocked my SoundSmasher card to run at 3 Megs, and then he wrote some software to do the filtering and added all sorts of other crap. It took him a month, but when he was finished, it sounded just like the real thing.

> *"I read somewhere that to get the true sound of an analog filter cutting off at 3 kHz, you have to use a sampling frequency of 3 MegaHertz."*

Why didn't you just buy a capacitor and a choke at an electronics store and do it analog?

Are you nuts, dude? That would mean going through at least two A-to-D converters. Do you know what those things do to the sound? They'd ruin it! No way, José. I don't compromise my integrity like that. But I gotta tell ya, it was the most expensive part of producing the record.

Because you needed so much storage space, or because the tech guy you hired was so expensive?

Oh, no—it turned out that the lady from Nebraska was union, and she was supposed to get a residual on every copy of the record we made. Well, Johnnie made her an offer she couldn't refuse, and she was cool, but it was a shitload of money just for a few samples. It really sucks that some people would take advantage of a creative artist like that.

Speaking of vocal sound, what do you use to get yours?

There was one of those Wollensak tape recorders in the garage with the mic that looks like a big silver bullet, you know? I'd been playing with that since I was about three, and I love the way the mic makes my voice sound, all thin and crackly. So, I had my tech build a balancing transformer for it, and I bought one of those really expensive Camelot tube preamps. I turned the input on the preamp way down and cranked the output, so I could pick up all that hum and tube noise. I'm down with how it sounds now, but I think it will be even better once the tube burns in for a while, or especially if it cracks.

I understand your studio was designed by Bau:wau:haus, and it's also pretty unusual.

Yeah, it was actually my folks' bomb shelter, which they dug back in the '60s. My dad was thinking of using it as a family mausoleum, but I got my lawyers on it, and they found out that the county health department wouldn't let him. So he gave it to me. It was already soundproofed, 'cause the ceiling is 12 feet underground, and it was air conditioned, too, although most of the Freon leaked out a long time ago, and you can't get that stuff any more, so it doesn't work all that good. It can get pretty warm.

What's your main gear?

There's a customized DAW—I forget what it's called, I think it was named after a city. Everything's 32-bit, 192kHz. I mean, the more data, the more accurate and pristine the sound, right? And I think what I'm doing is really, like, bleeding-edge, so I want to make sure my system captures everything. I want 20 years from now people to listen to my stuff and have them say, "Yeah, he knew his shit."

On the analog side, I have a Knave board, which was rebuilt by Humbert Knave himself, on account of he owed my dad a favor, and it sounds just incredible. I got a Strudel 2-inch 8-track, which I run at 60 ips with Dolby SR. And my Dad's Wollensak, which I use a lot 'cause the studio's only wired for 10 amps, and when I turn the Knave and the Strudel on, the lights go out. Which is a bummer when you're 12 feet underground.

How do you monitor?

Hamanahaha SN-100s, of course. I own 40 pairs, 'cause they're not making them anymore, and I blow them up a lot. Most people put tissue paper in front of the tweeter, but I found out they sound better with Saran Wrap. 'Course, it changes the balance, so I also tape a couple of layers of bubble-pak over the woofer. They rule.

What do you use to make your beats and loops? Are you Mac or Windows?

Neither. I don't like composing with software. You know, using a mouse is so restrictive and dehumanizing, and it prevents you from getting those expressive things that make a song musically meaningful.

I have a Valiant drum machine from 1974, and that's my main rig. It's got a great vibe, and the sounds are awesome—analog, of course. I also get all the new groove machines that Kong and Be-muse and those other companies put out 'cause I'm a beta-tester and endorser for them. So whatever I've got lying around when I'm working, that's what I use.

Did you build a MIDI interface for that drum machine, so you could sync everything to it?

Oh, no, man! MIDI sucks! Everybody knows that. You get timing problems and all kinds of slop, and it just destroys the groove. I do *really* tight beats, and the rhythms and the tempos have to be *right on*. So I just make sure I push all the start buttons at the same time, and that works great.

How about mastering? Do you use SACD or HDCD?

No, I just take the output from the DAW and run it through a couple of those real heavy FuzzyFaces from the '60s and then into a MiniDisc recorder. If you turn the distortion knob on the FuzzyFace up to about 5 o'clock, it sounds really awesome. But finding two that matched for stereo was a pain.

You mean in terms of signal quality and distortion characteristics?

No, I mean the color. 'Cause people would paint them all psychedelic, and I never liked that. I wanted to make sure the two I had were absolutely identical, that original dark brown, or I just wouldn't feel right mastering with them. I was thinking of sending my tech off to Russia to get them custom manufactured, but then a guy in New York called me and said he was cleaning out a back room at that famous studio in Greenwich Village, the one with the river in the basement? And he found all these FuzzyFaces that had been used to hold down the sandbags when it floods. So, I bought all of 'em. They even had the original batteries.

How do you like your new distributor, AOL?

I'm down with them. They're putting one of my cuts on those CDs that they send out in the mail to get people to sign up, ya know? That's 14 million units right there, and the RIAA says they all count. So I'm getting the first Uranium record that's ever been awarded. That should go pretty good with the decor in my studio. They're also taking off that little "N" with the comets flying around on the Netscape Navigator 7 and putting my picture there instead.

How do you feel about Napster and downloading services like that?

Oh, man, that shit's going to *kill* the music industry. If everyone gets their music for free, how are artists going to be motivated to create? There's going to be no one doing anything original any more. Everything's just going to be a rip-off. And that's going to be really sad.

"I've got a new record I'm doing of duets with Elvis. Johnnie and my other lawyers are working with Col. Sanders to get all the permissions."

What's next for Grump?

Well, I've got a new record I'm doing of duets with Elvis. Johnnie and my other lawyers are working with Col. Sanders to get all the permissions.

You mean Col. Parker. But he's dead.

Whatever, dude! That's why I got lawyers, to take care of those kind of shit details! But what I really want to do is more classical. You know, what Billy Joel did, but instead of writing like some dead guy, I'll just sample the stuff, like I did with *Beethoven Bytes*. That way, instead of imitating the dude, I'm actually using his actual *music*. You know, I studied piano, too, when I was a kid, and my mom has been bugging me to start taking lessons again.

Do you think you will?

Naah, I'm much too busy making records to spend any time learning anything about music.

Paul Lehrman is not feeling well.

Chapter 32

The World Above 20kHz
What Are We Missing?

Preface

The debate over sampling rates is one of the longest running and hardest-to-solve issues in professional audio. While I think there's a case to be made for longer word lengths in A-to-D conversion systems, I remain skeptical about the need for sampling rates over 48 kHz, and certainly over 96 kHz. It's actually one of the few industry controversies where Stephen St. Croix and I found ourselves in complete agreement. People whose ears I trust tell me they can hear a difference with higher sample rates, but they can't tell me exactly what it is or even, in some cases, whether it's better. Meanwhile, the bits pile up...

May 2002

Like most of us, when I was a kid, I suffered from a bad case of technolust. Among my favorite reading matter were catalogs from Allied Radio, the monthly *Popular Electronics*, and the publications of the American Radio Relay League, the organization of ham radio operators, of which I was a member—although at the age of nine, a not-very-accomplished one. One of my favorite books of theirs was a slim volume called *The World Above 50 MHz*, which talked in vague terms about how the hams of the future might be able to take advantage of what were then considered "trash" radio frequencies. Although these high frequencies (or very short wavelengths, as we used to refer to them) might be usable for things like commercial television and FM radio broadcasts, they were not much good for any sort of long-distance communication, which is what hams lived for. Novice ham operators (like me) were allowed to operate voice transmitters way up there around 144 MHz, where they wouldn't bother anyone. Much more valuable to experienced hams was the spectrum between 2 MHz and 30 MHz, since signals at those "shortwave" frequencies could bounce off the ionosphere and travel around the world. Above 50 MHz was basically of interest only to "experimenters."

Since those days, the VHF, UHF, SHF, and EHF ("S" for Super and "E" for Extra, in case you were wondering) bands have, of course, been used for a stunning variety of purposes and are now being viciously fought over by a plethora of different wireless services, both real and imagined. With the advent of the communications satellite, shortwave radio went more or less the way of the dinosaur. Congested spectra made signals that did not bounce but instead beamed right through the ionosphere much more valuable.

Today, we all talk nonchalantly about 700-MHz digital television broadcasts, 900-MHz wireless phones, 1.9-GHz digital cell phones, and Ku-band satellites, which use the 13-18 GHz band. In Europe, research and field testing is going on into frequencies as high as 60 GHz—which would have a great future in point-to-point transmissions were it not that they tend to be disrupted by things like snow.

But you don't want to hear me talk about radio, you want me to talk (if at all) about audio. Just as the radio amateurs of yore considered 50 MHz the top of the usable spectrum, audio engineers and enthusiasts have long regarded the 20-kHz upper limit of human hearing as an inviolate parameter, and signals above that simply didn't need to be dealt with. In the days of analog, this proved to be very helpful since the physics of audio transducers and media—the tape and tape heads, microphones, and speakers—made recording ultrasonic frequencies a difficult proposition indeed: Above about 10 kHz, for every tiny increase in high-frequency response, there was an enormous increase in cost.

Which is not to say that the world above 20 kHz has been completely ignored. Phonograph records have long been—at least in theory—capable of playing higher frequencies, and in fact the ill-fated '70s quadrophonic LP system known as "CD-4" (for "Compatible Discrete," not the other kind of CD) took advantage of this fact by putting the back/front difference signal onto a 30 kHz carrier, which meant that signals as high as 45 kHz were being cut into the grooves. (Even though they did tend to disappear after a few listenings.)

And there have always been laboratory instruments—both transducers and recorders—capable of handling ultrasonic frequencies. Some of these, like B&K microphones for example, have trickled their way down into the professional audio world.

In analog audio, the top-end response of a system generally sort of fades away gracefully the higher you go, not unlike the noise floor. In digital, however, because of the need for a fixed clock frequency, there is an absolute limit—the Nyquist frequency—above which signals cannot be processed, period. Ever since the first commercial digital systems—PCM-F1, DAT, and CD—put a brick wall up in front of any frequencies over 20 kHz, voices have been grumbling that this really wasn't high enough. Many of the grumblings were objections to the phase distortion that the low-pass filters engendered below 20k, but some were about the fact that we were losing "detail" in the higher frequencies, which could never be recovered, and that in order to achieve true "high fidelity," our audio systems needed to stretch further into the ultrasonic realm.

In recent years, as the cost of bandwidth and digital storage has plummeted, those grumblings have become a deafening roar. Much of the pro audio community now regards ordinary CDs (which were once described, lest we forget, as "Pure, perfect sound, forever") with something approaching contempt, while even sub-$1,000 home recording systems are boasting about the superiority of their 96-kHz sampling rates, so that those of us with plain old 44.1- and 48-kHz hardware are dejectedly feeling left behind.

But do we really need these higher sampling rates? Or is the whole thing, as some say, just a marketing scam to shame us into junking perfectly good equipment and buying all new stuff? Or is it perhaps something that we audio pros have latched onto to make us feel superior to the great unwashed millions, who are forced to listen to lo-fi audio that tops out at a paltry 20k?

Well, the question of whether we need to do this actually has to be broken down into three questions. First, can we hear sounds above 20 kHz? If not, do ultrasonic frequencies somehow influence sounds that we *can* hear? And if they don't, then is there something about higher sampling rates that makes the stuff in the audible band sound better? I'm going to deal with the first two parts this month.

An audiologist and former musician says that there's no way to measure a human's response to sounds above 13 kHz or so.

There's no question that there is plenty of sound energy far above 20 kHz in the musical and natural worlds. For some striking evidence of this, take a look at a paper (www.cco.caltech.edu/~boyk/spectra/spectra.htm) by James Boyk, a pianist and electrical engineer at CalTech, which shows, among other things, that the spectrum of a trumpet with a Harmon mute slopes down linearly and smoothly from 2 kHz all the way to *102* kHz—and probably beyond, but that's where his spectrum analyzer quits.

But do those frequencies actually reach us in some way? As I wrote here a couple of months ago, Dr. Chris Halpin, an audiologist at Massachusetts Eye and Ear Infirmary and an erstwhile electronic musician, says that there's no way to measure a human's response to sounds above 13 kHz or so. It doesn't mean we don't hear sounds up there; it just means that they have not figured out any objective means of quantifying our sensitivity to them—or lack of it. Whatever it is, however, it's awfully small. According to the tests Dr. Halpin gave me,

233

for example, my sensitivity at 10 kHz is down some 60 dB and plummeting. If the curve were to continue, then my sensitivity at 20 kHz would be -120 dB, which is probably comfortably below the noise floor of my nervous system.

When anything above about 12 kHz tickles the cilia deep in our inner ears, it registers in our brains as "high," and that's about all the information we get from it.

Interestingly, it seems we also can't differentiate between dissimilar frequencies in that range. When anything above about 12 kHz tickles the cilia deep in our inner ears, it registers in our brains as "high," and that's about all the information we get from it. It might appear, then, that as long as there is *something* going on in the top octave, it sounds perfectly okay to us.

But surely someone has done some hard research to see if we respond to frequencies above 20k, haven't they? Well, a search of the literature actually turns up one—count 'em, one—formal study in this area. A paper presented at the AES convention in October 1991 by five gentlemen from the National Institute of Multimedia Education in Japan is entitled "High-Frequency Sound Above the Audible Range Affects Brain Electric Activity and Sound Perception." (It's preprint number 3207 and available from the AES at www.aes.org.) It's quite a fascinating document, with some pretty weird results.

The researchers stuck electrodes on the scalps of a rather small sample of people—ten men and six women, ages 20 to 34—and played them the recorded sounds of a Gamelan orchestra, a source that is very rich in high harmonics. The subjects heard the recordings through two systems: one with response out to 40 kHz and the other with a low-pass filter at 26 kHz.

In A/B testing, the subjects could not hear any difference between the two systems. However, the researchers found that six of the 16 subjects showed a marked increase in brain electrical activity, which started anywhere from 20 to 80 seconds after the music started, when they were listening to the 40-kHz system. Six of the subjects showed a slight increase in brain activity, while the remaining four showed a slight *decrease*. There were a couple of other tests in the paper, whose results are equally curious but hardly more compelling. Among the remarkable conclusions that the researchers make from this experiment are not only that we do indeed respond to sounds above 26 kHz, but also that our standard method of real-time A/B evaluation of audio systems is not valid!

Interesting stuff, but a little out there, I think you'd agree. And it would seem we'd have a lot of company, since the results haven't been confirmed or followed up, as far as I know, in the 11 years since the experiment. So maybe I'm missing something, but I think that it's a bit much for the entire audio industry to reinvent itself based on this one, light-years-from-definitive study. It reminds me of that infamous paper that equated a person's ability to resist pressure on his outstretched arm with whether he was hearing digital or analog source material. Whatever happened to that guy? Perhaps he's working up an experiment to prove that subjects listening to 96-kHz digital audio on their Walkmans can run a marathon 73 seconds faster than those listening to 44.1-kHz audio!

There are less-formal experiments that purport to show that we can hear above 20 kHz, and perhaps the best known of these is the one that Rupert Neve—for whom I have almost unlimited admiration, although I think he's completely wrong on this—does. He plays his audience a 10-kHz sine wave and then a 10-kHz square wave, and everyone in the place agrees: They sound different. Therefore, he concludes, since the lowest harmonic above the fundamental in a square wave is the third, we are hearing 30 kHz!

Of course, this is, as the English say, "tosh," and many before me have pointed this out. There are a lot of reasons why we can hear the difference between those two tones, none of which have anything to do with ultrasonic sensitivity. One is simply that the energy of a square wave is higher than a sine wave at the same nominal amplitude, so the square wave sounds louder. Another is that any transformers in the signal path, unless they are exquisitely designed and constructed for passing such high frequencies, will introduce slewing and intermodulation distortion from the square wave—not only from the third harmonic, but from all the odd harmonics above it—that will have products well inside the audible range. And if somehow a perfectly amplified 10-kHz square wave *were* to make it all the way to the speakers, the speakers would create their own distortion, which would be quite different from the distortion a sine wave would make.

You can easily prove this for yourself by running a 10-kHz sine and a 10-kHz square through a guitar amp. You will readily hear the difference, even though the amp probably doesn't have much response at all above about 6 kHz. My friend Leon Janikian, a longtime audio engineer and a professor at Northeastern University, re-creates Neve's experiment for his classes but with an additional step. He plays the two signals from oscillators and then records those same signals onto a 44.1-kHz DAT machine and plays them back. Then he asks the group if they can discern any difference between the first pair and the second. Regardless of the order in which he plays them, the students can easily differentiate between the sine wave and the square wave, but they can't hear any difference between the pre-DAT and the post-DAT signals. Since the DAT isn't recording anything at all above 21 kHz, it's obviously *not* energy at 30 kHz that the students (whose high-frequency response is probably a lot better than Leon's) are hearing.

So it seems like the audio world above 20 kHz, unlike the radio world of my youth above 50 MHz, will probably not turn out to be very important. As I said, there may be other reasons why high sampling rates are helpful, and they are very much worth discussing, but they're not because your old technology, and mine, is missing anything.

Paul Lehrman is at long last beginning to get over his technolust. Thanks to Richard Elen and David Moulton for their contributions and suggestions.

Afterword

While we're on the subject of high-frequency hearing, here is some fascinating additional material on the subject that I wrote in my August 2005 column.

After I wrote my March 2002 column about tinnitus and age-associated hearing loss, I was contacted by a company called EarQ Technologies (not to be confused with the hearing-aid company called "EarQ"), who were selling an audiological self-testing system. The company claimed that the system could be used to custom-tailor a room's frequency response to an individual's own threshold-response curve, so that the result would be, from the individual's perspective, "flat." Their slogan was "Fit your mix to your ears." The system had received a favorable review in *Mix* and other plaudits from the musical and scientific communities, but these write-ups were strictly about how the product made it easy for people to monitor their hearing loss without having to go to an audiological clinic. They didn't address the issue of whether it could fix one's mixes.

I don't want to beat a dead horse, as the system is now out of production, but I do still get asked about it periodically. So I think it's worth sharing what I've been able to find out about the concept. According to Dr. Halpin, the EarQ system *can't* work that way. "An elevated threshold for a tone does not imply abnormal loudness above the threshold for that frequency," he writes. "In sensory hearing loss from age or exposure to noise, the apparent loudness does not shift with thresholds. You just lose the quiet tones.

"The loudness grows abnormally fast from threshold back to normal perception so that a loud sound, like 90dB SPL, for someone with normal hearing is the same loudness for someone with a threshold loss of as much as 60 dB. This is known as the 'recruitment' phenomenon and also happens in other sensory systems.

"To adjust a room or mix EQ based on thresholds is not a valid concept in sensory hearing loss. Instead, you should be thinking that when it sounds good to you, it will sound good to the audience."

But you already knew that.

Chapter 33

Like a Broken Record
The RIAA Tries to Outrun the Hackers

Preface

I'm one of those people who thinks that no one has done more to destroy the recording industry than the record companies. There are lots of reasons why record sales are down (although the figures aren't nearly as dire as they would have you think), but the RIAA only wants to focus on one—file-swapping—and in the process has done untold damage to the concept of copyright. This column describes some of the more dubious efforts the major labels made to thwart copying—which, like all others, were not at all necessary and were even less effective.

June 2002

Remember the saying, "You sound like a broken record"? You used it when you wanted to shut someone up who was saying the same thing over and over again. Its origin, of course, is from the (first) days of vinyl. When the stylus encountered a crack, a scratch or a piece of dirt, it would get knocked into the previous groove, so the same little bit of music would play forever. Today, of course, that would be considered an artistic choice, but in the days when the preferred mode of music playback was strictly linear, it was highly annoying.

Nothing sounds more like a broken record these days than the record industry itself.

Ironically, nothing sounds more like a broken record these days than the record industry itself. Like a needle stuck in a particularly irksome groove, the major labels are once again howling that record sales are being killed by piracy. If it all sounds very familiar, it's because we've been here before—often. When analog cassettes became a major delivery medium, when DAT machines were struggling their way onto the market (and failing), and when Napster was getting a million hits a minute, the record companies were making the same dire prediction.

This is not to deny that *something* is going wrong in the record biz. The revenues of the five major labels that control the RIAA (and it recently almost became four, but for reasons that are about to become obvious, nobody seemed to be interested in buying EMI) were off last year, for the first time in a long time. *[Not long after it did become four, when Sony bought BMG.]* But to put the entire blame on piracy ignores the fact that we really did have a recession, particularly in the music-loving high-tech sector; plus, we were targets of terrorist attacks, both real and imagined, which put a severe damper on commerce in general, especially of the leisure kind.

And let's not forget that minor accounting problem EMI had when it sacked Mariah Carey. Barely nine months after giving her the fattest recording contract in history, it bought her out, taking a $49 million hit. Then it cut 1,800 jobs to cover it and announced it was pulling its stake out of music retailer HMV. You gotta love this business.

Armed with dubious surveys that point to billions of dollars being lost because of teenagers downloading Limp Bizkit tracks from Napster and its more lawsuit-proof descendants Kazaa and Gnutella, the music conglomerates late last year took a bold step toward protecting their bottom line by introducing a new business paradigm: They started to put out—you knew this was coming, right?—broken records.

Several million compact discs have been issued with some kind of "protection" designed to prevent their audio from being extracted by computer CD-ROM drives. Four companies have developed copy-protection technologies for audio CDs, and some of them are very clever, but they all share some rather serious problems. One is that the discs don't seem to work on a fairly significant number of audio CD and DVD players, as well as Sony Playstations. Another is that a lot of computer drives, especially DVD-ROMs, have no trouble reading them. And a third is that, according to the folks who own the trademark, these discs are no longer CDs.

Most of the action so far in this brave new world of musical copy-proofing has been in Europe. A spokesperson for one developer, Midbar Tech, which is based in Israel, says that this is because European nations are ahead of the United States in terms of both writing copyright laws and enforcing them—and in terms of the incidence of piracy. Something like 15 million of the discs have found their way into stores so far. Avex, Japan's largest indie label, recently signed on as the first label in that country to use protection, while in the States, as I write, there are only two encoded CDs available: the soundtrack from the movie *The Fast and the Furious* and Charley Pride's *Tribute to Jim Reeves*. The former uses Midbar's Cactus Data Shield, and the latter uses MediaCloq technology from Phoenix-based SunnComm. Another developer is Macrovision, which you may remember from its vertical-drive-suppressing, copy-protection system for videotapes.

So how do they work? Well, they can't suppress a sync signal on an audio CD because there ain't none—PCM digital audio is self-clocking. Nor can they notch out a piece of the audio spectrum, the way some old and unsuccessful systems tried to do, because that would be painfully audible and consumers wouldn't stand for it. And they can't take advantage of the SCMS-bit idea that killed the domestic DAT market, because there are far too many computers out there that wouldn't know a SCMS bit if it (pardon the expression) bit them on the ATA.

The systems use one or more of three basic techniques. One, they deliberately put errors in the audio data, based on the idea that audio players, with their relatively robust error correction, are much more tolerant of media errors than data drives are. Two, they scramble the directory and the header (.cda) files so that the computer looking to rip the audio can't find the tracks. Three, they put non-audio data tracks on what are supposed to be audio discs, with the idea that computers will glom onto the data tracks and not see the audio tracks. One radio engineer reports that on a Michael Jackson promo CD released to stations last September, "The TOC tells a Windows PC that the disc has a Multisession/Hybrid CD-ROM portion. But that section of the disc is either corrupted or has a piece of code that the computer can't read. And so the CD just spins in the drive."

The SunnComm system goes further: If you try to extract the audio from it, it makes your computer go online to the label's site, where you can purchase a license to download the song you're trying to hear! So buying it once on CD apparently isn't enough: If you want to make a dub of it, you're going to have to pay twice.

One thing all these schemes have in common is that they have made Philips, which co-owns the Compact Disc patent with Sony, absolutely furious. Philips is telling those who do this to a CD that they may not print the "Compact Disc" logo on it, because it doesn't conform to their specs—it's broken. Meanwhile, Philips (which, until recently, owned PolyGram Records) is also saying that its next generation of CD burners will be able to both read and write all of the protected formats, which means no one's protected CDs will be very protected.

Another concern of Philips and many others is that pressing a CD that contains deliberate errors will shorten its life span. Yes, CD players have error-correction, but they are designed to deal with ordinary wear and the occasional scratch or piece of dirt. If the system is already working hard to play a new, clean disc, it may take very few additional errors caused by normal problems before the disc becomes unplayable.

Do these schemes work? Sort of. Not being able to pass up a challenge, hackers all over the world have been trying to break them since the first protected discs came out, and they've managed to do just that, generally without much trouble. One journalist found that an ordinary computer DVD drive couldn't see the copy-protection files on *The Fast and the Furious* disc, but it could see (and therefore rip) the audio tracks just fine—except for the first track, which refused to play under any circumstance. An English engineer analyzing the Charley Pride disc found at first that the files would rip with a plain old CD-ROM drive, but there would be significant errors in the resulting .WAV files. But when he listened closely to the disc, he found all sorts of problems with the sound, including non-random clicks and an almost total lack of stereo separation. Eventually, he did find a program called "X-tractor" that could copy the audio "with what sounded like perfect quality to my ears."

Since the first protected CDs came out, hackers all over the world, not being able to pass up a challenge, have been trying to break them.

So, if the hacker community can get past any of these systems, why do the labels bother? According to Marjie Hadad of Midbar Tech, "The point of the exercise is to keep honest people honest. We can put a dent in copying. There is no such thing as 100 percent protection, but we do our best to keep one or two steps ahead of the hackers. We make it a moving target, so there's no 'universal hack.' We're using multilevel protection—they might be able to get through one level, but it's unlikely they'd get through all of them."

It's hard to keep secrets, however, in the age of the Internet, and it's easy to search the Web and find the right application or the right procedure to get past the protection on any CD. While it may not do much for the record companies, it all leads to, as my editor says, lifetime job security for hackers.

But copy protection is only part of the labels' strategy to keep people from copying their discs. They're also looking to new legislation. The 1998 Digital Millennium Copyright Act (DMCA), perhaps the most big-corporation-friendly, small-guy-screwing intellectual-property law in U.S. history, made it illegal to make or sell any device that could circumvent copy-protected works. It's an absurd law in that it means that any DVD player that

The 1998 Digital Millennium Copyright Act is perhaps the most big-corporation-friendly, small-guy-screwing intellectual-property law in U.S. history.

just happens to be able to ignore the copy protection on any particular audio CD is in the same category as black-market cable TV descramblers. It would also outlaw video timebase correctors, thereby putting a total halt on television production everywhere on the grounds that these rather crucial components can also be used to copy Macrovision-encoded videotapes. Philips' new CD burners would, of course, be banned instantly. One congressman, Rick Boucher, D.-Va., has been trying to get the clause repealed, but he faces an uphill battle. More hopeful is that, as I write this, a federal judge is hearing final arguments that it is unconstitutional.

But there could be more to come. South Carolina Senator Fritz Hollings has proposed something called the Consumer Broadband and Television Promotion Act (don't you love the names of these things?) that would prohibit creating, selling, or distributing "any interactive digital device that does not include and utilize certified security technologies." In other words, your computer, DVD player, game machine, television, cell phone, and clock radio will all be required to have firmware that tells them when they're allowed to read a file and when they're not. Fortunately, this bill won't be going anywhere soon, thanks to the efforts of Vermont Senator (and well-known Grateful Dead fan) Patrick Leahy, who chairs the Judiciary Committee.

In another column, I'll talk about some ideas on how the record companies can get the most out of their assets—without stomping on your rights and mine and without sounding like a broken record.

Afterword

A very different set of perspectives on these issues, those of the people who are actually listening to and buying music, can be found in Chapter 37. Meanwhile, what should have been the final chapter (but no doubt won't be) in this saga was written in 2005 when Sony issued some audio CDs that installed a virus on any computer they happened to be inserted into. The lawsuits for that bonehead move should keep many legal firms happy for years.

Jo Rivers

Chapter 34

War Stories
Readers' Adventures on the Front Lines of the Industry

Preface

As I've said earlier, I had a lot of fun during the time that *Mix* let me take charge of their online presence. The most fun was creating with readers an online community of like-minded folks. MySpace and Facebook are doing this sort of thing now with millions of people (a lot of whom don't actually exist), but at Mix Online we had, at one point, a signed-up membership of something like 40,000 audio and music professionals, students, and wannabes. It was a great pool of humanity who could help each other and exchange experiences and ideas, and it was not incidentally a marketing tool to die for—just the sort of thing business types everywhere were hoping the Web would provide.

The most active area was the Forums, which were moderated (by me) so as to keep the bullshit and bullying down. One of the areas where we particularly encouraged contributions was horror stories. Members were invited to send in tales of their worst gigs, mistakes, clients, assistants, or whatever. We got so many, and so many that were really good, that I decided one month that some of them—ones that weren't slanderous or salacious—deserved to get into print. So I asked the writers' permission, and every one of them said "go ahead"—although a few asked for their names not to be published. Thus, the following column.

January 2003

One of the best parts of moderating Mix Forums online is that I get to read and, most of the time, approve all of the messages submitted by site visitors. I like reading your technical questions because they keep me up-to-date about what kind of problems you're having with gear, techniques, business, and a bunch of other topics. I like discussing and arguing issues like analog vs. digital and RIAA vs. everybody because they tell me where you stand and what's important to you.

But my absolute favorite part of the gig is reading the "horror stories" you contribute about recording sessions, live shows, and yes, even church services from Hell. You've told us about pompous producers getting their comeuppance, idiot clients finally (or sometimes never) realizing the error of their ways, and horrendous screw-ups that you admit to and laugh at now. As the great Steve Allen said, Comedy = Tragedy + Time.

We've got well over a hundred horror stories online now, and this month, I thought I'd share a few of my favorites. I've changed any identifying characteristics in the stories to protect both the innocent and the guilty, but I haven't done any serious checking on whether any of them are actually true. After all, as journalists since time immemorial have known, one should never let the facts get in the way of a good story. I'll just have to take your word for it.

This One Time, in the Studio...

Punch-in, rinse, repeat: Many years ago, I worked with my partner on a project with a famous producer. We only had a few days' time to record, overdub, and mix three songs. Late one night, we were working on punching in a vocal section of a song, and after the first take, I let the tape machine roll a bit further into the song. The producer (who was dozing in the corner of the room) said, "One more time." So we rolled it back and did it again. Again, he said, "One more time." We kept going like this for nearly an hour until we realized that "One more time" had been recorded on the tape at the end of the first take. But we kept on hearing it because after each new take, I would punch out right at the end of the vocal. We found out that the guy had actually been asleep for the entire hour we were going over and over the part.

Track 24 was, of course, timecode—and very loud. The executive producer looked shocked. "Are you guys using this on the song, too?"

Your highness: It was a 24-track analog mixing session. The producer and the mix engineer were hard at work when the executive producer came in and started to assert his presence by pressing some buttons on the mixing console: mutes and solos. At a certain moment, he pressed Solo on track 24, which was, of course, timecode—and very loud. He looked shocked. "Are you guys using this on the song, too?" "Yes, of course," said the engineer. "Well," said His Executiveness, "please keep the volume of this track pretty low."

The human metronome: I accepted a call to track a rock band's demo late last year. The band set up quickly and seemed on top of things. They wanted to loosen up by going straight to two-track for a little while. I was asked to set up a single vocal mic, and there was also this one extra fellow who appeared not to play anything but asked for a set of cans.

The female vocalist came in, smiled at me through the glass, adjusted the mic stand, and pretty soon the band started counting off. I noticed, however, that the vocalist was not wearing headphones, so I hit the talkback and asked her if she wanted cans. The "extra" guy said that I had to speak to her through him. Thinking that I was dealing with an ego here, I said, "Fine, please ask her if she wants cans." His reply: "It would be no use; she's stone deaf."

His role, it turns out, was to conduct her so that she knew when to come in: a human metronome who knew how to sign. You cannot imagine the sounds she created in her role as a "vocalist," although the "lyrics" were right on meter. The band has a strong local following north of Baltimore, or so they say.

Even the dog cried: A woman booked an hour of time in my studio and showed up on the appointed day with her husband of 25 years. They told me that they were about to redo their marriage vows, and he wanted to sing a particular song to her during the ceremony but was afraid that he might not be able to pull it off, as he might be overcome with the emotion of the moment. So they decided he should record the song, and they would play the tape at the appropriate point.

Made sense to me. I started to copy the background-music cassette they'd brought in over to the multitrack so he could overdub his vocal. The song was, unfortunately, "Wind Beneath My Wings." Now we *all* know how difficult that song is to sing for several reasons, not the least of which is that it was written for a woman's voice and that there are no drums during the whole first half of the tune. I was already starting to get a chill up my spine when she casually mentioned that her husband had never done this sort of thing before. Oops!

Well, I won't bore you with the gory details of how the session progressed. Suffice it to say, my wife took the boys out somewhere in the car, the dog howled at the door until I let him escape as well, and the cat threw up a hairball right on top of the console. To this day, I will never hear that song again without breaking into a cold sweat. I hope the ceremony survived the playing of that tape. I plan to be on vacation on their 50th.

Don't touch that button: Multitrack recording direct to the computer, running Cubase. Band in the studio. Several takes, many hours work. Had to eject a floppy that was used a few hours earlier to print a lyric for the band. Floppy-eject button? Nope. PC POWER SWITCH—Thump!! Off it goes!

Why They Invented Soundcheck

God, are you there?: Back in the early '90s, we were hired to do a rock/blues festival at the local music school here in our little town in Mexico. One of the headliners was a group who were all in their mid-40s, and none of them had ever used a monitor system before. We did our soundcheck, and the guitarist was the last one to set up. We asked him to play, which he did with his eyes closed: It seemed he had just smoked some hash before setting up, so he was pretty inspired and getting into a Clapton vibe. After a couple of minutes, I called his name through the monitors: "Luis…Luis" He started to slow down his playing and opened his eyes and looked around, not knowing what was happening. He closed his eyes again and kept playing. Again I called: "Luis…Luis" Again, he opened his eyes and this time started to look up toward the sky. Finally, he stopped playing and raised his arms up and said, "God!!" So I answered, "No, you dork, it's Antonio, and I'm in front of you!"

Stairmaster: I was mixing FOH sound for a college production of *Hair,* the musical. There wasn't any place in the house that they could put me, so they decided to put me above the house, in the catwalk. Things were a little awkward and a bit cramped up there, with the college's two 24-channel consoles, the ton-and-a-half of wireless mic receivers, the FX processors, and other assorted outboard gear. The power supplies for the consoles were right at knee level under the consoles.

Well, you can guess what happened when I got comfortable during a run-through. I shifted my leg, and all of a sudden, I had no power to the console. I had to run back down to the booth and turn everything off in order, run back up to the catwalk, turn on the power supplies and then run back downstairs to the booth to turn everything back on again. It was not fun, but the rehearsal just kept going as if nothing happened.

It wasn't until the second time that it happened that I became angry and so did the tech director. But, hey, I got in shape with all that running around, and I learned a valuable lesson: Never get comfortable while running sound!

What's that smell?: I had just started working for a band doing FOH sound. It was only the second night of what promised to be a six-year run with these guys, and I was eager to please. It was supposed to be an off night, but we got a call to fill in for another group that had cancelled.

I went to the club, laid out the gear, and tied my power into a convenient breaker panel. When I turned on the first monitors, I realized I had nothing! No power. I checked all of

I pulled power just in time to prevent flames from erupting out of the racks.

the gear; none of it was on, but the six-ways (indicator lights) were all on. And then I started to hear these repeated "pops" and smelled the telltale burning of insulation, plastic, etc.

I rechecked the breaker box and, to my horror, realized it was a three-phase panel, and, yes, I had tapped onto a 240VAC branch. I pulled power just in time to prevent flames from erupting out of the racks. A local country group was gracious enough to bring in their gear from down the street so that we could do the gig, but we never played there again.

Double-check the booking: A friend of mine is in a thrash-metal-meets-percussion-ensemble band: raging bass and double-bass-drum ostinatos over which xylophone, vibes, or steel drums play very loudly. The "vocal" portion consists of someone yelling one word on one pitch, sometimes for an entire song. Their whole set is nothing but their own music. Being fairly new to the performing scene, they tend to take any gig that is offered to them. Someone booked them for a party held annually at a local Elks club, most of whose members are retirees and older yuppies with children.

Confused about this and concerned that the Elks club wasn't going to get the type of music they thought they were going to get, I approached the man who hired them. "Did they give you a demo tape?" I asked. "Yes," he replied. I paused a bit and then asked, "And you listened to it?" Again, he said, "Yes." Well, I had to know, so I asked, "Why on Earth did you book *this* band?"

He smiled and explained, "There are eight of us on the board. Every year, the responsibility to hire a band for this event shifts to one of us. This was my first year, and after looking for weeks, I was so frustrated that I finally gave up and hired these guys, because I know they'll never ask me to do this again!"

Even Assistants Get the Blues

Not so helpful help: We were laying album tracks with an extremely well-known band and had successfully completed the second number, getting the basic tracks on to our trusty 3M 16-track. I was terribly efficient, and as soon as I heard the band approve the take after playback, I immediately leadered it up as I had the previous number. I even zeroed the big fluorescent SelecTake digital tape counter so that it was ready for the next song. But then, the producer had a quick word in the engineer's ear, and he said to me, "We just need to do a quick guitar overdub. Go and put an 87 on the amp and bring it up on 28." I was off like a shot to move the mic and repatch it.

It only took a short time to do it, but by the time I was back in my seat next to the tape machine, they had changed their minds. "We'll just go on to the next number," I was told, so I had to go out and move the mic back to its original position and channel. The band went back into the studio, and being well rehearsed as people were in those days, they were ready for a take in a little more than 15 minutes.

Not only were they ready, their first take sounded like it was going to be the master. The last chords faded away, and everyone was smiling. But as I turned to stop the machine, I was overcome by sheer horror as I saw a piece of leader tape run past the heads. I had just wiped the previous song! I dutifully admitted my mistake to the engineer, and he was kind enough to give the band some technical reason why they had to do the previous number all over again.

The engineer, it turned out, had done his best to help *me* get ready for the overdub. While I had been out moving the mic, he had kindly rewound the tape to the beginning of the song. He had even more helpfully re-zeroed the counter for me. Only he didn't tell me he'd done it—so we had now wiped the basic tracks of what was destined to be the band's next single. Luckily, we re-recorded the number in a couple of takes. And, luckily, it made the charts.

A regional situation: A couple of years ago, I was the Pro Tools engineer for a composer on a low-budget feature film. As this was my first gig as a Pro Tools engineer, I wanted to do everything perfectly, so I stayed up all night with the composer, making sure that everything was set up right, complete with guide tracks, click tracks, etc.

When the clock struck 9 a.m., we rushed to the studio, set up the mics, and prepared for the orchestra. Everything went perfectly for the next six hours as the composer conducted all of the cues. Then, around 4 in the afternoon, we finally got to the last music cue of the film. We were running low on hard disk space, and the take we had just recorded was no good, so I used the Delete Selected Regions command in Pro Tools to free up space.

When we went to record the next take, there was suddenly no click track, because I had inadvertently selected the click track to delete when I deleted the last take! It was the most complicated tempo map of the entire film, with meter or tempo changes about every 12 bars. Even after scouring the disk with Norton, we couldn't recover the click, so the orchestra had to wing it with the composer (who is no conductor) waving his arms without benefit of a click.

The session finished three hours late, and we spent three extra days of editing trying to get the track to sync to what was supposed to be the right tempo and meter. After all that, it still didn't sound quite right.

Moral of the story: *Never* use the Delete Selected Regions command in Pro Tools!

A tip o' the Insider Audio toupée to Prince Charles Alexander, Richard Elen, Mike Petit, Noel Quinlan, and those who wish to remain anonymous.

Afterword

Unfortunately, the very same month I wrote this column, the large, unwieldy, highly leveraged, multinational corporation that owned *Mix* at the time (who had initially made their money selling television advertising aimed at kids trapped in elementary-school classrooms) decided that having a real person in charge of the website wasn't cost effective. They folded Mix Online into a huge corporation-wide network they called "IndustryClick," whose principal advantages were that content could be flowed from the magazine directly onto the Web without human intervention (or any graphics) and that a reader could move from *Mix*'s site to any of their other magazine sites—including *Concrete Products Monthly* and *International Hog Farmer*—with a single click. The 40,000 members and all of their demographic information vanished, and I had to find another way to get health insurance.

All of the executives who were behind that brilliant decision were eventually tossed out of the company, and not long after that the company sold off *Mix* and the rest of its business magazines. But the opportunity for a *Mix*-oriented online community had passed. Referencing Kurt Vonnegut again, so it goes.

Chapter 35

Hacking and Hijacking
What's He Building in There?

Preface

Besides casting a spotlight on a student I really liked and admired for his ingenuity, my favorite thing about this column was that it shows that it is still possible to start a genuine revolution in the audio world at the grassroots level.

Last month, the most dangerous man in the music business turned 20.

March 2003

The most dangerous man in the music business is on his third, or maybe his fourth, company. He's been selling audio software on the Internet since he was a sophomore in high school, and his latest product looks like it's going to make at least one of his partners a functional millionaire. It's a little 2-megabyte Macintosh program that neatly circumvents any copy-protection scheme on any audio program, file, or stream and lets you make a digital copy of it. It costs all of $16.

Last month, the most dangerous man in the music business turned 20. And he works for me.

If nothing else forces the dinosaurs of the RIAA into the new millennium, this product will do the trick.

Say what? Okay, I'll back up a little. First of all, he's not *really* the most dangerous man in the music business, although since Napster collapsed, that title has certainly been up for grabs. But he and two youthful cohorts—hackers, in the original, positive sense of the term, who, by the way, have never actually all met in person—are working on stuff that the record industry really, really hates. And if nothing else forces the dinosaurs of the RIAA into the new millennium, this product will do the trick.

It has an admittedly provocative name: *Audio Hijack*. Running under Macintosh OS X, Audio Hijack takes advantage of Apple's flexible sound architecture, Core Audio, to intercept—at the digital level—any audio signal that passes through the Mac, process it, and store it as a high-resolution .AIFF file. It's like the old QuickTime Audio Extraction function on steroids; instead of just working with audio CDs, it can also handle Internet streams, DVDs, MiniDiscs, and external MP3 players. Whatever "protection" anyone tries to build into an audio file, *Audio Hijack* simply sidesteps it; if you can play it through the Mac speaker, *Audio Hijack* can record it.

So, where is this guy? Somewhere in a cellar in Eastern Europe, in one of the copyright-averse areas of the Far East, on a well-defended mountaintop in Idaho, or sunning in a tiny Caribbean tax haven? No, he lives about a mile from me, in a dorm room at the college where I teach. He's a second-year undergraduate majoring in computer engineering. And he happens to be the systems administrator and chief technician in my music and multimedia laboratory.

His name is Paul Kafasis, and he comes from New Jersey—"Exit 8A," he told me when we met last year, before I could even ask. (And if you don't understand that reference, then you need to spend more time on the East Coast.) Although he loves music and played the drums for a while in grade school, he doesn't think of himself as a musician. His tastes are eclectic: When I walk in on him working in my lab, he might be listening on his laptop to Soul Coughing, Eminem, or acoustic blues.

Unlike many of his contemporaries, he's well aware that there was a world before there was a Web. During the last semester break, he read Tom Wolfe's *The Electric Kool-Aid Acid Test*, and he wrote in his "blog" *[that's in quotes because almost nobody had heard of blogging when I wrote this]* that he is intrigued by Neal Cassady's constant striving (through drugs, unfortunately) to overcome the 1/30th-second delay between reality and humans' perceptions of it.

He's a big help in the lab, and I'm seriously considering asking some of my colleagues to flunk him so that I can keep him around another year or two. I have to admit, he reminds me of myself a couple decades ago, in that he's willing to put in insane amounts of time to keep up with the latest programs, prices, utilities, and system patches. And he's pretty enthusiastic about all of it. (Remember when we all felt that way?)

He did mention to me some time ago that he was working on music applications, but I didn't realize how serious he was until after a conversation I had with Apple's audio technologies manager Dan Brown. At Dan's urging, I visited the osxaudio.com site, and there on the front page was an interview with my lab technician. So I did some hunting around the Net for more on the lad (I discovered that he graduated from one of the top high schools in New Jersey with near-perfect SAT scores) and then sat him down and grilled him about his company and his product.

Paul was 16 when he first got involved with music software. He wrote a review for a Web magazine on *StripAmp*, a control-strip module for *MacAmp*, then the leading Macintosh MP3 player. *StripAmp* was written by Alex Lagutin, then a 25-year-old engineer who was in fact behind the former Iron Curtain (in Siberia, to be specific). It was freeware, but Paul thought people would pay for it. Being in Russia, however, Alex couldn't set up an account that would accept credit-card payments, so Paul convinced Alex ("I told him I was a college student, since I didn't think he'd take me seriously if he knew my real age.") to let him create a paper company, called "PK Industries," register it with e-commerce provider kagi.com, and start taking orders at $5 a pop. Users could download a time-limited version of the program for free, and when they decided that they wanted the full version, they'd send a payment to Paul, and then Alex would e-mail them a registration code. Every few weeks, Paul would arrange to wire-transfer the funds to Alex.

The team took in a couple of thousand dollars, and their work caught the attention of @soft Software, the Swedish company that distributed *MacAmp*. They both went to work for the company: Alex writing an equalizer plug-in for the program, and Paul taking care of "anything a native English speaker would do," like documentation, Web content, and PR. After @soft dissolved, Paul and Alex formed a new company, Subband Software, joining forces with the original creator of *MacAmp*, Dmitry Boldyrev, and a student at the University of Maryland named Quentin Carnicelli. "Alex had the idea to record an .AIFF file from another application within *MacAmp*," says Paul, and he wrote a plug-in that could do that. This was the first incarnation of *Audio Hijack*.

"*MacAmp* has its own DSP architecture," explains Paul, "which allows incoming audio to be filtered, processed, played on the speaker, or captured to disc. People mostly used our plug-in to capture streaming RealAudio files," which normally can't be recorded except as an analog signal from the Mac's output, "and to enhance playback of the audio on DVDs, adding EQ, reverb, or whatever. And it can also be used to rip audio from DVDs by intercepting the output from *DVD Player*," the free application that Apple supplies with each new Mac. "There are underground DVD rippers out there. They have to find the audio on the disc, recognize the codec, and do the conversion to MP3 or .AIFF. This is much easier, since you just use it with software that you have."

But *MacAmp* was soon made obsolete by another free piece of Apple software, *iTunes*. Apple's program, however, doesn't have its predecessor's DSP plug-in capabilities. Paul,

Alex, and Quentin realized that under OS X, *Audio Hijack* could be spun off as a stand-alone application, which could then accept plug-ins itself. So last fall, they formed yet another company. Around the same time, Alex moved a little closer to his partners—to St. Petersburg—but he has still never set foot outside of Russia.

"We didn't want to be known as an MP3 company and didn't want to be judged by our old companies," says Paul. Rogue Amoeba (www.rogueamoeba.com) was the name they came up with for the company after some three weeks of deliberations. "No, there's no significance to it," he says. It does, however, give them an excuse to have a corporate logo that's pretty hysterical.

How does *Audio Hijack* work? It's actually quite simple. First, you launch it and then launch the application you want to rip from. "It presents a spoof of *Core Audio* to the application you're using so that the audio is passed to *Hijack*," says Paul. In other words, it fakes out the operating system into thinking that the audio is going to someplace normal, like the Mac's audio output circuit, when actually it's being sucked up by the *Audio Hijack* "shell," which can process it in dozens of ways and store it on disc as an .AIFF file. It's then passed back to the real *Core Audio* so that you can hear what you're doing.

You can open multiple instantiations of *Audio Hijack*, which means that you can record several different streams at the same time: a DVD movie, an audio CD, an MP3 file from an iPod, music and effects from a game, and a streaming RealAudio file. "We're looking at how to combine multiple streams into a single pipe," says Paul. "A 'total jack.' We don't have the interface for it yet, but if we get a lot of requests, we'll add it."

Several DSP functions, written by Alex, are built into the software, like reverb, EQ, VU meters, and an oscilloscope. Although the folks at Waves don't have anything to worry about, Alex's modules are respectable. More importantly, however, the current version of the software—1.6.5—includes "VST Hub," a wrapper for VST plug-ins from any source.

Another feature is a timer that works just like a VCR but for Webcast audio. "If you're interested in hearing streams from around the world, like the BBC, they often come at inconvenient times," says Paul. "With the timer, you save a 'config' file that contains the input you want, the time, the destination, and any DSP you want to add. You can target it at a URL, a bookmark, or a RealAudio file. At the right time, it opens the appropriate application, loads the stream, and records it."

Version 2.0, which may be out by the time you read this, will be able to rip audio from running applications, so you can launch *Audio Hijack* and other programs in any order you like. Although it is OS X only (no Classic mode!), it can host many "noncarbonized" (that is, they haven't been updated for OS X) VST plug-ins. It will also support OS X's Audio Units, which will make it compatible with even more third-party plug-ins, as well as external audio cards and interfaces. "People have also asked for live input," says Paul, "and we're working on that."

They're also working on writing files at different sample rates, word lengths, and formats—most notably, MP3s. Their MP3 encoder is based on the open-source LAME, which, in true open-source tradition, stands for "LAME Ain't an MP3 Encoder." But because *Audio Hijack* is a commercial product, the company will still have to pay Fraunhofer IIS, who holds the patent on MP3, $2.50 per unit, which raises the retail price a bit.

Paul, who lists his company title as "CEO/lackey," is still handling the finances for the company and designs a lot of the user interface using Apple's *Interface Builder* for OS X. Quentin builds the working front end, while Alex toils away on the back-end code. They split the revenue more or less equally. "We're projecting revenues in mid-six-figures for the fiscal year," says Paul. Do the math, and you've got a couple of young men who are doing a nice job of putting themselves through two top colleges and a guy in Russia who is making—relative to that country's per-capita gross domestic product—the equivalent of about $20,000 a week.

And how about video? Is there a "Video Hijack" in Rogue Amoeba's future? "That's the single question we get most often," Paul says. "But it's completely different technology, and we're not planning to go there at all."

Naturally, considering the audience it's aimed at, a number of potential users will try to obtain *Audio Hijack* without paying for it. "We've had very good response from users and reviewers, and a lot of people have told us, 'I gotta have this,' and have tried to hack it," says Paul. "On the serial-number pirating sites, they love us. And there was a valid serial number being passed around for a while, but we found out about it and blocked it. Maybe 100 people all told will figure out how to pirate it, but the rest will pay for it. I mean, it's only $16!"

Apple's Brown considers *Audio Hijack* to be a shining example of how OS X's music and audio architecture lends itself to creative third-party development. But other companies—and their favorite legislators—may not be so sanguine. Under the various radical changes in copyright law that have been proposed in—and sometimes passed through—Congress in recent years, merely possessing a copy of *Audio Hijack* could be considered a felony.

"We realize that some people may believe that this is violating some laws currently in existence," says Paul. "However, in terms of fair use, *Audio Hijack* really is in the clear. Time-shifting was ruled legal by the Supreme Court in 1984. The idea was, 'Hey, you can watch this show at home, why shouldn't you be able to watch it on your own time?' We believe the same idea clearly applies to digital content. Why shouldn't you be able to record a Real stream that comes in the middle of the night, burn it to a CD, and listen to it on the way to work?

"Likewise, if you're allowed to have a Windows Media file on your local machine and play it whenever you like, why shouldn't you be able to convert that to MP3 and play it on your iPod? The RIAA fought the original Rio MP3 players, but the court ruled that they were legal. *Audio Hijack* simply aids this digital 'space shifting' by removing limitations set by file formats.

"However, these laws have not been well applied to digital content, and the DMCA [Digital Millennium Copyright Act] and other restrictive laws are making it more confusing. We're hoping, if it ever comes to this, that the courts will agree with us on both of these points."

And they have allies besides Apple. A small Missouri company called 321 Studios last spring sued nine major film studios in a pre-emptive move to have its $100 software "DVD Copy Plus" declared legal and parts of the DMCA declared unconstitutional. The designers are not stupid: They designed the software so that (just like the RIAA-backed SCMS that so efficiently killed the domestic DAT market) a copied DVD can't itself be copied, which means that real pirates won't find it very useful.

The suit was filed in a San Francisco federal court—"a more friendly jurisdiction," according to Paul. "Hopefully, the case will force a fair-use provision into the DMCA, and that will help us." The boys from Rogue Amoeba are not the only ones who are watching this very carefully. If the suit is successful, the media conglomerates will no longer be able to scream "piracy" at the appearance of every new format and tool. They may just have to come up with better reasons for people to buy their products than merely because they've put a permanent legal hammerlock on intellectual property. And they'll have to find better ways—more flexible and appropriate for a thriving, truly open market—to sell them, too. Imagine that.

Paul Lehrman would feel much safer in a world where more drivers were listening to last night's Webcast and fewer were yakking on their cell phones.

Afterword

The battle rages on. 321 Studios lost their suit in February 2004 and were ordered to stop selling their product, but there's still plenty of DVD-ripping software out there. Legislation to reform the more draconian aspects of the DMCA was introduced in 2003 and 2005 but has yet to pass.

Rogue Amoeba, still lawsuit-free, is going strong and now has six employees. Its products have received a bunch of awards from various Macintosh magazines and trade shows. A "pro" version of *Audio Hijack*, which along with many other features adds the ability to record both sides of Skype and iChat conversations, is now available, and other new products include *Nicecast*, for creating your own Internet radio station; *AirFoil*, which routes audio to an AirPort Express; and several free utilities such as a *Pong* screensaver/clock. And Alex has still never met his fellow Rogues.

Chapter 36

Posting and Beaming into the Future
Grumpmeier Builds His Dream Studio

Preface

April again? How the months fly by! Well, time to check in with Grumpmeier. Leave it to my old buddy to take the concept of the "virtual studio" further than anyone else....

April 2003

"Welcome to the GSPoT!" the kid grinned at me. "Mr. Grumpmeier told us you were coming. We're really happy you're going to write about us in *Mix* magazine. Around here, you know, we don't only look at the pictures, we sometimes even read it!"

That's nice, I thought, and smiled back at the young assistant. His purple hair matched the plush, yet hideous, heavy-duty indoor/outdoor carpeting that ran on for what seemed like miles, under which you could still smell the glue drying. I was amazed by how fast this place had gone up. Four recording rooms, three control rooms, a post suite, a screening room, a CD/DVD duping operation, a tape-baking kitchen, a sushi bar, and a Starbucks were now occupying what had just a few months ago been the tire and automotive section of a busy department store.

"There you are!" Grumpmeier came out of a doorway, giving me a hale-fellow-well-met grimace that was the closest he could ever come to a smile. "You found us!"

"It wasn't hard," I replied. "The big red 'K' in the parking lot helped a lot. But tell me again what you call this place."

"The GSPoT!" he said triumphantly. "Stands for 'Grumpmeier Studios Post and Transformation.' I figured that would get people in here faster than if I named it after some drink or the godforsaken part of town we're in. But you can't beat the rent. That discount chain's stuck with a 30-year-lease that they can't get out of, and with the commercial real estate market in the dumper, they were desperate."

"So you got a good deal on the rent?"

He once tried to sell me a Mac SE for Pro Tools, saying it was better than a new G4 because of its "vintage sound."

"No, we got *no* rent. All we have to do is pay the utility bills so the pipes don't freeze and the landlord doesn't sue the store. 'Course, I'm working on getting out of that, too." It's comforting to know that no matter how successful my friend Grumpmeier gets, he'll always be the same cheap S.O.B. who once tried to sell me a Mac SE for Pro Tools, saying it was better than a new G4 because of its "vintage sound."

"So show me around," I said, pulling out my notepad. "This is quite a step up from the place you used to have in your basement. And that fallout shelter in the yard your kid was using for a while. What have you got here, like nine rooms?"

"More or less," he waved his hands vaguely. "We're constantly changing things, so it's hard to say exactly. But I'll tell you all about that later. Right now, I want to show you this really sweet new system I picked up." Grump loves to go to trade shows that no one else seems to know or care about, like the Kirghizstan Broadcast Union & Winter Wheat Farmers Fair, and has been known to come home with some pretty strange stuff.

"I found this really tiny company in Colombia called Morningside Hockwerks," he said as he opened the door to a control room that bore a striking resemblance to the main room in the old Hit Factory. He picked up a small half-rack box with a single knob and several odd-looking jacks on the front. "They've taken a vocal processor and a reverb simulator and combined them into what they call a 'Vimulator.' They give you this whole library of FIR analyses of the nose, throat, and chest cavities of famous singers who are retired—or should be—like Grace Slick, Diana Ross, and Tony Orlando. Then you can apply those algorithms to any vocal track, and they'll come out sounding like the model. In tune, out of tune, tight or sloppy, dynamic or condenser mic, whatever you like."

"But don't those singers object?" I asked. "I mean, didn't Bette Midler win a lawsuit against some 'soundalike'?"

"Yeah, well, Bette's not in here. And neither is Springsteen. Neither is Tom Waits, but if you take Louis Armstrong and turn up the 'smoke' parameter, you can get pretty close. The company pays royalties to all the singers they model, and most of those folks are happy to get them. See this thing that looks like a parking meter? You drop a quarter in there, and you can use any of their models for 15 minutes. At the end of the week, someone from the RIAA comes by and empties it.

"But you can do more than that. The company also throws in a set of nasal and esophageal probes, which you use to make your own models. Of course, if you've got some kid who wants to sound like Eminem or 50 Cent, you have to get special probes that go into different body cavities. And there's beginning to be a big underground market—literally—for models of singers who aren't with us anymore. Hey, want to hear me sound like Jim Morrison? *This is the end...*"

"Uh, no, that's fine. I'll take your word for it." I cut him off. "But that doesn't seem like something a lot of clients will use. I mean, besides Harry Connick, how many Frank Sinatra wannabes are out there?"

"Oh, no, there's tons of ways we can make money with this sucker. The government keeps us real busy. We have profiles for a lot of political types in the can, and whenever one of them says something really idiotic, they send us the videotape. We bring in an actor to redo the voice and replace the dumb stuff with something more innocuous. Do you know how many ways there are to mispronounce the word 'nuclear'? Since our audio quality's usually much better than what the network news shows have—what with those cheap camcorders they're all using now—they're happy to throw out their own tapes and use ours. And so nobody ever has to hear what the jerk actually said. And the networks? They adore us because of the reality shows."

"Huh?" I was getting dizzy. "You mean those, uh, bachelorettes all want to sound like, I don't know, Jennifer Lopez?"

"No, the girls all want to *look* like Jennifer Lopez, but we can't help them there. I'm talking about the cop shows and the desert island shows and the dumb games. There they are slogging through some swamp or being chased down an alley by a couple of patrol cars or hanging on a cliff while stuffing maggots up their nose. How're you going to get a decent audio track out of any of that? They're all amateurs, and none of them know how to loop dialogue, so you can't fix it in post—even if they're not in custody. But if we can get them to come in for 15 minutes, even in handcuffs, we can create a profile on them, and then any time we want, we get a professional actor to do the looping, and it sounds just like them. We've saved a lot of shows that way. And since you never hear the actors' real voices, the producers don't even have to pay them scale."

I had to sit down. This was deviousness beyond even what *I* thought Grumpmeier was capable of. But it turned out I hadn't seen anything yet. As I slumped down in a huge leather chair that felt suspiciously like a milk crate, I noticed a dusty sign in the corner that said "Grump Post and Beam." I figured it might be a relatively safe line of questioning, so I asked him about it. "Oh, that was a name we came up with for the place a long time ago. Sort of a pun, but not really. We didn't use it 'cause it gave away a little too much."

"What do you mean?" I puzzled.

"I'll show you," he snickered, as he pushed through another door, this one marked "Folodeck." All of a sudden, we were in what I could have sworn was the Taj Mahal. "The simulation stuff we do isn't just audio. It's visual, too. And even tactile. We tell the clients this is our Foley room, but it's much more than that. In this room, we can build any kind of space, from a downtown nightclub toilet to Middle Earth exteriors, and make it absolutely right. Remember the Total Information Awareness program the Justice Department wanted to set up? Well, even though the Senate cut off its budget, they went ahead with it, but they needed to find, uh, alternate means to fund it."

"Don't tell me," I said, "Some colonel in the White House basement is shipping pirated CDs to Chinese school kids?"

"Nothing that lame," he scoffed. "Besides," he intoned somberly, "that would be *wrong*.

"See, they set up tons of surveillance equipment all around the world, tapping into wireless LANs, Webcams, and cell phones, and they're using technologies I'm not even allowed to talk about. They got together this unbelievable database that makes Google look like an iPod. Not only has it got complete credit, medical, political, educational, and employment histories of every person on the planet, but it also has analysis of every *place* on the planet, with dimensions, colors, lighting data, temperature, humidity, textures, ambient noise, and acoustics. In order to pay for it, they came up with this brilliant idea of a government/industry partnership: They're selling access to it. It's called the Official Repository of Worldwide Environments and Landscapes: ORWEL."

"How many people know about this?" I gasped.

"Not many," he cackled. "They're starting slow. They're only bringing in partners who are absolutely trustworthy and who they know aren't going to abuse the data. I got friends in the Agency"—I didn't know exactly which agency he was talking about, but the capital "A" was unmistakable—"so we're one of the first commercial subscribers. The only others I know about are a group who are direct-marketing really revolutionary ways to improve your sex life and a former government minister from Nigeria, or maybe it's Zimbabwe, who seems to have gotten his hands on a bunch of venture capital and is looking for partners."

"But what do you use it for?" I still didn't get it.

"Don't you see?" he looked at me condescendingly. "We can create any setting a client wants and then record in it. We can do music, Foley, or ADR. We can make a two-chord garage band feel like they're playing Shea Stadium. A guy doing a voice-over for a wild-animal series can think he's in the Amazon jungle. Last week, we put the Three Tenors on top of Mount Fuji. With all that simulated wind around them, they really had to sing loud. One of 'em, Fiorello or whatever his name is, got pneumonia, but they sounded great! We're booked up in here 18 months in advance."

A guy doing a voice-over for a wild-animal series can think he's in the Amazon jungle, and last week, we put the Three Tenors on top of Mount Fuji.

"That's amazing," I said, truly amazed. "Are you going to expand past this one room?"

"Well, that's what I wanted to tell you earlier," he said, lowering his voice. "As it happens, the whole facility was actually set up with ORWEL before we got here. The last tenants, that department store? They wanted all of the housewives buying the cheap linens and kitchen stuff think that they thought were in Martha Stewart's house. So they put it in, but they never got the chance to use it. When we turned it on, we realized we could get profiles of some places that *our* customers would like: All of the best control rooms all over the world, or those great old recording spaces that don't exist any more, or a place that's just loaded with gear, like a Guitar Center. So, that's what we did. Thanks to ORWEL, we're literally beaming all those places in." He pulled a car-key remote out of his pocket that said "Kia" on it. "That's so nobody even *thinks* of stealing it," he chuckled as he pressed a small button.

In an instant, the entire studio complex disappeared. All that was left was the ugly carpeting and bare concrete walls, stained a sickly blue where the stacks of antifreeze bottles had once stood. The chair I was sitting on really *was* a milk carton. On the other side of what was now a huge open space, the young assistant who had first greeted me sat at a cheap bridge table, headphones clamped on his head tightly, staring intently at a laptop. After a few seconds, he looked up, smiled, and waved at us.

"Sammy here is taking care of our whole operation," Grump said, with some pride in his voice. "We often have him handling four sessions or more at a time. He's got control over a couple of hundred tracks of audio, more processing than he'll use in his entire lifetime, instant video sync, surround encoding, 20,000 loops, 30,000 sound effects online and 350,000 samples, and all those vocal models. Everything's in that iBook. When there are no clients around, we turn off the projectors to save power. All that expensive gear with the dials and knobs and lights? We don't need it anymore. We sold everything from my old place on eBay, and I never bothered to replace a thing."

Of course, I was horrified. "So, the whole place is just an illusion? All those clients think they're sitting in a state-of-the-art facility, and it's really a *hologram*? None of this is real?"

"What's 'real'?" he scoffed. "You don't have to be able to sing to have a hit. You don't have to know jack about music to be a producer. You don't have to play an instrument to write songs or soundtracks. You can make all the records you want without ever actually recording anything. So what do we need all that hardware for? We've got no overhead, which means we can finally make some money. Everyone's hurting, everybody's low-balling. You pay the bank for the equipment, you pay the staff and the rent and the light bill, and there's nothing left. How long has it been since a client gave you a decent budget to do a project? But get rid of all that stuff, and you get to take something home.

You can make all the records you want without ever actually recording anything, so what do we need all that hardware for?

"Go virtual, bucko," he bellowed, slapping me hard on the shoulder. "This is the future. Get used to it."

Paul Lehrman is recovering nicely, thank you.

Afterword

I have to say I surprised myself with how prescient this column turned out to be. In less than four years, we've found out the "Agency" actually *has* been tapping all our phone conversations; we've seen computer graphics replace not only movie sets, but the actors, too; and we've been given new toys like Google Maps, Google Earth, and Zillow that give us clever ways to access unimaginably large databases. No doubt as soon as the holographic projectors are perfected, some real Grumpmeier is going to start working on *his* dream.

Jokes: Part 4

A man goes to a marriage counselor and tells him that his wife won't talk to him. "I know just what to do," says the counselor. "Take her to a nice nightclub. Buy her dinner and listen to the band. When they take a break, buy her a drink. At the end of the second set, the leader will introduce the band. Then there will be a drum solo, and that will be followed by a bass solo. And your problem will be solved."

"It will?" asked the astonished man. "How can you be so sure?"

The counselor replied, "Hey, *everyone* talks during the bass solo."

■ ■ ■

Q: If you were lost in the woods, whom would you trust for directions: an in-tune tenor sax player, an out-of-tune tenor sax player, or Santa Claus?

A: The out-of-tune tenor sax player. The other two show clearly that you are hallucinating.

■ ■ ■

A lighting designer, a sound engineer, and a tour manager are sitting around at a gig one day when they spy a very ornate bottle under a riser. The tour manager uncorks said bottle and in a wisp of smoke, out pops a genie.

"Oh thank you for releasing me!" says the genie. "To show my appreciation, I will grant each one of you a wish." The lighting designer steps up first and says, "I want a million dollars and a beautiful woman on a tropical island." The genie says, "It shall be done," and POOF!—off he goes.

Next it was the sound engineer's turn. Being a bit more clever than the lighting designer, he says "I would like *TEN* million dollars, *TEN* beautiful women, and on my island there's a five-star private resort." The genie says, "It shall be done," and POOF!—off he goes as well.

The genie then turns to the tour manager and says, "And now you, master, what shall be your bidding?" The tour manager thinks about it for a bit and replies, "I want both of those guys back here in five minutes."

■ ■ ■

An orchestra musician calls the symphony office to talk to the conductor. "I'm sorry, he's dead," comes the reply. The musician calls back, and asks for the conductor. "I'm sorry, he's dead," comes the reply again. He calls back 25 times, always getting the same reply from the receptionist. Finally, she asks him why he keeps calling. He replies, "I just like to hear you say it."

■ ■ ■

Jesus and Satan have an argument as to who is the better programmer. Finally, they agree to hold a contest, with God as the judge.

They set themselves before their computers and begin. They type furiously, thousands of lines of code filling up the screen, for several hours straight. Suddenly, seconds before the end of the competition, a bolt of lightning strikes, and the electricity goes down.

Moments later, the power is restored, and God announces that the contest is over.

He asks Satan to show what he has come up with. Satan is visibly upset, and cries, "I have nothing. I lost it all when the power went out."

"Very well, then," says God, "Let us see if Jesus fared any better."

Jesus clicks his mouse, and the screen comes to life in a beautiful vivid display, while the voices of an angelic choir pours forth from the speakers.

Satan is astonished. He stammers, "B-b-but how?! I lost everything, but Jesus's program is intact! How did he do it?"

God chuckles, "Everybody knows that Jesus saves!"

■ ■ ■

A young boy decides to take up the bass guitar and so he finds a teacher. After his first lesson, his dad asks, "What did you learn today?"

"I learned the first three notes on the E string," the boy replies.

After the second lesson his dad asks, "What did you learn today?"

"I learned the first three notes on the A string!"

The next day the boy doesn't come home until after 2 a.m. His dad is furious. "Where the hell have you been?" he screams.

"Well, hey, Dad, I've got all these gigs…"

■ ■ ■

The wedding was going along just fine until all of a sudden the drummer and the bass player started to pummel each other in a ferocious punching match. The bandleader quickly climbed to the back of the bandstand and separated them and yelled at the bass player, "What the heck is that all about?"

"He grabbed one of my tuning pegs and twisted it, so I'm all out of tune!" the musician said.

"Well, you don't have to punch him," said the bandleader. "Why don't you just turn it back?"

"Because the son-of-a-bitch won't tell me which one!"

■ ■ ■

A sax player got to town early for the gig, so he decided he'd practice for a little while in his hotel room. As he was getting into it, he leaned back against the window in the room. Suddenly, the window gave way, and the player and his horn fell 18 stories onto the sidewalk. But much to his amazement, he found that he wasn't hurt at all—not even a scratch. He picked up his sax, and saw that it too was in pristine condition. So he joyfully dusted himself off and started to play right there.

The hotel doorman witnessed the whole thing. He ran up to the musician and said, "I can't believe what I just saw! You fell out of a window from 18 stories, landed on concrete, and you don't even have a bruise! You just stood up, picked up your sax, and began to play like nothing ever happened! You must be the luckiest sax player alive!"

The musician smiled and responded, "Nah! That's still Kenny G."

■ ■ ■

Two women are walking in the woods when they hear a tiny voice calling them. They look down and see it's a frog who's talking to them.

"Hey chicks, hey chicks, c'mere and help me out!," says the frog. They lean closer so they can hear it better, and it says, "Dig, I'm a jazz musician, see? I was just minding my own business playing my gig, and when I wasn't watching I got turned into a frog by an evil witch. But if one of you kisses me, I'll turn back into my old self."

One of the women picks up the frog and places it in her coat pocket. The other looks on horrified and asks, "Why didn't you kiss him?"

"Are you kidding?" says the first. "He's worth a lot more as a talking frog than as a jazz musician!"

■ ■ ■

The young producer was so inept that all of the session musicians were totally lost. But he refused to stop and fix anything, so they played gamely on. At one point the drummer played a huge cymbal crash 20 bars early, in the middle of what should have been a flute solo. The producer punched the talkback button and screamed, "Who did that?!?"

■ ■ ■

Top 14 reasons why Microsoft shouldn't make cars:

14. For no reason whatsoever, your car would crash twice a day.

13. Every time they repainted the lines on the road, you would have to buy a new car.

12. Occasionally your car would die on the freeway for no reason. You would have to accept this, restart, and drive on.

11. Executing a maneuver such as a left turn would sometimes cause your car to shut down and refuse to restart. You would have to reinstall the engine.

10. Only one person could use the car. If you wanted to lend the car to your wife, you would have to buy her her own seat.

9. New seats would force everyone to have the same butt size.

8. Apple would make a car that was powered by the sun, was more reliable, five times as fast, and twice as easy to drive, but would only run on eight percent of the roads.

7. The oil, water, temperature, fuel, alternator, seatbelt, and airbag warning lights would be replaced by a single "general car fault" warning light.

6. The airbag system would say "Are you sure?" before deploying.

5. Occasionally, for no reason whatsoever, your car would lock and refuse to let you in until you simultaneously lifted the door handle, turned the key, and grabbed hold of the radio antenna.

4. All car buyers would be required to also purchase a deluxe set of Microsoft road maps, even though they neither need them nor want them. Attempting to delete this option would immediately cause the car's performance to diminish at least 50 per cent.

3. Every time Microsoft introduced a new model, car buyers would have to learn how to drive all over again because none of the controls would operate in the same manner as the old car.

2. The chassis would arrive full of small holes, and every time you got in the car you'd discover that someone else had been in it and left garbage all over the place.

1. You'd press the "Start" button to turn off the engine.

Chapter 37

The Kids Are Alright
Who's Really Going to Determine the
Future of the Music Industry?

Preface

In the face of continuing and escalating panic among the record companies and consequent unease in the parts of our industry that are dependent on them, the May 2003 issue of *Mix* came out with an all-black cover bearing only the words "What Can Save the Music Industry?" Most of the articles in the issue dealt with the changes in the world of records and recording that the RIAA was screaming were going to destroy us all, and my column was no exception.

In my usual non-conforming fashion, however, I decided that the many "players" in the field didn't need any more coverage, and instead I sought out members of a group who are *really* going to determine what the music industry is going to look like in years to come: the young folks who are our present and future customers. I tried to get as diverse a sample within that group as possible, in terms of geographic origin, ethnicity, professional interests, and educational level. What they had to say was instructive, to say the least.

May 2003

My literary career started more or less in high school, when I specialized in incendiary articles for the school paper about then-fashionable topics like war, racism, drugs, and music (gee, not much has changed in 30-odd years...). One day I wrote a particularly outrageous satirical piece and asked the editors to use a pseudonym in the byline. At first they hesitated, but I assured them that if anyone asked who actually wrote the piece, they were free to disclose my true identity. So they ran it.

The article caused a huge uproar. Parents were outraged, letters were written to the local newspapers, committees were formed, meetings were held. The article contained not a single grain of truth, but that didn't stop anyone from overreacting to it. Grave statements were made by administrators about how "the author" came by such damaging knowledge. But nobody ever bothered to ask any of the paper's editors (or me) who the author actually was or what the article was really about. The tempest boiled for months, wasting lots of breath, time, and even money, before it gradually faded away, having accomplished nothing except making a lot of people look very foolish.

Which sort of reminds me of what's going on in the record industry these days. Sales are down, and listeners are downloading music. But outside of that, despite the hot air, apocalyptic predictions, and high-toned moral judgments being tossed around, no one seems to really know what's going on.

Maybe it's because no one has asked the people who are really going to decide the future of the music business: the kids. The 18–25 demographic is a crucial one for any market, but especially for entertainment. Young people are forming the tastes and preferences that will rule their buying habits for the rest of their lives. I see lots of efforts being made by media companies to influence their tastes, not only through traditional multimedia ad campaigns, but also through guerilla marketing techniques like finding the "coolest" kids in a crowd and buying their sway over others. But I don't see much effort in finding out what normal teenagers and young adults really think. So I asked. And I got some really interesting answers and insights.

We need to listen to them because, like it or not, our future depends on them.

I talked to seven young people, four men and three women, aged 20 to 22. Six are in college, one is a high-school dropout. They came from all over the country. Some are looking to pursue a career in music, while others are just enthusiastic listeners. They all have two things in common: They are highly articulate when it comes to talking about music, and they think the major record companies and media outlets are doing a miserable job of providing them with the music they want to hear. I won't pretend that this is any kind of scientific sampling—these are students at my school, students of friends, and friends of friends—but that doesn't mean that what these kids have to say is any less valid. We need to listen to them because, like it or not, our future depends on them.

The participants (not their real names):

Terri: from Texas, in her last year of college as a music industry major and looking to have a career in music marketing. She plays the piano "for my own amusement."

Christopher: from Los Angeles, graduating this year with a degree in electrical engineering. He has also seriously studied songwriting and plays in a band.

Amelia: from New York, a psychology major. She plans to go to law school after college.

Rob: from Pennsylvania, majoring in biomedical engineering. He's also a singer and works with a semi-professional *a cappella* group.

Wayne: from Tennessee. He didn't finish high school and now works with cars. Many of his friends are going to music school, and his stepfather is a successful studio session player.

Anna: from Chicago, an environmental engineering major, also very interested in cultural anthropology and ethnomusicology.

Eric: from Massachusetts, enrolled in a music industry program, plays bass in a band "for fun." He's the only one in the group who's married.

Insider: Where do you get the music you listen to? Do you pay for it or get it free?

Rob: The music I listen to regularly is off of CDs, but when I'm at my computer or when I'm traveling, I listen to MP3s downloaded from one of the P2P services. When I'm going on a long trip, instead of waiting to rip all my CDs to MP3, it's often just faster to download it and burn it directly onto an MP3 CD.

Amelia: I buy CDs, burn them from friends, download music, and also listen to the radio. I download more than anything. I pay for maybe 30% of what I listen to.

Anna: I don't download anymore, since Napster shut down. I buy CDs, more used than new. There is nothing I enjoy more than buying used CDs. I would much rather spend my money on a CD than clothes, and nothing makes my day like a cheap CD.

Eric: I haven't bought a CD in a long time. When Napster was getting put down and Metallica and the others were making so much noise, I thought a lot of the bands were crybabies, so I stopped listening to mainstream stuff. I know the people in a lot of the local bands, and they just give their CDs away for promotion, to get their sound out. I don't really use Kazaa much any more. I used to, every once in a while, but I go through newsgroups now. You get the whole CD, you don't just pick and choose one song, which might not even be what you want.

Wayne: I don't buy new music—mostly. I used to work at Tower, so I try to go to Tower, but like everybody else says, it's too damn expensive.

Terri: I don't buy many CDs. The last time was a few months ago, for a gift. My little sister still buys them. She's 13, and for her they're still cool. I listen to the radio when I know a station that's good, but radio gets old, bland. I just listen on my computer, getting music from Kazaa.

What would you consider a fair price for a CD?

Chris: Under nine dollars.

Anna: For used CDs, about $7.99 or $8.99. New ones I try not to buy for over $14.

Rob: Sub ten dollars, unless it's a new release and I'm really into the band, then I'll pay $16 or $17. There have been times when I was going to the store to get one $17 disk, and I ended up not buying it but spent $20 on two other disks.

Wayne: You pay $20 and there would be two good songs on it. You get home, and you're pissed off that you bought it. I go to used stores, but mostly for vinyl. It sounds better to me than CDs.

"I honestly don't feel that going out and buying a CD is worth it now."

Terri: For the price of a CD I can eat for a week. I'd pay nine or ten dollars. You can find those, but it's usually in used CD stores, or else they're really old, and I don't want to listen to them.

Eric: I honestly don't feel that going out and buying a CD is worth it now. Any other company that would still have the same product for 20 years wouldn't be in business, without upgrading their product a substantial amount. It's the labels saying "we own 80% of the market, and we can do anything we want. This is the product, you buy it." And it came to a point where, don't we have a say in it anymore?

Are you happy with the sound quality of the music you download?

Wayne: I don't really hear the difference between the MP3s I download and a CD I buy in a store. On the vinyl, the ranges are bigger: Instead of a flat sound, it's more spread out, more of a live feel. It does sound better.

Rob: I've downloaded enough now to hear the difference. I used to think that MP3s sounded good, and I still do, but when I started getting MP3s and then the CDs, I'd hear all this other stuff. The more I listen to MP3s, the more I notice little compression artifacts like poor stereo separation or a smearing of higher frequency content like hi-hats. So, I'll typically go out and buy the album, turn off the PC, and listen to the disc with headphones.

Especially if you've got a really carefully made album, with really good engineering, it's just not worth it to throw it to an MP3. I'd rather just listen to the original.

Amelia: Sometimes you get bad ones. We'll download it and say to each other, "Wait a minute—does that sound right to you?" You can tell. Sometimes there's a difference between the better MP3s and the CDs, but not really. I'll download a song, and then I'll listen to a friend's CD, and it's "Well, same thing to me."

Chris: I sometimes forget it's compressed, and I'll listen to a song, and I'll think this band is great, but the sonic quality isn't very good, and then I'll think, oh, right, it's MP3. Maybe the CD version is really good.

Terri: The audio quality on the downloaded stuff is fine. I have a pretty good speaker system, so it's not like wimpy computer sound, and that makes up for any lack in quality. I don't really notice a difference between when I play CDs and when I download stuff.

Eric: I don't think there's much of a difference. A lot of programs out there can convert MP3s into WAV files, and that creates a clearer sound. It's just a notch below the quality of a CD.

Are there advantages to having a CD versus downloading an album?

Amelia: The booklet. I read a lot about artists, and the booklet has pictures, and credits, and thank-yous. And since everyone's using samples, with every song they tell you who they sampled from, so you can go and listen to the original. And also lyrics, if you want to know the words of the song. I have all my discs together in a little zipper container, and I arrange it so I have the covers outside and the CDs inside, which looks kind of nice.

Rob: I have a couple of friends who have record collections, and it's really satisfying for them to go over to the shelf and take out a record and put it on the turntable and put the needle on. For me, the same thing goes for CDs. And you're not just hearing one song by the artists, but you're hearing the entire picture of what the artist has to present. I like to take the CD off the shelf and listen to everything the artist has to say, straight through.

What happens when you leave school, and you don't have a free broadband connection any more?

Chris: I become much more frugal in what I listen to. I spend a lot more time listening to the CDs I already have.

Terri: I can't imagine not spending the money for a somewhat speedy Internet. That would drive me insane. You want to use it for Internet anyway, so the music is a bonus.

Rob: If I didn't have that connection, I would probably not have had nearly as diverse music tastes. Over the past few years, I've switched back and forth between a high-speed connection and a modem, and my musical interests have expanded at a more rapid rate when I have had access to a broadband connection. I have AOL DSL at home; I pay for it myself.

Wayne: Everyone uses cable. I don't know anyone who uses a dial-up anymore.

How do you hear about new artists?

Amelia: Usually I get recommendations from my friends whose taste I like, or I see a new artist on television. When artists first come out, you'll hear them on the radio or see them on TV, or there's an article in the paper.

Rob: I'll read articles about the bands that I like, and if I read in an article of another band that's one of their influences or is like them, I'll go and check them out.

Chris: I like to look at Amazon.com lists: A customer bought this one, he also bought these. Go to that, listen to the samples, hey, that's not bad. Read some of the editorial reviews: this CD was at the top of the indie rock charts in 1994, and they were a really influential band, and this should be in your collection. Okay, so I go out and I get that. From e-mail lists I get announcements about different shows or people opening up for other people, you get into them there.

When I'm looking for a song on the P2P networks, maybe I'll find a guy who has six songs by the band I want. So I listen to more songs.

Could the record labels be doing more to get you to listen to new artists?

Eric: On a DVD you have coming attractions for stuff that's the same genre. You could do that on a CD or on the Web. The labels should figure out a way to get together with Kazaa, so that when you type in a band you like, a pop-up comes up for a different band.

"You flood everybody with something more and more, and after a while they think they like it."

Terri: How are you going to reach people? What are people really doing? Maybe commercials on TV—kids are sitting and watching TV. Or doing pop-ups: different things that will let you to listen to something for ten seconds and see if you like it. Or they could buy a word in a search engine, and when someone looks for it, it shows all the new people in that genre and what they're doing, and you can listen to a little snippet of it. Isn't that how you grow a fan base? By familiarizing a person with a band. So that would personalize it to the listener, to be more familiar and connect with the band.

Wayne: The music hasn't been so bad—it's good. But I don't know where they get these singers, they're whining and pissing and moaning about nothing. They sound like they're getting their ass kicked while they're trying to sing. I won't buy that. That's why everybody I know hasn't bought any new CDs in a long time. It's, for lack of a better word, propaganda. You flood everybody with something more and more, and after a while they think they like it. People think when they buy a CD they're getting a life. We're just running around like a chicken with its head cut off looking for the right clique. They're going to have to start thinking for themselves.

Can radio help?

Terri: People are in their cars and traveling, and they want to listen to music, so it's never going to go away, but as a way of pushing new artists, it's on the way out.

Eric: I don't think XM and satellite radio are going to do that much, because people aren't willing to pay for a CD right now, never mind a fee every month for a radio station. They do offer a lot, but how do you get 10-15 dollars a month out of someone's pocket when they can listen for free? I don't think Clear Channel is doing a very good job. You don't hear a lot of new music promotion on it.

Wayne: I turn on the radio and immediately turn it off. I'll go to the oldies station or the classic rock station in hopes that they'll play Zeppelin. Radio's dead. It's like a busted wheel. It's paid advertisements for crap. I listen to the music channels on cable. You hear some good stuff every now and then.

What would get you to spend more money on recorded music?

Rob: More albums by bands I like. And if there were extra content, I would pay for it. One thing that comes to mind, which I personally would find interesting, would be if they could give you more than two audio tracks, so you could mix it yourself. If it was a band I liked, I would have no trouble spending $50 on a disc that had a lot of tracks I could do that with. I would play with that to no end. And they should do a "making of the CD" like they do on DVDs. I've downloaded some things which have outtakes from CDs, and they're pretty cool. You can hear them talking at the beginning, you hear more of the personality of the artist.

Eric: I would suggest three different things. One is (guitar) tab music. You see all the commercials for "music makes you smarter"? That's a booming industry right now, and to go along with that, you put tab music in there. So you can buy a band's CD, and you can learn their songs right off the bat. I think a lot of people go through stages where they want to pick up a guitar and learn how to play, and they never really end up playing, but try to learn a couple of songs.

Two, I think PC-enabled CDs, with interviews with the band, are a great idea. They should put that on every disc instead of one in a hundred. This is why they took a year to do it in the studio, and this is how they wrote the song, and this is how it came about. People would start buying stuff like that for 15 or 16 bucks.

And then, like on DVDs, there's coming attractions on the disc itself. You put the freeware for playing the stuff on the website, so consumers have to go there, and you can promote more stuff. You're telling the consumer, "This is our gift to you when you buy the CD. You come to our site, and you can check out other bands and maybe buy their CD or DVD."

Wayne: If it's quality music, I'll support the band. If I like it, I'm more inclined to buy it, to show support. If something is out just because it's trendy, I'm not going to spend money on it, I'm just going to download it. Whoever *Rolling Stone* says is the god of rock and roll and is saving rock and roll now, it's just not it for me. To me that stuff is just as bad as the Backstreet Boys. They go into the studio and say this is what we want to do, but the label says no, it's going to be this way, and that's the way you do it. It's just being a whore.

Amelia: I can't think of any reason to spend more money on music. If there were better artists, more artists that I liked, I would buy their CDs. I would download it first, of course, but then I'd go out and buy it. But there are so few that I like.

Chris: CDs under nine bucks. Avril Lavigne did a CD for 7-8 dollars, and they sold four million of them. I'd buy more CDs, even to the point that the dollars I was spending would increase from my total budget.

Are the record companies still necessary?

Eric: They are to the extent that they are able to market a name nationally or worldwide. But that's pretty much all they're good for.

Terri: I think they should cut back on all the people they're paying. It seems like they pay a lot of people to do...what exactly? (laughs) They need the musicians, but why do you need legislative executives? It seems a lot of bands need a business manager and the people that are marketing them, and that can pretty much be it. They don't need hundreds of people, not with the Internet, and fax, and the telephone. I think that would cut out a lot of the money that they're having to spend, and that would be a little more fair towards who's doing the work and who deserves it.

Rob: I think that things have to change. As negative and depressing as that is, I think that some parts of the industry are just not going to be around much longer. My dad told me there was a place near where he grew up that made stagecoaches. Even in the age of cars, that's all they made. And they were around even up until my dad's lifetime. They were this completely stubborn company, and of course they went out of business. If someone wants to make money in the record industry, and the industry's changing, it doesn't make sense for someone to stay and do what they've always been doing.

Chris: My grandfather was a studio musician in Hollywood. Back then he would play in the background ensembles in movies, when they'd come out and dance. That job isn't there any more.

Terri: It might be a little scary for them, but I think if one of the major five labels were to just step out from that whole circle of monopoly and say, you know what, we're a good company, we're going to treat our artists right, and this is what our name stands for, I think more people are going to honor and respect that. And in turn they'll get more artists and consumers that way. If people hear that there's support by a label for this act, they tend to connect that with, "Oh, that must be a good label." If they can fix their image so that it's seen as a good thing, that they know music and they know how to support it, then they're needed. So many more people are aware of what is going on, that there's going to have to be a change.

Eric: I think the RIAA is going about it in totally the wrong way. It's like, no you can't do this; this is illegal. If you keep saying that, more and more people are going to download it. Just to piss them off more. Looking around at sites like that, there are so many out there that say "Boycott RIAA" or "RIAA sucks." The more they get involved to represent all these companies, the worse the companies look.

They're trying to represent themselves as promoting new ideas, when really, they have none. The scariest part for them is that they can't point a finger at anyone. They can't say, the guy on the street corner, this business exec, he's downloading the most. It's everybody. The numbers for downloading are showing that what they're doing is not working. If they got their hands on it when it first came out, they could have done anything. There would have been infinite possibilities. But they let it grow too big for them to hop on it now. The thing that really shows me how badly they're doing, how desperate they are, is this new "kidpop": reissuing their old catalog and aiming it towards kids, so that the baby-boomer parents will buy it all over again.

I feel this is kind of a good thing that's happening to the major labels, that this is coming about. The industry needs to realize that they need to treat the band, the product they're promoting, better. There are a lot of pop stars that make a lot of money, but there are also a lot of bands out there that are suing the companies they're contracted with. You hear the RIAA complaining that people are stealing music, but then you see Incubus, trying to sue Sony to get out of their contract, because they're not getting as much money as they should. That goes along with a lot of peoples' feelings toward the industry. You're pretty much screwing the bands that we like, so you can keep more of the money, so why don't we, as consumers, do the same to you?

Should the record labels set up their own downloading networks?

Anna: I personally don't like having to have my computer on all the time if I want to listen to music. If a record company's really looking to make money for an artist, I don't think selling MP3 singles on the Web is going to do it. I think their main objective should be to gain loyal fans, fans of the artist, not the single track. That's why I prefer CDs, because you see more of the depth of the artist when you listen to more of the songs. If they're looking to have a solid fan base, the way to do it is to sell the artist, not the single.

Terri: They could offer something more than just the music from the site. Like a drawing: win Dave Matthews tickets, or go backstage, or meet the press, something that's going to attract people who say, "Wow, I might be able to do this extra thing and get involved."

Rob: I wouldn't pay to download an MP3. I think that what they should do to make people buy CDs should be what they did with VHS. Originally, VHS players were just for people to tape off their TV. But then the studios went out and saturated the market and made VHS tapes of everything they had, movies and all kinds of stuff. If the record companies would just saturate the MP3 market with free or very easily duplicatable copies of the songs at, like, 96 kilobit or some really low quality, I think that people would download it and notice the difference in quality. People who are really interested in an artist and hear a really bad quality MP3 floating around would go out and buy the CD. If there were plenty of low-quality MP3s floating around, I don't think people would bother making really nice encodings of them.

Eric: It might make sense to set up a network through a label, instead of through Sharman Networks (makers of the Kazaa software). But not like Pressplay. With Pressplay you pay ten bucks a month, and then when you download a song, it's a dollar. That's crap—it ends up being more than you would pay for the CD if you went out and bought it. I don't even understand why they came out with that.

Afterword

The response to this article, and indeed the whole issue, was very strong, but the most concern was expressed by readers who bemoaned the fact that some of the "kids" couldn't tell the difference between an MP3 and a CD.

It's interesting to see how many of the suggestions that my interviewees made have actually come to pass, some on the very day that this issue of *Mix* hit the newsstands: April 28, 2003, the day that Apple announced its iTunes Music Store. And Apple, at least for now, seems to have done it right: Even though they've taken in over a billion dollars and own 80% of the downloadable music market, except for the occasional lawyer for The Beatles and some European copyright commissions, you don't hear any complaints about them ripping off listeners *or* artists.

Thanks to Rick Clark, Leon Janikian, Karen Panetta, and all the great kids who let me pick their brains for this column.

Chapter 38

Funk Brothers Ed Willis and Joe Messina.
Photo courtesy of Allan Slutsky.

The Shadows of Motown
You've Got to Catch This Flick!

Preface

Whenever a new delivery format is introduced, it has to wait for a product that really takes advantage of the format before a large number of people will buy into it—a "killer application," as it were. For many of us in the entertainment industry, the CD-ROM version of The Beatles' *Hard Days Night*, with its script, trailers, additional songs, and commentary served as the killer app for that medium. Of course, CD-ROM didn't last long, since DVDs holding eight times as much material were right around the corner, but it pointed the way. This wonderful project was the first movie I saw in a theater that made me want to go out and get the DVD, not only so I could show it to friends, but so that I could check out all the fantastic background material. It was definitely worth it.

September 2003

No, it's not *Harry Potter and the Invisible Weapons of Mass Destruction* or *The Matrix Regurgitated*. For us in the music biz, this year's superhot multimedia property is *Standing in the Shadows of Motown*, a 16-year-long project that just keeps getting better and better. The latest incarnation is so good, in fact, that it actually inspired me to go out and buy a DVD player.

It all began in the late '80s when Philadelphia-based musician/writer/arranger/guitarist/fanatic Allan Slutsky, who publishes under the name Dr. Licks, decided to write a book about James Jamerson, probably the most influential bassist in rock 'n' roll history. Jamerson was one of the legendary jazz-trained Motown session players who called themselves The Funk Brothers and whose work supported hundreds of hit records; as the opening titles of the movie (based on the book) tell us, the Brothers have "more Number One records than The Beatles, the Beach Boys, the Rolling Stones, and Elvis Presley combined."

Jamerson never garnered much attention for himself, but as anyone (especially a bass player) who has ever listened closely to his tracks knows, he was nothing less than a genius. He drove the Motown rhythm section with lines that were melodic, inventive, and constantly in motion, defining the beats and harmonic structures by filling the spaces between them rather than simply coming down straight on them. Slutsky's biographical/instructional book, *Standing in the Shadows of Motown—The Life and Music of Legendary Bassist James Jamerson*, which came out in 1989, supports Jamerson's reputation with the strongest possible evidence. Besides detailing Jamerson's life, which ended tragically at the young age of 47 after years of alcohol abuse, Slutsky's book also faithfully transcribes some four dozen of Jamerson's most amazing bass parts, from "Ain't No Mountain High Enough" to "You Can't Hurry Love."

And there's more: Recordings of the transcriptions, along with some great interviews of Jamerson's friends and fans, are featured on two CDs that are stuck into the back of the book. (In the first printings, these were cassettes.) The 24 players on the recordings include luminaries like John Entwistle, Will Lee, Jack Bruce, John Patitucci, and Jamerson's son, James Jr., who also talk about their love of and respect for the Motown bassist's work. The recordings are in the old "music-minus-one" style: The bass part is on one channel and the rest of the instrumental tracks are on the other. Slutsky's book is still available, and for about the cost of a six-pack of rewritable DVDs, you can't ask for a more valuable educational tool.

But Slutsky, who knew he was onto a good thing, wasn't finished there. Paul McCartney's opening greeting on the CD says, "I hope this project goes on to greater heights"—he had no idea how well that hope would be fulfilled. After the book came out (and won a few awards), the author, having made friends with many of the musicians who worked with

Jamerson, began to think about a more comprehensive project—aimed at a wider audience—that would involve all of the Funk Brothers. He linked up with documentary producer and director Paul Justman and producer Sandy Passman and got financing from a couple of other musicians who were major fans of Motown. The team organized a series of live shows at the Royal Oak Music Theater in Detroit, featuring seven of the surviving original Brothers and a supporting cast of a couple of dozen other first-class players and singers. The musicians, who hadn't played together in years, rehearsed for a week, using Slutsky's transcriptions to support their own memories, some of which were hazy. ("Did I really play that?" Slutsky heard more than once.) The concerts were shot with multiple 35mm cameras and recorded and mixed by Kooster McAllister and the Record Plant Remote.

Surrounding the concert footage, we get to see the Brothers rehearsing, reminiscing, and articulately explaining the elements of their musical success. Because many of the original singers are retired or dead, the lead vocals at the concert were handled by some newer talents—Ben Harper, Méshell Ndegéocello, and Chaka Kahn among them—but the point is well made that the vocalists in Motown were often not the most important factor in the label's musical success: It was the band. "You could take a chicken, bring him into the studio and have him squawk on two and four, and you would have a hit record," one of the Brothers declares in the DVD's supplementary material, and you realize that he's probably right.

> *"You could take a chicken, bring him into the studio and have him squawk on two and four, and you would have a hit record."*

There were, for example, three guitarists on many of the sessions, and when a new arrangement came in, they would divvy up their parts in seconds: one playing a riff down low, another the backbeat high up the neck, and the third a syncopated pattern in the middle. They created textures that were, well, funky and unique to Motown, which acolytes—even those as brilliant as The Beatles and the Stones—could only hope to approximate, never duplicate.

The performances from a mad-hatted Bootsy Collins on "Cool Jerk" and "Do You Love Me" and by an ecstatic Joan Osborne on "Heat Wave" and "What Becomes of the Broken Hearted" are fabulous, as is Tom Scott's alto sax solo on "Shotgun." But it's the Funk Brothers, cooking along on tracks that they defined 30 and 40 years ago, and the joy in their faces, who really catch your eye and put a lump in your throat. Drummer Uriel Jones says, "After so many years, we were all a little unsure about playing together. But we surprised ourselves—we had the Motown sound." Correction: They *were* the Motown sound.

The filmmakers do a fine job of framing the music in the context of the tumultuous world that inspired the sound. As the film's narration notes, "Motown played a pre-eminent role in the cultural soundtrack" that accompanied, and commented on, the events of the '60s.

When the film then segues into Chaka Khan's rendition of Marvin Gaye's "What's Going On," arguably the pinnacle of the Motown era (and the first record on which the individual musicians were credited), it is at once joyous and chilling. *[It also won her a Grammy for Traditional R&B performance.]*

None of the Motown session players became rich, but they weren't ripped off as badly as many musicians of the time, and some were able to afford respectable middle-class existences on what they earned in Berry Gordy's studio and elsewhere. The movie, which was produced with Gordy's cooperation (he still controls a large share of the music, after all), treads lightly on this area, but in one interview, drummer Jones, who still does some music teaching, makes an apt allusion to the economic dichotomy: "The kids say, "If you played on all those hit records, what are you doing teaching us?""

While Motown was predominantly a black enterprise, not all of the players were African-American. Joe Messina was the "white boy" sitting between two black Brothers. "They called us 'The Oreo Cookie Guitar Section,'" he says with a laugh. But then he and percussionist Jack Ashford recall a tense moment after a late-night session in July of 1967, when tensions between police and the black community reached a fever pitch and Detroit was rioting. "Everything was burning down," says Ashford, "and you protect your family. These were my brothers here. I didn't think about color. I would have gone down for them, even at the hands of a black brother." Méshell Ndegéocello interviews white bassist Bob Babbitt, who breaks down when he recalls how he was treated by the other players after Martin Luther King Jr.'s assassination the next year. "Had the role been reversed and we had been in a predominantly white area and something broke out, I would have took a bullet for Jack," he says.

There are many other poignant scenes, such as when the players visit the long-unused basement of Gordy's old Detroit home. Now a museum, the old Studio A at Hitsville USA was otherwise known as "The Snakepit." "It's still in there," says Ashford, referring to the spirit and prayers of Gordy and all who worked there. There's great sadness and frustration associated with the place, too. Slutsky relates one tale when he was at a restaurant with normally articulate guitarist Robert White, who played the lead line on "My Girl." When that song came on the sound system, White started to tell the waiter that it was he who was playing on the record but got too embarrassed to finish his sentence and, instead, just ordered his barbecued chicken. Says Slutsky, "I knew at that point, Robert desperately needed some recognition in his lifetime." That recognition is finally at hand, but sadly, White didn't live long enough to receive it.

To see the movie in a theater, which I did last year, is wonderful. But even so, the DVD adds a lot to the experience. On disc, the film is divided into 35 intelligently chosen chapters, which makes it easy to jump around and also makes it possible to just watch the music sequences. There are the usual extra audio tracks, which include two-channel, 5.1 Dolby, and 6.1 DTS surround; running commentary from Slutsky and Justman; and a reasonably informative *MST3K*-style on-screen "trivia track." Extra material (much of which comes on a second disc) includes a black-and-white video of interviews with some of the Brothers (including Robert White) from 1993 that helped raise funding for the film; biographical interviews; tributes to the Brothers who've died; scenes that had to be cut from the film due to time constraints; a bunch of onstage, club, and studio jam sessions, some of which are done "multi-angle"; and a delightful and touching segment entitled "Dinner with the Funks," which I would have been happy to watch for an hour or more.

And the project keeps going. The Funk Brothers themselves have gone on tour around the U.S., and this fall and winter they are scheduled to go to Europe and Australia. Slutsky is continuing to explore the old tracks and is planning a release of some remixes of the original Motown multitrack masters, which will showcase instrumental parts and licks hidden in well-known songs that no one has heard before. "Pushing up faders and punching mute buttons, and hearing all of this amazing stuff," he says, "it's a musician's dream."

Afterword

Slutsky's remixes of the Funk Brothers' vaults came out in 2004 in a two-CD "Deluxe Edition" set. Besides the Grammy for Chaka Khan's performance, *Standing in the Shadows of Motown* won the award that year for Compilation Soundtrack Album, and in 2004, the Funk Brothers received a Lifetime Achievement award from NARAS. The DVD is reported to have sold over a million copies.

Kooster McAllister and mixers Ted Greenberg and Clive Taylor won the 2003 TEC Award for Remote Production for their work on the film, and they were up against some pretty stiff competition, Springsteen and the Stones among them. It couldn't have happened to a more deserving team or a more deserving project.

Chapter 39

Joel Elrod

Audio Products Go Wild!

New Stuff You Will *Not* See at AES This Month…

Preface

This one was really popular among readers, a lot of whom wrote that they were jealous they hadn't thought of some of these ideas themselves—and a number of whom sent in their own variations on the various themes.

October 2003

It's AES time. Thousands of us will flock to the Javits Center to drink overpriced lukewarm coffee, eat three-day-old sandwiches, lose our voices from shouting over the din, and try to figure out which way to jump so as to keep ahead of the competition. And if you wonder why all of the engineers in the booths look like they haven't slept for two weeks, it's because they haven't. They've been working around the clock trying to get their prototypes up and running for the show or at least working well enough so no one can tell that production is actually still a year away.

But for those of us in the know—and that includes me, as I've been going to these things for more than 25 years (yes, I was there when the New York show was held at the

Waldorf-Astoria)—the real action isn't on the floor or even in the private demo rooms or high-priced hotel suites. It's in the corridors, the cheap motels, and the alleyways where you will find the truly revolutionary products, from manufacturers too hip—and too cheap—to have an official presence at the show. And that's what this column is about: new products that you *won't* see at this month's AES because they're simply too revolutionary for the public to know about yet. Like the products on the show floor these days, they break down almost entirely into two categories: control surfaces and software plug-ins.

It's too bad that Mackie wasn't audacious enough to trademark the words "user interface" and its attendant acronym, because we're about to see dozens of products that will piggyback on the popularity of its "HUI" and "Baby HUI" control surfaces. Most of these will be coming from an Indonesian company well-known for its poor-quality knockoffs of other companies' gear. Its first products, which will follow the tradition of being named after old comic-book characters, will be the "Donald's Nephews" line, comprising "LUI" and "DUI" (pending dismissal of the expected lawsuit by Disney).

LUI® is the Lazy Users Interface. It has but one physical control: a 2-inch-diameter, trackball-like thingie that can be placed on a flat surface, held in the lap, worn on the wrist, or put in your pocket. It is accompanied by a 15-inch LCD screen equipped with an eyeball tracking system that determines which parameter you are looking at and assigns the controller accordingly. (If you want to operate more than one control at a time, sticking out your tongue is the equivalent of pressing a Shift key.) A built-in speakerphone allows hands-free communication with producers, record company executives, and tech support, and a voice-operated automatic dialer connects to local sushi and pizza suppliers (small delivery charge).

The system is supplemented with a brainwave interpreter, so the user doesn't even have to be conscious to have full use of it.

DUI® stands for, depending on your predilection, either Drunk or Drugged Users Interface. It's actually a deluxe version of the LUI and comes with cup and can holders, roach clip, self-extinguishing ashtray, and optional mirrored surface and nasal cauterizer. The eyeball-tracking system is supplemented with a brainwave interpreter, so the user doesn't even have to be conscious to have full use of the system. The speakerphone auto-dialer has an additional feature: It calls a cab at the end of each session. Another option is a miniature blood-analysis lab designed by a well-regarded government subcontractor; its results are admissible in most traffic courts.

Should these devices prove successful, reliable reports say that there are three more models already in this company's development pipeline: SUI® is a special workstation controller that will be sold exclusively to record companies. It will operate in conjunction with the Watermarker plug-in (described below) to prepare legal cases against artists and consumers suspected of copyright infringement via sampling, downloading, recording streams, or just humming something that they heard on the radio. It promises to be very expensive (most likely charging by the hour) and very, very mean.

SKRUI®—Simulated Kinesthetic Recursive User Interface—A highly intelligent device that uses the latest force-feedback technology from advanced game controllers. It is so intelligent, in fact, that it knows what it's doing far better than you do, and if you try to make a mixing move it doesn't like, it will resist hard enough to break your fingers. So while you may think that you're controlling it, it's actually controlling you. (Due to the potential for intense violence, this device is rated M by the Entertainment Software Rating Board.)

> *It knows what it's doing far better than you do, and if you try to make a mixing move it doesn't like, it will resist hard enough to break your fingers.*

The last in the line, for reasons that should be obvious, is KABLUI®, the KAmikaze BorderLine User Interface. This device, which requires an enormous amount of both AC and CPU power, is brought online only when a project is so awful that you wish it would just destroy itself. Like LUI, this device has only a single control, but it's best operated with a long stick or while wearing protective gear. A new concept in warranties protects the product against failure right up until the moment it is used.

Going inside our computers, the best of this year's crop of not-ready-for-the-show-floor plug-ins reveals how comfortable our industry is with both the past and the future: They reflect the new digital realities of the music business, while reaching back to vintage sounds and ideas of yesteryear.

The software instrument ArpIdiocy® is the first "true" analog synth module to take advantage of recent modeling technology, which simulates leaky capacitors, dirty potentiometers, self-destructing heat-sensitive resistors, and other heretofore impossible-to-imitate relics of the pre-IC era. In this model, realistic oscillators and filters produce random drift of master-pitch and scale intervals; changing parameters gives rise to random, loud crunching noises, whose levels are in inverse proportion to the signal level (at elevated levels, the crunching sounds are replaced by momentary dropouts); an authentic-sounding spring reverb can be triggered by keyboard velocity to produce that famous, annoying "boing" sound; and a patented Human Pitchwheel® redefines its zero point after each operation. Unlike the original, the plug-in allows storage of your carefully designed patches, with parameter repeatability guaranteed to be "pretty close."

If you're looking for unique processors, check out That70sSound®, a virtual 8-track tape deck that automatically stops every 15 minutes, thinks for a few seconds, executes one of several skull-shattering mechanical noise samples, and then starts up again in some random spot. It also slowly, inexorably, and not-so-subtly increases wow and flutter over time, requiring the user to periodically virtually smack it with his virtual palm. At the end of every session, it breaks opens and spools out the entire session file, leaving it in a virtual tangle by the side of the virtual road.

Another relic of a bygone era is Gesundheit®: The Tissue Paper Simulator. This package contains two plug-ins: The first will make any speaker sound like a vintage Yamaha NS-10 (worth the price all by itself for studios lusting after an '80s vibe), while the second inserts digital models of a wide variety of paper products in front of the first plug-in's virtual tweeter. The parameters include tissue type (facial, kitchen, or bathroom), thickness (one- or two-ply), price (bargain or name-brand), color (white, pastel, or patterned), and embossing and roll format (regular, double, or 1,000-sheet). Users are asked to please not squeeze the software.

Producers who are tired of the "Cher effect" (and who isn't?), in which every note is dead-on in tune whether the singer is capable of producing such notes or not, will welcome the Vocaldroid RS® (Real Singer) plug-in. Modifying a glitch-filled, over-vibrato'ed, flat or sharp vocal track so that it comes out absolutely perfect is child's play these days in the digital world. But going the other way—making it sound like a real human being produced the sound—is a genuine achievement. The Vocaldroid takes even the finest classically trained vocalists and brings their level of artistry down closer to what you would expect in a typical session with typical backup singers or singing band members. Entrance timings are adjustable from one-half beat to three bars, early or late; harmony lines are reconfigurable into inappropriate modes, keys, or scales; and a special function does a convincing (but nondestructive) digital simulation of the singer tripping over the mic cord.

"Strike back with the Antimaximizer®!" That's the slogan for the upcoming marketing campaign behind an ingenious plug-in for pop music producers who are sick of hearing all of the dynamics of their mixes totally flattened when they are mastered by a major label or played on the radio. Because no one at radio stations actually *listens* to what they're playing anymore, leaving it instead to various machines to make sure that the instantaneous modulation level never drops below 98%, the designers of the Antimaximizer have come up with a way to fake out broadcasters and restore true dynamic levels to mixes.

Their work is based on an algorithm that uses a combination of noise-shaping and psychoacoustic masking, similar to MP3 coding but turning it on its head. Instead of detecting frequencies that won't be missed and eliminating them, the plug-in finds frequencies that aren't audible in the first place and raises their level enough so that the whole signal gets continuously slammed up to -0.001 dBFS. Because no audible frequencies are affected, the dynamics of the music are maintained faithfully, but anyone glancing at a signal-level monitor will see a barely moving needle or a constant red-plasma glow: a sight to warm the heart of any label or radio executive.

And finally, some farsighted (and very well-funded) developers who truly understand the future of the music business are about to release The Ultimate Watermarker®: "Protection for your precious assets."

Three versions of the plug-in will be available. The basic version, which is freeware, places a 64-bit digital word into each track every 536 milliseconds. This watermark, which on a 'scope looks like a tiny staircase wave piggybacking on a few audio cycles, is almost undetectable, but when it is audible, it actually enhances the bass response of the track, especially if the track is at 112 bpm. The watermark's data encoding is robust enough to withstand mixing, down-sampling, MP3 or AAC conversion, multiple A/D stages, compression, multiband broadcast limiting, Dolby and DTS surround expansion, and being played through a cell phone speaker.

The 64 bits contain a wealth of important musical information: names of the composer, lyricist, publisher, performing rights organization, artist, engineer, and producer; and the passport and Social Security numbers, as well as the library card, video rental, and voting records of all creative personnel. Also, there's the recording's date and time, studio longitude and latitude, microphone model and serial number, recording medium, the recording computer's IP number, iLok account ID and password, and an analysis of the lead vocalist's DNA.

If you want to *read* the digital watermarks, however, you need to pay for the "pro" version: Watermarker DRM® ($ classified). Available only in the United States—and only to individuals who can prove they have never been sued by the RIAA—Watermarker DRM automatically extracts the encoded information, displays it, and forwards it to the appropriate private or government bodies. For example, author and publisher information is sent to the Harry Fox Agency, which ignores it for a minimum of six months and then randomly changes the title, misspells the composer's name, and passes it along to ASCAP, BMI, SESAC, TAXI, the DEA, the NRA, and the U.S. Copyright Office. Technical and personnel information is sent to the AES, SPARS, NARAS, and the editors of *Mix* magazine, while information about microphone usage is forwarded to the mics' manufacturers and their respective PR agencies.

But that's not all. With funds from the major record labels and various black-budget intelligence agencies, the developers have also come up with a "stealth" version of the software called *Watermarker Mandatory Deployment* (WMD), which Congress is now considering legislation to require in all consumer electronic devices. With this software (which incorporates the "SUI" technology described earlier) installed, the IP number of the device playing any recording is transmitted (using 802.11x) to the nearest McDonald's, where it is sent on to a central database that cross-checks it against the ID of the device that created the recording. If this database doesn't show a legitimate sales transaction between the two devices, then the software interrupts playback and erases the file and then issues a subpoena to the user.

If the playback device is registered to a college student, then the software contacts the school's administrative computer (with the school's permission, of course) and changes all of the student's recent grades to "F"s, while revoking his financial aid. An RIAA spokesperson says enthusiastically of these features: "We can't think of a better way of increasing customer loyalty to our products."

In addition, any tunes, lyrics, or samples that are known to have been created by the Dixie Chicks or Steve Earle or are in French or are sung by anyone named "Ahmed" or "Yussef" are intercepted, and the offending device's IP number and GPS location are relayed to the appropriate local law-enforcement agency's anti-terrorism unit and to the Department of Homeland Security. A high-placed Washington source explains the rationale behind the system: "Keeping track of what everyone is listening to, everywhere, all of the time, is one of the best tools we can use for maintaining the freedoms that have made this country great."

Have a good show.

Paul Lehrman isn't paranoid. Yet.

Will Terry

Chapter 40

Bungling in the Jungle
Studio Life in the Third World:
A Memoir

Preface

As I mentioned in the Introduction to this book, I actually started my career as a pro audio journalist writing about my adventures in Trinidad, the place where I more or less started my recording studio career. While I'll admit it was a great educational experience, as you will see, it was also a nightmare. When I got back to the U.S., quite broke, unemployed, and homeless, I contacted a magazine in England called *Studio Sound*. They published short horror stories from the world of pro audio under the column heading "Agony," a feature that used to be common in British newspapers, usually consisting of stories of personal heartbreak or searches for missing friends and relatives. I sent the magazine two short accounts of my brief tenure in the tropics, and their response was "More!" Thus began a beautiful relationship and a whole new career path for me.

January 2004

Okay, kids, it's the longest night of the year, so it's time to gather 'round the simulated virtual fireplace, and I'll tell you some more stories from the bad old days, when I started out in this here recording business. It was 25 years ago this month when my girlfriend and I boarded a plane at JFK International Airport for Port of Spain, the capital of Trinidad and Tobago, for my first full-time gig as a recording engineer.

They must have known something—either about the owners or about the joys of running a high-tech operation in the Third World—that I didn't.

I was lucky, or perhaps unlucky, enough to start at the top. Unlike most of the folks you read about in this magazine, I didn't break into the studio biz as the assistant ashtray-emptier at a great metropolitan studio, nor did I open my own little 8-track studio and record local bands at loss-leader prices until one of them signed with Columbia. No, my first studio job was as the manager and chief engineer of a beautiful, brand-new 24-track recording facility. The reason I got the gig was, well, because everyone else in New York had turned it down. They must have known something—either about the owners or about the joys of running a high-tech operation in the Third World—that I didn't.

Actually, this story should have happened 25 years ago *last* month, but life in the Caribbean being what it is, we had to wait for things like a freight handler's strike at the airport to be settled and delays in getting work visas and import licenses for our household goods, all aggravated by phone service that was, to put it very politely, spotty.

At the time, the two-island nation boasted of having the highest per capita income in the English-speaking Caribbean, but that wasn't saying much, as most of the population was still desperately poor. While the tiny Tobagan economy was built on tourism, in Trinidad, where the studio was, there was little of that. Instead, there were oil refineries. Thanks to its proximity to Venezuela and harbors deep enough to handle transoceanic tankers, as well as a lack of government regulation in general, Trinidad was home to some very wealthy natives, most of whom had direct financial interest in the (foreign-owned) refineries. The rest of the populace lived in hope that the extreme levels of pollution they suffered would someday make them rich, too. In the meantime, many took advantage of the castoffs of the local industry and turned them into musical instruments: steel drums, which are, of course, made out of empty oil barrels.

The music scene was actually very exciting. Calypso, that super-energetic, irresistible dance form, was at its height, and reggae was making major inroads. A new type of Caribbean hybrid, soca, was gaining popularity, and local musicians, many of whom had spent time in New York or London, were beginning to understand how the modern recording studio could enhance their music. There was also a burgeoning film industry, at least according to the expatriate American filmmaker and his well-connected Trinidadian wife who had built the studio and hired me. They already had shot one feature film (something to do with lost cities of gold, protected by Amazon women, which, according to the lead review on the Internet Movie Database, is "the worst movie I ever saw") and were gearing up to do more. They also had plans for a record company, complete with pressing plant and a music publishing arm, and they had built the studio in hopes of attracting American and European artists who wanted a tropical experience but couldn't afford George Martin's recently opened AIR Montserrat.

When we touched down in Port of Spain, my boss impressively had us waved through customs and took us to the apartment he'd found for us in a residential neighborhood upstairs from an elderly landlady. As is true in most countries that have suffered long periods under colonial rule, many Trinidadians adopted some of the more obnoxious attitudes of their English oppressors without really knowing why. In our landlady's case, she had an impenetrable Victorian sense of decorum, which took the form of a prohibition on any music being played in her house. Of course, I spent a lot of time listening to music, and because my girlfriend was a pianist, this created a bit of a problem. To keep peace in the house, I agreed to play my stereo mostly through headphones, and somehow, a few weeks after we arrived, we convinced the landlady to let us rent an upright piano. But when the movers arrived and she was confronted with the actual instrument, she abruptly changed her mind and physically blocked them from coming up the stairs.

If someone happened to be around to pay off the driver (a bottle of rum was the preferred currency), then maybe we'd see more water in a few days.

The boss found us another place, which we fell in love with right away. It was high on a hill above Port of Spain, with the most gorgeous view of the city, the glowing refinery towns beyond, and the coast of South America beyond them. The sunsets, thanks to the high particulate content of the atmosphere, were spectacular. It was a building of 12 terraced apartments set into the hill, accessible only by a harrowing one-and-a-half-lane mountain road, which ended just above the top of the building. There was no landlady, but there were a pair of Canadian doctors, an oilfield worker from the U.S. (whose last job was in Iran), a young lawyer just back from school in England, a local automobile tire (or "tyre") magnate, and (rumor had it) the mistresses of several high government officials.

There was just one problem with the place: There was no water. The local water company wasn't legally required to pump higher than a certain altitude, and our little aerie was at least 100 feet above that limit. So instead, the water arrived in huge trucks that filled a large tank at the top of the complex, and if someone happened to be around to pay off the driver (a bottle of rum was the preferred currency), then maybe we'd see more water in a few days. But if not, it could be weeks.

Inevitably, when the tank had run dry, some poor soul in the building would get up in the morning, discover that he couldn't take a shower, and leave for work without bothering to close the tap. The water truck would arrive later that day and drop its load, and within a couple of hours, the entire tank would empty through our neighbor's bathtub, onto his floor, out the living room and back down the hill from whence it came. And we would be without water, again.

My work life was like that, too: occasional progress followed by major, often absurd, frustrations.

One of the first sessions I did was to record a steel band, the local equivalent of a symphony orchestra, for a single to be released just before Carnival, the annual Trinidadian pre-Lent bacchanalia that is rivaled in its over-the-topness only by Brazil's. The writer of the tune was a young man named Len "Boogsie" Sharpe, an absolute genius (and still very active today) at writing for an unusual ensemble that comprised two conga drums, a cowbell, brake drum, standard drum kit, and some 30 "pan" players, each responsible for between one and four hand-hammered, hand-tuned, carefully matched steel drums.

Steel drums are notoriously hard to record because the sound up close—which is a lot like banging on a tin can—is completely different from the sound at a distance, which can sometimes sound like an ethereal carillon crossed with a non-harmonic-overtoned pipe organ. The first time I got Boogsie in the studio for a solo recording, it took the whole session to figure out how to mic him. What finally worked was to put him at one end of the room in the vocal sweet spot and put a crossed pair of AKG 414s in figure-8 mode as far away from him as possible.

The studio was in a huge concrete building with corrugated steel walls 40 feet high, surrounded by several acres of asphalt, which was surrounded by jungle. It was on the site of a U.S. Navy tracking station that had been built during World War II and given back to the local government in the 1970s. For the dozens of pans we were trying to record, there was only one solution: Go outside. We had a 150-foot, 24-channel snake for film work, so getting lines out the door was no problem.

The session was scheduled for late afternoon, as most of the players had day jobs. Boogsie drew up a plot of where the different sections (with names like "double tenors," "guitar pans," "cellos," and "quadrophonics") should be. I marked up the diagram with mic model and cable numbers, handed it off to one of my eager new assistants, and set off to find dinner.

An hour later, I came back to find the mics in place and the whole orchestra ready to go. The only problem was, the assistants had placed the band right up against one of the steel walls. We tried a take and the resulting slapback would have sent Sam Phillips running into the jungle. I asked the guys where they got the insane idea to put the pans so close to the building, and the owner stepped in and said he was the one who ordered it; the last time they recorded steel pans, they did it there. It was mono, for a film, and "I kind of liked the echo." Needless to say, the track was useless.

So for the next hour, we moved everyone 20 yards over and then reset the mics and the levels. By now, the sun was setting, and in that part of the world, the temperature and humidity can change very rapidly as day turns into night. We tried another take, and during the final fade, I started to hear strange popping sounds and then some shouting, first on one channel, then another, and within a few seconds on all 24 tracks. I rushed outside and found that the players (and my trusty assistants) had all dived inside the building or into their cars to take refuge—leaving two dozen brand-new AKGs, Shures, Electro-Voices, and Neumanns to soak in the tropical downpour.

One more story. The studio had hired some local carpenters to build the control room furniture. They did some fine-looking work, but as most of their previous experience was in the domestic sphere, they were not terribly familiar with the concept of ventilation. The Dolby rack, for example, was built into a lovely hand-rubbed, completely sealed hardwood cabinet. By the time I was able to convince the boss to let me cut some holes in the back, we had lost several of the *Cat-22* channel cards. We wired the folks at Dolby UK, and they were very nice and promised to send us replacements right away.

Two months later, we were still waiting, while we tried to convince clients that they didn't really need Dolby on *all* their tracks. Someone went downtown to the main customs office and found that, yes, the cards had arrived some time ago, but customs was waiting for us to give them a "classification." (Our pointing out that they hadn't bothered to notify us about this didn't seem to impress them.) So the next day, I went down and explained that they were electronic subassemblies. Because we didn't pay for them, they had no cash value, and therefore we didn't have to pay any duty. But there was no such category on their forms. Instead, I was asked whether they should be considered "electronic parts" or "electronic equipment," the closest they could find.

"Call them parts," I said. "But we make electronic parts in this country," came the reply, "and you cannot import anything that's also made here without special dispensation. You don't have a license to import parts." I had never heard of a parts factory in Trinidad—all that came to mind was an image of some poor soul filling transformer cans with waste oil in his bathtub—but I wasn't going to argue. "Okay, then let's call them 'equipment,'" I said. "Ah!" came the swift rejoinder. "But then the equipment must have a cash value. And you must pay duty!"

I reached in my pocket and pulled out the first thing my fingers found: a $5 bill (worth about $2 U.S.). "How much cash value would this cover?" I demanded. The customs man dragged over a mechanical adding machine and, with great seriousness, punched in some numbers and pulled the crank. "At 17-percent duty, that would be $29.41," he intoned. "$29.41 it is," I said, leaving the five bucks on his desk and walking out with the cards.

I didn't last too long in Trinidad. My boss, who had been a respected filmmaker in the U.S., turned out to be a sleazebag and a bully. He bounced my paychecks, physically threatened me, and tried to confiscate my passport. He had recruited me with all sorts of promises to bring in foreign acts and promote the local music scene, but others later told me that wasn't the idea at all: He was in reality building an international film and music bootlegging operation, for which the studio was a front.

After six months, I had had it, and I got out in a scene like the one at the end of the Mel Gibson film *The Year of Living Dangerously*. Six months after that, the place was liquidated. The equipment was scattered to the winds, the site was eventually leased to someone else, and most of the projects I worked on never saw the light of day. I lost touch with everyone I had met there. My girlfriend and I stayed together a few more years, and then we went our separate ways, too. The experience left such an awful taste in my mouth, I wouldn't go anywhere south of Florida for more than 10 years.

But now it's 25 years later, and I have this strange hankering to go back. I want to see what became of the place and see how the recording scene in Trinidad has evolved. There were some beautiful places and lovely people there, and I would like to have a memory of them untarnished by the painful ones. I have some free time this month and a bunch of frequent-flyer miles burning a hole in my pocket. But this time, if I go, it'll be on my own terms. I'll let you know what happens.

Paul Lehrman is working on a lot of things, among them his tan.

Afterword

Actually, I didn't go back to Trinidad that year, since I got an invitation to go to England the next month to work on a terrific new music festival, which I wrote about later on. It wasn't very warm, but there was no trouble taking a shower.

Chapter 41

Andrew Shachat

In a Silent Way
Why Is Everything so *&!@%# LOUD?!?

Preface

Besides watching the trailer for *Timeline* (which really did turn out to be a turkey) and listening to my wife complain about the noise levels in her performing spaces, this column was inspired by going to some painfully badly miked theatrical shows. It struck a real chord with readers, especially those who worry about the hearing of the younger generation and those who think that most of the records being produced today have no dynamic range and are much too loud.

March 2004

> *"Beautiful, isn't it?" Gomez said. She seemed to sense that he was uneasy.*
>
> *"Yes, beautiful," he answered. But he didn't feel that way at all; something about this forest struck him as sinister. He turned round and round, trying to understand why he had the distinct feeling that something was wrong with what he was seeing. Something was missing or out of place. Finally, he said, "What's wrong?"*
>
> *She laughed. "Oh, that," she said. "Listen."*

I knew the movie version of *Timeline*, Michael Crichton's latest Cassandrian sci-fi tome to get the Hollywood treatment, was going to be a stinker when I saw the preview. It came on before *School of Rock*, and it was way, way louder than anything Jack Black could coax out of those precocious kids and his van full of amps. It featured stampeding horses, clashing armor, and various and sundry explosions, all of which had precious little to do with the 14th-century world that Crichton, in his usual convincing fashion, had constructed in his novel:

> *Chris stood silently for a moment, listening. There was the chirp of birds, the soft rustle of a faint breeze in the trees. But other than that...*
>
> *"I don't hear anything."*
>
> *"That's right," Gomez said. "It upsets some people when they first arrive. There's no ambient noise here: no radio or TV, no airplanes, no machinery, no passing cars. In the twentieth century, we're so accustomed to hearing sound all the time, the silence feels creepy."*

And not only do we hear sound all of the time, but it's loud sound, and it's getting louder. The amount of noise that we put up with in our average existence is, when you think about it, pretty awful. So I thought I'd talk this month about noise, environmental and otherwise.

When was the last time you really heard silence? I mean outside of a well-built studio or when you didn't have heavy-duty headphones clamped on your skull? The neighborhood where I live is known as one of the quietest in the Boston suburbs. When a teenage driver honks his horn at night to announce his arrival at a friend's house, neighbors complain to the parents. People tend not to set their car alarms, because they know how annoying they can be when they go off. Stepping onto my front porch on a calm January weekend evening, when there are no insects spreading their aural blanket and birds aren't yet rolling out their mating calls, the world seems, at first blush, silent. But after a few seconds, I realize I can easily hear the traffic on the freeway over a mile away, the buzz of a transformer on a pole overhead, a distant police siren, someone on the next block starting his car, and the endless procession of jets arcing up from Logan Airport, eight miles distant. It's noisy out here.

Inside my house, with the Andersen double-paned windows shut tight against the cold and noise from outside, I can hear the furnace in the basement, the 60Hz hum from the light dimmers in the kitchen, the low rumble from the oil delivery truck down the street, the ticking of the security timer in the closet, and of course, the fan and disk drive in my computer. It's noisy in here, too.

Few of us today really know what silence is, and since the beginning of the Industrial Revolution, the level of background noise has been constantly rising. Ironically, city streets may be one of the few environments where this trend has managed to reverse itself, at least a little. Recent efforts to improve traffic flow, make horn-honking a violation, and tighten restrictions on car and truck exhaust noise have successfully reduced the ambient level in many urban cores. But as the streets may have become slightly less oppressive, many indoor environments are significantly more so. Who can walk into a modern office building or hotel lobby without feeling assaulted by the awful background music, the splashing from fake waterfalls, and the walla from the coffee shop and bar amplified a hundredfold by the vaulted glass ceilings?

> *Few of us today really know what silence is, and since the beginning of the Industrial Revolution, the level of background noise has been constantly rising.*

Even spaces that are supposedly designed for listening are becoming aurally unfriendly. My wife, a professional storyteller, performs for children in schools and libraries. When she first started, it was no problem to do a show for 100 children without electronic assistance, but in newer buildings, she finds that she needs a sound system for groups of 50 or even fewer, unless she wants to come home with laryngitis. It's not that the kids are noisier—she's really good at getting them to be quiet—it's that she has to make herself heard over the ubiquitous "air exchange" systems: positive ventilation systems that seem to have been installed primarily to protect the builders from lawsuits resulting from "sick building syndrome." Teachers, librarians, and even custodians are often powerless to shut them down, as they're on undefeatable timers. No doubt that representatives from the schools carefully considered lots of data when they spec'd these systems, like air volume and energy use, but unlike when you put in that ventilation system in your control room, no one at the school board thought to ask how loud it was going to be. That's too bad, because those systems deny the students the power and magic that come with direct, personal contact with a performer. Not to mention they throw away any effort or money spent on room acoustics.

There's a new trend in doctors' offices that you may have noticed. As medical practices get larger, and more practitioners are crammed into smaller spaces, patient confidentiality is endangered because it's harder to keep those in adjacent treatment rooms from overhearing each other's complaints. So have office designers tried to acoustically isolate the rooms better? No, they buy doctors machines that generate white noise to cover up the conversations. They are effective unless the patient has a hearing problem, in which case, the whole office can overhear the doctor shouting.

Theaters are getting louder, too, but not because of bad design. The days when someone like Rex Harrison, whose singing voice could hardly be called operatic, could be heard in *My Fair Lady* as clear as a bell in the back row of the balcony at the Mark Hellinger Theater are long gone. Harrison, or for that matter a vocal powerhouse like Bernadette Peters, can't keep up with the elevated sound levels that people expect to hear today, especially if they're going to make it through eight shows a week. Audiences are accustomed to loud music in their homes, in their cars, at the movies, and at concerts, and so they expect to get the same impact from theater orchestras, which means that even the best singers need help to be heard.

It's not a good trade-off. I know I'm hopelessly old school, but I can't think of a single theatrical performance I've ever seen that used amplification and didn't suffer because of it. I recently saw a one-man, one-set historical play in a 350-seat theater performed by an actor with a well-trained, but not overwhelming, voice who didn't need a sound system to be heard over the minimal music and sound effects. The audience came out chattering excitedly about how close they felt to the character and how extraordinary it was to spend all that time in the same "room" with him. You don't hear that kind of reaction when actors wear mics, no matter how well-concealed and amplified.

People are so used to oppressive noise levels that they don't even know when they're being assaulted. Some years ago, I moved to a town where a fire horn (the locals called it a "whistle," but it was actually around 300 Hz) blew three times a day. The first 18 months I lived there, the horn was broken, so I was completely unaware of it. But then they fixed it, and when I first heard the thing—which was well over half a mile from my house—blow at noon one day, I literally fell off my chair. And when it blew the next morning at 6:45 a.m., which I found out it was supposed to do *every day* (as well as at 6:45 p.m.), I got furious.

A few of us recent arrivals who hadn't known about the horn—a group that included healthcare workers, teachers, psychologists, scientists, journalists, and other low-lifes—started a referendum drive to get it shut off. (We also considered getting a bylaw that would require real estate agents to show properties in the area only at noon and 6:45 p.m.) But we were outvoted by older members of the community who wanted to keep the monstrosity for its nostalgic value: Once upon a time, it seems, the signal was used to wake up local mill workers so they could be sure to get to their jobs on time—menial, dangerous, and underpaid as they were—and a whole lot of people felt it was somehow crucial to the character of the town to preserve that miserable tradition.

Eventually, we got an engineer from the state's Environmental Protection Agency to come in with a sound level meter and measure the thing from inside the apartment of one of our members—a nurse who worked the night shift—in a new high-rise right across the street from the monster. It checked in at 138 dB, which was high enough for the state agency to tell the town that if they kept blowing the wretched thing, they would be fined $1,000 a day.

Sadder still is when people—and governments—don't know when the sounds around them are actually beneficial. At the end of last year, the agency that runs the Boston subway system declared that live music played in the stations created a safety hazard and tried to shut down the practice. The recommendation to do so, the agency said, came from a task force on security that was set up in response to the September 11th attacks. The music, the agency conjectured, might drown out crucial security announcements on the P.A. system. The decision set off a flurry of activity in the newspapers and on the Web, and within a couple of days, 8,000 supporters of subway music—including Grammy-winner Tracy Chapman, whose career was launched in these same subways, and singer Peter Mulvey, who actually had the guts and patience to recently record an album in the Boston underground—signed a petition supporting the performers.

In the face of the petition, and after a number of newspaper articles pointed out that the musicians are often the only ones who actually *understand* what the P.A. systems are saying, and that they, with their reasonably good vocal mics and modern amplifiers, would be much more effective at getting an important message to a crowd of people than a station agent with a Dorchester accent in a glass booth 50 yards away squawking through a moldy carbon mic and a 50-year-old grime-encrusted speaker, the transportation agency backed off. But they stipulated that there were to be no drums or even electronic simulations of drums and no trumpets, although French horns, soprano saxes, and electric violins were perfectly okay. So Roland Kirk would be fine, but not Miles.

What's the point of being able to deliver 24-bit recordings to a world where the ambient noise level never drops below 60 dB?

Furthermore, sound levels were limited to 80 dB SPL at 25 feet from the source (not, as one of the local NPR stations reported, 800 dB SPL, which would be roughly the sonic level of the Big Bang). That rather odd spec works out to about 98 dB at three feet, which is pretty respectable, even on a subway platform. One official described the new spec as "akin to positioning your ear directly over a garbage disposal while it's operating." While he's not too far off, my guess is that this guy is not a music lover. I imagine he's happy that there's little danger the music would ever cover up the hideous sounds the train wheels make as they grind their way around the old system's tight curves.

Like children who grow up in the city having never seen the Milky Way, we've lost our appreciation for silence. Those who question how their world is changing for the louder and noisier are few and far between and are easily drowned out. And it's particularly ironic that it's getting worse while the dynamic range of our audio systems is getting bigger. What's the point of being able to deliver 24-bit recordings to a world where the ambient noise level never drops below 60 dB? Well, I guess if we can't find a time machine, there's always headphones.

Afterword

As I write this, the Metropolitan Boston Transit Authority is experimenting with new sound systems that deliver "crystal-clear" announcements. While many riders have noticed them, most would be happier if the trains would just show up once in a while. Meanwhile, earlier this year I saw the national tour of "Spamalot," and even though I was sitting right in front of one of the columns, the sound was excellent. So I take back some of what I said about theater sound.

Chapter 42

Dave Ember

Alone Again, Virtually
The Ups and Downs of All-in-One-Production

Preface

As the book *Bowling Alone* points out so well, technology is turning us into a society of people who play by themselves. In the music production field this is particularly evident, as home and project studios have become predominant, and one-man bands, whether they're doing rap, dance music, or electronica, have infiltrated the charts, clubs, and concert halls. The kind of empowerment this gives many of us is a good thing, but something important is being lost.

July 2004

Just as millions of Americans have come to believe that "You can have it all," in our industry the new mantra is, "You can do it all." It's hard to open a magazine, go into a music store, or get through the security gates at a trade show without being bombarded by this-is-all-you-need workstations and software, from digital multitrackers to Pro Tools to GarageBand. And it's true that what you can buy these days for very short money is absolutely mind boggling and—this month bringing Summer NAMM—it's about to become more so. In a couple of weeks in Nashville, the art and science of stuffing more functionality into smaller, cooler-looking, and cheaper packages will no doubt take yet another quantum leap.

Of course, the one-man-band recording concept is nothing new. When Les Paul invented multitracking, he didn't do it for a band, he did it for himself. On Paul McCartney's first solo album, the former Beatle played all of the instruments by himself. Part of the draw of electronic music from its earliest days was that the composer had complete control over the finished product, without any intermediaries to change things. I first tried the be-the-band idea during my freshman year of college: To get out of writing a term paper on William Blake for an English class, I set a bunch of his poems to music and wired two stereo tape recorders together so I could layer several instruments and sing harmonies with myself. A few years later, while on a mercifully brief songwriting binge, I walked into a high-end 8-track studio in New York with all of the money I could scrounge up and managed to come out with a pretty decent four-song demo on which, like McCartney, I overdubbed all of the instruments: guitars, bass, keyboards, and even drums. Unlike McCartney, however, my efforts were not well rewarded.

It was when cheap "semi-pro" multitracks came along that the cost of entry to the solo private studio fell off its first cliff. Multitrack hard disk audio was another milestone, and the fall off that cliff continues to accelerate as hard disk space keeps getting cheaper. How's this for a statistic: Between 1984, when I bought my first 20-megabyte hard drive for $1,200 (at an academic discount), and last week, when I bought a 120-*giga*byte hard drive for $120, the cost of random-access digital storage has gone down 99.99833 percent!

Who could have foreseen the day when producers would pass the time on a transcontinental flight editing their next album?

MIDI had its role in promoting the one-person-orchestra concept, as you didn't need the actual instruments anymore. But there was still a cost factor: When Yamaha first ruled the synth world, if you needed multiple FM voices, then you bought multiple *DX7* keyboards at $2,000 or so apiece. But pretty soon, you could get a *TX816* rack, saving more bucks and space. Then manufacturers figured out how to make multitimbral synths that could take the place of 16 or 32 modules. Since then, synths and processors have shrunk to the point where they take up literally no space at all. As the pundits at *Wired* magazine like to put it, they're made of electrons, not atoms.

Then there's the peripheral hardware. Who could have foreseen the day when producers would pass the time on a transcontinental flight editing their next album on a computer on their lap? The world of education has been affected just as much. Only five years ago, when I would do any kind of a talk on music and multimedia, I'd have to take a car. That's because I needed a desktop computer stuffed with PCI audio and sampler cards, a CRT monitor, a full-size keyboard synth, a video deck, and a SMPTE synchronizer.

Now I can take a plane or a subway (or in the case of this month's MacWorld Expo—which is back in Boston for the first time in seven years and happens to land right in the middle of my vacation on Cape Cod—on a ferry boat) with only my lowly iBook in tow. The synths and samples are in a *Reason* patch, the audio comes out of the computer's headphone jack (if the audience is really picky, I can schlep a Mark of the Unicorn *828*, which weighs 25 percent less than the iBook), and the video is a QuickTime movie that syncs up perfectly in *Digital Performer* without a SMPTE bit to be found anywhere. All I need are audio and video patch cords, and I'm in business.

In my home studio, I still have three VCRs and as many CRTs, two mixers, and four racks of hardware modules, but a lot of that stuff is not getting very much use. I could take that same iBook (which is already three years old but still kicks butt) and add one of the new, cheap, but highly functional MIDI/USB keyboard/control surfaces, a couple of much-better-than-you'd-expect-at-the-price Chinese large-diaphragm condenser mics, and an inexpensive FireWire audio interface (they're finally here!) with S/PDIF I/O and not-at-all-bad mic pres and end up with a pretty darn good little production facility that can be thrown, with room for cables and stands, into a carry-on suitcase. And the total cost would be less than any 8-track deck that was ever made—or, for that matter, my first Mac.

The studio-in-a-box is now so common that it's hard to imagine that there was a time, not so long ago, when top-selling acts would agonize over the decision to build their own studio: Would the investment be justified by the money they'd save *not* making their next two or three albums somewhere else? Now that formula seems ludicrous: What I spent on that four-song demo in the '70s was more—in *1970s* dollars—than I would need to spend in *today's* dollars to get a computer-based rig that could blow the socks off of anything I could have done in that studio.

So obviously, this is the end of the recording industry as we know it, right? Well, no, not yet, because most of us, it seems, are still working. And just as "You can have it all" is but a propaganda slogan as opposed to a practical way of life (you can't, for example, have a functioning government with no taxes, and you can't have peace in the Middle East with two SUVs in every garage), "You can do it all" is a nice way to sell toys, but it falls short in reality.

It's true that thanks to products like *Absynth*, *Kontakt*, and *Reason*, you can load up racks and racks of the most sophisticated synthesizers you could ever imagine. With *GigaSampler*, you can have at your disposal entire virtual symphony orchestras that are capable of making nearly every individual and collective sound that a real symphony can make. With Synthogy's new *Ivory* virtual instrument, you can have a $175,000 9-1/2-foot Bösendorfer Imperial Grand piano, beautifully recorded in an exquisite hall, at your beck and call. (Full Disclosure Department: I'm currently helping this company with its documentation.)

And it's true that tools like *Sonar, Logic, Nuendo,* and *Digital Performer* have made entry into the world of high-end production a lot easier. To take advantage of what these products have to offer, you no longer have to know how to handle a soldering iron, or which end of an electrolytic capacitor is which, or even how to gain-stage a mixer to keep the signal comfortably between the noise and the distortion. But the fact is, the greatest tools in the world are no good if you don't know how to use them. And what you do have to know, and which no computer by itself can teach you, is music.

If you don't know how a guitar is played, you can't possibly take advantage of even the greatest virtual guitar software. If you've never sat in a horn section, or at least written music for one and heard it played by real players, then you can't do a convincing simulation of it with a keyboard, no matter how brilliant the samples under your fingers are. And if you don't play the piano and have never learned about dynamics, phrasing, and pedaling, any piano track you come up with is likely to be mechanical and boring.

Learning how to work with music without knowing about music itself is extremely difficult and no fun. In traditional college recording programs, teachers all agree that it's generally much easier to teach engineering and studio techniques to a musician than it is to teach music to an engineer. Unless you're planning to give up all originality and spend the rest of your musical career using samples and loops made by others (yes, I know there are such people, and I feel very sorry for them), you have to know how music is made, played, and structured. And the best way to know that is to be a player.

With not many exceptions, the folks who are behind the records that make the top of the charts, who will be remembered after they drop off the charts, and who win Grammy and TEC Awards, have a real grounding in real music. Superhot rap producers The Neptunes met in a high school band class. Shania Twain didn't learn how to sing from a machine. Bob Clearmountain and Bruce Swedien were both into electronics and recording at a very early age, but Clearmountain was also a bass player, and both of Swedien's parents were professional musicians, so he grew up surrounded by the Minneapolis Symphony. Nile Rodgers is one of the greatest all-around producers in history, but before that, he was a killer guitar player. Meredith Brooks started playing guitar at the age of 11 and worked hard in bands for 25 years before she made *Blurring the Edges*, the first album on which she sang and played everything. And me? I played 11 different instruments in high school, some of them not too badly, in rock bands, folk groups, jazz combos, stage bands, orchestras, chamber groups, and percussion ensembles. When I lay down a saxophone line, whether it's on my *VL1* or in *Reason*, I not only know what a saxophone is supposed to sound like, I know what it *feels* like.

On the other side of the coin, while the one-person studio has been so empowering for people like me, something has been lost. When I used to play in bands, as annoying and frustrating as I often found my bandmates, we never ran out of ideas. There was always something else that somebody wanted to try. Nowadays, working by myself, composer's block seems like a constant threat. If I don't at least get out of my studio occasionally to see how someone else responds to what I'm creating, I can feel the creative juices drying up. If I don't play with other musicians at least once in awhile—and it hardly matters whether I'm playing Dave Brubeck, Neil Young, or four-hand piano arrangements of Mendelssohn symphonies—I feel like what I'm doing lacks context, and my muse gets lethargic. That recharging I get from interacting with other musicians, even if it's just a few times a year, is critical.

As annoying and frustrating as I often found my bandmates, we never ran out of ideas.

More than other musicians, though, it's the audience we need. When I was a kid, I saw a terrific stage show performed by the great actress Mary Martin called *It Takes Three to Make Music*, the premise of which was that someone has to write it, someone else has to play it, and someone has to listen to it. (The recording of this show won a Grammy in 1959, but you can't get it on CD.) Of course, that equation has been slimmed down a bit in the intervening years, now that so many of us are taking care of the entire composition and performance chain. But we still need someone to listen to what we do, or it isn't music.

As I write this, an interesting event is unfolding in Vienna called *Internethausmusik*. It's a performance project, sponsored by companies like IBM and Telekom Austria, in which 23 classical musicians sit in their apartments and "phone in" their parts (over Telekom DSL lines, of course) to a theater downtown, where a "conductor" mixes the parts and streams the result to the world. The musicians, the conductor, and the audience are never in the same place at the same time.

The music that's being played is designed specifically for this occasion, and in that context, it may work pretty well. But the publicity surrounding the event is hinting strongly that this might be a wave of the future. Instead of dealing with large, expensive concert halls where musicians meet to play, we can have them all sit at home with cheap microphones and Internet hook-ups playing their parts individually, leaving it up to a central conductor/engineer to make it all come together.

Of course, it's ridiculous to apply this concept to any kind of traditional music for any number of reasons. First is timing. For musicians to make sense out of their ensemble, they have to hear each other in real time or be playing against prerecorded tracks that they can lock up to. But even the fastest Internet connection is going to have enough latency—what with codecs, packet-switching, and repeaters—to make it impossible for the musicians to hear each other in any way that they can possibly relate to.

A second reason is that there are no extra-aural cues. Musicians constantly play off of each other visually, using facial gestures, eye contact, hand signals, and limb and body movements, both conscious and unconscious. It's why drum booths have windows. Cutting players—especially classical players—off from each other's sight completely would require a pretty major, and maybe impossible, readjustment on everyone's part.

But perhaps the most serious problem with creating this kind of bodiless music is that it insulates the musicians from their audience. The vast majority of us do this music thing because we want to communicate with people. We have ideas, emotions, and concepts that we want to get across. Isolation, whether it's sitting in front of a computer putting together beats and tracks and sending them out to faceless CD buyers or playing into a glorified telephone along with others whom you can't hear to an invisible Internet audience, is antithetical to what music is supposed to be about. Without each other and our audiences, we might as well be staring into a mirror 24 hours a day. Some narcissistic types might find that fascinating for a little while, but for most of us, it gets pretty old, pretty fast. Maybe you *can* have it all—but it doesn't mean anything if you don't share it.

As a child, Paul Lehrman was never warned not to play with himself—and just look what it led to.

Chapter 43

A Law unto Itself
Why Misusing the Legal System Hurts Us All

Preface

I wrote about one misuse of the legal system in June 2001, when I covered bogus patents and how they stifle innovation. This column is a follow-up to that and talks about a particular egregious use of patent bogosity, as well as other nasty legal tricks that can adversely affect how we create, distribute, and listen to music and other entertainment media.

August 2004

"The first thing we do, let's kill all the lawyers."
—Shakespeare, *Henry VI*

Actually, let's not. The Shakespearean character who utters this line is preparing to throw the kingdom into chaos and sees getting rid of lawyers and other educated people as the first step toward that goal. I think we've got enough chaos in our business already.

Lawyers can be forces for good, especially when they're on your side. What makes lawyers go bad is when people hire them to misuse the law. And those people deserve, well, maybe not to be killed, but it would be nice if they could be put out of business.

One of the primary purposes of a legal system, at least in a free society, is to protect the weak against the strong. Every individual is entitled, so they say, to his day in court, and all individuals, so they say, are equal under the law. This means that bullies who beat up on smaller individuals are supposed to be punished, whether they are neighborhood thugs stealing kids' lunch money or large corporations taking advantage of trusting customers, employees, or shareholders. And the law also protects bullies from themselves, restraining them from their worst impulses so that their nefarious deeds don't come back to bite them. We all know it doesn't always work out that way, and too often, justice is the sole property of those with the most resources, i.e., money. But sometimes, especially when legal issues are thoroughly examined by the system expressly set up to deal with those issues, the results can be very good indeed. They even allow us to get beyond our own limited vision and open ourselves up to the future.

A case in point is *Sony Corporation of America et al. v. Universal City Studios Inc. et al.*, usually referred to as "The Betamax Case." For you young 'uns who may not remember this (or you oldsters who have forgotten), in 1976, Walt Disney and Universal Studios sued Sony Corporation over the fact that Sony's newly developed home VCRs could record copyrighted television programs off the air, and therefore Sony, and anyone who used a VCR, was violating the studios' copyright. The studios were positively apoplectic. Their side of the fight was led by a former politician-turned-movie industry lobbyist named Jack Valenti who proclaimed, "The VCR is to the American film producer and the American public as the Boston Strangler is to the woman home alone."

After a couple of seesaw decisions in lower courts, the case was finally decided by the U.S. Supreme Court by a one-vote margin in favor of Sony. The court's decision was based on the fact that individuals making recordings of television programs for their own consumption should be considered "fair use" under the copyright laws.

After that, of course, movie studios got into home video themselves—in a big way. In fact, it could be said that home video *saved* the movie industry: Today, something like 50 percent of the studios' revenues comes from VHS and DVD sales and rentals. Nonetheless, like a dinosaur that refuses to accept his extinction, Valenti (who as I write this, has, at long last, announced his retirement) continues to argue that home video hurts the movie industry.

Ironically, Sony's Betamax format lost out to the technically inferior VHS, but that had nothing to do with the court case. The important point that emerged from the battle was the preservation of fair use as a crucial aspect of the principle of copyright. Fair use is supposed to promote the exchange of ideas, and the Betamax decision did exactly that: Without it, we would not only *not* have VHS, but we also wouldn't have DVD, miniDV, iMovie, or TiVO.

Like the courts, regulatory agencies are at their best when they work to promote new technologies in a fair and firm way. The '60s rock 'n' roll explosion might never have happened had not the FCC in 1964 changed the rules so that radio stations who had licenses for AM and FM transmitters were, all of a sudden, required to broadcast separate programs on each band. (Of course, the radio lobby fought this bitterly and managed to delay its implementation for three years—just in time for the release of *Sgt. Pepper*—and then in the early '90s, hat-in-hand and bemoaning the decline of AM radio audiences, got the rules changed back.)

Stereo television might not have happened—or would be in the same chaotic state as digital television is today—if the FCC didn't mandate one system that every broadcaster had to implement. Anybody remember stereo AM radio? I didn't think so. The FCC dropped the ball on that one and, bowing to pressure from the industry, allowed four competing systems to coexist. No one could figure out which one to invest in, and it soon sank without a trace.

But of late, regulatory agencies have gone into hiding (except when handing out favors to corporate donors), while the most significant legal fights have taken place outside of the courtroom; for example, the Recording Industry Association of America vs. file sharing. Is this case wending its way through the courts like the Betamax case so that each side gets to rationally argue its position before impartial judges? Not exactly. The RIAA (of its five members *[now four]*, only one—Warner Bros.—is actually headquartered in the U.S.) has as of this writing sued close to 3,000 individuals for song-swapping, yet not one of those cases has made it to court or even mediation. So we don't have any idea whether any of these people who have been accused are actually breaking any laws.

Four hundred of the defendants have cried uncle in the face of the association's legal muscle and forked over a reported average of $3,000 each (although some sources say that figure is way too low). Add it up, and you probably get a sum somewhere close to the lawyers' bills. One thing you can be sure of is that not a dime of this money has made its way to any recording artists.

Many defendants in these suits are college students. Picking on them is a brilliant strategy: What parent, already facing tens of thousands of dollars in tuition costs, is going to want to spend *more* money fighting a giant organization with unlimited resources so that his kid can continue to download the latest releases by big-label artists whom the parent can't stand anyway? In the latest round of lawsuits, a couple of dozen defendants have decided *not* to settle, so perhaps our judicial system, as creaky and flawed as it may be, will at least get a crack at sorting out the issue. Maybe.

To date, there has been only one significant court decision relating to this mess. A Federal District court ruled that when the RIAA (or any other copyright holder) engaged in fishing expeditions to sniff out suspected file sharers, it couldn't force Internet service providers to divulge customers' personal information. Score one against Big Brother.

Meanwhile, as new technologies emerge, new ways for bullies to misuse the law at the expense of the creative community expense and its consumers are sprouting up right behind them. Sarah Benzuly wrote in the May 2004 issue of *Mix* ("On-the-Spot CD Releases") about companies that are making recordings of concerts that the audience can take home the same night. All it takes is a rack of fast computers, a boatload of storage, and a mobile CD-pressing plant. It's a win-win situation for everyone. The recordings are far better than the typical Walkman-under-the-jacket bootlegs of the past, the audience gets a more meaningful souvenir than a T-shirt, and the bands stand to make a pretty decent amount of money as there's no record company or distribution chain to suck up the profits.

The three largest players in this field are Hyburn, DiscLive, and Instant Live. Phoenix-based Hyburn has been around since 2001, when it produced the first on-site live disc for the Phunk Junkeez. DiscLive started in the spring of 2003, founded by two college students and two industry veterans. This past April, it was acquired by Dallas-based Immediatek, a small company developing new delivery systems such as Net-Burn, which aims to make it possible for artists to sell music on the Net without worrying about it being copied.

Instant Live's story is slightly different, as it's owned by Clear Channel Communications, the 600-pound gorilla of the entertainment industry. Clear Channel owns about 1,200 radio stations, which is roughly one-third of all of the stations in the entire country. (They would own a lot more by now had Congress not succumbed to a massive public outcry and over-ruled an FCC decision that would have raised the limits of ownership of broadcast stations even further.) Clear Channel also owns 130 concert venues in the U.S. and Europe and claims to have staged some 32,000 events in 2003.

Not surprisingly, the parent company's reach has created some problems for others who are involved in the various areas in which it operates, and thus it is no stranger to the court-room. In May—after being told by a federal judge that, yes, it would have to stand trial—Clear Channel settled an antitrust suit filed by a Denver concert promoter who accused them of refusing to play the music on their stations of any acts who performed at non-Clear Channel venues. In the settlement, Clear Channel, of course, "admitted no wrongdoing."

The company is also making Instant Live's rivals pay royalties if they want to get into any of Clear Channel's concerts. "If they own the venue, then we can pay them a reasonable fee for that," says Zach Bair, CEO and chairman of Immediatek. "It's up to the band. If the band chooses them over us, so be it. I think the live disc industry is a big enough sandbox for all of us to play in."

But it's gone further than that. In April, Clear Channel bought the rights to a patent (number 6,614,729) that, as *Mix* editor George Petersen mentioned in his July 2004 "Editor's Note," the company claims gives it the exclusive right to record any concerts and sell the CDs on-site *anywhere*. "We want to be artist-friendly," Steve Simon, the director of Instant Live, told *Rolling Stone*, "but it is a business, and it's not going to be, 'We have the patent, now everybody can use it for free.'"

The patent—filed in September 2001 by two brothers, an electrical engineer and a lawyer—describes a generic system to record, edit, and duplicate CDs using redundant systems. (You can view it at http://patft.uspto.gov/netahtml/srchnum.htm; just type in the patent number.) It's clever and looks like it should work, although the brothers apparently never built a working version. But one of the requirements of a patent is that it be "non-obvious," and I have at least a half-dozen engineering students who could have come up with the idea in about an hour.

"We provided Clear Channel with a lot of documentation for older patents showing this technology has been out there since 1994," says Bair. "The patent examiner must have been asleep." Nonetheless, Clear Channel is using the patent as a bludgeon on its competitors. "Last year, they sent cease-and-desist letters to our president, Sami Valkonen," says Bair. "We had no idea about the patent. They bought it at the same time it was made public." Furthermore, Hyburn and DiscLive say that the systems they use don't infringe on Clear Channel's patent. "We don't practice what their patent is claiming," says Bair. "We use off-the-shelf software like Steinberg's WaveLab, along with our own technology. How can you patent the way someone uses a retail product?" And to add insult to injury, according to Bair, "From what I understand, the process they do at Instant Live is different from what's in the patent."

But Clear Channel is forging ahead, telling anyone who will listen that its patent makes the company the only game in town. "Band managers are continuing to be told that DiscLive will not be able to record and issue CDs on-site," says Bair. The manager of The Pixies, one of the most popular artists to have worked with DiscLive, told *Rolling Stone* that they may switch to Instant Live. "It may be best to feed the dragon rather than draw swords," he said. "Still, I'm not fond of doing business with my arm twisted behind my back."

Besides being a businessman, Bair is also a musician. "As an artist," he says, "I look at this, and it makes me angry. I would find it hard to pay Clear Channel to record my own band. Sooner or later, there will be a big artist backlash against them from artists with a lot of money.

"On the other hand, the business side of me says I'd rather come to an agreement with these guys than fight it out in a courtroom. But if I'm pushed to the wall, I'm not going to throw in the towel."

Let's hope not. As many of us learned in high school, sometimes a well-aimed towel is the best way to fight off a bully.

Paul Lehrman isn't a lawyer, but he knows a lot of them. So be warned.

Afterword

As of now, Clear Channel is winning this war. Hyburn, while still in business, hasn't recorded any concerts in two years, and DiscLive is only doing a handful of shows each year. A 95-percent interest in DiscLive's parent corporation was bought in early 2006 by Dallas Mavericks owner Mark Cuban. Clear Channel now says it handles 153 venues, and its Instant Live subsidiary is recording new shows just about daily.

Chapter 44

Out of the Garden
One Man's Journey to Woodstock—
and Why He Left Early

Preface
Robin Williams is famous for (among other things) his remark about how if you remember the '60s, then you weren't there. There's a corollary to that having to do with the 1969 Woodstock Music & Art Fair: If everyone who says they were there really was there, then New York City would have had to be completely devoid of people for three days. My own personal story is about being there *and* not being there, and after 35 years, it finally seemed safe to tell it.

September 2004

The other day at a party for a soprano friend (she's a singer, that is, not a member of a certain fictional family), I found myself performing with several other musicians I had never met before in an impromptu chorus, serenading the birthday girl with a medieval German canon. Shortly thereafter, a slightly inebriated guest confronted me to ask if this little group could do a request. "We can try," I said. "Sing 'Woodstock,'" he said.

Because we didn't have any electric pianos (which Joni Mitchell, who wrote the song but wasn't at the festival that the song commemorated, used) or electric guitars (which Crosby, Stills, Nash & Young, who had all the chart action with the song and *were* there, used), we would have had to whip up a quick *a cappella* version. For a group who had worked together all of five minutes (which was even less than CSN&Y had on that historic occasion), that would have been difficult. So we begged off. Instead, I offered to tell the gentleman a story. "I was at Woodstock," I said. He looked at me in admiration and confusion as to how someone so young-looking (hah!) could have accomplished such a thing. "But," I added, "I left." His admiration immediately turned to disgust. "How could you do that?!" he yelped. So I told him. And because it all happened exactly 35 years ago, I'll tell you.

I was in high school on Long Island, about 20 miles outside of New York City. Being a conscientious sort at an early age, I bought advance tickets to the festival as soon as they came out, which made me one of approximately 186,000 (according to the Woodstock Statistics page at woodstock69.com). As I didn't yet drive, I hooked up with my friend Roger (not his real name), who was a couple of years older. In college and at home for the summer, Roger arranged to borrow his mother's Plymouth Valiant to get us up to White Lake, N.Y. I had big plans after the festival, too. I had a girlfriend up in Montréal whom I had met the year before at music camp, and when the music was over, I intended to hitchhike up to visit her for a few days. I even had a plane ticket for the trip home. It was going to be the teenage adventure of a lifetime.

Early on Friday morning, the first day of the festival, we left Long Island equipped with two sleeping bags, two rain ponchos, a couple of changes of underwear, and a canned ham, figuring—as the posters promised—there'd be plenty of food available once we got to Max Yasgur's farm. It was normally a two-hour drive up the New York State Thruway and Route 17, but we figured to allow some extra time for traffic. A little after noon, about 10 miles from the site, we stopped dead. For the next several hours, we crawled around the back roads and cow paths of Sullivan County, watching the local farmers and Hassidic Jews on their tractors and front porches with as much curiosity and trepidation as they were watching us.

Around 6 p.m., we were waved off of a dirt road by someone vaguely official-looking and directed into a field where we would park. It was the only sign of authority we would see the entire time we were there. We left the ham, the underwear, and the sleeping bags in the car, but grabbed the ponchos. We could see several streams of people who seemed to be headed in more or less one general direction, so we followed as best we could. We couldn't see or hear anything resembling a concert as we trekked over fields and downed fences, through clumps of bushes, and around oddly placed tents and trucks. After a while, we began to hear a kind of roar in the distance. We came over a ridge and caught the faint strains of a singer named Bert Sommer wailing about losing his virginity. Over another ridge, we found ourselves at the edge of what could only be described as a sea of humanity.

The scale of it was not to be believed. The huge stage looked like a small city and the performers and stage techs like insects scurrying around. The perimeter of the natural amphitheater was lined by Porta-Sans, and way off in the distance were cone-roofed tents surrounded by hordes of people, which we figured must be where the food was. People were seated on blankets, straw mats, their jackets, or just in the dirt.

Roger and I found a spot between two blankets, laid our ponchos down in the dust, and sat down. Soon, Tim Hardin took the stage. Although we could hardly see anything, the sound was amazingly clear. What we could see, however, was that Hardin, a great songwriter, was having a lot of trouble staying vertical. (Apparently, he had recently resumed a heroin habit, which eventually killed him.) After just a couple of songs, he left the stage. I told Roger that I needed to use a toilet. "Please don't move," I begged, "or we'll never see each other again."

I did a broken-field walk up the hill, stepping as lightly as I could over blankets, backpacks, coolers, and conscious and unconscious people, and got in line for one of the Porta-Sans, where I waited for about 15 minutes. Inside the unit, it was dark and putrid beyond belief. After I accomplished my mission, I inched my way back down the hill to try to find my spot. It was getting dark, and by the time I rejoined Roger, nearly three-quarters of an hour had gone by. As I sat back down on the lumpy poncho, Ravi Shankar was making himself comfortable on the stage, which was now covered by colorful carpets. From the distance, he looked (with apologies to Robert Klein) like a raisin poking out of a dollop of whipped cream on a bed of flowers. As the sun fell behind the Porta-Sans and the lights around the amphitheater came on, he announced "a raga to night." The tamboura droned, he plunked out a few mournful notes on the sitar, and it started to rain.

Roger and I looked at each other and wordlessly stood up, grabbed the ponchos, put them—dust and all—over ourselves and started the long trek back to the car. Somehow, we found it. When we managed to dry ourselves off a little, we cracked open the canned ham. After a few bites, we said to each other, "This is really stupid," and started the car.

We didn't get very far, however, because what had earlier been a grassy field was now a vast muddy ditch, and our back wheels spun helplessly. Out of the darkness and the rain, eight hippies, unbidden and silently, lifted the car up and pushed it forward a few feet, just enough so the wheels could grab. We lurched along the rain-soaked field, and 50 yards later, we got stuck again. Another phalanx of hippies appeared and helped us on our way. After four such incidents, we finally found ourselves on pavement, inching through the still-arriving crowds and randomly abandoned vehicles. By around 2 a.m., we were back on Route 17 heading south. Exhausted, we pulled over on the shoulder as far as we could and, heedless of the tractor-trailers barreling past us in the night, went to sleep.

When daylight broke, we resumed our journey down the freeway, listening to the road-closings and other disaster reports on the radio, marveling at the steady stream of abandoned cars on the northbound side of the road. We got on the Thruway and had breakfast at the first rest stop we came to, which looked like a Red Cross shelter after a major earthquake. We finally pulled into my driveway around 9 a.m. to the great astonishment and thinly disguised relief of my parents.

For the next two days, I watched the news reports from the festival on television and was very happy I wasn't there. A lot of the people being interviewed said they were having fun, but it didn't look like much fun to me.

On Monday, the day the festival was to end, no longer able to follow my original plan of sticking out my thumb on an upstate New York road in hopes of being picked up by some joyful Canadian concertgoers on their way home, I took a commuter train into New York City and got on a Trailways bus to Montréal. When I got there at long last, I found myself in for another disappointment. In the several months since we'd seen each other, my purported girlfriend had been seeing another guy, a local, and she had decided that she couldn't handle more than one relationship at a time. So I was being dumped.

Unfortunately, my plane ticket home couldn't be changed without paying a $25 fee (which, to put it in perspective, was about 50 percent of the price of the youth-fare ticket itself), and I literally didn't have the money. So I hung around for five days in a foreign country, in a suburban house with a family who really didn't want me there, with no means of escape. And, being a cultured family, the only pop record they had in the whole house was the debut album of the dolorous bard of Canada, Leonard Cohen. So I listened to "So Long, Maryanne" and "That's No Way to Say Goodbye" a *lot*.

In the weeks that followed the Woodstock festival, I didn't tell too many of my friends the story, because I was a bit embarrassed that I had chickened out and split from what was supposed to be the defining event of my generation. People I knew who had stuck it out regaled me with tales of what an incredible time they had, and perhaps they were telling the truth, but I could tell, even in their enthusiasm, that this would have been an experience I really wasn't ready for.

When the movie came out a year later, I finally got to see some of the performances I had missed, and they were, without exception, incredible. I saw it on a starlit night at a drive-in in rural Vermont from the comfort of the back seat of a Plymouth Fury convertible, with a brand-new girlfriend, plenty of popcorn, and a lighted, fairly clean men's room just a few yards away. To my way of thinking, it was definitely a much more enjoyable way to experience the event.

I've driven up Route 17 many times since August 1969 and passed the signs for the turnoff to White Lake. Though I still don't regret my decision to leave, I can't help but wonder,

"What if?" What if I had been a looser kid, more adventurous, less concerned about mundane things like food, sleep, and hygiene?

I didn't go back to Montréal again until just last year when I had a gig there. As the plane approached, I thought I could see my old girlfriend's old house. I Google'd her and found her living in Western Canada. I sent her a note, and she was delighted to hear from me. She'd married the guy she had dumped me for, had two children with him, and then got a divorce after 30 years. It took a while, but I've developed a tolerance for Leonard Cohen, and when a song by him comes on the radio, I no longer instantly change the station.

My friend Roger went back to college and then to medical school, and we lost touch with each other. Bert Sommer died in 1990. The *Woodstock* movie made $50 million in its first release, and two of the guys who had put the thing together retired very young and very rich. My original poster (which places the event in Wallkill, N.Y.) is framed on my office wall, along with my $6-a-day advance tickets, never collected. I'm told they're worth a lot of money.

As for the performers at the Woodstock festival, I never did get to see Janis Joplin or Jimi Hendrix, and it wasn't until just a couple of years ago, after half the band was dead, that I got to see The Who live. Those seats cost me $100 each. But in the weeks and years to follow Woodstock, I got to see Jefferson Airplane, Richie Havens, the Grateful Dead, Santana, Arlo Guthrie, The Band, Joan Baez, Sha-Na-Na, Joe Cocker, John Sebastian, and the Incredible String Band. They were all great, and I didn't need to sit in the mud and the rain for three days to have the experience. So even though I didn't make it through all of the actual event, I still think of myself as part of the Woodstock generation.

A final coda: At a high school reunion about five years ago, I ran into Roger's younger sister, Susan (also not her real name), who was in my class. Roger was a successful doctor in the Midwest, she told me, and has a good life. And then she added, "But he's still angry at you." I was flabbergasted. "Why?" I asked. Did he think I was the one who forced him to leave the Woodstock festival and miss the event of a lifetime?

"Oh no," Susan said with a laugh. "That wasn't the problem. He didn't want to stay there either. He's pissed off because you made him sleep in the front seat of the car, which wasn't nearly as comfortable as the back seat."

Roger, if you're reading this, you know who you are (and what your real name is), and I want you to know I'm really sorry. I had no idea that you wanted the back seat. But I'm not sorry we shared a little bit of history together. Despite what Robin Williams says, we were there, and we remember.

Paul Lehrman is having trouble figuring out what happened to the '70s, '80s, and '90s.

Afterword

I was amazed how many letters and e-mails I got after this piece appeared from people who had pretty much the same story: They came, they saw, they bailed. Some didn't even get that far, but were turned back miles from the site. One reader who stuck it out (although his friends didn't) wrote, "It helped that I had been a Boy Scout—I never had to visit those outhouses." And I heard from my friend "Roger," too—who loved the column and told me his sister was full of it, and he was never mad at me at all.

Chapter 45

Back to the Future
Ancient Tomb Reveals Low-Cost Audio of Tomorrow!

Preface

The line between "pro" and "consumer" audio gear, in many quarters faint but still visible, has utterly vanished in this unusual, pioneering installation. And so, apparently has the line between "home" and "theater." If you're a manufacturer of this sort of stuff, perhaps there's more to fear than just a mechanical mummy.

October 2004

There's an interesting conundrum in audio these days: As our tools get better and the quality of what we produce achieves new heights, the delivery system for those products in many ways gets worse. Data-compressed audio files; tiny, tinny, under-powered "multimedia" sound systems; and—God help us—cell phones have all somehow become significant elements in the chain that brings music from our 24-bit, 192-kHz, six-channel discrete, tri-amplified production systems to our audience.

As "low-end" audio delivery becomes more prevalent, it's finding its way into unexpected new areas. One of these is illustrated in a terrific high-tech "haunted house"—type attraction called "Tomb," which should be open by the time you read this. The design and the technology behind it are the very latest, but the audio is surprisingly low tech. Perhaps even more surprising, it sounds just fine.

The philosophy behind Tomb can be described something like this: Start with a computer game that has several layers of puzzle-solving. Get the player out of his seat and make him walk through different spaces. Use a whole lot of scary content based on ancient myths and classic horror movies. Make the lights flash, the walls groan, creatures crawl over the player's feet and fly around the room, long-dead folks talk from behind waterfalls, the floors shake, and the ceilings drop precipitously. Throw in a complex interactive soundtrack of dialogue, sound effects, and music. Make it multiplayer so that every player can hear every other player scream. Call it the future of entertainment and put it in a high-traffic area full of students and young professionals. Charge admission.

Tomb is located in a former warehouse in Boston's Fenway neighborhood. It's the first of what the creators, who call themselves "5Wits" (www.5-wits.com), hope will be many such shows. They chose a great location—right down the street from the home of the perennial second-place (yet passion-inducing) Red Sox—*[that is until the month this column appeared, when they won the World Series—go figure]* in an area teeming with clubs, bars, movie theaters, stores, and restaurants, only a stone's throw from some of the city's largest universities.

It's the brainchild of Matt DuPlessie, a designer who has done work for Disney, Universal, and the Boston Museum of Science and who holds an engineering degree from MIT and an MBA from Harvard. In fact, it started out as a business school project. "It was an entrepreneurial studies assignment," he says. "I was supposed to get investors and creators together—and I did."

In Tomb, groups of between five and 15 would-be Indiana Joneses move through a series of rooms that resemble an ancient Egyptian crypt and solve a series of puzzles at each step before they can move on to the next. The walls use art taken from the real thing. Pharaonic tombs were photographed and the images digitized and cut by a computer lathe into foam and Fiberglas. "We don't have to worry about copyright issues," says DuPlessie, "since it's all over 3,000 years old."

When a Tomb-bound group begins their 40-minute journey, they're told that the original discoverer of the tomb never came out, and his crew deserted. The goal is to find out what happened to him and to see if the mummy he was searching for is actually there. When the first door closes and the group is plunged into darkness, they switch on flashlights, but it isn't long before the lights start winking out.

Suddenly, there's a splash, and the face of the ancient Pharaoh appears on a curtain of falling water. The Pharaoh speaks, challenging the group to solve puzzles based on each of the "Five Wits," which are either the five senses or, according to Shakespeare, the faculties of common sense, fantasy, memory, judgment, and imagination.

There are hidden buttons in the walls, hieroglyphics, snakes on the floor, falling ceilings, a descending mummy, more puzzles, and screams.

"Whether you live or die," says DuPlessie, "you end up in the gift shop," where you can buy books and videos about Egyptian history and, of course, have a cappuccino. It's too soon to tell whether it will be a financial success, but the concept and execution, which combine the idea of a haunted house, a "dark ride," and a special-effects show, are a highly effective combination of old and new technologies. "I researched heavily to see if anyone had done this and could maybe advise us," says DuPlessie. "No one has."

Music and sound, naturally, are critical to a project such as this, and for that, DuPlessie hired two New York composers, Scott Shapiro (who happens to be a former student of mine) and Rich Jacobs, who call themselves Composers' Collective. "Believe it or not," DuPlessie says, "I met them through Craigslist." Shapiro and Jacobs have been working together for about a year-and-a-half, making music and sound effects for clients such as CBS, NBC, Showtime, ESPN, and the Discovery Channel.

"There are five basic pieces of music," says Shapiro, "which we did based just on Matt's descriptions. When we finally got together with him, we found they all worked with just some minor tweaks. We also did a couple of hundred sound effects, some adapted from libraries and some we recorded ourselves." Borrowing from techniques used in video game scoring, they broke the music down into loops so that, for example, when a group solves a puzzle or accomplishes some other task, the music can jump quickly to the end of the track or to a new piece. Making the transitions between loops seamless was a critical task. "We did the entire score right in *Pro Tools*, even the MIDI stuff, since we didn't need to do much editing," Shapiro says. "The sound sources were *GigaSampler* and *Reason*, and we used some samples of Egyptian instruments. We mixed the files to .WAVs and put them on an FTP site where Matt could download and audition them."

There are a number of alternate shows built into Tomb for different types of groups. One program is for a typical college/post-college walk-in audience, while another is for corporate team-building events, "where everyone sees that it's the secretary who makes the hard decisions and solves all the puzzles, while the CEO doesn't do anything," says DuPlessie with a laugh. One morning a week, school groups are scheduled, and the place goes into "educational" mode. Besides a specialized show, workstations in the café are set up for students to make papyrus and explore hieroglyphics. Each version of the show has its own soundtrack, using different versions and mixes of the tracks.

Tomb is totally automated and totally modular, which makes sense for a show that DuPlessie hopes will be able to travel after its initial shakedown. Every aspect of the show is operated by a self-resetting show-control control system made by AVStumpfl, an Austrian manufacturer of high-end audio/visual systems. The system is made up of multiple modules linked together with Cat-5 Ethernet cable and speaking a proprietary protocol called *SC Net*. Each module has 16 contact closure inputs, which are programmed to generate commands using the lighting industry-standard DMX protocol to activate more than 200 different devices.

The show is programmed using software developed by AVStumpfl (for Windows) called *Wings*, which looks a lot like a music sequencer, in that each show has multiple tracks that can cue other tracks and subroutines. How and when the various tracks are executed is largely based on user input: what the visitors do inside the tomb. "Disney and Universal rides aren't this complicated because they're not really interactive," says DuPlessie. "Tomb gives everyone the illusion of control."

DuPlessie can sit in the middle of his show and program it on his laptop. "We're beta-testing a version of the software for the company," he says. "They've never had anyone do something of this complexity before." When the programming is finished, it gets burned onto a 512MB Flash card, which goes into a slot on the AVStumpfl system's control module. "There are no crashes, as you would expect if we had a PC controlling everything. That just wouldn't be tolerable."

The lighting is mostly intelligent LD fixtures made by Color Kinetics under DMX control, as are the mechanics, which are handled by dimmer and relay packs from Light Stream Controls. "You know them as 'American DJ,'" says DuPlessie. "They're that company's theatrical arm. It's the highest of the low end." The mechanics are relatively simple: direct-drive electrical motors to open and shut *Star Trek*-style sliding doors between the chambers and a pneumatic system to move buttons, statues, and walls. "Air is safer," he explains. "If something gets in the way, like someone's hand, the pressure drops and the movement stops until the obstruction is removed."

Much of the intelligence in the system is distributed. For example, the flashlights winking out are triggered by a single command from the master controller, which starts a routine built into a custom radio transmitter. The transmitter generates various coded signals according to a set schedule, each of which triggers a dedicated chip inside one of the flashlights, which causes that light to blink a few times and then turn off. It looks random to the player, but of course, it's not. "Everything that can be driven by an on/off control is," says DuPlessie. "It makes it much simpler. Why do you need proportional control?" The complex mechanical systems that drop the ceiling and levitate the Pharaoh's mummy are similarly hard coded: "The DMX system just says, 'Go.'"

For one of the major effects, input to the system is translated into MIDI. The buttons and touchpads that the visitors interact with are wired to an Alesis *D4* drum module, which has eight trigger inputs. "It's the cheapest multichannel MIDI trigger ever made," says DuPlessie, "and it was even cheaper since we got it on eBay." The *D4*'s output goes to a MIDISolutions *R8* relay box, which, in turn, feeds the AvStumpfl system.

The audio is handled by another pair of AvStumpfl modules, *Master 16 Players*. Each module generates eight stereo pairs under the control of the master system. The output goes through four Crown *660* amplifiers, delivering 24 channels at 60 watts each. The audio is also stored on the 512MB Flash cards so that it, like the master controller, is essentially fail proof. To get all of the segments and their individual tracks onto the cards, the files are converted to MP3.

All of the chambers in Tomb have multiple speakers for the music and sound effects, which serve to provide a surround general environment and effects at specific locations. Subwoofers handle the ominous rumbles and other low-end effects, and in the chamber in which the ceiling comes down, bass shakers are installed in the floor, adding to the players' anxiety.

Surprisingly, except for the amplifiers, almost none of the audio components are from the usual professional sources. "Only recently has home-theater stuff become powerful and robust enough for this kind of operation," says DuPlessie. "For these sound levels, home-theater speakers work fine. The acoustics are horrific in the Tomb, and there's no way you could EQ these rooms to make them sound better, so under these circumstances, people can't tell the difference between this and high-end audio."

A foot of airspace and 12-inch-thick doors separate each of the rooms from the others, but there is still plenty of leakage. "Since it's haunted house-style, leakage is okay," explains DuPlessie. "People coming in want to know that it's an emotional experience, and they like to hear the screams of the people in the other rooms. The sound in each room is overpowering enough so that you know what's background and what's foreground."

The speakers DuPlessie and his team decided to use are from Cambridge Soundworks, the consumer electronics company started by the late Henry Kloss and then acquired by Creative Technologies, creators of the infamous *Soundblaster* computer sound cards. Even the subwoofers come from there: 15-inch, self-powered, down-firing *Bass Cubes*. The floor shakers are from a similar consumer electronics source: *Car Audio Bass Enhancers* from a company called Aura Systems. Sold in pairs, these are typically wired in parallel (through an internal 100-Hz active crossover and 100W amplifier) with a sound system's main speakers to provide that added *oomph*. But in Tomb, they are sent their own dedicated track, which is designed to be felt and not heard.

It's not just the low initial cost that attracted Tomb's designers to these components but also their practicality for the long term. "The usual approach is to make a bulletproof installation in a steel cage," says DuPlessie, "but that's expensive, and it can still fail. When a show at Disney goes down, the whole thing is down—they put tape over the entrance for a month while they fix it. Here, I have a shelf with spares of everything in the show, so if something goes down, I just swap it out. And since the show will be traveling, it's important to be able to get spares quickly anywhere in the field. If we have to replace everything two years down the road, that's fine. If I need 20, I buy 25. When I have to replace a box, I just plug in the new one and set its address." Even the lighting control boxes are easily replaceable. It's an eminently sensible approach and reflects the realities of today's electronics marketplace—much like the early adopters of Alesis's 8-track ADAT knew they needed at least four units if they wanted to promote themselves as a 24-track facility.

As a symbol of how the line between professional and consumer electronics has become increasingly vague, the ADAT serves well. But today, the distinction has gotten even more confusing, and as the newest technologies often find themselves in mass-market mail-order catalogs before they make it into our studios, Tomb can be seen as an indicator of where things are going.

Besides creating an exciting new form of entertainment, DuPlessie and his team are valuing replaceability and quick and easy repair over making sure their sound systems are of the highest possible quality. MP3 audio and home-theater and car-audio speakers are easily good enough for Tomb—and that means, as disturbing as the concept may be to some of us, they're good enough for a lot of things.

To tell the truth, Paul D. Lehrman prefers his multiplayer games outdoors, preferably using some kind of ball and plenty of beer.

Afterword

Tomb received unanimously positive reviews from the local media when it opened, and after two years continues to attract good crowds. As I write this, I have just returned from a party where a 15-year-old girl who recently experienced it at a friend's birthday celebration pronounced it to be "really awesome." And it's made me famous—well, sort of. Since it opened, this column is quoted every single day in the theater listings in the Boston *Globe*: "Tomb: The Future of Entertainment!—Mix Magazine." Plans are to take Tomb on the road in 2007 and install a new spy-themed adventure game at the Boston location.

Jokes: Part 5

Did you hear what the Deadhead who ran out of pot said?

"This band sucks!"

■ ■ ■

The doctor said to the jazz musician, "I am very sorry to tell you that you have cancer and you have only one more year to live."

The jazz musician replied, "And what am I going to live on for an entire year?"

■ ■ ■

Q: What do you do with a horn player who can't play?

A: Give him two sticks, put him in the back, and call him a percussionist.

Q: What do you do if he can't do that?

A: Take away one of the sticks, put him up front, and call him a conductor.

■ ■ ■

Q: Why do violin players have that little cloth tucked under their chin?

A: Because violins don't have spit valves.

Q: How can you tell when a rock-and-roll guitar player is particularly well hung?

A: When you can just barely slip your finger in between his neck and the noose.

Q: What's the last thing a drummer says before he's thrown out of the band?

A: "Let's play one of *my* songs!"

Q: How do you get two soprano sax players to play a minor second apart?

A: Have them read off the same chart.

Q: How do you make a million dollars singing jazz?

A: Start with two million.

Q: What's the definition of a gentleman?

A: Someone who knows how to play the oboe but doesn't.

■ ■ ■

In the middle of the set, the piano player pulls over the singer and says, "Okay, now tonight we'll try a special version of this song: After five and a half measures of intro you come in with the second verse a minor third up, go to the bridge after 11 bars, modulate twice a half-step down, and then halfway through the last A-section you start the tag, but a tritone lower. Are you ready? One, two..."

"Hey, wait!" the singer interrupts. "I'll never be able to do that!"

The pianist replies, "But you nailed it last night!"

■ ■ ■

Q: Why are music jokes so short?

A: So the bass player can understand them.

Q: Why are a violist's fingers like lightning?

A: They rarely strike the same place twice.

Q: What is "perfect pitch'?

A: That's when you lob a clarinet into a toilet without hitting the rim.

Q: How do you improve the aerodynamics of a trombonist's car?

A: Take the Domino's Pizza sign off the roof.

Q: Why are orchestra intermissions limited to 20 minutes?

A: So you don't have to re-train the cellists.

■ ■ ■

An orchestra was on the last day of a long series of rehearsals for a big upcoming tour. Suddenly, in the middle of a piece, the conductor had a heart attack and was rushed to the hospital. Word quickly got back that he would be okay, but he couldn't possibly go out on the tour. The orchestra board knew there wasn't time to hire a replacement, so in desperation they asked the members of the orchestra whether any of them could conduct.

One of the viola players spoke up, saying, "I took some conducting in college. I think I can do it." They gave him the job, and he ended up doing just fine, and the tour was a success.

After they came home, the regular conductor, now rested and ready, took the podium, and the violist returned to his chair. The player sitting beside him looked at him and asked, "Where the hell have you been!?"

■ ■ ■

An upscale hotel bar has a sign out front announcing that the management is looking for a new piano player. A presentable young man walks in one day and asks to speak to the owner. "I'm the guy you're looking for," he announces. "I write and play my own stuff, and audiences love me."

"Okay," says the owner, a little skeptical. "Let's hear something."

It turns out the young man isn't lying. After just a couple of minutes, the owner is in awe of his talent. "That's the most beautiful piano playing I have ever heard!" he exclaims. "What's the name of that song?"

The pianist says, "I call it 'Your Mother is Screwing the Milkman and There's a Stinking Mess All Over the Kitchen.'"

The owner gasps and says, "Jeez, that's a terrible name for such a lovely song. What else do you know?" The guy smiles and plays a different piece. If anything, it's even more beautiful than the first. The owner is almost afraid to ask the name of the piece, but he does.

The pianist answers, "Dogshit on the Sidewalk and Cat Vomit on the Rug." The owner again is shocked. He asks the pianist if all of his tunes have names like that. "Well," comes the reply, "two others that people really like are 'I Nailed Your Little Sister in the Back Seat of My Hummer and Left Her Naked in a Ditch' and 'Vultures Plucked Out My Liver and Fed it to the Wolverines.'"

The bar owner takes a deep breath and says, "Well, you play gorgeously and your songs are incredible. I'll hire you, but only under one condition: You have to promise never, *ever,* to tell the name of your songs to my patrons." The pianist agrees, and they shake hands on the deal.

That night the guy is playing, and the crowd is just as amazed as the owner was with his musical abilities. People are lined up at the door, the bar is doing great business, and even after three straight hours, the audience won't let him stop playing. But he desperately needs to take a bathroom break, so he runs off to the men's room. As he's standing at the urinal, the owner barges in and yells, "Hurry up! They're screaming for more!"

"Okay, okay!" says the pianist, and rushes back out to the stage. But in his hurry he forgets to zip up his fly. As he stands next to the piano and takes a bow, a drunk at one of the front tables hollers, "Hey buddy! Do you know your dick and balls are hanging out and you're dripping piss all over your shoes?"

The pianist smiles at the drunk and says, "Know it? I *wrote* it!"

■ ■ ■

A man walks into a new private club and asks what kind of members they are accepting. "Oh, we'll take anybody," says the cheerful doorman. "but you have to furnish proof of your IQ, and then we put you in a room with similar people."

"Sounds fair," says the man. "Can I look go look at some of the rooms?"

"Sure," says the doorman. He opens a door marked "175" and inside are three physicists discussing the merits of string theory. Then he goes to a door marked "150" and finds a half-dozen brain surgeons comparing notes. Then he goes to a door marked "85" and encounters four guys arguing over whether Rush Limbaugh is smarter than Bill O'Reilly. Finally, he finds a door marked "62" and goes in.

There he sees two men smoking cigarettes and drinking beer. One of them looks up at the newcomer and says, "So what kind of sticks do you use?"

■ ■ ■

Top 11 Things You Don't Want To Hear From Tech Support

11. "Do you have a sledgehammer or a brick handy?"

10. "That's right, not even McGyver could fix it."

9. "So—what are you wearing?"

8. "Duuuuuude! Bummer!"

7. "Looks like you're gon' ta need some new dilithium crystals, Cap'n."

6. "Press 1 for Support. Press 2 if you're with *60 Minutes*. Press 3 if you're with the FTC."

5. "We can fix this, but you're gonna need a butter knife, a roll of duct tape, and a car battery."

4. "In layman's terms, we call this the Hindenburg Effect."

3. "Hold on a second…Mom! Timmy's hitting me!"

2. "Okay, turn to page 523 in your copy of *Dianetics*."

1. "Please hold for Mr. Gates's attorney."

■ ■ ■

A musician who's spent his whole life trying to break into the big time is at the end of his rope. He's been turned down by every record company, club manager, and publisher in the country, and if it wasn't for his dog he wouldn't have any audience at all. So he dreams up an ingenious plan to get back at all those creeps who have failed to recognize his talent all those years. He goes into a recording studio with a list of everyone who ever rejected him and tells the engineer to record exactly what he says, burn it onto 1,000 CDs, and send them out to all the names on his list.

He goes into the vocal booth, the red light goes on, and he begins: "This is a message to all you sycophantic, greedy, talentless bastards who've ignored me all these years. I dedicated my life to writing beautiful, emotional, soul-baring music, and all you assholes are interested in is phony gangster rappers, pretty-boy bands, and teenage vamps. Well, I've taken all I can of your shallow, vicious, money-grubbing industry, and you're the ones who have driven me to it!! See you in Hell, you murderers of art!!" And with that, he pulls out a revolver and sprays his brains all over the studio wall.

The engineer glances up and says, "Okay…good…that's fine for level. Wanna go for a take?"

Chapter 46

A Talk with John Chowning

Preface

When I saw John Chowning speak about the future of musical instruments at the 2004 AES conference, I was so taken with what he said that I decided I needed to discuss it in a column. As you can see from the length of this chapter, it went much, much further than that. Chowning is one of the heroes of the computer music age, with a lot to say about a large variety of important subjects, and he deserves all the recognition and accolades he gets—and more. After you read this two-part interview, I think you'll agree.

February & March 2005

Part I: Extreme Vibrato and Other Accidental Flashes of Genius

John Chowning pretty much sleeps when he wants and works when he wants. That is why when I'm talking to him at 10 a.m. East Coast time—and he's on the West Coast—he's been up and composing for about four hours already. "Now that I don't have institutional obligations, I find it's really great," he says. "I remember hearing

Buckminster Fuller give a talk about his lifestyle, and he said he'd work all the time, and when he was tired, he'd just take a nap. So I was inspired by that. Of course, Fuller says it's really hard on the rest of the family."

Chowning, for those of you who just got up, was the inventor of FM synthesis, the computational technique that ushered in the era of digital synths, MIDI, desktop music production, and much of what we've all been doing for the past 20 years. At the age of 70, he's now a professor *emeritus* at Stanford, where he was on the faculty for more than 25 years, and the *emeritus* part means he doesn't have to show up for classes anymore. So what's he doing? He's devoted himself full-time to what a great many of us would like to be doing: composing with all the neat new tools he and those who learned from him helped develop.

Chowning was the founding director of the Center for Computer Research in Music and Acoustics (CCRMA, pronounced "karma") at Stanford, one of the most successful think tanks for music technology in the world. Some of the most important research in music synthesis and digital signal processing that we use today emerged from there, and among the many major figures who worked there were Andy Moorer, developer of the legendary *SoundDroid* for Lucasfilm and founder of Sonic Solutions; David Ziccarelli, writer of Opcode's original *DX7* patch editor and now head of the wildly innovative software company Cycling '74; and Julius O. Smith, creator of what was to become known as physical-modeling synthesis.

I ran into Chowning at the recent AES in San Francisco, where he was on a terrific standing room-only panel about the early days of electronic music in the Bay Area. A question came from the audience about the future of electronic musical instruments, and his answer was short but highly thought provoking. So I went up to him afterward and asked him if he would be willing to elaborate on it. A few weeks later, we had a fascinating 90-minute phone conversation covering that and many other subjects, which led to him being the subject of two *Insider Audio* columns.

Chowning was always a musician, never a scientist.

Chowning was always a musician, never a scientist. He grew up listening to the big band music of the World War II era and started violin lessons in public school at the age of 7. A few years later, his junior high school band needed a cymbal player who could read music, so he became a percussionist. He served in the military and went to the U.S. Navy's music school where he learned jazz. "It was an amazing place during the Korean War," he recalls. "The Adderley Brothers were there and a future member of the vocal group The Hi-Lo's. There was a very high level of playing."

He then went to college on the GI Bill and studied composition, which he followed up with three years in Paris, studying under the legendary Nadia Boulanger, teacher of generations of composers from Aaron Copland to Quincy Jones. In Paris, he heard and was seduced by electronic music for the first time, thanks to a concert series produced by Pierre Boulez. "It wasn't Boulanger's music," he recalls. "She was more fond of Stravinsky and the romantic composers, but she had a fascination with it—Boulez in particular—and she encouraged us to go." There he heard many of the great pioneers of the early electronic era like Luciano Berio, Henri Pousseur, and Karlheinz Stockhausen.

After Paris, he went to Stanford for graduate study, but there was no electronic music there at the time, although that would soon change: "My second year there, someone gave me an article from *Science* by Max Mathews who was at Bell Labs. I tried to understand it. It made this fantastic claim that any sound that could be perceived could be produced by a computer. So I went down to the computer science department and took a course in ALGOL (one of the first computer languages). I contacted Max, who was at Bell Labs, and visited him. He gave me a stack of punch cards, which was the BEFAP compiler (Bell Labs' custom FORTRAN language) for the IBM 7094, which you needed to use Music 4, the music composition software that was available. I didn't understand much of what he told me, but then I read an article by James Tenney in Yale's *Journal of Music Theory*, and after that, I understood everything in Max's article.

"So I had this stack of cards, and I was wondering how I was going to get this to happen," he continues. "One day, I was standing outside the computer center and this student walked up whom I knew, since he was the tuba player in the orchestra where I played timpani, and he asked me if he could help. That was David Poole, who was a sophomore math major, and he was hanging around what was going to someday be the AI lab. He taught me everything I needed to know. Among other things, he figured out a way to transfer the computer sample data in a dual-buffer arrangement, so it could be output as a continuous stream. Up to that point, it was a two-step process: At Bell Labs, they had to write the output to a computer tape and then send it to a separate D-to-A converter. So this was probably the first online (real-time) computer music system."

This process of going to various sources until he could get his hands around a concept came to define Chowning's development. "I thought maybe I should go back and take some math," he says. "So I enrolled in Algebra A; I think they called it 'Bonehead Algebra.' I was already 30 or 31-years-old, and my last math class had been in high school. I struggled through it. I understood everything; I just didn't have the capacity to get through these tests in the few minutes we had. I had to beg the teaching assistant for a passing grade. I said to him, 'Imagine you were taking a music course, and I asked you to play an augmented sixth chord in the key of A-flat major. Musicians can do it right away. You could figure it out, but it would take some time.' He said, 'Yeah, yeah, I understand.' So he didn't give me an A, but he did pass me. But I decided this was no way to learn what I felt I should know. Finding out answers to the immediate questions at hand was more important, but I needed to find the right person to explain it to me.

"If there was something I wanted to know, I would ask the same question of all these people, until I could finally get an answer in a way I could understand it."

"At the computer center, the environment increased the number of timeshare users from eight or nine to 20 or more, and now there were all these people there I could talk to: engineers, psychologists, philosophers, linguists. So I built up an incidental education. If there was something I wanted to know, I would ask the same question of all these people until I could finally get an answer in a way I could understand it. That's how I learned physics and acoustics."

Chowning's first work at the computer center at Stanford in the early '60s was with reverberators and other spatial illusions in a four-channel surround environment. "When I started out," he says, "someone told me I would need vector algebra, and I said, 'Yeah, right,' but instead I thought, 'How else can I capture this information about distance and Doppler Shift?' Well, I just did it graphically. The lab had an arm with potentiometers in two angles, like a drafting machine, that plotted points on a CRT—sort of a precursor of a mouse. It plotted the points at a constant rate, so if you moved more slowly, the points were closer together, and if you moved faster, they were further apart. So I would just measure the points and that would give me the velocities. And it worked. Some of the mathematicians there laughed at me, but I got this four-channel system to make these sound paths.

"That was the single most important point of learning for me: the importance of programming. I couldn't solder—I still can't—but I could make all these things with just a modicum of programming skill. I could bypass all the (engineering) detail and go directly from brain to output with just programming. I would write a subroutine to do a spatial path and another to do a circular path and just use them whenever I needed to. The essential notion of efficiency came to me like a knock on the head."

In Chowning's view, musicians and computers are not at all an unlikely combination. "Music is a symbolic art," he says. "A painter gets the sensory feedback immediately, but musicians are used to writing things on paper and hearing them later. So they have to deal with symbols, things that are some distance away from where they are at the sensory level. It might be why music was the first of the arts to make so much artistic use of the computer. I know that other artists were working with computers at the time, but there wasn't this rush of activity—'I've got to get back to the computer center to work on my piece'— that musicians had. And this wasn't the electronic music I had heard in France. There was now this whole other dimension, besides just producing electronic sounds."

The idea of a musically oriented research environment with a variety of brains to pick resulted in the founding of CCRMA. Chowning usually gets the credit, but he says, "I didn't create it—it just sort of happened. Andy Moorer, John Grey, and Loren Rush were grad students there, and we were doing projects that came out of a collegial need. We'd ask each other, 'What are you doing?' 'Can you modify that?' Lots of applications would develop from that. Because what we were doing was interdisciplinary; it didn't fit in the music department, which was dominated by musicologists. So we decided we should form some sort of center that would allow us to apply for funding. I was the one on the faculty, and so I became the director. I chose good people—the idea was to make an open, accessible system and then leave people alone. The downside was that I became the administrator. There were fights to keep it intact and funded."

Initial money came from the National Science Foundation and the National Endowment for the Arts, but a big break came when Systems Development Corporation came across with $2.7 million. "Systems Development Corporation was a Defense Department contractor, and they had made an enormous amount of money," says Chowning, "which they had to dispose of. We were one of four centers to get grants for computer music." The grant came in large measure because of the efforts of John R. Pierce, another Bell Labs scientist (among whose myriad major accomplishments was coining the word "transistor"), who was so enamored of the center that he worked at CCRMA for more than 12 years as a "visiting" professor without ever asking for a salary.

By varying the amount of frequency modulation over time, he could control the spectrum of a sound by using just two oscillators.

It was in 1967 when Chowning first discovered the idea behind FM synthesis. "I was experimenting with extreme vibrato," he recalls, "and I heard these inharmonic sidebands. I did a bunch of experiments, and I brought in an engineer to see whether what I thought I was doing was what the science would say that I was hearing. He looked at the equations and said, 'Yeah, that's right.' It was all very counterintuitive: Not a theoretical discovery, it was an ear discovery.

"But I was deep into the quadraphonic stuff, so I put it on the back burner," he continues. "In 1971, I was thinking about work that Jean-Claude Risset had done in additive synthesis (among Risset's contributions was showing that the harmonic spectrum of natural sounds changes with overall amplitude) and that Max Mathews had done in analysis synthesis, and I realized I could do the same sort of thing by coupling an amplitude envelope to a modulation index." In other words, by varying the amount of frequency modulation over time, he could control the spectrum of a sound by using just two oscillators. "I realized it was all predictable, and within a few tens of minutes, I had some pretty passable brass tones. So then I wrote an article for the *AES Journal*, which was published in September 1973."

Like The Beatles being turned down by the first few record companies their manager went to, Chowning's ideas on FM synthesis were rejected by several companies that Stanford's

Office of Technology Licensing tried to get interested. Among them were Hammond and Wurlitzer. Chowning says of these companies, "Frankly, I don't think their engineers understood it—they were into analog technology and had no idea what I was talking about.

"But then the office put a Business School graduate student on the project, and he found out that the world's largest manufacturer of musical instruments, even though they didn't have much of a presence in the U.S. at the time, was Yamaha. One of Yamaha's engineers was visiting their American office, so he came up to Stanford for the day. I guess they had already been working in the digital domain, because in ten minutes, he understood exactly what I was talking about." The rest, as they say, is history.

Although not exactly linear history. "Of course, the Yamaha patents made a huge difference," says Chowning, "but they didn't begin to pay off for a number of years." And in the meantime, Chowning had lost his job. "Like many universities, at Stanford you teach for seven years, and then they either give you tenure or you're out," he says. "No one understood what was going on in computer music, so they didn't promote me, and in 1973, I had to leave."

Part II: Making Electronics Sing
"I understand why they did that," he says now. "Except for Leland Smith, I think it scared the music faculty a little bit: the idea of machines in this deeply humanistic department full of musicologists."

But meanwhile, by the late 1970s, Yamaha began to get very serious about building digital synthesizers using FM technology. The company had put together a couple of prototypes called "MAD" and were working on what was going to be its first commercial FM synth, the fantastically complex (and expensive) *GS-1*. So Yamaha came back to Stanford looking to extend and make exclusive the license it had bought for the patent that Chowning had created and had signed over to his then-employer. Only Chowning wasn't there: He'd been invited to do an artist-in-residency in Berlin (arranged by famed composer György Ligeti) and was also asked by Pierre Boulez to help design the new French government musical research center, IRCAM. It was, no doubt, a bit of an embarrassing moment for the university.

Chowning hadn't completely severed his ties with Stanford, however and, in 1975, had come back to CCRMA as a research associate to work on a piece that IRCAM commissioned. And a couple of years later, he was given an offer to return to academia. But it wasn't from Stanford. The University of California wanted to appoint him as a full professor. Stanford, finally realizing what it had lost, asked him to come back with tenure. "It was the only time they had ever let a junior professor go," he recalls with a laugh, "and then hired him back."

The economics would soon make the wisdom in Stanford's decision clear. Yamaha's first popular FM synth, the *DX7*, came out four years later and sold something like 180,000 units, which was an order of magnitude more than any synthesizer had sold before. FM technology remained at the center of the company's electronic keyboard line, including home organs and pianos, through the *TX, TG,* and *SY* series for well into the next decade. The royalties received by Stanford for Chowning's patent totaled $22.9 million, making it the third most lucrative patent the university ever licensed. (Number two on that list is a gene-splicing technique for building recombinant DNA, and number one is a text-searching technology dreamed up by two graduate students that is now commonly known as *Google*.) Even though the patent expired in 1995, FM synthesis is still available as an option on Yamaha's current flagship synth, the *Motif*.

Those who were around at the time have their own ideas about why the *DX7* was so popular—and all of them are right. The instrument was groundbreaking and amazingly useful in many ways. But Chowning's thoughts are a bit different, and they cast an interesting light on what makes for a successful electronic musical instrument.

One of the primary goals of a new instrument, he says, if it is to be successful, is that it be able to sort out the good players from the not-so-good. "Two of the most enduring electronic instruments are the Hammond *B3* and the Rhodes," he opines. "That's because they have unusual acoustic attributes: They have instantaneous attacks, which pianos don't. So they offer rhythmic precision that someone like Jimmy Smith can take advantage of. That has real musical consequences, and it reveals the deficiencies in lesser performers. The same thing is what was important about the *DX7*: It gave really good keyboardists expressive control that a keyboard without velocity sensitivity wouldn't have. Velocity is one of the things that pianists spend thousands of hours learning how to control. And when you coupled the velocity sensitivity to the modulation index, it gave a dimension to the timbre, not just the loudness, that was different from earlier synths and which our ears are very sensitive to."

Chowning recalls that soon after the DX7 was introduced, English musician David Bristow, who was one of the primary sound designers for the company (and still is, although his current work is on ring tones), did an experiment that showed how important minute timbral changes could be to a musician. "I was working with him in Paris at the time," Chowning says, "writing our book (*FM Theory and Applications*, a seminal tome published by Yamaha). He convinced professional keyboard players that he was changing the action and the keyboard sensitivity on a *DX7* and getting their reactions. Actually, all he was doing was increasing or decreasing the amount of what he called 'stuff' during the attack: the noise. It was an impression based entirely on acoustic feedback; he did nothing to the keyboard at all.

"The relationship between energy, force, effort, and the acoustic result is a part of all musical performance," he continues. "More effort results in greater intensity or spectral complexity. I guess the exception to that is the pipe organ, but then again, in the early days you had this little guy in the back working the bellows. The *B3* is a little different because the key velocity doesn't matter, but in that case, the precision of execution really does. So if you have a synth with *both* a sharp attack and velocity sensitivity, good keyboard players can get a high degree of expressive control out of it. So it reveals virtuosity, or lack of it, and separates out the really good performers from others.

"That's also why the *WX7* (Yamaha's unique MIDI wind controller, which has been in production for some 18 years) works. It's easy to distinguish between a good player and a bad one.

"Here's what I would consider the ultimate test of expressivity. I proposed this to a concert pianist to get his attention. Now, I don't play the piano, so if I tell him to hit a note and then I try to hit it the same way, it will take me a few times to get the velocity just right. If he plays two tones, it might take me 100 times to replicate it perfectly. If he plays a phrase, just four or five notes, I'm lost. I could never do it. I could never convince a listener that it's him and not me. It's not in my hands; it's not in my training. So we need to look for instruments that expose that kind of technique, that have richness and can reveal virtuosity and expressivity. Those instruments will find users who will be able to highlight some or all of that expressive neural-motor connection."

Chowning doesn't think that breakthroughs in new instruments will look entirely different from what we're familiar with. But he does think that musicians can be encouraged to experiment with new techniques, as long as the encouragement is given in the right way. "Controllers that make use of existing technique ought to be the top issue," he says. "I would look for instruments that play upon instruments we already use. Piano, cello, and violin are the three great virtuoso instruments—that's what kids learn to play. If you're looking for a population willing to be experimental, you'll find them in those three groups. And also wind players and horn players.

"For example, you could work on finding ways to use violin technique," he adds. "Not a 'virtual' violin where there's no physical object there—although we've worked with that, and it's interesting—but a real object that lets players slap their fingers down and touch the strings; for example, Chris Chafe's 'celleto.' Some of the controllers we have today a dancer could do much better with than a musician. They have a sense of body movement that musicians aren't trained to have."

One instrument of the future, Chowning thinks, will be a fully programmable piano in which the soundboard and the strings—the heavy, temperature-sensitive part—disappear. "The measure would be if you could take a great pianist and blindfold him and sit him down, and he can't distinguish it from a grand piano. And then you move him to another piano, which is identical or maybe even the same one, but you've changed the key reaction characteristics and the sound quality, and he thinks that he's no longer at a Steinway; now he's at a Baldwin."

Another characteristic that he thinks makes for a useful new instrument is its ability to control large musical parameters, as opposed to minute ones. "The most successful controllers are those like Max Mathews' *Radio Baton* or Don Buchla's *Lightning* (which are both systems that track the motion of two wands in space), where a simple gesture can produce a result that has meaning at the highest musical level, such as loudness or tempo. It relieves the performer of dealing with all of the details. Think about an orchestra conductor who doesn't know how to play the violin or the bassoon, but she animates all these well-trained machines—the players, who have spent thousands of hours learning from the masters of their instruments, going back generations. Expressivity in machines has to have this kind of top-level control."

In addition, and this was the surprising answer that Chowning gave at the panel discussion at the AES conference, "For a controller to persist, it needs repertoire. It can be written repertoire or oral, or a tradition of jazz or folk or ethnic music. People who begin to play it have to have models of excellence or know that the music is rich because of a long tradition." He points again to the *B3* organ as an example. "The *B3* could never reach the popularity of the piano because it is missing the idea that more effort equals greater volume, but it has a solid tradition in pop and jazz and gospel, and so it persists."

Commercial manufacturers, although they have been very, very good to Chowning, are not necessarily going to be the ones to produce these instruments, in his opinion. "People like Buchla have different ultimate interests than a company like Yamaha. He senses an opportunity and builds a device that extends the performance capability in ways that performers never asked for. His nose is ahead of the pack. Yamaha, on the other hand, is looking for ways to engage the public. If in doing so they can make a more expressive instrument, that's desirable, but they need to make money. Their grand pianos are their great tradition, and fortunately, they make money with them, because if they were marginal, they'd stop making them."

Chowning is very happy that the state of electronic music technology has reached the point that it has, just at the moment when he is able to retire from teaching and concentrate on composing. "The present is the dream for me," he says. "It's all software and real time and portable. I sit here with a laptop that has more power than I could ever use. With a laptop Mac or PC and a MOTU *828*, it's like I have everything I've ever had in all the labs we've ever built, in all the years at Stanford, in 10 stacks of Samson boxes put together"—referring to refrigerator-sized, computer-controlled synths that were state-of-the-art in the late 1970s. "Software synthesis is the take-off point for ultimate freedom. The only hardware devices you need are controllers; there's no real reason anymore to build a synthesizer.

"We still do need controllers, and the difficulty is how to put that extra piece, that performance knowledge, into them."

"But we still do need controllers," he says in conclusion, "and the difficulty is how to put that extra piece, that performance knowledge, into them." Fortunately, musical expression, according to Chowning, is not an unfathomable art, although we have much to learn. He points to studies done by a scientist at the Royal Institute of Technology in Stockholm named Johann Sundberg, an eminent researcher who, among his many accomplishments, showed why you can hear an operatic soloist over an entire orchestra. "Sundberg did some wonderful work on the voice: how the vocal tract changes, how the timbre changes, how to shape a phrase using little gradations in the intensity and the linkages with pitch glide. That's an area that if we understood more, we could make our machines more expressive. It would be extremely enriching. Because once you understand that, you can apply it to a violin or to any other instrument. After all, the voice is the instrument of instruments."

Paul D. Lehrman teaches a course in electronic musical instrument design at Tufts University but knows that he, too, has a lot to learn.

Afterword

The topic of new musical controllers—how to make them, how to use them, and what they mean—occupied me a lot that year and ended up filling two more columns, which you'll find in Chapters 49 and 50.

Chapter 47

On the Road with Kronos
Chamber Music That's Eclectic
and Electric

Preface

When I was a little kid, all that I heard around the family home was classical music—especially Mozart, Beethoven, Brahms, and Haydn—Broadway musicals, and traditional folk music. My father was a good amateur violinist, my brother played the piano, and I played the piano and the guitar. At about the age of 12, like millions of kids whose lives were utterly changed by The Beatles, I started playing rock and roll. But not long after that, thanks to the wonderful non-profit New York radio station WBAI, I discovered another kind of music: the great composers of the first half of the 20th century like Varèse, Cage, Stravinsky, and Bartok. From there it was a short leap to the ultra-modern and electronic masters Berio, Stockhausen, Boulez, and Ussachevsky. And I've had a deep love of what's now called "contemporary concert" music since then.

It's a type of music, however, that seems to be played less and less, as "classical" orchestras and ensembles struggle for decreasing funds and, in order to keep their audiences happy, program fewer and fewer challenging works. And with the near-collapse of music education in public schools in the U.S., there are fewer young people coming of age who want to hear it. Sure, every large city has an ensemble or two who specialize in modern music, but few of these ensembles are more than a blip on the cultural radar of the city, and none of the players actually can make a living doing nothing but "new" music.

The Kronos Quartet, happily, is a shining exception to this and is doing well by doing exactly what many other ensembles wish they could do: combining electronics and the finest acoustic instruments, commissioning and performing new works, and continuing to expand their audience's consciousness and horizons, without losing them. And they've been at it for 30 years. It was a privilege to sit down and talk with one of their team about this very special group and the technology they use.

May 2005

When a string quartet gets on an airplane, they get five seats, with the extra one for the cello. But here's a question: Does the cello get a baggage allowance? For most groups, that may not be a big deal, but for the Kronos Quartet, who schlep along the electronic equipment they need to create their unique sound (as well as a modicum of lighting gear) packed into nearly a dozen hard-shell Pelican cases, it can mean a huge difference in what a tour costs.

If you don't know the Kronos Quartet, you should. Not long ago, the group celebrated its thirtieth anniversary as one of the most daring and innovative "classical" music groups in the world. Violinist David Harrington founded the group in 1973 in response to hearing a performance of George Crumb's revolutionary (and fervently anti-war) quartet *Black Angels* for amplified string quartet.

Since then, they have recorded more than 40 albums under their own name, one of which earned a Grammy for Best Chamber Music Performance in 2004, and dozens more with other artists ranging from Nelly Furtado to Joan Armatrading to the Dave Matthews Band, as well as soundtracks for films such as *Heat*, *Requiem for a Dream*, and *21 Grams*. They have commissioned more than 450 new works and arrangements and have performed the works of almost every major composer of the 20th century, and promise to do the same for the 21st. And they're fantastic.

I'm ashamed to say that despite all my years following the contemporary classical scene, I had never heard Kronos play live. But I finally got my chance to hear them at an arts festival in the dead of this past winter—called, appropriately, "Light In Winter"—in Ithaca, New York. They played a typically eclectic program: works by composers from Mexico, Nicaragua, India (with a prerecorded track by tabla virtuoso Zakir Hussain), and

Azerbaijan, as well as a new work by renowned American composer Terry Riley. The encore was their rendition of Jimi Hendrix's interpretation of *The Star-Spangled Banner*, complete with gobs of distortion, feedback, screaming rockets, and bombs bursting all over the stage—all played live through a couple of small racks of processing gear. They blew the audience, and me, away.

Kronos is the only string quartet in the world that travels with a full-time sound engineer.

Unique problems call for unique solutions. Kronos is the only string quartet in the world that travels with a full-time sound engineer (actually, two engineers alternate) because they're the only string quartet in the world that uses amplification at every performance. Shortly after the concert that I saw, engineer Scott Fraser took some time away from the group and let his cohort Mark Grey take over for a tour of Australia and New Zealand. "We leapfrog over each other," he says, "so we can accommodate each other's schedules. I tend to do the gigs in Japan because the Japanese promoter we work with likes to have consistency, and I do Latin America because I get by in Spanish fairly well. Mark gets to do Scandinavia."

Fraser, whom I met at breakfast the morning after the concert I heard, has been working with the group for 14 years. He started his career, like so many of us, as a musician with a tape recorder. "I was playing guitar in rock bands in the '60s, and when I discovered Hendrix, I discovered electronics," he recalls. "That led to an appreciation of Pink Floyd, and I got a tape deck and started doing my own *musique concrète* in 1971. Other musicians realized I had a tape recorder, and so they asked me to record their band demos."

He went to college to study music and theater-sound design. "I couldn't get a music degree where I was," he says, "because there was an ensemble requirement, and they didn't have any way to accommodate someone who played electric guitar. Meanwhile, they had one little room with a modular Moog system and a Putney synth. So I spent every spare minute I had in there teaching myself synthesis."

After college, he found work in the shipping room of Burbank, California's legendary Location Recording Service, where "I hung around with great people. *[Transformer guru]* Deane Jensen ran his business out of there. Eventually, I worked my way up." He went freelance around 1977, starting out with a TEAC *3340S* 4-track reel-to-reel, and has never looked back. At the same time, he started doing live sound for a wide variety of artists, including jazz and big band acts, folk festivals, and "square stuff," such as Peter Nero, Mel Tormé, Leslie Uggams, and Sid Caesar. On the classical side, he toured with piano duo Katia and Marielle Labèque, and on the rock side with The Residents.

One of his favorite gigs was a 20-year relationship with the Aman Folk Ensemble, who performed authentic folk dance music from all over the world. "I got to work with every possible kind and variation of stringed instruments and weird horns," he recalls.

He got the Kronos job through connections with the quartet's first resident sound engineer, Fred Stites, and his successor, Jay Cloidt. "They brought Fred in when they decided they needed to have consistency," he explains. "I had toured with him on a few acts. After it became too much for him to be on the road all the time, he recommended me."

Kronos tours for about five months every year, with an enormous repertoire to draw on. "On any given tour, there are usually no two nights that are the same show," says Fraser. "A given piece, if it's good, they'll do for years. Some promoters or producers want specific pieces, so they'll work a program around that. Sometimes they'll set up a tour around a new CD. Usually, they'll have up to 20 pieces ready at a time for a tour, and they'll do about six a night.

"They feel that an evening's program should have the same structural integrity as an individual piece; in other words, the whole program is a composition, and they work the programs out months in advance. Sometimes, they'll have to make a change if the promoter prints something different in the program or if it's a big outdoor festival and they see that quiet pieces won't work." At the Ithaca show, in fact, they made a last-minute decision to switch the order of two works.

Kronos is amplified for two reasons: so that the audience can hear the music better and because a lot of composers call for—and take advantage of the group's willingness to use—electronic effects on the instruments.

"Ideally, you don't want it to sound like a sound system," Fraser says. "What we're trying to do is make everyone in a 2,000-seat concert hall, even the people 150 feet from the stage, feel like they're sitting in the fifth row. We don't do it by cranking it; we do it by paying attention to image and detail. I've brought in an Ivie analyzer, which showed that the increase in level is only about 1 dB over the acoustic sound of the instruments. But the increase in clarity is significant. They do a piece by Alfred Schnittke in which he specifies they play *ppppp*: one hair of the bow on the string. You can't hear that 80 feet from the stage, but you can with our sound design."

One of the key strategies Fraser uses is to make the amplified sound image not much larger than the original image. "The idea is that the musicians should be the apparent source, not speakers that are separated spatially from the acoustic source. We bring the stacks in from the wings and angle them in—all the stuff you're not supposed to do," he says with a laugh. "Part of it is to keep the sound from bouncing off the side walls, and part of it is so that you can be sitting outside the stereo field and still hear left and right. We don't want people to hear stuff coming from one speaker or another. When I see the performers in the middle and the sound is coming from 50 degrees off-center, that doesn't work.

"We'll sometimes take out all of the house's main speakers and build pyramids out of wedges and monitors. And if they have a center cluster, even if it's garbage, we'll always use it, taking the sound out of the left and right speakers a little so that the reinforcement is not as easily discernible as if it were emanating solely from the left and right stacks.

"We have a pair of Meyer Sound *UPM-1P*s with us—they fit in the Pelican cases—which are designed for under-balcony fill, but we use them for frontfill in mono, putting them in front of the quartet. We'll use a delay to push the system 'back' a few feet since the stacks are usually about six feet in front of the fiddles. We always bring the sound back to the players.

"Our biggest problem is that many venues fly their systems. We put it in the rider in capital letters that the main system must be ground stacked. You just can't be up in the air, and no amount of delay can bring the sound out of the air when it's flown. Sometimes, like at a big festival, we have to back off from that—it is what it is, we're here for only one night, and there are a lot of other things going on."

There are two sets of microphones on the group, reflecting the two purposes of the system. Neumann *KM150*s are mounted on sidearms attached to the music stands, facing upward. "We use those for the more 'acoustic' pieces," says Fraser, "to give a transparent sound. They had been using cheap AKGs, and one day I brought in some *KM140*s and David *[the first violinist]* right away said, 'We have to get these.' The second set are Countryman ultra-miniature *Isomax* omnis taped to the instruments' bridges. These are used for pieces that have processing, and when there is a lot of processing, the Neumanns are taken out of the mix completely.

Though many different types of processing are called for in the group's vast repertoire, Fraser and his colleagues have reduced their touring kit to just three devices. The work-horse is a Boss *VF-1* half-rack multi-effects box. "It's great for analog-style distortion," says Fraser. "It's good at the really radical stuff; it's nowhere near as polite as the others. It has a very flexible architecture. In *The Star-Spangled Banner*, I'm using a distortion preset that emulates a Strat going through a Dallas Arbiter *Fuzz Face* and a Marshall stack, with a little *Univibe*-y chorus and some delay and reverb."

A terrific piece that I heard the group play called *Potassium*, by Michael Gordon, involves long slides on all of the instruments resolving into major chords. The composer heightens the effect tremendously by pushing the fiddles through distortion so that all of the odd harmonics clash really nastily until the resolutions. "Originally, *[Gordon]* called for an Ibanez *Tube Screamer*," Fraser says, "but after we toured it for about a year, I programmed the Boss to do the same thing. It's hard to interface a stomp box with a Midas console, and now I also get more gain before it feeds back."

The second box in the processing rack is a Yamaha *SPX-990*. "Mark and I use it differently," says Fraser. "Mark uses it as a general-purpose reverb, but I use it to emulate the hall we're in, which means reprogramming it every day. The whole idea of the P.A. is not to make it louder, but to move the critical distance so that more people are in the direct field. But I don't want the P.A. to sound different from the hall, so I program the *SPX-990* starting with the "Echo Room" program, and I match the parameters to the room using an impulse generator to measure it. That's sort of the opposite of the way you're supposed to do it, but it ends up working. When everything coming out of the speakers sounds like the hall's acoustics, it blends with the acoustic sound better, and it draws less attention to the fact that you're listening to a P.A. system." In addition to simulating hall reverb, Fraser uses the *SPX-990* for some amplified effects, such as "super-heavy" flanging and a 20 second reverb.

> *"When everything coming out of the speakers sounds like the hall's acoustics, it draws less attention to the fact that you're listening to a P.A. system."*

Finally, there's a TC Electronic *FireworX* box, which Fraser uses when he needs to stack three or more high-quality effects in series, like a reverb, delay, and phase shifter.

Kronos plays a number of pieces that have prerecorded tracks, and for that reason—and not much else because, as classically trained musicians, they are most attuned to hearing the natural sounds of their instruments—they have always needed stage monitoring. "Until about three years ago, we had two wedges," says Fraser. "But it was always unwieldy, and it often crashed the front-of-house sound. When the new cellist *[Jennifer Culp, who replaced Joan Jeanrenaud, the group's only personnel change in the past 25 years]* joined, the balance changed, and we went to three wedges with active individual monitoring. But then the level started rising. So one day, I pulled the Furman headphone monitoring system out of my studio and plugged it in for them. I explained how they each get their own little mixer with control over themselves and everyone else and the playback tracks. Since then, I've never heard a word about changing monitors. Soundcheck now takes about a half-hour less, and the stage sound got cleaned up immediately.

"All of them use just one ear, and all the 'phones have to be on-ear: They don't want to have anything blocking them acoustically. I told them to go out to the store and buy whatever they wanted, and I'll make it work. The violinists use Audio-Technica ear clip-on types, which swivel out so you can move them off. The violist uses a Sony *Walkman* earphone; it was a pair, but I just cut one off. The cellist uses an over-the-head *Walkman* single headphone."

Fraser's unconventional approaches and attention to detail can even be seen when he tunes a system before a concert using a MiniDisc player for source material. "I have a recording of a male vocalist that I did in my studio that I use to EQ the room," he says. "I can't use *Aja* because, well, I wasn't there.

"I check channel identity and leakage with that old 'Left, Right' file that came with the original *Sound Designer* software. We need to make sure there's isolation when the group is playing with a click track, since we don't want the audience to hear it. I also have signals with reversed polarity to check phase—I've come across more than one system that was wired backward. Then ten minutes of pink noise, during which I walk the room, move speakers around, and balance the center cluster with the stacks, then clicks, 2.2 seconds apart, to program the reverb."

When I met Fraser that morning at breakfast (and he told me he was an avid *Mix* reader), all I could think of to say was to tell him what a great gig he had. He hardly disagreed. "I get to hear incredible music played fantastically every night," he admits. "There are moments of illumination when I'm standing close to the ensemble. There is a vibrancy and detail and juiciness to that sound, which is just overwhelmingly wonderful. That's what I want the sound system to do. In smaller rooms, you're really aware of the presence of the instruments and the way they move air, and that's what I'm trying to do in a 2,000-seat concert hall. When it works, it's great."

And he has one more treat: Later this year, Kronos, who have recorded with the likes of Leslie Anne Jones, Joe Chiccarelli, and Craig Silvey, will release their first album project that Fraser engineered (and co-produced). It's a collection of Indian "Bollywood" film-score music and features the quartet playing instruments they've never played on record before, such as electric sitar, accordion, and autoharp. A lot of it was done at The Plant in Sausalito, but true to form, Fraser didn't use a conventional workstation or tape recorder. "We did it all in *Digital Performer*," he says. "I ran it on an 800-MHz *G4* with up to 120 tracks, dozens of plug-ins, and tons of automation. As soon as it's finished, I'm going to send a copy of it to Mark of the Unicorn. I want to let them know what can be done with their program when you don't know what you can't really do."

Paul D. Lehrman amplified his bassoon in 1969 and immediately blew out his best friend's guitar amp.

Afterword

After some seven years with the group, cellist Jennifer Culp left in 2005 and was replaced by Jeffrey Zeigler, so for the first time in its history, Kronos is an all-male quartet. Reports from the critics say they sound just as good.

Chapter 48

Do You Hear What I Hear?

Learning to Listen in a Mediated World

Preface

My March 2004 column on why the whole world is so loud got me thinking about how we perceive sound and music and what we're gaining, or losing, in terms of that perception as more of what we hear is filtered through or produced by electronic means.

June 2005

There's a priceless moment on the Firesign Theatre's third album when an authority figure (a prosecutor who is somehow also an auctioneer) bellows, "What do I hear?" and a stoned voice from the back of the room responds, "That's metaphysically absurd, man. How can I know what you hear?"

This brings to mind two questions. First of all, inasmuch as we're professionals who depend on our hearing to produce sounds that will appeal to other people's ears, how do we know what our audience is actually hearing? And second, for that matter, how do we know what *we're* hearing? These two questions are becoming even more prevalent today, as most music listeners are "enjoying" sounds on low-fi playback systems or headphones—far from the quality of studio monitors.

When it comes to our audience, you might as well ask, "What do you mean by 'green'?" Physicists can agree on a range of wavelengths for "green," while everyone else can point to different objects and get a general consensus from those around them that these objects are or are not the color in question. But no one can possibly put themselves into someone else's mind to see exactly how they experience "green." As conscious beings, our perceptions are ours alone. Lily Tomlin's character Trudy the Bag Lady, in *The Search for Signs of Intelligent Life in the Universe*, put it perfectly when she said, "Reality is nothing but a collective hunch."

Similarly with sound, we can measure its volume, look at its spectrum, see how it changes over time, and analyze the impulse response of the space in which it's produced. But there's that subjective response to the sound that's within our heads that can't be measured—at least not without a sensor on every brain cell and synapse involved.

No amount of visual or data analysis will allow us to decide that a sound is "right" without hearing it.

Because we're in the business of shaping the reality of sounds, it's fairly important that our "hunches" be correct. And it's our ears that we trust. No amount of visual or data analysis will allow us to decide that a sound is "right" without hearing it.

How do we make that decision? A crucial part of the act of hearing is making comparisons between what our ears are telling us at the moment and the models that live in our memory of what we've heard before. From the moment our auditory faculties first kick in, those memories are established, and baselines are formed. The first sounds all humans hear are their mothers, and then they hear other family members, then domestic sounds, and gradually they take in the larger world outside. I imagine it's a safe bet to say that for most of us in this business, among those earliest aural experiences were the sounds of singing and musical instruments. Not only did these sounds intrigue and inspire us, but they also provided us with the context in which we would listen and judge the sounds we would work with in our professional lives.

So we know what things are supposed to sound like. As professionals, we learn something else: What we're hearing through the studio monitors isn't the same as what we hear when there's a direct acoustic path from the sound source to our ears. Ideally, speakers would be totally flat with no distortion or phase error and with perfect dispersion, but even the best monitors are still far from being totally "transparent." In addition, every indoor space that's not an anechoic chamber has its peculiar colorations, which are different from any other space. We need to be able to compensate for these distortions, consciously or unconsciously, and block out the sound of the speakers and the room as we listen. Our experience and training as professionals teach us how to eliminate the medium and concentrate on the source.

But this weird thing has happened in the past hundred or so years, and the trend is accelerating: The proportion of musical sounds that people are exposed to throughout their lives that are produced by "organic" means has been decreasing and is quickly approaching zero. This means that the baselines that we and our audiences need to determine what sounds "real" and what doesn't are disappearing.

Before the end of the 19th century, the only music anyone heard was performed live. The sound that reached an audience member's ears was that of the instruments and the singers, with nothing mediating between the mechanism of production—whether it was a stick hitting a dried goatskin, the plucking of a taut piece of feline intestine, or the vibrations of a set of vocal cords—and the mechanism of perception.

But with the invention of the radio and the phonograph, all of that changed. People could now listen to music 24 hours a day every day if they wanted and be nowhere near actual musicians. Compared to real instruments, wax cylinders and crystal sets sounded dreadful, but the convenience of hearing a huge variety of music at any time without leaving home more than made up for the loss in quality for most people.

The "hi-fi" boom that started in the 1950s improved things, as listeners began to appreciate better sound reproduction and the price of decent-sounding equipment fell to where even college students—who soon became the music industry's most important market—could afford it. Today's high-end and even medium-priced home audio equipment sounds better than ever.

But as the media for music delivery have blossomed—from wax cylinders to XM Radio—fewer people experience hearing acoustic music. Symphony orchestras are cutting back seasons or going out of business altogether all over America, and school music programs, which traditionally have given students the precious opportunity to hear what real instruments sound like from both a player's and a listener's perspective, are in the toilet. While there are certainly parts of the "live" music scene that are still healthy, they depend on sound systems that, as they get bigger and more complex so as to project to the farthest reaches of a large venue, serve to isolate the audiences even more from what's happening onstage acoustically.

And as electronic sources of music have become more prolific, another thing has happened: Because it is now so easy to have music available, people actually *listen* to it less, and it has become more of an environmental element like aural wallpaper. Because audiences aren't focusing so much on the music, the quality of the systems that many listen to has been allowed to slip backward. Personal stereos have been a major factor in this: From the Sony *Walkman* to the *iPod*, people are listening to crummy sound reproduction at top volume, screening out any kind of sonic reality and replacing it with a lo-fi sound. People can now have their own private soundtrack, as if they were perpetually walking alone through a theme park, without any other aural distractions, with a 15-dB dynamic range and nothing below 100 Hz.

I remember this hitting me like a ton of bricks one day in the summer of 1979. I had been out of the country for several months *[bungling in the jungle, as I wrote in Chapter 40]*, and soon after I returned to the U.S., I was walking in New York City's Central Park and came upon an amazing picture: On a patch of blacktop were several dozen gyrating disco-dancing roller skaters, but the only sound I could hear was that of the skate wheels on the pavement. Each of the dancers was sporting a pair of headphones with little antennae coming out of them. Inside each of the headphones, I soon realized, was an FM radio, and they were all dancing to music that I couldn't hear. But it became obvious—after I watched them for a few minutes—that they weren't all dancing to the same music; each was tuned to a different station.

The "multimedia" speaker systems that people now plug into their computers so they can listen to MP3 streams have taken us farther down the same road. Companies that decades ago revolutionized speaker designs—such as Advent, KLH, and Altec Lansing—have had their brands swallowed up by multinational electronics foundries that slap those once-revered names on tinny little underpowered speakers connected to "subwoofers" that produce a huge hump at 120 Hz so that consumers think they're getting something for their money.

More recently, the tools of personal audio wallpaper have entered the production chain. Again, one incident sticks out in my mind that showed me clearly where this was going. A couple of years ago, I went into a hip coffeehouse—where the blaring post-punk music makes it impossible to hold a normal conversation—and sat down at a table near a young man wearing earbuds and peering intently into a *PowerBook*. I glanced over, and to my amazement, I realized he was working on something in *Digital Performer*.

How many composers live in apartment buildings where they work late into the night and, for fear of disturbing their neighbors, never turn on their monitors but only mix on head-phones? How many of your colleagues, or even you, boast of doing some of your best audio editing on a transcontinental plane flight?

A pessimist looking at this might conclude we were approaching a kind of "perfect storm" in which we lose complete control over what our audience hears. No one ever finds out what a real instrument sounds like; the systems that we use to reproduce and disseminate music are getting worse; and because most people don't even listen closely to music anymore, they don't care.

> *A pessimist looking at this might conclude we were approaching a kind of "perfect storm" in which we lose complete control over what our audience hears.*

In my own teaching, I've seen how the lack of proper aural context results in an inability to discriminate between good and bad, real and not-real sound. In one of my school's music labs, I use a 14-year-old synth that, although I really like it as a teaching tool, I'll be the first to admit has a factory program set that is a little dated. But one of my students recently said, "The sounds are so realistic, why would anyone need to use anything else?"

There are nine workstations in that lab, which means the students have to work on headphones. We use pretty decent closed-ear models, and the students generally don't have any complaints. That is until we play back their assignments on the room's powered speakers. "Why does it sound so incredibly different?" one will invariably ask. I take this as a splendid opportunity to teach them something about acoustics: how reflections and room modes affect bass response, the role of head effects in stereo imaging, and so on. They dutifully take it in, but then they say, "Yes, but why does it sound so incredibly different?" The idea of the music and the medium being separate from each other sometimes just doesn't sink in.

If you're looking for an answer or even a conclusion here, I haven't got one. But I do know that the next generation of audio engineers and mixers—if there's going to be one—will have a hard time if they don't have more exposure than the average young person to natural, unamplified, and unprocessed sound. If every sound we ever hear comes through a medium—and if most of them suck—then how are we ever going to agree on what we hear?

Which means that our ears and our judgment are still all we have. Try to take care of both of them. And keep listening and keep learning.

Paul D. Lehrman has only heard one MP3 he's liked, which was on a collection of Goon Shows.

Afterword

Many readers responded strongly to this piece, telling me I had put my finger on one of the most important, and unspoken, issues facing the music world today. Some considered it the most successful "think piece" I had ever done for *Insider Audio*. One reader, the notorious Fletcher, proprietor of the high-end pro audio shop Mercenary Audio (and a loyal *Mix* advertiser), liked it so much he asked me if he could put it on his company website.

Chapter 49

Student Dana Price plays the Laserharp

Bikes, Harps, and Yo-Yos
Teaching Engineers and Artists to Talk to Each Other

Preface

I always tell people that one of the best ways to learn a subject is to try to teach it. The course I describe in this column is a sterling example of this: Except for the MIDI part, when I began working on it, I hardly knew anything about designing electronic musical instruments. But when my school asked me to create this course, and I started to get into it, I found out how much there was to learn and how much fun it would be to learn it right alongside the students.

August 2005

One of the hottest fields in the academic research world is Computer/Human Interfacing (CHI), which has several other names, such as Tangible Interfaces, Human Factors, Design Psychology, and probably many more. A mixture of psychology, physiology, industrial engineering, and computer science, CHI tackles how humans interact with machines to make those interactions more efficient, more productive, less fatiguing, and from the humans' standpoint, richer. In other words, how to make tools that do something useful, are fun and rewarding to use, and can be used for a long time.

Because there are so many disparate disciplines in this field, schools don't have an easy time figuring out how to teach it. Getting the students from all these areas to meet on common ground is a problem. For example, in the school where I teach, a relatively small liberal arts-oriented college, there is a strong engineering program, but engineers and arts and humanities students rarely cross paths and almost never collaborate.

Regardless what he is studying, however, almost every student is into music. So a few years ago, the engineering faculty decided to face the challenge of how to get their students to work with non-engineers, and the answer was to create courses around music technology. But they weren't thinking about what most schools consider music technology, that is, computer composition and sound manipulation. (I already teach that.) In this program, the students would build musical instruments.

The first course they created was called Musical Instrument Engineering. It's strictly acoustic: Students build flutes, guitars, zithers, and bagpipes and do research that requires them to measure various environmental effects on things like trumpets and piano actions. But the course still draws students primarily from the Mechanical Engineering department. To enlarge the pool and make the course attractive to a wider variety of students, they decided to create a course called *Electronic Musical Instrument Design*.

"The first time you teach a course, it owns you. The second time, it's a draw. The third time, you own it."

Because I'm pretty much the only faculty member who knows a lot about electronic music (I told you it was a small school), they asked me to write the course curriculum and teach it. I've created a lot of college courses, but this one felt quite a bit beyond me at first. I'm not a mechanical engineer, most of my electronics knowledge is self-taught, and although I've played a lot of instruments, I've never built any. Nevertheless, I took heart in a friend (also a part-time professor) of mine's maxim: "The first time you teach a course, it owns you. The second time, it's a draw. The third time, you own it."

As I write, I've just finished teaching the course for the third time, and I think I've got a handle on it. I can say it's become one of the most rewarding enterprises I've undertaken in my teaching career despite—or because of—the fact that it's an insane amount of work. Better yet, the students concur. Many of them tell me they've never put so much time into a course, and they've never had so much fun.

The premise behind Electronic Musical Instrument Design (EMID) is straightforward: Students design and build working musical instruments that use electronics to produce and control the sound. The course is listed in both the Music and Mechanical Engineering departments' catalogs. But because the college doesn't have an Audio Technology program, the number of students who can handle every aspect of the course is somewhere between few and none. Think about it: You need to know how to make objects of wood, metal, or plastic that people can push, pull, swing, or bang on; how to put sensors on them to measure what you're doing; how to translate the sensor data into something a computer can understand; how to communicate it to a synthesizer of some kind; and how to set up the synthesizer to make meaningful sounds out of the data.

When students sign up for the class, I poll them on their backgrounds to make sure all of the different skill sets needed to undertake the projects are present. I ask them if they play an instrument, if they've ever worked with MIDI and synthesis, how they are at designing and building small electronic circuits, how their wood and metal shop skills are, and what they know about acoustics and object-oriented computer programming. If a student doesn't have some experience in at least two of these areas, he doesn't make the cut.

The result is we end up with a wide cross section of majors. Mechanical engineers form the largest group, although by no means the majority, and just about everyone plays an instrument or at least has some DJ chops. I've had several music majors; other students have been electrical engineers, chemical engineers, computer scientists, business or economics majors, art history majors, and even a few from the School of the Museum of Fine Arts in Boston, with whom we have a cross-registration agreement.

Midway through the semester, I divide the students into teams, arranged so that each group has all of the skills needed to complete the projects. Interestingly, electronic tinkering is the most poorly represented skill, perhaps because electrical engineering these days is taught largely using computer models, and hands-on circuit construction isn't as prevalent. Fortunately, my teaching assistant this semester—a graduate student in electrical engineering—had a lust for designing clever circuits using standard op amps and other components and threw himself into the task of supporting the other students.

Before we start building anything, the students get some technical and historical background. I go over the history of electronic musical instruments, from the Theremin to the latest experimental devices from places such as the Paris research center IRCAM, MIT, and Stanford. I introduce them to the concept of "gesture controllers" and have them do creative exercises in thinking about a wide range of body movements, what devices might be used to measure them, and what musical effect they might have.

I also bring in guest lecturers who are developers or virtuoso players of unusual electronic instruments. Among these have been Mark Goldstein, an expert on Don Buchla's *Marimba Lumina* and *Lightning* systems; Mario DeCiutiis, who makes the KAT percussion controllers and is the drummer for Radio City Music Hall's Christmas shows; Bruce Ronkin, one of the top Yamaha wind-controller players in the country; FutureMan, the very-far-out electronic drummer in Bela Fleck & The Flecktones; and Theresa Marrin Nakra, whose doctoral thesis at MIT involved wiring a jacket with position and muscle-tension sensors and getting Boston Pops conductor Keith Lockhart to wear it during a performance. *[You can read more about Nakra's work in Chapter 54.]*

I give the students a thorough grounding in MIDI; in *Max*, the object-oriented MIDI "construction set" developed by IRCAM and now distributed by Cycling '74; and in the subtractive synthesis and sampler modules in Propellerhead *Reason* software. For all of the projects, the audio chain is extremely simple: *Reason* feeds the audio outputs of our two desktop Macs, and these go to a pair of Edirol powered monitors. (If the students want to make their own samples, we have an M-Audio USB audio interface and BIAS *Peak*.) Data comes into the computer using a set of voltage-to-MIDI and switch-to-MIDI converters made by the German analog synth company Doepfer, which we've customized to give us 16 controller channels and 64 binary note-on controls. The incoming MIDI commands go into *Max*, which interprets and processes them in a variety of ways, performing logical operations, filtering and transforming the data, and triggering sequences. The processed data then goes on to one or more *Reason* modules.

The front end—what goes *into* the Doepfer devices—is the real challenge for the students. As long as something closes a contact, produces a DC voltage, or changes its electrical resistance, they can use it to input data into the system. We've used buttons of all shapes and sizes, rotary and slide potentiometers, force-sensing resistors, strain gauges, tiny bits of piezoelectric film, infrared and ultrasonic transceivers, contact microphones, hacked wah-wah pedals, photocells, accelerometers, flex sensors, reed switches, and thimbles rubbing against a washboard.

An ethnomusicologist, a violinist, and a mechanical engineer created a musical yo-yo.

What do they come up with? One group—an ethnomusicologist, a violinist, and a mechanical engineer—created a musical yo-yo: A $2 yo-yo was equipped with four tiny rare-earth magnets on each face. A glove was equipped with magnetic reed switches on each finger that, when they closed, triggered different samples. When the yo-yo left the hand, *Max* would start a sequence, and an ultrasonic sensor would measure the yo-yo's distance, closing down a low-pass filter on the sound as the yo-yo approached the floor and opening it back up again on the return. Meanwhile, flex sensors attached to the wrist and forearm controlled other filter and vibrato parameters as the player moved his arm.

Another group—a violinist, a different mechanical engineer, and an optics engineer—created a laser harp. Starting with a small wooden harp, the group replaced the 12 strings with the same number of lasers and photocells so that putting one's hands where a string used to be interrupted a beam, which sent a note-on to *Reason*. Buttons on the front of the harp selected the scale: diatonic, chromatic, or blues. More buttons along the frame next to the strings controlled vibrato depth and note durations. Foot switches transposed the instrument up or down by an octave, and a foot pedal added an FM component to the sound, making it more bright and metallic.

Then there was the "über-Theremin" built by a guitar-playing math major, an engineering science major, and an economics major. Three infrared sensors, each with a 15-degree cone of sensitivity and each using a unique pattern of amplitude modulation so that they wouldn't interfere with each other, were mounted on a piece of cardboard. The plan was to have the sensors somewhat overlap and read values created by the player's hand position and translate them into *Reason* parameters. But the students realized that none of them had the math skills to handle the 3-D conic projections to make this work. So they separated the sensors and assigned each one to a different parameter: One controlled pitch, the second a low-pass filter, and the third duration. "The only problem with this instrument," one of the members explained, "is that you need three hands to play it."

"The only problem with this instrument is that you need three hands to play it."

Two engineering students came up with the Schwinnophone: An ancient 10-speed bike was fitted with flex sensors on the front and rear brakes, the pedal crank, and the derailleur, and three of the magnets from the yo-yo project were attached to the rear wheel. A reed switch was mounted on the frame so that each time a magnet came near the switch, a note-on was sent to *Max*. The *Max* patch stepped through a five-channel sequence playing "Born to Be Wild" using *Reason* sampler and drum modules, with the speed of the incoming notes determining the tempo. When the rider sat down and started to crank and the rear wheel began spinning, the sequence started. As he switched gears and changed speeds, the tempo and note velocities of the sequence changed accordingly. The left-hand brake lever made a convincing whammy bar for the lead guitar. When the bike stopped, the *Max* patch switched to another sequence, which played a convincing rock 'n' roll ending.

One of the most enjoyable parts of teaching the class was watching them evaluate and modify their plans while they built the projects. Besides the technical issues—perhaps a flex sensor didn't respond if it was mounted in a certain way or the sensitivity of the ultrasonic detector wasn't as linear as the specs said—there were musical considerations at work. They constantly asked themselves, "How playable is this? What can we do to make it more responsive, more dramatic, more fun?" Perhaps the only thing missing from the course was having the students learn how to really *play* the instruments they had made. As they were solving technical problems right up until final presentations, none of them had the time to practice and master their creations.

So as much as we all got out of this class, we could see that building new interfaces is only half the battle—making them into truly expressive musical instruments is a whole 'nother beast. Next month, I'll take you to a remarkable conference in a beautiful city where a couple of hundred people were engaged in battling that beast—and many came out victorious.

Paul Lehrman can be found on a beach on Cape Cod with a pennywhistle and a ukulele— at least until the next semester starts. Details on the EMID class are at www.tufts.edu/ programs/mma/emid.

Chapter 50

The Overtone Violin

More Than Mice

Tomorrow's Musical Instruments at the NIME Conference

Preface

NIME '05 was one of the two most interesting conferences I've ever attended, and as it happened, it took place in the same city as the other one: Vancouver. This chapter is an expanded version of the report on the conference that I wrote for *Mix*. Parts of it also appeared in the English magazine *Sound On Sound*, but the bulk of it is appearing in print here for the first time.

September 2005

The class I wrote about last month, in which students from various disciplines got together and designed new electronic musical instruments, had some pretty unusual aspects, but I don't want you to get the impression that it was unique. Far from it.

There are dozens of courses and development projects dealing with the same subject matter happening at universities and research centers all over the world. So many, in fact, that they have their own convention: New Interfaces for Musical Expression, or NIME, which met for the fifth time this past May in the beautiful city of Vancouver, British Columbia. And when I submitted a paper that described my own undergraduate course, they were kind enough to accept it. So I had no excuse but to go.

Vancouver is stunningly set between the island-filled Strait of Georgia and Canada's Coastal Mountain range. Although real estate values are among the highest in the country, thanks in large part to an influx of people and capital from Hong Kong in the years preceding the Chinese takeover of that city, Vancouver is still a very reasonably priced place for Americans, as the film industry well knows. I had been there only once before—22 years ago—and I've always wanted to go back.

I was there for an event called *Digicon '83*, which billed itself as the "First International Conference on the Digital Arts." You probably never heard of it, but for almost everyone I encountered there, it was a life-changing experience: dozens of digital luminaries and soon-to-be luminaries in one place, talking about music, video, graphic arts, digital communications, and what would eventually become known as *multimedia*. I met Bob Moog, Herbie Hancock, Todd Rundgren, and Andy Moorer there and saw for the first time toys and tools the likes of which would soon take their place at the center of the production world, such as Lucasfilm's *EditDroid* and *SoundDroid*, which evolved into Avid's *Media Composer* and Sonic Solutions' *Sonic System*, which in turn begat the non-linear digital tools we all use today; some of the very first CGI systems used by Hollywood; a sampling instrument called the *Fairlight CMI;* and something called MIDI. *[You can read a report on Digicon that I wrote for* Creative Computing *magazine on my personal website, paul-lehrman.com.]*

Among the speakers at Digicon '83 was a prescient Canadian composer and computer scientist named Bill Buxton, who said, "It's time to rethink the interface between electronic instruments and the user. We have to get away from the 'overblown electronic organ' syndrome. If we want to expand the range of musical expression, why can't we use new gestures—blowing, sucking, squeezing, kicking, caressing—instead of emulating the past?" He spoke, for the first time that I can recall, of devices he called "gesture controllers."

Flash forward to 2005, and gesture controllers are what NIME is all about. And Buxton, who had left the music world to work on projects such as Alias/Wavefront (which garnered him a Scientific and Engineering Academy Award), is back, delivering one of the keynote speeches and still preaching the same gospel.

At Digicon, Andy Moorer opened his presentation about the *SoundDroid* with a slide of a Moviola and the words, "This is the enemy." He was talking about how hard it was for film sound editors to keep up with the changes that the picture editors constantly make during the production of a film. I don't know if Buxton remembered Moorer's speech, but he started his presentation exactly the same way—only the picture was of a Revox reel-to-reel tape deck. In the days when electronic music was brand new, he explained, concert performances would too often comprise someone walking onto a stage, pushing a button on a tape deck, and walking off. But those days aren't entirely over: People still do the same thing with laptops and expect the audience to respond to the music.

"If you're sitting at a computer and typing, why should I care?"

"If you're sitting at a computer and typing, why should I care?" he asked. Audiences at a live performance want to see someone doing something interesting to create the music, he said. "The goal of a performance system should be to make your audience understand the correlation of gesture and sound." It was a well-applauded point, and many of the systems in evidence at NIME showed strong agreement with that idea.

Another keynote speaker was Don Buchla, who has been actively developing new electronic instruments for four decades, and whose original analog synthesis systems are still cherished by many composers. He presented a comprehensive history of electronic performance instruments, starting with the Musical Telegraph designed in 1876 by Elisha Gray, who he said might have been the real inventor of the telephone, "but Alexander Graham Bell beat him to the patent office." Among the less-familiar devices he showed was the SalMar Construction, built in the late 1960s by composer Salvatore Martirano, which looked like a giant switchboard with almost 300 switches, so sensitive they could be operated by brushes, and surrounded by 24 ear-level speakers.

"The purpose of a controller is to transfer a performer's intent into sound," he said. "What we as designers are concerned with is linkage. Acoustic instruments have no linkage, but keyboards, even acoustic ones, do. MIDI allowed us to get a gesture controller from one manufacturer and link it with a sound vocabulary from another."

Buchla discussed a number of his own fascinating instrument designs, some of which made it to market and some of which didn't. There was *Lightning*, a pair of batons with infrared sensors that could be mapped to a wide variety of musical gestures; *Thunder*, a touch-surface that measured independent finger-position and pressure; *Wind*, a disc that looked something like an electric turtle, with a breath sensor that responded to both positive and negative (sucking) pressure, a tongue sensor, eight holes for fingers, and sensors for rotational and absolute position, which sadly didn't make it past the prototype stage; and *Rain*, based on an African rainstick, which Buchla said was designed to make "sonic clouds and densities, faster than MIDI," but which he never finished. He also described an EEG-to-control voltage converter that he designed some years ago, which responded to alpha waves. "I did a performance in Copenhagen," he recalled, "but while I was up on stage, I found I couldn't generate any alpha waves, so I didn't make a sound for 15 minutes. It was the longest silence I've ever heard."

Oddly enough, only one of Buchla's instruments was actually at the conference: a *Marimba Lumina*, which was given a fine demonstration by Joel Davel. It turns out, as Davel told me later, that all the gear Buchla was planning to bring up from his home in San Francisco had been confiscated at the Canadian border. His car full of musical instruments and three passengers aroused the suspicions of a Customs officer. "The Customs guy didn't believe we were coming to a conference," Davel said. "He figured we must be a band, and we were going to play some gigs, and we didn't have a work permit for that. So to make sure we didn't play in a bar somewhere, he held onto all our stuff." The *Marimba Lumina* Davel played was hastily supplied by the Audities Foundation, in Calgary, Alberta—on the right side of the border.

Over three intense days, the 180 attendees at the conference, which was held on the campus of the University of British Columbia, situated on a peninsula sticking out into the bay, were introduced to all manner of new ways to make music and to enhance expressiveness and creativity. I had never before been to a conference where I sat through every one of the presentations—but at NIME, you didn't want to miss anything. There were three dozen papers and reports, along with 18 informal "poster" presentations, five large interactive sound installations, and four demo rooms showing a wealth of gadgetry and software. There were also jam sessions, which in terms of the weirdness of the musical gadgetry bore more than a passing resemblance to the cafe scene in *Star Wars: Episode IV*, and each night there was a concert in the University's recital hall.

The presentations were primarily about new one-of-a-kind instruments and performance systems, as well as new ways of thinking about performance. Some of the instruments were variations on conventional instruments. For example, Dan Overholt of the University of California Santa Barbara showed his "Overtone Violin," a six-string solid-body violin with optical pickups, several assignable knobs on the body, and a keypad, two sliders, and a joystick underneath the scroll where the tuning pegs usually go. In addition, a miniature video camera was mounted at the top of the neck, and an ultrasonic sensor kept track of the instrument's position in space. It's played with a normal violin bow, but the player wears a glove containing ultrasonic and acceleration sensors, which allow him to make sounds without ever touching the strings. The whole thing was connected to a wireless USB system, so the performer didn't have to worry about tripping over cables.

Then there was the "Self-Contained Unified Bass Augmenter," or "SCUBA," built by researchers at Stanford University. It started with a tuba, adding buttons and pressure sensors to the valves. The sound of the instrument was picked up by a microphone inside the bell and sent through various signal processors like filters, distortion, and vibrato, all user-configurable and -controllable. The processed sound was then piped through four bell-mounted speakers and a sub-woofer under the player's chair.

Perry Cook, of Princeton University, who started his career as a singer and then got his doctorate in Electrical Engineering, was in one of the demo rooms showing his outrageous controllers for synthesizing the human voice, many of which also started as conventional instruments. There were two that he called "Squeezevoxen": "Lisa," based on an accordion, and "Maggie," based on a concertina. ("Bart" and "Santa's Little Helper" were the names of earlier models, showing how much *The Simpsons* has infiltrated high-tech culture.) Lisa's piano-style keyboard had a pressure sensor next to it to control pitch and overtones, and the 64 buttons on the opposite side triggered phonemes, words, and phrases. Four bend sensors controlled formant filters, and a small trackpad simulated vowels by changing filter resonance. The bellows, of course, were the equivalent of the lungs and control volume, and a vent button could be used to stop the vocalization and generate breath noises. Lisa we quite a bit simpler, but also impressive, and it had internal speakers, which helped contribute to the illusion that the instrument was really singing.

Another keyboard-based instrument of Cook's was the attractively named "VOMID," or Voice-Oriented Melodica Interface Device, in which a modified Korg *MicroKontrol* keyboard, with 37 notes, 16 buttons, 16 potentiometers, a joystick, a ribbon controller, an extra touchpad, and an accelerometer, was attached to the two-way breath sensor of an old-fashioned Melodica.

A hotbed of development for new musical toys has been the Media Lab at Massachusetts Institute of Technology. One of the more well-known of these is the Beatbug, a hand-held gadget with piezo sensors that respond to tapping. A player can record a rhythmic pattern, watch it be displayed on internal LEDs, and then change it while it plays using two bendable "ears." An internal speaker makes the player feel he is actually playing an instrument. But Beatbugs work best in packs, as Israeli-born Gil Weinberg, who is a graduate of the MIT program and now director of a new music technology program at Georgia Tech, showed in a new system called "iltur." In the system, multiple Beatbugs were connected to a computer through *Max/MSP* software and produced a variety of sounds from *Reason* modules. The *Max* program allowed a high degree of interaction and transformation of the input patterns, which encouraged the players to bounce musical ideas off each other, and it was designed to let both novices and experienced musicians improvise together with equal comfort levels.

If you've ever wanted a set of MIDI wind chimes, you would have been interested in the "Swayaway" from a group at New York University. Ambient sound from the room was continuously picked up with a microphone, analyzed and processed by *Max/MSP* Max/MSP, and converted to MIDI, which was sent to a module containing a number of preprogrammed sounds. Seventeen vertical plastic stalks, each with a wooden weight at the top, were attached to a base containing flex sensors. The action of the sensors was translated into MIDI controllers, which affected the sound and also caused green LEDs in the base to brighten in proportion to the amount of bend of each rod. Played by waving one's hands among the stalks, it was a soothing and involving experience.

John Bowers and Phil Archer, of the University of East Anglia in the UK, presented their concept of "Not Hyper, Not Meta, Not Cyber but Infra-Instruments": reductionist musical devices that could fit into one of several dubious categories. For example, using the philosophy "Take an Instrument and Make It Less," they showed how one could use a smashed violin to make music: scrape the strings lengthwise or make them "thunk" and use the wooden shards as scrapers or beaters. Under the "Take Something Non-Instrumental and Find the Instrument Within" banner, they showed the "Victorian Synthesizer," which used a battery, a bare wire, and a small speaker, set up so that scraping the wire along a surface caused the cone of the speaker to fluctuate in step with the contour of the surface. To enhance the effect, a number of metal washers were put inside the speaker to rattle.

Other categories they described included "Take Materials Partway to Instrumenthood" and "Build an Instrument but Include Obvious Mistakes." Other infra-projects they showed included the Strandline guitar, comprising strings, a pickup, a whammy bar, and a bunch of odd objects found on a beach at low tide; and the Percussive Printer, in which ball point pens were mounted on motors removed from an inkjet printer so that they acted like small drumsticks, and the motors were sent text information as if they were still inside the printer, but instead they waved the pens around and produced various bangs, rattles, and scratches.

Some of the presentations used interfaces borrowed from completely different fields to produce musical sounds. Golan Levin, also recently of MIT and now at Carnegie Mellon University in Pittsburgh, Pennsylvania, described in his keynote speech his famous "Dialtones: A Telesymphony," which had its first performance in 2001 at the Ars Electronica Festival in Linz, Austria. In this project, some 200 members of the audience had their cell phones programmed with specific ringtones and were told where in the hall to sit. A computer performed the piece by dialing the phones' numbers in a prepro-grammed order. In addition, whenever a phone rang, a spotlight in the ceiling illuminated its seat location. "There's an accuracy of plus-or-minus about a half second," Levin noted.

Describing himself as "an artist whose medium is musical instruments," while admitting he "can't read or write a note of music," Levin told the audience, "Music engages you in a creative activity that tells you something about yourself, and is 'sticky'—you want to stay with it. So the best musical instrument is one that is easy to learn and takes a lifetime to master." He also made the point, which had attendees nodding in agreement, that "the com-puter mouse is about the narrowest straw you can suck all human expression through."

He next showed his "Manual Input Sessions" project. Using an old-fashioned overhead projector and a video projector, the player of this system made hand shadows on a screen, while a video camera analyzed the image. When the fingers defined a closed area, a bright rock-like object filling the area was projected, and when the fingers opened, the rock "dropped" to the bottom of the screen. As it hit, it created a musical sound, whose pitch and timbre were proportional to the size and the speed of the falling rock. It was fascinat-ing to watch, and no doubt easy to learn.

Another borrowing, after a fashion, from the world of visual art was the "Scrubber" from a team at the MIT-created Media Lab Europe in Dublin. Described as "a general controller for friction-induced sound," the device was based around an ordinary white-board eraser fitted with two tiny microphones and a force-sensing resistor. The system analyzed the sound created by the eraser as it rubbed against a surface and applied it to a wavetable or sample, playing it in granular fashion. The sound controlled the sample's speed, volume, or other parameters, and the system could even detect whether the eraser was going back-wards or forwards. One convincing demo used a garage door closing: It was cool to see its speed and direction being controlled in real time. Sadly, the Dublin Media Lab closed down the day after the authors submitted this paper, a victim of funding problems.

Some of the systems shown didn't require the "player" to use any hardware at all. A group from ATR Intelligent Robotics in Kyoto, Japan, showed a system for creating music by changing one's facial expressions. A camera image of the face was divided into seven zones, and a computer continuously tracked changes in the image, so that any change in any of the zones resulted in a particular MIDI note being triggered. "The displacement in a region," said the presenter, "controls the flow of a particular synth parameter."

Niels Böttcher and his team from Aalborg University in Copenhagen described a work in progress in which they attempted to use interactive music to connect strangers at a train station. "People waiting for trains in Denmark usually don't communicate with each other," said Böttcher, "and this has the potential to make them aware of the people across the tracks." Two video motion-tracking systems were focused on a 2- by 3-meter rectangular area on each platform, and movements detected in those areas were fed to a computer that produces the sound, which was then piped through speakers on both platforms. But Böttcher and his group found that the choice of what kind of sounds and controller mappings would engage people the best and make them aware of each other wasn't an obvious one. They experimented with having movement on the two platforms affect a single sound but in different ways, as well as with having them produce sounds independently and also with linking the two inputs so that movement in one platform by itself did nothing until there was also movement in the other. "You don't want to require people to make weird gestures to get interesting sounds," Böttcher said, "but at the same time you don't want to make the system so simple that they would get bored and just walk away."

Another work in progress was the HandySinger from ATR Labs and Nagoya University in Japan, which used a hand puppet to control the tone, and more importantly, the emotional content of a sampled singing voice. A woman was recorded singing a Japanese nursery rhyme using four different types of voice character, which the researchers called "normal," "dark," "whisper," and "wet." They wrote software that could morph in real time from one recording to another. Then they constructed a hand puppet that had flex sensors on both sides of the thumb, forefinger, and middle finger, plus one on the back of the wrist, and two touch sensors on the tips of the thumb and middle finger that would sense when the puppet clapped his hands. By mapping different combinations of sensor readings to different voice qualities, they were able to create a fairly convincing correspondence between the body language of the puppet and the emotional tone of the voice.

And then there was "Bangarama: Creating Music with Headbanging," from Aachen University in Germany. This extremely low-budget project used a more-or-less guitar-shaped controller made out of thin plywood. Along the neck were 26 small rectangles of aluminum arranged in pairs, which were used to select from a group of prerecorded samples, most of them guitar power chords. The player wrapped aluminum foil around his fingers so that moving his fingers along the neck closed one of the circuits. The headbanging part consisted of a 50-pfennig coin mounted on a metal seesaw-like contraption, which was attached to a Velcro strip on top of a baseball cap. When the player swung his head forward, the metal piece under the coin would make contact with another metal piece in front of it, closing a circuit, triggering the sample. When the head went back up, the note ended. One problem the designers had was that the mechanism would sometimes bounce on the downswing, creating false triggers, so they put in a timer which ignored new notes that were less than 250ms later than previous notes. "We predicted that typical users would not headbang faster than 240 beats per minute," they said—and who could argue with that?

As perhaps a counterpoint to the human-played instruments, several presenters showed instruments that played automatically. One was a group from New York City called the *League of Electronic Musical Urban Robots*, or "LEMUR." Director Eric Singer showed how they made musical robots equipped with small motors, cams, and various striking and spinning devices that vibrated, banged, scraped, plucked, slid, and spun, all under MIDI control. Most of the robots were small, but the centerpiece of the family was the ForestBot, which consisted of 25 ten-foot vertical stalks with egg-shaped rattles at the end, which were slowly spun in eccentric orbits by motors in their bases. The rattles swayed and knocked into each other, while the rods bounced and hummed. Singer had a couple of the smaller robots present, but more impressive was a kinetic video of the whole family playing together at an installation built earlier this year at a college in Southern California.

And last, but not least, thanks to Roger Dannenberg of Carnegie Mellon University, we were presented with "McBlare," a MIDI-controlled bagpipe. This was certainly a fun project for Dannenberg, who has been involved in the more serious side of computer music for over 20 years. "The founder of the university, Andrew Carnegie, was born in Scotland," he explained, "and the school has its own Tartan." In fact, *The Tartan* is the name of the school newspaper. So using the formidable resources of the university's School of Computer Science and Robotics Institute to make a robotic bagpipe player seemed eminently logical.

The result looked like a hospital recorder hooked up to a soprano saxophone with solenoids.

McBlare started with a genuine set of Highland bagpipes. The two mechanical tasks the team faced were building an air compressor that would precisely match the breathing and arm pressure of a human piper, and another was outfitting the "chanter" pipe with electrically controlled mechanical keys. The result looked like a hospital respirator hooked up to a soprano saxophone with solenoids. The chanter's keys had to respond at least as fast as a player's fingers, and in fact Dannenberg's team were able to make it perform even better than that: It could execute about 25 notes per second. Just as crucial a task was analyzing how a professional piper played the thing, using slurs, grace notes, and other idiomatic gestures—and the group did a great job with this, too. Their robot, under the control of an old Yamaha *QY10* portable sequencer, could not only do a convincing imitation of a real piper, but could also go several steps further into frenetic, complex riffs no human could ever—or would ever want to—play.

Dannenberg said that McBlare's first public performance was at the graduation exercises of the School of Computer Science. At the end of his demonstration, some wag in the audience (okay, it was me) asked, "Why is that bagpipers are always walking?" and Dannenberg immediately responded with the correct answer: "To get away from the sound." (After his talk, Dannenberg told me the great joke about the octopus and the bagpipe, which appears elsewhere in this book.)

NIME is not a trade show, so there were few commercial products on display, but there was one that drew a lot of attention: *Lemur* (no relation to the robotics group), a marvelously versatile combination touch surface and LCD screen made by a French company called JazzMutant. Users could set up buttons, faders, knobs, and moving, colored balls on the 12-inch surface, all of which responded to multiple fingers simultaneously. It communicated with a host computer over Ethernet and was compatible with any software that conformed to the Open Sound Control protocol. (MIDI users could use *Max* to translate between the two protocols.) *Lemur* comes with its own graphic editing software, which is especially important since it has no non-volatile memory. It looks like it could be a brilliant addition to any studio, although the price of $2,500 will no doubt limit its market a bit. A number of speakers bemoaned how difficult it was for new electronic instruments to survive in the marketplace, despite the amount of ingenuity, inspiration, and just plain hard work going on in the "alternative controllers" world that was evident at NIME, and many attendees nodded in agreement. But one presenter gave a potentially bright picture for designers of these devices, thanks to the growth of other forms of electronic entertainment.

Tina "Bean" Blaine, co-chair of the festival, is a percussionist, vocalist, inventor, "musical interactivist" (at Interval Research, the exciting but short-lived Silicon Valley company founded by Microsoft billionaire Paul Allen), and student of African drumming, who is now on the faculty of the Entertainment Technology program at Carnegie-Mellon University. Her presentation was called "The Convergence of Alternate Controllers and Musical Interfaces in Interactive Entertainment," which translates to "Everything you're doing, the game industry can use."

There are a number of categories of games that have interactive musical components, she explained, and they are growing all the time. The most common are beat-matching games, starting with the mid-'90s arcade game *BeatMania*, and evolving into Konami's *Dance Dance Revolution* and Namco's *Donkey Konga*. But there are also games that require one of a variety of specific actions by the player in response to musical cues, like Sega's *Samba de Amigo* and Hasbro's *ZingIt*, and those in which the player pretends to play a musical instrument like Sony's *Guitar Freaks* and Koei's *Gitaroo-Man*, or sings, like Harmonix Music Systems' *Karaoke Revolution*. And there are other games that make music when the player moves his body or hands in free space, like Sony's *Groove* and Discovery's *Motion Music Maker*.

Blaine went on in some depth about what makes a game successful, describing a "regime of competence," which allows the player to simultaneously experience both frustration and pleasure and motivates him to move on to progressively more difficult levels. She also discussed the positives and negatives of multiplayer games, those that require physical immersion, and those that are played out in front of an audience—which can create an experience similar to performing music. But her most salient point was that none of the game manufacturers develop their own controllers: All of their technology is licensed from someone else. And who better to develop that technology than the musicians and scientists who are tinkering away in their labs trying to build the next generation of electronic musical instruments?

Each night of the conference, there were concerts. At computer-music conclaves, performance events are too often deadly boring affairs, as high-brow programmers and theorists show off their latest algorithmic compositions by pushing buttons on laptops and projecting lines of code. But at NIME, since the emphasis was on interactivity, the concerts were anything but dull. By Bill Buxton's standards regarding the correspondence between gesture and sound, all of the 18 works presented over three nights were worthy, and many had the crowd roaring their approval.

An example of the latter was *Ligature*, by Giorgio Magnanensi, an Italian-born composer who now lives in Vancouver. Seated at the mixing console in the middle of the audience, and looking like a cross between Albert Einstein and Napolean Dynamite, Magnanensi frantically manipulated a dozen modified electronic toys of the old "Speak&Spell" variety, creating an ungodly landscape of screaming, ripping, "circuit-bent" sounds, which were thrown around the hall by a 16-channel digital matrix mixer, made all the more hideous by the sounds' roots in (badly sampled) human voices. The one glitch, when a motorized Furby with a tiny speaker in its stomach stopped moving, was adeptly overcome by the composer, who ripped a wire-filled twist-tie in his teeth and shoved it into the critter's back, bringing it back to life. (He told me later a solder joint had failed, and he knew exactly where it was.) It was a masterful, completely insane, performance.

The pace slowed down for *The Appearance of Silence (The Invention of Perspective)* by Laetitia Sonami (born in France, now resident in California), which featured a performance system she helped develop at the Amsterdam research center STEIM called the "Lady's Glove." Sonami has been working with the system, which contains a formidable variety of sensors, allowing control of up to 30 simultaneous musical parameters, for 15 years, and it is now in its fifth version. Her performance, a sinuous, highly expressive mix of concrete and abstract sounds, was a shining example of what can happen when a performer has enough time to become a virtuoso on an instrument, no matter how unusual or complex— something that few of us, especially us adults, find we have the time to do.

Another collaboration between musician and dancer was performed the second night by Luke DuBois, a faculty member at New York University, who is also the author of Cycling '74's *Jitter* software, and Turkish dancer Beliz Demircioglu, a graduate student at the same school. DuBois held a video camera while Demircioglu athletically moved around the stage, as a stylized image of her was projected on a video screen behind her. The music was created by a motion-capture system, with various musical parameters being controlled in real time by the dancer's position in space and by specific physical gestures that the system was trained to recognize. It was an evocative performance, and the connection between dancer and music was, even by Buxton's standards, very clear.

Another winner in the "gesture vs. sound" contest was Yoichi Nagashima of Hamamatsu, Japan (where last year's NIME was held, and for which he served as chairman), a former designer for Kawai and now a researcher and educator, as well as a composer. His *Wriggle Screamer II* used two sensing systems. One looked like an empty picture frame, which was divided up into a grid of 13 vertical and three horizontal optical beams. As the performer put his hands and wrists through the frame, various sounds of harps, bells, strings, percussion, and orchestral hits emerged that reflected whether he was stabbing, poking, caressing, plucking, slapping, or karate-chopping the space. The second system used muscle (EMG) sensors in his arms and legs to provide more complex control over the sounds, as he wriggled his fingers, rotated his wrists and elbows, and kicked up his heels. "I want...to express the sound that the body grates and the spirit to struggle," he wrote in the program notes for the evening—perhaps not in perfect English, but it certainly got the point across.

Finally, on the last night we heard the simplest and in some ways the most effective piece of all: *boomBox* by Jamie Allen, another grad student at New York University. Allen's only equipment was a featureless injection-molded hard travel case, like the kind you'd take your gear on the road with. But he subjected the thing to tortures you hope your gear never experiences. He punched, kicked, slammed, rolled, flipped, and threw the case down on the ground. Inside the case were piezo, tilt, flex, and motion sensors, wired up to processing circuitry (encased in thick foam rubber) and a wireless transmitter. As he tortured the case, agonizing noise samples emerged from the speakers that made you instantly sorry for the thing. The performance ended, to the great hilarity of the audience, with Allen kicking the box into the second row of seats as it let out a final, exasperated grunt.

I would be remiss if I left out another NIME event: It wasn't in a recital hall, but it could certainly fall under the heading of "performance art." After Friday night's concert, the organizers had scheduled a beach party, with drums and a bonfire and the promise of a fine sunset over the sea. Not far from the concert hall, a wooden staircase led precipitously down a heavily forested cliff to a small sand spit known as "Wreck Beach." Some of the participants descending the 200 or so stairs noticed a sign that said: "Beach closed after dark," but said to themselves, "Hey, the organizers must know what they're doing!" As they arrived, drum circles were forming, the sun was sinking, a bonfire was rising, and cold Canadian beer was emerging from bags of ice.

Not long afterwards, however, two uniformed gentlemen (Greater Vancouver Regional District Park Rangers, I found out later) appeared and politely told the assemblage to put out the bonfire. Everyone just as politely ignored them, so they tried to snuff out the fire by kicking sand on it, which didn't work at all. (It should be mentioned that forest fires had been a serious problem in the Vancouver area last year, so the Rangers' action wasn't as arbitrary as some thought at the time.) A few minutes later, however, a hovercraft appeared on the horizon, its powerful spotlight aimed squarely at the beach and growing rapidly. When it arrived, its crew politely told partiers to move away from the bonfire and doused it. I have no doubt it was the first time in history that a party at a computer music conference had to be broken up by the Coast Guard.

It was the first time in history that a party at a computer music conference had to be broken up by the Coast Guard.

Military intervention notwithstanding, once again, a trip to Vancouver has left me in awe, both of the beauty of the place and of the concepts I encountered there. I left the conference with all sorts of new ideas for my own course and my own music ringing in my head.

Perhaps what comes out of NIME will not be as instantly earthshaking as what I saw at Digicon '83, but it eventually may be just as influential, in more subtle ways, as the science of computer/human interface design becomes more important in all of our activities. Better still, NIME is now established and will happen every year, so more and more people will be exposed to this tremendously exciting field. NIME '06 is going to be at IRCAM in Paris. I wonder whether I can come up with another idea for a paper?

Paul D. Lehrman started piano lessons at age five, got his first soldering-iron burn at nine, sang in his first opera at 11, and bought his first electric guitar at 12. He's still learning, playing, singing, and occasionally getting burned.

Afterword

I *did* come up with an idea for a paper for NIME '06. The very month that this column appeared, the National Gallery of Art in Washington, DC, commissioned me to build a robotic installation that would play *Ballet mécanique*, with no human intervention, as part of a huge exhibit on Dadaist art they were planning for the following spring. I contacted LEMUR director Eric Singer, whom I had met for the first time in Vancouver, and his team and I put the thing together. It was a pounding, screaming, wailing success, and you can read about it and watch a video on www.antheil.org.

Singer and I proposed a paper about the installation for NIME '06, and to our delight, it was accepted. Unfortunately, I couldn't go to Paris, so Singer had the privilege of presenting it. But we wrote a second paper for the 121st Audio Engineering Society convention in the fall, and that one I got to present. Meanwhile, NIME '07 is in New York, so I have no excuse for missing it. But what am I going to write this time?

Chapter 51

To Preserve and Protect
The Library of Congress Gets Busy with Our Recorded Heritage

Preface

Cooperation between an industry organization and a branch of the Federal government very often means trouble for consumers, taxpayers, and others without much political or economic power, but when you are talking about a pair of good guys, like the Audio Engineering Society and the Library of Congress, it can mean something else. In the case of the subject of this column, it means that sometimes very important and valuable things can be accomplished, which one institution couldn't do without the help of the other.

October 2005

Should you ever encounter the words "recording industry" and "legislation" in the same sentence, your reaction—usually—should be to run away as fast as possible. For those of us trying to make an honest living in this business, most of the bills that affect us that have crawled onto the floor of Congress in the last couple of decades have not been our friends. From the failed tax on blank tape in the early 1980s to the more successful Miscommunications Act of 1996, the Sony-Bono-and-all-his-Descendants-unto-the-Seventh-Generation Term Extension Act, and the Dismal Millennium Copyright Act (my names, not theirs), these bills have been designed to promote and protect the interests of the major corporate players in the entertainment world at the expense of just about everyone else.

But there are exceptions to every rule, even this one. In November 2000, while the world was enthralled by Florida's inability to distinguish between a dimple and a hanging chad, a bill was quietly signed into law by President Clinton called the National Sound Recording Preservation Act. The NSRPA stipulated that the Library of Congress was to establish the National Recording Registry, which would contain recordings that "are culturally, histori-cally or aesthetically important, and/or inform or reflect life in the United States." Beginning in 2002 and each year following, 50 recordings—out of scores of nomina-tions—have been added to the registry. The idea for the Recording Registry follows on the success of the National Film Registry, which was established four years earlier, and which includes 25 new entries each year.

The sound recordings in the registry cover a tremendous amount of territory, from Edison cylinders to rap records, from ethnological field recordings to political speeches. The most recent list, for example, includes Sophie Tucker's first recording on a 1911 cylinder; Woodrow Wilson's Armistice Day broadcast of 1923, believed to be the earliest surviving electrical recording; Glenn Miller's 1939 recording of *In the Mood*; 1953's low-budget smash *Songs by Tom Lehrer* (about which you read quite a bit in Chapter 6 of this book); a set of 1989 recordings of Asian elephants by Cornell University scientist Katharine B. Payne, which revealed that the animals use infrasonic sounds to communicate with one another; Public Enemy's *Fear of a Black Planet*; and Nirvana's *Nevermind*. The only rules are that a nominated recording be at least ten years old and that a copy of it actually exists.

The selections are made by a standing advisory committee, known as the National Recording Preservation Board, which is made up of members from some 17 organizations involved with music and sound recording. These include NARAS, ASCAP, BMI, the RIAA, the musicians' union, the Society for Ethnomusicology, the American Folklore Society, and the Audio Engineering Society. Each organization gets to name a committee member and an alternate, and there are also five "at-large" members appointed by the Librarian of Congress, among whom are such luminaries as Mickey Hart, Michael Feinstein, and Phil Ramone.

While having a recording in the registry would be an honor for any artist or producer, there's more to the Library's efforts than just singling out recordings of merit. The NSRPA also specifies that the Preservation Board study and report to the Librarian of Congress the current state of preservation techniques and practices, as well as how best to make archived materials available to researchers and educators. According to the two delegates to the board from the AES, George Massenburg and Elizabeth Cohen (who's the alternate), this part of its mission is critical to the health of the recording industry, looking both backwards and forwards, and gives the AES an important role on the board.

"The AES was approached to recommend someone to the Librarian (of Congress) who had good experience in both music and engineering," says Massenburg, who with his extensive track record in engineering, production, design, and education certainly fits that description, "and would be able to help with discussions on any number of levels, working with preservationists and archivists. I loved the idea that we were going to cherry-pick recordings of great cultural significance. I learned about a lot of things that I'd missed. There are some brilliant people on the board with great long careers in music-immersive fields. And everyone deeply cares about music and preserving it. That's the key.

"We're tracing the roots, looking back at the great thread of musical styles, how one influenced another. Given that perspective, you see that only a small percentage of the artists in any given genre are really inspired—their work is transcendent and influential—while the others you view as 'entertainers.' The process gives us a chance to look at the really important innovators and how seminal their work was. Criticisms of the day fall away, so you can see the work better in perspective. For instance, at the time he was composing, Gershwin was thought of as good with melodies, but not as much of symphonist.

"Some of the early flat acoustical discs are extraordinary work. I never knew about this before, but when electrical recording was introduced, people complained it was too cold and brittle and wanted the 'warmth and natural intimacy' of acoustic recordings. Now what does that sound like?"

Cohen, a leading acoustical engineer with academic appointments at Stanford and UCLA and also a former president of the AES, helped write the original legislation. "The major contribution of the AES to the board, as regards the registry, is to speak up for recordings that demonstrate important changes in technology," she says. "We spoke up for Edison recordings and recordings that couldn't have been made without new mic techniques."

For example, there was a 1951 recording by Rafael Kubelik and the Chicago Symphony of Mussorgsky's *Pictures At An Exhibition*. Massenburg explains, "It was a single-mic recording: they set up a [Neumann] *47* in the middle of the hall and rehearsed the orchestra really well. It was a major departure because, before then, electrical recording had been all about close mics and technicians doing the balancing, without much in the way of ambience. This was, 'Let's play music in a hall and record what it sounds like.'

"We wanted to include *Sgt. Pepper* as a turning point in modern recording: the use of technology to tell an interesting, focused story, and which also stood the test of time. We wanted to emphasize methodologies that were unique and innovative: the lyrical use of technology. Of course, Les Paul had to be in there—a guy who will stop at nothing to try an idea. But we're not going to recommend a technology for its own sake, like list a record just because it was done on *Pro Tools*. Nobody's getting a listing for Best Plug-In."

> *"Of course, Les Paul had to be in there-a guy who will stop at nothing to try an idea."*

"There's a rich variety of music in the United States," says Cohen, "and a rich variety from all over the world that has impacted us in the U.S."

There's also a larger context for the board, she explains. After all, she points out, the invention of audio recording was a major event in human history, but ironically, it's not an event that will preserve itself. "The cultural shift that happened when you first preserved the human voice was tremendous," she says. "When a loved one was gone, you never heard his voice again. So the shock of hearing someone speak after their death was astounding.

"We now have 100 years of recorded sound, and our job is to make sure that that legacy is accessible to future generations. It's an act of cultural preservation, preserving that record of human creativity across time. But there are so many endangered recordings. We have an enormity of challenges: Obsolete formats are becoming harder for us to hear, hardware and the technical expertise to operate the hardware is becoming harder to obtain, the materials are deteriorating, and people don't know how to handle the materials to preserve them. You can't imagine how much material has been lost due to bad labeling or boxes that corrode.

> *"The cultural shift that happened when you first preserved the human voice was tremendous."*

"Part of our work is to do a study on the state of audio preservation and to develop a comprehensive national preservation program. We have to become intelligent advocates to management and show them why preservation is an important issue: how you store things and how to establish a data migration policy for a studio, especially in terms of metadata, like session and track information. We're working with recording companies and individuals, making sure that deliverables have migration advice with them."

"A newborn digital project is a lot more difficult to keep track of than anyone imagined," notes Massenburg, who has also worked on this issue at the behest of NARAS and the non-profit Council on Library and Information Resources. "In the old days, there was a master tape. With analog multitrack, even with digital multitrack, there was almost always a master with a track sheet inside and some descriptive notes on the back. But with hard disk recording, looking at your 'master' tells you little. There's no established protocol to name things and no archive structure to handle it, much less preserve it. In time, certain new technologies become unreadable, and evolving computer applications can't read old project files. We've been told, in confidence, that some records have indeed been lost. One thing we found at the major labels was that their libraries were incompatible—each of them was making it up as they went along. Many of us feel that it would be an asset to music preservation to just help libraries coordinate metadata."

"Preservation and handling of the data itself is an important market that shouldn't be left just to IT (information technology) people," says Cohen. "Audio people have to communicate with the IT people to tell them what the requirements are for us. Usually, when you are asked to talk to IT people, it's groan and complain, but those days have to be over.

"We need to develop a series of best practices for how to move the bits from point A to point B before the media decays, or the hard drive or tape drive fail, or the software collapses. Even today, if you have digital audio on Beta tapes or memory sticks, just try to read that! And we need hard disks that last more like a decade than just two years. Everything comes with error-correction, but you have to know how to read it and use it. Amateurs can do this, too: We can educate individuals how to handle their own collections. But there's a four-letter word that people have to use: 'plan.'

"There is a whole array of related technologies, such as compression and lossless compression, that other fields deal with, like data storage, medical imaging, and supercomputing. And we need to look at where things are going: Nanotechnology, RAID arrays, grid computing, holographic storage, or whatever—all of these are vital. I would like to see leadership coming from audio engineers in these fields, so our applications are on the radar screen of the people developing them—not just the banks'."

Of course, not every studio or library or small record label has the resources to deal with all this, but Cohen feels the audio industry can help itself. "A lot of local archives can't afford to do transfers of analog-to-digital or afford best practices," she says, "so we need to coordinate things so that they can go into a studio that is equipped to do this and get it done. It would behoove engineers to help, to serve the public-interest needs."

Cohen also sees a large role for educational institutions in the effort to preserve our past. "Young engineers have to be learning the techniques of data recovery," she says. "One of the roles the board has is to improve education in this area and make restoration and preservation of analog and digital objects part of an audio engineer's basic education. So many people proficient in the analog world are passing, those skills are disappearing, they have to be taught. In film school, it's very common to have classes that cover everything from the most ancient projectors to modern digital technology. We rarely have that in audio: what the equipment was, what its capacity was, and how it's maintained for its purposes. And now, because of the tremendous variety of digital media, we have a big problem of simple bit preservation. When you can store terabytes and petabytes on your desktop, that's a lot of audio. Students need to know about audio longevity, all the different types of media, magnetic and optical, what current practice is, and what are the alternatives and future storage technologies and models."

"In film school, it's very common to have classes that cover everything from the most ancient projectors to modern digital technology. We rarely have that in audio."

Around the time you read this, the physical repository will be opening for the very first time at the National Audio Visual Conservation Center in Culpeper, Virginia, some 70 miles from Washington, DC. But the work is slow. "They're already overtaxed, and they only get $250,000 a year in government money," says Massenburg. "I don't think they're even halfway through the first year's list. They wanted 25 items a year, and we wanted 100, so we compromised on 50. There's a radio station in New Orleans, WWOZ, 'Jazz & Heritage' public radio, and we elected to list their entire archives. But that's a huge job, and it's just one item on the list. When we wanted to list the entire 9,000-mother Edison collection, they declined."

And according to Cohen, a single physical location is not necessarily enough. "We've learned enough from floods and fires that we need to mirror these repositories," she says. "Networks make that easy, but you need good practices and coordination between various archives."

And there's another issue, which is particularly tricky given the current state of copyright law. "The public today equates preservation with access," says Cohen, "and there's a public demand for preserved recordings. The idea of 'preservation' is no longer museums with objects under glass that have restrictions around them. People want to be able to reach their own cultural heritage. It shouldn't be so far away from them that they're deprived of hearing those recordings.

"This requires greater access than is allowed by copyright restrictions. So we need to determine how to handle orphaned recordings, how to deal with copyright issues over unidentifiable or unreachable sources. Sometimes, there's no known provenance or originator for recordings, but they're locked up because someone may have an economic interest in them. There's a huge amount of material that could be released if we could deal with these legal issues. We're working to find a balance between the need for broader access and respecting international property rights. I feel very strongly about providing access, and so do a lot of other board members. The intent of a lot of works was to be heard and performed, and locking it up in a way that makes it inaccessible to an audience is very disrespectful."

As for getting your favorite recordings into the National Registry, there are ways to do that. "There's no limit to public nominations," says Massenburg. "Anyone can bring a nomination to Elizabeth or me. Public nominations have a decided edge in consideration. On the other hand, you can imagine how many times people nominate a Beach Boys record. We had a preservation session at the 2003 AES in New York and passed out a form. Now you can do it online at the Library of Congress's site. The procedure changes every year, but if something doesn't make it one year, we can roll it over and nominate it the next year."

"There's a great expertise in the board," says Cohen, "but there's greater expertise in the public at large. The public can be advocates for things the board may not be aware of. If you make good arguments, then you might be persuasive. We'd love to see an increase in nominations from the AES membership and *Mix* readers. As long as it's had a cultural historical or aesthetic impact on the U.S., it can be nominated. It doesn't have to have been made in the U.S."

"We don't know what will be important in 50 years," says Massenburg. "Some obscure record might turn out to be very influential. We need everybody's support and participation to help us uncover that work."

The National Recording Registry's site is at www.loc.gov/rr/record/nrpb/nrpb-nrr.html, and the submission form is at www.loc.gov/rr/record/nrpb/nrpb-form.html. Feel free to, as Elizabeth Cohen says, "Vote early and vote often."

Paul Lehrman has several thousand LPs, all of which (he hopes) are in pretty good shape.

Afterword

Hurricane Katrina, which roared into New Orleans just a few weeks after I wrote this, blew off a large chunk of the roof at WWOZ, the New Orleans station, and wrecked about $200,000 worth of equipment. But the station managed, through extraordinary measures, to save its entire library of 25,000 recordings, including some 3,000 hours of live performances. If nothing else, Katrina showed how valuable the preservation efforts of the AES and its partners in the National Registry are.

The 2005 registry included records by Jimi Hendrix, Stevie Wonder, The Mothers of Invention, Wendy Carlos, and our dear friends at the Firesign Theatre.

Chapter 52

Marketing to Myself
The Promise of the Web…
the Reality of the Business

Preface

Sometimes it's important to step back from looking at techniques and technology and even the people who use it and think about what it's all for. The last 20 years have seen huge changes in the way music is produced, distributed, and experienced. But when you balance them all together, it's an open question whether those changes have been for the better.

February 2006

Whatever happened to the democratization of music production? Wasn't that supposed to be here by now? And wasn't it supposed to be a good thing? Wasn't every musician going to be able to make records in his home, and weren't all of the giant record companies going to come crashing down in the wake of the home studio revolution and the Internet explosion?

In fact, some of it did happen the way we thought it would, but some of it didn't. I have a home studio, and I couldn't live without it. But the record companies are still out there, strong as ever. And you know something? I'm glad they are. We need them. But we need them to do a much better job than they're doing because the alternative could actually turn out to be worse.

Back in the 1980s, we all knew this would happen. We were going to be able to frolic in the musical playrooms of our dreams, with minimal financial investment and no restrictions on what we could do or how long we wanted to take to do it.

There was to be a renaissance of creativity, in which millions of artistic flowers would bloom, and all of us cultivating those flowers would be justly compensated.

Then in the '90s, thanks to the World Wide Web, we would be able to funnel our creations directly to a waiting audience, who would enthusiastically embrace the new models for seeking out and buying music, thus eliminating the greedy chain of middlemen consuming every crumb of the economic pie. There was to be a renaissance of creativity, in which millions of artistic flowers would bloom, and all of us cultivating those flowers would be justly compensated.

Well, here we are in the mid-Aughts, and it's awards season. The Grammys, the Oscars, and all of the others are going to the same movie studios, the same record companies, and even the same old artists. Has downloading, the technology that was going to change everything, actually done so? Well, it made the record labels paranoid beyond belief, but this year's blockbuster acts aren't much different from last year's: The first million-downloaded song was by the not-exactly-underground Gwen Stefani. How about the other new media opening up paths for new talent? For example, Cingular signed an agreement with an artist that lets the company's cell phone customers hear her next releases (in all the hi-fi glory that medium delivers) before they hit the stores—pretty cool, if you like that sort of thing, and with definite revolutionary potential. Whom did they sign? Gwen Stefani. Meet the new boss, same as the old boss.

The music-making part has worked out pretty much the way it was supposed to. Any kid with a laptop has access to tools that would have cost as much as a house 20 years ago. The studio business has tilted sharply toward the low end. Remote trucks have been replaced by *PowerBooks* and MOTU *Travelers* strapped onto the monitor board's direct outs. High-end studios are being used less to make records and more to score films and videogames. Mid-level commercial studios have all but disappeared as their customers squirrel themselves away in personal and project rooms.

It's the other part that we're still waiting for. And we may be waiting a long time. True, there are people who are making some money selling music on the Internet or through genuinely independent distribution channels such as Broadjam and CD Baby. But mass-marketing is still in the hands of, well, the mass-marketers. And they don't show any signs of letting go.

As you may recall, the record industry was supposed to be eaten up by small fry, and experts were predicting that traditional mass media, like *The New York Times* and the major TV networks, were going to die and be replaced by personalized sources of entertainment and information that would organically grow out of audience needs and desires, using the Web as the medium.

It takes a lot more than a few recommendations on a website to sway a significant number of people and bring a book, movie, or CD into mass consciousness.

To some extent, this has happened. There are some terrific new ways to get information. I subscribe to several online news services that give me important political stories that my local paper ignores and business news that's too specialized even for *The Wall Street Journal*, to say nothing of *USA Today*. When it comes to things like books, movies, and music, recommendation lists on Amazon, user reviews on the Internet Movie Database, and playlists like those on musicstrands.com and the iTunes store are helping people decide what to buy or see or listen to.

But it takes a lot more than a few recommendations on a website to sway a significant number of people and bring a book, movie, or CD into mass consciousness. It's still up to the old media to do that. They haven't gone away. I still read *The Boston Globe. The Times* (which not long ago bought *The Globe*) is still very powerful, even if readership, especially among young people, is down, and ABC is still responsible for getting the news to millions of Americans (even if they once tried to get David Letterman to replace Ted Koppel). *Rolling Stone* is doing better than ever, and even *Time* and *Newsweek* are gaining influence in the entertainment world.

Much of what we think of as new voices are merely extensions of the old: Comedy Central, for all its attitude and appeal to the younger generation, is owned by the people who own CBS. Spike TV, the Cartoon Network, and almost all your favorite "alternative" cable channels are owned by Viacom, Time Warner, or NBC/Universal. Even the Sundance Channel is only partly owned by the Sundance Institute; the rest of it is in the hands of two media giants. *Wired* magazine, where a lot of these predictions were first uttered, didn't take long to morph into a techie version of *Vanity Fair*—not surprising, as both magazines are now part of the same publishing empire, Condé Nast, whose other properties include *The New Yorker*.

And for the record industry, as we can see on the awards shows and the *Billboard* charts (whose Dutch parent company also owns *Hollywood Reporter* and AC Nielsen) and hear on the radio, music that's really popular (and thus makes real money) comes from only a few sources. And the number of those sources continues to shrink. Who could have predicted even ten years ago that RCA and Columbia—once bitter arch-rivals in everything from which opera singers sang on their labels to which color television format would be approved by the FCC—would end up being divisions of the same company, to say nothing of being owned by a Japanese conglomerate?

These media behemoths have the marketing, the advertising, the exposure in multiple mediums, and the sheer financial muscle to make the biggest splashes in the entertainment world. And, of course, that's the primary reason why they remain so influential. But the flip side of that is audiences *like* to be told what to like. We want people and institutions to look up to, to tell us how to behave and what to pay attention to. If a friend tells you something is cool, well, *maybe* it is. But if Warner Bros. tells you something is cool—especially if it can dress its marketing machine up as some kind of super-hip teenage online community and keep repeating it, using the glitziest of music and graphics and costumes and toys and whatever—then it *must* be.

In the classroom, we want the teacher, not the other students, to tell us what we need to know. We may know some people who make us laugh sometimes, but we *always* laugh at Jon Stewart and Jay Leno. In concert, we want the artist to speak to us, and we're not interested in what those around us have to say. (Would you please shut up!?) We watch talking-heads television and listen to talk radio because we want to hear what those people are thinking—that is, once we get past the narcissistic impulse of trying to get our phone call on the air.

These institutions filter what comes our way, and we need them. There's just too much stuff out there for us to do it ourselves. Too many news stories, too many comedians, too many indie rock bands, too many cartoons for us to deal with, so we look to filters to help us. When we find a filter that we like, we stick with it, whether it's *Utne Reader* or Fox News. The magazine *[well, the book actually]* you're reading right now is a filter, and you're reading it because you approve of what we choose to present to you.

The media companies, especially the record companies, are in desperate need of a plunger or a good shot of Drano.

The problem with any filter, however, is how it behaves when it gets, for lack of a better term, clogged. To stretch a metaphor much too far, a clogged filter fills up with hair and other bodily wastes, refuses to let anything pass through untainted, and before long, begins to stink. And the media companies, especially the record companies, are in desperate need of a plunger or a good shot of Drano.

The clogging in the media marketing world is caused by the unimaginable sums of money that are at stake. The cost of marketing a property so that it can attract enough attention to make money has risen to ridiculous levels, and it's a phenomenon that feeds on itself. The result is that every marketing effort has to pay off big and fast. Movies have to make back the bulk of their nut during the first weekend, and new artists' first CDs have to ship Platinum. Making a record costs far less than it did 10 or 20 years ago, but the cost of *promoting* records far outweighs any savings on the production end. The idea of slowly building an artist—of supporting several releases that don't initially make a big profit so that the artist has a chance to mature and build an audience—is anathema to companies that need to see an immediate return on every investment. When you've got that much at stake mucking up the works, very little can get through.

The son of a friend of mine is an executive at one of the major labels, and he recently got a big promotion. The label, according to my friend, has only one really big act, and so his son is desperate to find a new act that will be as big. "He tells me there's just nobody out there," my friend says. Now I agree that there is a plethora of lame bands and singers trying to be heard (and not just on *American Idol*), but I also know that there are plenty of genuinely talented and appealing musicians who would die for the chance to record for that label and who would be able to attract a good-enough following to make decent bucks for everyone. But the label doesn't want that—they want an act to appear who can, overnight, goose the balance sheet of the whole operation in one fell swoop. That's not a filter, that's a brick wall.

> *The labels want an act to appear who can, overnight, goose the balance sheet of the whole operation in one fell swoop. That's not a filter, that's a brick wall.*

So is it time for the big record companies to go? A lot of people think so. Certainly, the labels themselves aren't doing much to win sympathy, what with suing college students and random Internet users and placing nasty irremovable Trojan horses on customers' computers. In other industries, as in the animal kingdom, this is known as "eating your young," and it's not recommended.

Now that broadband is within reach of a majority of American homes and businesses, certainly the mechanism for completely bypassing the Big Four is in place. We have other sources of information that can tell us what we want to buy. Computers that record people's buying and browsing habits are already making decisions about what other items we might want to spend money on. Just as online news services are getting better at customizing news for each reader and eliminating anything that the reader might consider disagreeable, automated recommendation algorithms in online shops can focus our choices so that we only know about things that we are considered likely to purchase—and in the case of creative products, we never learn about new authors, films, or recording artists.

As screwed-up and self-defeating as the record companies are, the potential for this kind of extreme "narrowcasting" could be even worse. There's a well-done and quite frightening *Flash* presentation from a fictional museum some years in the future at www.EPIC2014.com. EPIC stands for Evolving Personalized Information Construct, a system that uses "his choices, his consumption habits, his interests, his demographics, his social network" to determine what a user should see and buy. Without active participation from respected and authoritative human-based filters, which should include the record companies' A&R departments, many people will depend more and more on these automatons to make their buying and listening decisions for them.

For some people with open minds and expansive tastes, the machines will make interesting conclusions, propose novel juxtapositions, and open up new areas of exploration. But for others, whose purchasing habits are less broad, the machines will shrink their focuses even further. New acts and genres will never have a chance to get their attention. All users will be exposed to will be what the machines, in their cold logic, consider "safe" for them. The market will become even more fragmented, as each user becomes his own filter. And the ability of music to reach out to people, to open their eyes, to change their minds, to teach them something they don't already know, to do anything at all except reinforce their own beliefs—and perhaps get them dancing—will be gone.

Paul D. Lehrman is expecting his royalty check to arrive any day now from the four people who downloaded his latest musical effort.

Afterword

Actually, by now I've sold a few hundred CDs and DVDs on the Internet, thanks to PayPal, Amazon, CD Baby, a few public television stations, and a huge mailing list, and I've made back my production costs and even a small profit. But I wouldn't yet call that a paradigm shift, exactly.

Chapter 53

False Sense of Security
How Not to Get Caught in the Web

Preface

Have you ever been ripped off? I don't mean at the gas pump or the ticket scalper's. I mean, has anyone ever picked you out deliberately and tried to steal your money or worldly goods? I was, about 20 years ago, when I left a rear window in my first-floor apartment open and went out for dinner, and a little while later someone invited himself in. They stole some expensive cameras, a cheap portable recorder, and a bit of fake jewelry. Insurance paid for almost everything, but it was not a fun experience and has left me very security-conscious ever since.

Today, however, you don't need an open window to make a criminal feel welcome in your home or, especially, your bank account. All you need to do is participate in the online world. The bad guys know that as the tech gets higher, the scams need to get more clever, but there will always be plenty of suckers. Here's another true story (why do these things always happen to me?) with a lesson for everyone.

April 2006

One of the words on everybody's lips these days is "security." National, job, personal, data—security of all kinds is the topic of countless conversations and news stories. As was the case with Y2K, Africanized killer bees, and the horrors of copying LPs onto cassettes, a great deal of the information flying around about threats to our security is complete nonsense, but nonetheless, there are some real dangers out there.

My local newspaper, for example, recently wrapped bundles of papers going to dealers with "scrap" paper, which happened to be printouts of subscribers' credit information. (Haven't you guys ever heard of a shredder?) In the days after that leaked out (and the publisher's subsequent full-page apology), the paper had to field several hundred thousand phone calls, and no one yet knows how much damage might ensue from the incident. It's hardly a unique occurrence: Almost every week there's a report about some tape or disk or laptop containing personal information about thousands of people being misplaced by, or stolen from, a bank or credit agency. Sometimes these breaches are the result of criminal intent, but they often occur due to sheer stupidity.

Security is a serious issue to us in the recording business because in a number of ways, we're a tempting target for thieves of all kinds. We've all heard stories of low-level studio employees or band hangers-on e-mailing MP3s of mixes to bootleggers; of break-ins by screwdriver- and wire-cutter–equipped thugs who leave behind empty equipment racks; of studio personnel who forget to erase the hard disks in a rented DAW; of masters that are put into a taxicab and never seen again; and of late-night sessions that turn into rounds of Grand Theft Microphone. We need to keep reminding ourselves to keep the doors and equipment cabinets locked, to keep our servers firewalled and our wireless networks encrypted, to turn on the alarm when we leave, and to check the credit and credentials of new clients, as well as new employees, lest things go very wrong in a session and we lose a lot more than just the cost of the studio time.

In my humble opinion, though, one of the most serious threats to our security these days— besides the RIAA and the clowns in Washington—is the scumbags who have figured out how to use the Internet to implement clever scams against just plain folks like you and me. Con men (and women), swindlers, and bunco artists are as old as civilization, but the Internet has made their jobs so much more interesting, easier, and more lucrative. The Internet is still young and growing, and not everyone has developed the kind of radar that serves them well when, for example, a sleazebag on the street tries to sell you a Rolex from inside his raincoat.

The Nigerian-dead-bank-manager-leaves-$15M-with-no-heirs scam is so old and hairy it's amazing it's still going around, but I still get several of those a day, some with amusing twists involving Christian missionaries and Russian orphans. There are, of course, the ever-popular penny stocks "due to increase 400 percent!" that you've never heard of and those *urgent* notices that someone has tapped into your PayPal or VISA account and put a second name on it—which are designed to get you to contact the fraudster who sent you the notice and give him your confidential information so that *he* can tap into your account.

Many of these fall under the category of "phishing," which means (and even if they aren't together any more, I can't imagine the band Phish being happy about this coinage) using a phony but authentic-looking e-mail to get you to disclose your presumably secure information to someone who would very much like to use it to your disadvantage. Some phishing scams are easy to spot and some are not, but a great many of them can be identified if you know where (and take the time) to look. Open up the raw code of the message and look for an originating Web address or a URL under a click-on link, which is different from the organization the message claims to be from. If you find one, it's a scam.

Considering that all Web domains are publicly registered and the names of the registrants are easily available, it's amazing that, even though some phishers are quite skilled at covering their tracks, law enforcement hasn't been able to track down and prosecute more of these jerks—but in fact, there have been very few charges brought against these miscreants. I guess some agencies figure it's more important to keep tabs on people wearing inflammatory T-shirts.

The biggest Internet-related fraud problem in the country today, according to the Federal Trade Commission, is online auction fraud, with a typical loss per incident of more than $1,100. This takes many forms: There's the tried-and-true "ship a brick instead of a computer" gambit; the phony "Xbox case with nothing inside" ploy; and the "you pay by cashier's check, and you never hear from them again" routine.

Well, progress, as one great American company used to boast, is our most important product (that was before they shifted the bulk of their operations to television networks and financial services), and there's progress on the Internet fraud front, as well. This month, I found out about a new twist that combines a number of these tactics and is aimed at an economic sector that a great many of us belong to: equipment buyers and sellers.

Here's how it works. You have a piece of gear you want to sell at auction on eBay, so you list it. You get a number of bidders, and when the auction ends, you sell the item to the highest bidder. But for quite some time after the auction is over, the eBay IDs of the other bidders, and the prices they bid, stay up on eBay on your item's page.

Now, eBay has a comprehensive set of procedures for dealing with transactions that don't work out for one reason or another. One of these—which is also useful if you have more than one of a certain item to sell—is called Second-Chance Offer. If the highest bidder's transaction goes sour, this gives you the option to sell to one of the other bidders at the price that they bid rather than the highest bid. For the seller, it's a good backup, and for the buyer, it's a good deal because he doesn't have to pay any more than he wanted.

The Second-Chance Offer is made through eBay's website. You, the seller, go to a special page and select which losing bidder you want to make the offer to and how long you want the offer to remain open, typically one to three days. Then eBay generates a message to the bidder, telling him the item is available and how to purchase it from you.

The scam involves sending a phony Second-Chance Offer message to the losing bidders that looks like it comes from eBay, but it doesn't.

The scam involves sending a phony Second-Chance Offer message to the losing bidders that *looks* like it comes from eBay, but it doesn't. The message includes genuine eBay graphics, complete with all sorts of "seals of verification" and legitimate links to other places on eBay's site. It lays out all sorts of procedures and policies that sound reassuring and just complicated enough to be true: how the transaction is "guaranteed," how the seller has a whole lot of money in a "purchase-protection account" to make sure the buyer doesn't get ripped off, and how the buyer has five days to examine the merchandise and can return it for a full refund if he doesn't like it.

The buyer is told that in order to pay for this item, he has to send a Western Union money transfer to the e-mail's sender, which is on Yahoo or Hotmail or some other impossible-to-trace service. The original seller's eBay ID is prominent in the message, but the seller's real name and address (which the buyer doesn't know) have been replaced with a bogus name and the address of a mail drop in a foreign country, London and Rome being two popular locations. To further entice the buyer, the message says that the seller will pay all of the shipping charges and split the fee with the buyer for sending the money transfer, usually around nine percent of the total amount.

The notice is even cheeky enough to "warn" the buyer, "Never use Western Union money transfer or money gram to pay a seller which *[sic]* credibility and payment address was not verified by us. You are most likely to lose your money and never receive the merchandise you paid for. If a seller requires cash transfer and you do not have this kind of purchase protection, please do not participate."

Of course, the "purchase-protection account" doesn't exist, so when the mark does send a money transfer, the money disappears. The item itself doesn't exist, either, because it was already sold to someone else—the highest bidder. The mark blames the seller, a nasty dispute follows, and the real culprit, wherever he is, goes and cashes in the money transfer, while laughing at the idiots trading accusations and insults on eBay. The crooks pick their marks carefully. All of the scams I tracked down involved losing bids of $1,000 or more.

So how did I find out about this? Someone tried to scam the bidders on a piece of gear I sold on eBay. A sharp-eyed *Mix* reader in California, who was the second-highest bidder on the item, received one of these bogus messages, and he noticed that the original location of the equipment (Massachusetts) didn't match the address he was supposed to send the money to (London). In fact, because I use my buddy Grumpmeier's name as my eBay ID (and I used to have an ID that was even easier to link to me), he figured out that I was the seller. He wrote me through eBay's messaging service to tell me what was going on, and he also notified eBay's fraud department, plus he wrote all the other bidders on the list to warn them that they might receive a similar message. Because anyone who might have been taken in by this would have first gotten mad at *me*, he did me almost as much of a favor as he did them.

I tried some Google searches on the address and the modus operandi of the scamsters and turned up incidents dating back about a year and a half. They have gone after bidders on a collectible 19th-century $5 bill, a Nikon camera, a chip from a defunct Las Vegas casino, a Mesa Boogie amp, a dirt bike, a National steel guitar, a high-profile domain name and, yes, a sarrusophone, which is a rare, mid-19th-century musical instrument that's an unfortunate cross between a saxophone and a contrabassoon. Sarrusophone aficionados are, as you might imagine, a small and relatively tight group, and word got around quickly, so none of them fell for it.

No technology or law can protect us against our own carelessness and gullibility.

Are there ways we can make ourselves secure against this sort of thing? Well, there are certainly things that governments and the corporate world can do. In January 2006, the British division of eBay announced that it would no longer recognize wire transfers as a legitimate form of payment. Of course, that means more business for eBay's wholly owned subsidiary PayPal, but in truth, PayPal has a lot fewer security holes. It would be nice if some state attorneys general would generate a little publicity about this scam so that the media might pick it up. And it might be good if some of that enormous amount of money being spent on "homeland security" could be used to chase down these crumbs and put them behind bars.

But the scamsters' most potent weapon is what's called "social engineering": figuring out how to make suckers bite. And no technology or law can protect us against our own carelessness and gullibility. As Sgt. Phil always said to the Hill Street cops, "Let's be careful out there."

The major reason schemes like this succeed is that we let them. Too many of us accept the things we're handed at face value without the proper examination and skepticism. It's true whether we're being told we can get an unanticipated bargain on a piece of gear, we will be rewarded with a veritable fortune just for being nice to a stranger, or that by waging eternal war on an invisible enemy we will achieve world peace. As long as we are willing to get fooled and fooled again, those who would compromise our security will always find a target.

Afterword

With more and more scamsters taking advantage of the anonymity of sending money by Western Union, many online services are now refusing to accept transactions through that company, and Western Union itself posts fraud warnings prominently on its website, advising customers not to send money to people they don't know. So that loophole, perhaps, is closing. No doubt another will open up soon enough.

Chapter 54

Two Hearts
Do Musicians and Audiences Beat as One?

Preface

When you think of academic research in music technology, you generally think of designing new instruments (as I talked about in Chapters 49 and 50), creating new models for sound synthesis, or developing new algorithms for signal processing. But these days, there's also research going on in how people *perceive* music. Our knowledge of the physics and acoustics of sound and how it gets to the ear is far ahead of our understanding of what happens between the ear and the conscious brain. This experiment is in the latter category and should give our investigation of that realm a good kick-start.

July 2006

Music is one of the most powerful forms of communication the human race has come up with. When it comes to sending purely emotional messages of joy, despair, exhilaration, languor, or what scientists call "dynamic" emotions—like when you're excited and terrified at the same time—few languages communicate as efficiently and effectively as music.

Psychologists and others who study the human brain know that emotions have a strong physiological component. Smiling lowers the blood pressure, anxiety constricts capillaries, anger makes your adrenal glands secrete. But when someone plays music and someone else listens to it, what changes in their bodies and how, if at all, are those changes linked? Can the transmission of emotions through music be measured and studied?

That's the question behind a fascinating experiment that took place on a sunny Sunday in April at Boston's Symphony Hall, with the Boston Symphony Orchestra and an audience full of children and their parents. The results of the experiment aren't going to come quickly, but the group of musicians, psychologists, and technicians in the Green Room that afternoon gathered enough data about the physiological effects of music to keep them busy for months and, just as important, to point the way toward further research.

If you're going to measure how music affects an audience, you will need a high-fidelity transmission medium, and there are few such media better than Boston's Symphony Hall.

If you're going to measure how music affects an audience, you will need a high-fidelity transmission medium, and there are few such media better than Symphony Hall. Its acoustics are world renowned, and everyone involved in music there—audiences, musicians, and the many recording engineers, including myself, who have plied their trade there—loves to work in the place. As it happens, my first gig when I moved to the Boston area was to mix the radio broadcasts of the Boston Pops orchestra under the late Arthur Fiedler from the stage of Symphony Hall. Since then, I've attended many concerts, rehearsals, and recording sessions, but none that required as much audience participation and as much technology spread throughout the hall as April's event.

The project was dreamed up by three researchers whose fascinating resumes straddle the worlds of music and science. Teresa Marrin Nakra, who happens to be a personal friend, got an orchestral conducting degree from Harvard and then did her doctoral work at MIT's Media Lab, where her thesis was a "conductor's jacket": a wired-up garment equipped with sensors to measure motion, muscle tension, and other physiological factors while the wearers—Boston Pops musical director Keith Lockhart among them—conducted symphony orchestras. She's the artistic director of a nonprofit group that develops new technologies for the performing arts called *Immersion Music*, and she recently became an assistant professor at The College of New Jersey.

Her teammate, Daniel Levitin, dropped out of both MIT and Stanford as an undergraduate and spent his 20s and 30s as an A&R man for a small record label in San Francisco, at the same time freelancing as a musician, engineer, producer, standup comedian, and music journalist, counting among his clients Mel Tormé, Steely Dan, Blue Öyster Cult, Jay Leno, and *Mix* magazine. Eventually, he went back to Stanford for a degree in psychology and went on to receive a Ph.D. from the University of Oregon, where his thesis was on absolute (or "perfect") musical pitch. He joined the music faculty at McGill University in Montreal in 2000 and now has a joint appointment as an associate professor in music and psychology. His book *This Is Your Brain on Music: The Science of a Human Obsession* will be published this summer by Dutton.

The third team member, Stephen McAdams, is also at McGill and also with a joint appointment. An expert on musical perception, he has a Ph.D. in hearing and speech sciences from Stanford and a doctorate in cognitive psychology from the University of Paris.

The project originated, says Nakra, when Levitin called her up about a year and a half ago and told her he had received a grant, which he wanted to spend on some kind of collaboration with her and McAdams. "We met in Montreal and came up with this idea," she says. "It took in a bit of all of our research: Steve had worked with slider boxes as response tools, and Dan had worked with audience response to music. So we decided to combine our methodologies and do a project that was bigger than anything each of us could do alone.

"We wrote up a proposal and then asked, 'What orchestra might agree to do this?' I called a friend in the BSO's education office, and they immediately saw the value in the experiment and that it would be best to integrate it into a concert with both kids and parents present. They also knew that Keith Lockhart would be the right guy to conduct."

In fact, Lockhart was scheduled to conduct one of the orchestra's Family Series concerts. Myran Parker-Brass, the BSO's director of education and community programs, approached him over the summer. In the hall's parking lot on July 4, as Lockhart was getting ready to conduct the Pops' huge outdoor Independence Day extravaganza, "he gave her the thumbs up."

What Lockhart agreed to was to be wired up with an updated version of Nakra's jacket, made from a Lycra biking jersey. Inside the jacket were an electrocardiogram (EKG) sensor, an accelerometer, and six electromyogram (EMG) sensors from a company called Delsys. These were all wired to a beltpack and then through a 100-foot audio snake to a computer backstage in the Green Room.

Electromyograms measure muscle tension. Delsys, which makes these sensors and others for the medical and sports-training industries, has an academic origin—it grew out of a program in neuromuscular research at Boston University—which may be one reason why they were so helpful to the project. They've sponsored Nakra in her research in the past, but she says, "I didn't expect them to come through like this. They loaned us about $60,000 worth of gear. The project would have been unaffordable without their equipment. Plus, they helped us build a custom isolation unit for each of the musicians so they wouldn't be harmed by stray electricity—like if lightning struck the hall." What does the company get out of it? "Well, they get nice pictures of Keith for their website," she says with a laugh. "They like the idea of having arts applications for their products, too."

In addition to the sensors, Lockhart wore an armband made by the Pittsburgh-based company BodyMedia, containing a two-axis accelerometer, a body temperature gauge, and a galvanic skin response monitor, which measures a person's excitement: As the excitement level increases, skin resistance goes down. The armband, which is the sort of thing you might see worn in very posh health clubs, wasn't wired to anything; it collects data by itself. The data can then be downloaded via a USB port. However, the team time-synced the device with the main computer before the concert to make sure all of the data would be coordinated.

In her previous work, Nakra was able to determine that a conductor experiences physiological changes along with the music, but with this experiment she was able to ask, "How are those signals received?" The first people to receive them would be, of course, the players in the orchestra. So five musicians were wired up similarly to the conductor, with armbands, EKGs, and two EMGs each. "All of the members of the BSO got a letter explaining what we were doing," says Nakra, "and the five we ended up working with were the first to respond. They were among the younger, more science-y types in the orchestra—definitely not the older crowd." The players were nicely spread throughout the orchestra: one player each from the bassoon, percussion, trumpet, bass, and violin sections.

And finally there was the audience. "The orchestra has a 'Kids Club,' who are regular subscribers to the Family Series," explains Nakra. "We sent all of them a letter inviting them to participate. We told them we were doing an experiment in how science can reveal emotions in music. Several wrote back and signed up, but we still needed to recruit some audience members at the last minute. We had a bunch of volunteers from McGill, Immersion Music, and Northeastern University greeting people in the lobby and getting them equipped."

Sixteen audience members—children and parents—got the BodyMedia armbands, as well as finger cuffs made by Thought Technology, a Montreal biofeedback company, to measure blood pulse volume, heart rate, and galvanic skin response. Four more were given wireless heart-rate monitors. In addition, 30 concertgoers were given boxes with slide potentiometers on them marked "weak" and "strong" at the two ends. They were given instructions to "continuously rate your impressions concerning the strength of the emotional reaction you have to the music as you are listening" and move the slider accordingly. The instructions were careful to point out that their response should not be determined by whether or not they *liked* the music—just how strongly they responded to it, either positively or negatively.

Who got the sliders depended on where they sat. The researchers didn't want to run the ribbon cables connecting them more than 100 feet, and so only people in the front few rows on the side of the hall closest to the Green Room could get them. "Through the education office, the box office sent letters to everyone who had tickets in that section," says Nakra, "and people responded. But the hardest part was getting everyone to sign releases just before the concerts, and so we had a big team of guys running around with clipboards."

Another interesting chore was running the cables, which couldn't commence until after 10:30 the night before the experiment as there was a concert in the hall that evening. It kept the researchers and volunteers very busy until past two in the morning. "We could get under the stage, which was a big help," recalls Nakra. "And it was important to protect the cables. The ones connecting the beltpacks to the isolation boxes cost about $700 each; they're very lightweight and were built for laboratory experiments, not heavy-duty use. One hit from a stiletto heel, and they would have been toast.

"It was pretty strange under there," she continues, laughing. "Piles of cables and some evidence of rodents, but the weirdest thing is that there are holes in the stage, and so there are these odd streams of light coming through. Crawling around down there, I sort of felt like Indiana Jones."

The concert-cum-experiment, which was also recorded and videotaped in HD by a crew from the local PBS station, went off almost without a hitch. During the first number, a Mozart overture, one of the accelerometers fell off Lockhart's wrist. The researchers realized that something had gone wrong when that sensor's data stream, which was being processed using custom software that Nakra's husband Jahangir wrote, turned into gibberish. After the piece ended, they could see on their video monitor the sensor hanging down and flopping around, so after a brief debate, one of the technicians went out onto the stage with a roll of duct tape. "Be careful," warned Lockhart as the man started to reattach the sensor to the conductor's Lycra sleeve, "it's Armani." It got a big laugh, at least from the parents in the audience.

So what did the researchers get out of all this? They don't know yet. "It's our summer project," says Nakra. Not counting the video and audio, they gathered 4 GB of data, which they now have to sift through. "The first task is to look at the muscle activation of the performers. We expect to see the score realized in that data pretty clearly. We're most curious about heart-rate activity. It was the first time we have collected high-resolution, clean EKG data. We're wondering how the heart rates of the performers and the audience will correlate. Not that they'd beat in sync, but whether they'd move up and down together.

"Then we'll look at the skin response, the excitement level. We expect that the performers' response will be more intense than the audience's, but we don't know for sure. Performers are so used to this and comfortable with it that they might be more casual about it than the audience. And we're looking at delays. The conductor's responses will be a little ahead of the music; the performers will be in the moment, although there is some anticipation there, too, when they prepare to play a phrase; and the audience's will be a little behind. But we want to see how large those delays really are."

A second experiment is scheduled soon that will play the *recordings* from the BSO concert to a similarly wired audience. The main question this experiment hopes to answer is how different, and in what ways, an audience's response to a recording is from an audience present at a live event.

Nakra, Levitin, and McAdams know that they're just getting started on this idea of quantifying physiological responses to music, but their work could turn out to be very important to the way people make, hear, record, and, dare I say it, sell music. Not that we need any more bean counters determining what music we listen to, but these are scientists and musicians, as well. Besides, as Lockhart said in a television interview just before the concert, "they're measuring something that musicians intuitively have always known is there: the power of music to transport you." It will be interesting to see what kind of science can be found driving that mode of transportation.

Paul D. Lehrman wrote a satirical article on the practical uses of perfect pitch in 1977 that was never published. But it has all come true since.

Afterword

The summer after this experiment, the Boston Symphony Orchestra replaced the stage floor at Symphony Hall, which had been there since the building opened in 1900. To preserve the acoustics, the designers worked hard to match the species and geometry of maple that went into the original and installed the new boards by hand, with custom hand-cut nails. The replacement floor does not have any holes in it, so the next time Nakra crawls under the stage she won't feel like she's in a Spielberg movie. Nor does it have the large, square trap door that used to be in the middle, since no one can remember why it was there in the first place.

As for my article about perfect pitch, a reader who actually has perfect pitch wrote to ask if I could send him a copy of it. It's around here somewhere....

Chapter 55

For the Benefit of Mr. Harrison

How a Nice Guy from L.A. Filled the Albert Hall

Preface

This is a column that means a lot to me. I loved writing it, and I did so with pride, nostalgia, and not a little bit of envy. Although I wrote it over two years ago, this is the first time it's been in print.

It was written in 2004, at the time when the *Concert for George* aired on PBS, but after I finished it I found out that Harrison's family and friends had requested that there be restrictions on the way the media covered the event. The reasons for this were complex, and I won't go into them here, but the editors of *Mix* and I agreed that those restrictions should be respected, and we decided not to run the piece.

Now that a couple of more years have passed, however, the restrictions have eased, and I now have permission to tell the story.

I'll bet you know someone who wanted to grow up to play lead guitar for The Beatles. In fact, if you're reading this, I'll bet you *are* that person. I know I am—the first time I played an electric guitar in public was at my junior high school Spring Concert, when the choral-music teacher (thanks, Mr. Taglino!) enlisted me and Izzie on guitars, Jeff on bass, and Janie on drums to back up his brand-new Beatles medley. The parents were pretty shocked, but we were in heaven.

Of course, no one could ever replace the real lead guitarist for the Fab Four, either while they were still together or in the decades since. Except that a year after George Harrison died, at the memorial concert that his family and friends put together for him in November 2002, someone needed to play lead guitar. That someone turned out to be a journeyman musician/programmer/mixer from Los Angeles, someone whom few people had ever heard of, and who happened to be an old friend of mine. His name is Marc Mann, and when I saw him on the screen in the wonderful movie they've made of the *Concert for George*, up there along with Paul, Ringo, Eric Clapton, Jeff Lynne, Ravi Shankar, Tom Petty, and the rest of the literal hall of fame who performed that night at the Royal Albert Hall, I was so insanely jealous that I had to talk to him and find out how he got there.

Tracking him down, however, wasn't easy. We actually hadn't seen each other in a number of years, and his e-mail address on the PAN network where we had first met back in the mid-'80s was long out of date. He's incredibly busy, working mostly on high-profile projects, yet he doesn't have a website of his own or even his own domain name for e-mail. It took a bunch of sleuthing around Harrison- and Lynne-oriented discussion groups (where most references to him were in sentences that began, "Who the heck is...?") before I found a link to a page on a five-year-old site that had an AOL address for him. I shot a message into the cyber-ether, and a few days later Marc replied.

He was very happy to hear from me but reluctant to talk about the concert. Not because he didn't want to, but because he was up against a wall working on Danny Elfman's score for *Spiderman II*. "We've got 58 cues, an hour and 22 minutes of orchestral music. And we had six weeks to do it in. I've been putting in 18-hour days. Our downbeat at Sony is Friday, with the setup on Thursday, and today I'm doing all the synth pre-mixes." Like I said, busy. Working as a programmer and orchestrator for Elfman has been one of Marc's bread-and-butter gigs for 16 years. But how did something like that lead to playing slide guitar on "My Sweet Lord" in front of 5,200 fans of George Harrison and The Beatles?

Well, we finally did talk, and our conversation started with the late '70s, when Marc was a graduate composition student at UCLA. "I was straddling both sides of music, the 'classical' and 'popular'," he says. "I would be doing papers on Mahler or studying Stravinsky scores by day and playing in bands around town at night. As for modern composers, I got into all the usual suspects, but I decided that, for me, musicality had to do with melody and harmony and rhythm."

Marc's father had bought him his first guitar, "and I learned to play around campfires." He taught himself rock and roll by listening to "the usual Boomer music list: Clapton, Page, Harrison, and Howe." But in college he saw that the recording studio itself could be just as interesting an instrument. "I got the key to the electronic music lab, with all the modular Moogs and Buchlas and a Stephens 16-track," he recalls, "and that's when I started staying up all night in the studio. And that's never stopped." He picked up his first national album credit in grad school: a 1981 Dan Fogelberg LP, *The Innocent Age*, on one cut of which he conducted the UCLA choir. After he finished his degree, he continued playing in bands, conducted musical theater, and worked for a number of music production companies around L.A., doing advertising work and writing some of the music for the ABC series *Coach*.

In the fall of 1984, he caught the computer bug when a production company he was working for bought a Kurzweil *250* and an original 128k Macintosh to edit and sequence with. He jumped on the new technology: "My partner Rich Aronson and I put together a state-of-the-art computer/MIDI studio, with two computer rooms and a large live room," he says. "We did TV, radio, and records, and I would play keyboards or guitar, or bass, whatever was needed." He also established himself as a "computer music evangelist" to musicians and studios all over Southern California and helped them get Macs through a West L.A. dealership called Personal Support Computers. "It was a great way to meet a lot of musicians in town," he recalls. He also set himself up as an independent dealer for many of the protean Macintosh music products from Opcode, Digidesign, C-Lab (which later became Emagic), and Mark of the Unicorn. Since I was doing the same thing on the East Coast, Marc and I found ourselves corresponding a lot on PAN to compare notes and swap war stories, and we met a few times for drinks at NAMM shows.

Elfman was one of his early clients. "I ended up playing keyboards in (Elfman's band) Oingo Boingo for touring and recording, and around the time he was scoring *The Nightmare Before Christmas*, I showed him what music notation software had become capable of. He asked me to do some orchestra sketches of cues and songs used in that film, and I've worked on every film he's done since."

Jeff Lynne, leader of the Electric Light Orchestra, was another. "I met the folks at Fogelberg's management company, and one of them, Craig Fruin, later became Jeff's manager. He got me together with Jeff about the time they were doing the *Traveling Wilburys* album at a big house in L.A. they called 'The Wilbury Mansion.' Jeff wanted to get into computers a bit and see what music stuff there was, and I helped him. I was around when he was working on the Roy Orbison *King Of Hearts* album."

"Jeff called me one night, and he really didn't want to tell me what was going on. He just said, 'Can you come over? I want to show you something.'"

A major turning point in his relationship with Lynne came in 1994 when Yoko Ono turned over to the three surviving Beatles several cassette demos her husband had recorded shortly before his death. "George suggested they send the tapes to Jeff," his fellow Wilbury. "Jeff called me one night, and he really didn't want to tell me what was going on. He just said, 'Can you come over? I want to show you something.'"

Marc was the right guy in the right place at the right time. He brought in his Mac, equipped with Opcode's *Studio Vision*, Emagic's *Logic Audio*, and Digidesign's *Pro Tools* with the *DINR* noise-reduction plug-in, and massaged the noisy cassettes, moving passages around to cover weak spots, and time-stretching and -shrinking phrases to make consistent tempos. He and Lynne overdubbed temp tracks to make sure that the cleaned-up tracks would work when the other Beatles put their parts down, and then they put Lennon's voice and piano on one track of a DAT and a click on the other and sent them back to Paul McCartney's studio in Sussex. *Free as a Bird* and *Real Love* both went Gold.

"Jeff is very creative, and the computer stuff was another tool for being creative, in music and in graphics as well," says Marc. "He is an amazing musician and a really generous man. He is a friend and mentor—I've learned so much working with him in the studio. To have his trust to ask me to help with the Beatles tracks was very gratifying." They continued to work together, and over the years Marc got to know the remaining Beatles. "Harrison would come by Jeff's, and we'd put some of his guitar on things we were working on. McCartney would come by, and we recorded him doing Buddy Holly's *Maybe Baby* for a film of the same name."

More recently, Marc played on and engineered ELO's 2001 *Zoom* album, and when Lynne decided to take out a touring band, he asked Marc to join him. "I got to do all the string arrangements for the record, and then I did the live strings, as well as keyboards and guitar," he says.

The tragic death of George Harrison from cancer in November 2001 led to another opportunity. Lynne was asked by Harrison's family to work alongside Harrison's son, Dhani, to finish production on the *Brainwashed* album. In turn, Lynne asked Marc to do some string arrangements, and Marc ended up with two engineering credits on the album as well.

When Harrison's widow, Olivia, began working on a tribute concert for her husband, she enlisted long-time friend Eric Clapton to put it together. Meanwhile, Marc had told Jeff that if he needed help, "I would do anything he wanted. Eric came by the house to talk to

Jeff about the concert and told him that Paul had agreed to sing *All Things Must Pass*. Eric said, 'How're we going to do the slide guitar and the sound effects?' Jeff pointed to me and said, 'Marc can do it.'"

The rehearsal period lasted for two and a half weeks at a hall outside of London. "I was staying at the Royal Kensington Hotel, which is just down the street from the Albert Hall," Marc says. "So one of the first days I was there, I walked over to take a look at it. It's a pretty amazing venue. And yes, I now know how many holes it takes to fill it.

"Eric isn't a man of a lot of words. If it goes well, he just turns around and says, 'Lovely.' I use a Roland *Virtual Guitar* system, and I had the sounds I thought I'd need preprogrammed. I walked into the rehearsal and told Eric I had the sounds for *All Things Must Pass*, with all the different tunings. And we did the rehearsal, and he just said, 'Lovely.'"

Since Clapton wasn't used to singing lead on Harrison's songs, having someone else take over some of the lead guitar work seemed like a good idea. "One day he turned to me at lunch," says Marc, "and said, 'Do you know the lead to *Something*?' And of course I did, since I had worn out *Abbey Road* learning it when I was a teenager. And it turned out to be something useful to know. We played through it, and Eric said, 'Well, you'll be playing that.' So whenever they needed something, I would come up with it, and they kept saying, 'Okay, give it to him.' It took some of the pressure off of him and Jeff, so they could concentrate on the singing.

> *"He showed me a few tricks and things about how he did it, and I'm thinking 'Omigod, Eric Clapton is showing me how to play like him!'"*

"One thing that made me nervous was when we were working on *While My Guitar Gently Weeps*. Eric said, 'I'm going to be singing on this, can you play all the bits?' So I said, 'Can we do it tomorrow?' And I woodshedded all night in the hotel. The next day he showed me a few tricks and things about how he did it, and I'm thinking 'Omigod, Eric Clapton is showing me how to play like him!' And then at the concert, he played an amazing solo. So full of emotion. I was also a little fluttery when Paul came by when we were doing *For You Blue*, and here I am playing the slide lead in front of him.

"We originally thought that all the different artists would have their own backups, but then it developed that we had this core band, with Gary Brooker and Chris Stainton on keys, Jim Keltner and Henry Spinetti on drums, Dave Bronze on bass, Dhani on acoustic, and Andy Fairweather-Low and me on guitars. I had been standing off to one side, but at one point Eric said about me, 'Move his amps to the middle, he's staying.' It was a fantastic time, working through George's songs. I had to pinch myself and say, like the Talking Heads song, 'How did I get here?'

405

"Olivia thanked me at one point and said, 'Hey, you're playing all the hard bits, which leaves the guys in front to concentrate on presenting and singing the songs.' It was a real honor. And Eric and Jeff said, 'We're glad you're here, you're helping us through this.' Everyone was so generous. It's really nice when you meet your heroes, and they turn out to be really nice people. They are where the fire came from for me to learn to play guitar. There's a reason they are who they are—they're just good souls."

All of those good souls put together an amazing concert. If you haven't had a chance to see the film (it only played in theaters in a few cities, but was on PBS nationally in February), it's now out on DVD, so you have no excuse. It's an uplifting, moving, exciting, and beautifully produced tribute to one of the true giants of our world. The film sound was produced by Lynne, with Marc and Ryan Ulyate getting additional mixing credits. Personally, I feel honored just to see a guy I used to hang with, up there pulling off those timeless licks. Woody Allen once said, "80 percent of success is showing up," but Marc Mann's work in *Concert for George* is proof that the other 20 percent consists of knowing what you're doing and being able to give people what they need. And if you can do that, maybe you can grow up to play lead guitar for The Beatles. At least once.

Paul Lehrman learned his first guitar solo from The Beatles' recording of Matchbox. *He misses George, too.*

Chapter 56

A Bradbury Moment
Grumpmeier Gives Up a Grudge

Preface

Here's another column that never ran in *Mix*. I wrote it early in 2006, and it's based on true events, although some of them happened to me and some to other people, and of course the names have been changed and identifying facts smeared (it's hard to pixelate, like they do on TV cop shows, in a magazine). The *Mix* editors told me they liked the piece, but they didn't feel comfortable running it. Was it because Grumpmeier turned out to have a soft, squishy side? Was it because they feared a lawsuit from whomever it was ol' Grump was talking about?

No, the real reason was far more prosaic: They didn't know why it should be published in *Mix*. After all, it had almost nothing to do with pro audio or even music. And after we argued about it for a while, I found I couldn't disagree with them. So it didn't run. I thought about trying to place it elsewhere, but then I started working on this book, and I realized it would fit well here, almost at the end.

If you've read this far, you know the characters by now. And as in any book, it's okay for the characters to, well, evolve. Because we as human beings evolve. No matter where you are in your life or in your career, how you feel about things today, even if you feel very strongly, will quite likely not be how you feel tomorrow. That's even true of my friend Grumpmeier.

I ran into Grumpmeier at my local coffee shop the other day, and he was looking mighty happy. Not that smug, self-satisfied, cat-that-swallowed-the-canary expression he often gets when he's done something shifty, but a real calm, sunny, almost Zen-like happy look, like he was actually at peace with the world.

I asked him if anything was wrong.

"Oh no," he said. "Everything's right. I had a Ray Bradbury moment last night."

What the heck is that? I asked.

"You know, Ray Bradbury the writer. *Fahrenheit 451, The Martian Chronicles...*"

Yeah, yeah, I replied, I know the writer. I read him a lot as a kid. But what the heck is a Ray Bradbury moment?

"Did you ever read a story of his called 'An Utterly Perfect Murder'?"

You killed somebody?! Jeez, Grump, I knew you had a temper, but I never thought....

"I didn't kill anybody, stupid. The story is about a guy who *doesn't* kill somebody."

All right, I give up. What are you talking about?

"Okay, the story goes like this." He settled back into one of those faux-leather almost-beanbag chairs. "A middle-aged man wakes up one day and decides he's going to travel all the way across the country, back to the town where he grew up, and shoot the guy who used to beat him up when they were both 12. And through the whole trip, all he can think about is the moment when that guy opens his door, and he gives him six quick shots to the heart. Only when he gets there, something else happens."

What happens?

"Well, before I get to that, you remember I used to be in the manufacturing side of the audio business?"

He could still jump subjects like a 16-year-old Russian girl in tights doing a triple Lutz. Yeah, what was that, 20 years ago? You had a startup with that guy with the funny name. It all sort of fell apart, and you got pretty bent out of shape.

"That's it. For a little while, we had some of the hottest stuff out there. Rock and roll stars, producers, jazzers, funk bands, film composers: They were calling us 24 hours a day trying to get their hands on our product. The only problem was, it never worked right, and the guy designing it, my partner, who unfortunately was the majority owner of the company, could never be bothered to fix anything. I was in charge of sales, which meant I had to deal with all the nasty calls. So when I realized the thing was never going to be finished, I quit."

"We should have made millions. Instead, we ended up pretty much inventing the idea of turning paying customers into Beta-testers."

I remember this wasn't one of your finest moments.

"I was really pissed off, not just because the thing was a bust, but because I thought what we had started out to do was great, plus I figured this was gonna be my one big chance to make a lot of money. My wife and I were already pricing houses out in the expensive 'burbs. We should have made millions. Instead, we ended up pretty much inventing the idea of turning paying customers into Beta-testers. Not to mention one of my dealers claimed he was the one who coined the term 'vaporware,' and it was about our stuff. I was mad at my ex-partner for years and would badmouth him to anyone who'd listen to me, and anyone else, for that matter. And I vowed never to get involved in a startup again."

What happened to his company?

"It sort of hobbled along for a little while longer, but then he had the *cojones* to sue the company that was assembling his stuff for shipping defective product. But that company wasn't dumb, and they were a whole lot bigger than he was, so they counter-sued. They showed that it was the design itself that was no good and cleaned his clock. All that was left was a bunch of ex-employees with worthless stock, a bunch of customers with useless product, and a bunch of dealers with dead inventory they couldn't return. He was not a popular guy. Even today, you mention his name to people who were around at the time, and they just laugh: 'Oh, that shmuck!'"

What happened to him? Did he ever do anything else in the audio business?

"No way. But he was a shrewd bugger when it came to money, and somehow he pulled enough out of the company to buy a vacation house and still had some left to do a dot-com startup. That crashed and burned too. But after that he ended up with a boat. Go figure. I hated him for it. I used to drive by his house every few months, hoping that it had burned down, or thinking of how I could make that happen."

So what's this got to do with Ray Bradbury?

"I'll get to that. The guy had two kids, who were little when I was working with him, but by now they're grown up. One of them turned out to be a real loser: dropped out of school, hung out with lowlifes, got involved with drugs, and a couple of years ago somebody ended up dead because the kid was stoned and did something stupid. His old man got him the best-connected lawyer he could find, but they couldn't get the kid off: He's in the state pen for a good long time."

Geez, that's terrible. Did you feel bad for his father?

"Are you kidding? I laughed when I heard about it. I figured it was the chickens coming home to roost. He deserved it."

Always count on you, Grump, to kick someone when he's down, can't I? So is that why you're so happy?

He grinned. "Actually, no. There's more. The other kid was a different story: went to college, got involved with high-tech music, and is already pretty well known around town as a composer. In fact, there was a concert of his stuff last month in a really prestigious hall. Some of my friends were in it, and it got all sorts of great write-ups in the newspapers before the event."

Did the write-ups say anything about his father?

"Yeah, one of the reporters quoted the kid as saying that his old man had invented this and that, which I knew wasn't true, but I guess that's the story he told his kids."

So don't tell me—you called up the reporter to complain.

"Of course I did!," he snapped. "Seeing that got me furious all over again. I went into all this detail about what the guy did and didn't do and how the kid had got it all wrong. But I guess I overdid it, 'cause the reporter didn't do squat about it. He probably figured I was some kind of nutcase, and I can't say I blame him."

Did you go to the concert?

He grinned again. "Wouldn't have missed it for anything. Got a ticket in the third row. And guess who was two rows in front of me? The old man, with a really expensive video camera."

You knew he was going to be there, didn't you? In fact, I'll bet you were planning to go there and confront him and say something nasty to him about his other son. Like, 'Well, one out of two isn't bad!'

"Aaah, you know me too well! Yeah, I figured I could do something like that. I was even sort of hoping the concert would be a bust, and he'd be even more embarrassed when he saw that I was there."

So was it a bust?

"No, it was really good! The kid's got talent, and the music was pretty interesting. The audience loved it, and I could see the old man was very proud."

So I guess you didn't bother to say anything to him.

"*Au contraire, mon ami*. That's when I had my Bradbury moment.

"In the story, you see, when the bully opens the door, the guy who came all that way to kill him doesn't see the bully who tortured him: He sees an old man, short, bald, bent over, who doesn't even recognize him. So he puts his gun down and walks away. He didn't have to kill the bully. Life had already done that.

"So after the concert I went up to the father with a big smile, and stuck out my hand, and said 'Hi, Fred.' And there was a look on his face—it lasted just a second, but it told me everything I wanted to know. It was fear. It said, 'I think I know this guy, and I must have screwed him somehow, and now he's come back to get me.' And after a second he realized who I was, but all he could do was croak my name. So I smiled some more and said, 'Been a while, hasn't it?' And he's stammering, so I said, 'You should be proud of your son,' and he managed to get out, 'Yeah, he's done really well,' and I gave his hand a good squeeze and walked away.

"Then I said hello to the son, who said he recognized my name because he reads *Mix*—but I don't think he even knew about my history with his father. And he was genuinely happy I had come."

So you got your revenge, eh? Is that why you're smiling?

"No, it's not revenge. It's more like...balance. That fear I saw—that someone he ripped off and ran over so long ago is going to get back at him some day—it's made him old and it's made him miserable. He ended up with all the toys, but it didn't do him any good. And when one of his kids turned into a total disaster, some part of him *had* to think that was part of the payback.

"What he did to me or anyone else doesn't matter any more. Because whatever he did, he did far worse to himself. And he's got to live with that."

"The reason I'm smiling is because I don't hate him any more. In that moment, all that stuff I'd been carrying around about him all those years just vanished—poof! He's not the devil, he's just another shlub who has to muddle through what he's made of his life. What he did to me or anyone else doesn't matter any more. Because whatever he did, he did far worse to himself. And he's got to live with that.

"But you know what? *I* don't."

He finished his latte and got up to leave, flashing that Zen-like sunny smile again. I told him I had never seen him look better, and I meant it. Nothing like dropping old baggage to make the trip lighter, I said.

"You're right. I don't need to get back at ol' Freddie. I like my life. I got my own work to do. I'm just going to do it."

He walked out of the coffee shop, whistling. He was right, of course. We all have work to do, and too many of us have old stuff that's holding us back, keeping us from doing it. But time moves on, and we don't need a lot of that stuff any more. I thought about Ray Bradbury and the guy who didn't have to shoot his old nemesis, and I smiled. And then something made me smile even more: I never knew Grumpmeier could whistle.

Chapter 57

Remembering Stephen St. Croix

My fellow *Mix* columnist, Stephen St. Croix, died on May 6, 2006. Stephen was only 58 years old. In recent years, he had suffered two (perhaps more) major motorcycle accidents, and a tree fell on his bed while he was in it, but none of those stopped him. What did stop him was cancer, which began as melanoma, and which he fought for some five years. He did, in fact, outlive by a wide margin most of his doctors' predictions. But that was hardly a surprise to anyone who knew him: Stephen always did things that were bigger than life and always confounded expectations.

Even though he was only a few years older than I, Stephen was already a huge presence in the audio industry when I first started working. In a red T-shirt, his hair down to his kidneys, he graced a gorgeous full-page ad in the very first issue of the venerable *Recording Engineer/Producer* magazine that I ever saw—June 1980—sitting in front of the mammoth Midas console in his personal (wow!) studio, looking for all the world as if he were the hyper-alert captain of a starship—an image he told me years later reflected exactly the way he felt.

In that same issue was an article he wrote called "Hassling Haas," about the ramifications of the precedence effect in the mixing process, and about how time interacts with volume and spectral characteristics to give us location information. Written in a highly friendly style, it was enormously influential over the next few years in the DSP world, especially to engineers working on digital reverb and stereo synthesis. I still use it in the classroom today, and I continue to be impressed with it, not only for the practical information it presents, but also as a shining example of how an independent researcher, without burying himself in formalized jargon, can make a major contribution to a scientific discussion.

I'm sorry he never got to finish his work restoring the notorious 18-minute gap in the Watergate tapes. I'm sure his explanation of how he did it would have been every bit as fascinating as what he actually found.

My first direct contact with Stephen was when he was preparing a review of a software product I helped to design, and which I wrote the manual for. Discussing the program on the phone as he put it through its paces, he was argumentative, demanding, and highly critical. After our final conversation, I was in a panic thinking about what his review was going to look like. But when it did appear, it was one of the most enthusiastic reviews of any audio product I had ever read. And he made special mention—which hardly any reviewer ever did—of what he referred to as "the owner's 'novel'…I read it cover to cover, and the text is actually interesting!"

It wasn't until several years later that I met Stephen in person for the first time, after I had started writing for pro-audio magazines myself. *Mix* wasn't the first magazine in whose pages Stephen and I lived next to each other: In *Recording Engineer/Producer*, he had a column called "Living with Technology," and I had one called "Managing MIDI." My writing, since I was still fairly new at this, was careful and measured and tried to make considered, persuasive arguments on a fairly narrow range of topics. Stephen's was gonzo personified and flew all over the place, sometimes hitting the nail on the head, and sometimes wandering off into areas where none of us knew what the hell he was talking about—but he always made us *want* to know. He wasn't afraid to be totally wrong—but he rarely was. He was the first writer, as far as I know, to write for any magazine in the entertainment production industry with that kind of latitude and attitude, and it was very refreshing, if sometimes a bit scary.

He wasn't afraid to be totally wrong-but he rarely was.

When we did finally meet, he was in fact about to leave *RE/P*. Mel Lambert, whose leadership had nurtured both of us (as well as many other writers), had stepped down as editor, and Stephen wasn't happy with the new regime. *Mix* had made him an offer to jump ship, and the rumor was he was going to accept it. I took it on myself—callow youth that I was—to try to convince him otherwise.

The meeting took place over breakfast at the Warwick Hotel during a New York AES conference. The conversation, as everyone who ever talked with Stephen experienced, ranged far and wide, touching on areas I had no idea he was involved with and couldn't imagine he had any knowledge of—but which I was later able to confirm he was indeed an expert in. When we finally came to the subject of why he was giving up on *RE/P*, he put down his fork and stared at me.

"You trained as a writer, right?" he demanded. I hadn't really, but I wasn't inclined to disagree at that moment. "So you think through what you write, and you're very careful to be clear and dispassionate. Well, I don't do that. I write fast and get all of it out at once and say what I feel I have to say. That's my voice. And you know what those people want to do?" he almost screamed, referring to the staff at *RE/P*.

"No, what?" I replied meekly.

"They want to *edit* me!"

I nodded and took a sip of my orange juice, and we didn't speak of it again.

A year later we saw each other again at the New York AES (there were shows every year on both coasts in those days). He was showing the DAW design he had done for Symetrix—the first such system most of us had ever laid eyes on—which crammed an entire console's functionality onto an 11-inch Macintosh monitor. It was way ahead of its time, and the screen was so dense that some wag dubbed it "The Stephen St. Croix Astigmatism Test," which he didn't like much. Though it created quite a stir, it unfortunately never made it into production, but many of the same concepts ended up in the *Paris* system Ensoniq released some years later.

On this particular occasion, I was taking a break in a hallway at the Hilton, and he came over and said hello. He spotted a famous female composer at the other end of the hall whom he knew and asked me if I would like to meet her. "Sure," I said. We walked over, and Stephen began innocently enough, "Barbara *[not her real name]*, I'd like you to meet a friend of mine, Paul Lehrman."

The woman barked, "Paul Lehrman!? I never want to hear that name again. I do *not* want to meet him!" It turns out that in my earliest writing days I had penned a rather snotty review of one of Barbara's albums for a little weekly paper in New England. I suppose in my naïveté I never thought (or perhaps cared) that she would ever see it, but that was before I knew about clipping services. I tried to look invisible as I snuck away. (Barbara and I are now good friends, by the way—I loved her next few albums and made sure I told her so.)

That same evening, I was invited by a friend to join a large group for dinner at a Japanese restaurant, one of those places where the table is sunk down so you can pretend you're sitting on the floor, but your legs have room to stretch out under it. A few minutes after the appointed hour, there was still one empty seat at the table, and I asked my friend who was missing. "Oh, we're waiting for Stephen St. Croix," he said innocently. I briefly considered extricating my legs from under the table and making a run for it, but it was too late.

Stephen arrived, immediately spotted me, stepped up onto the table, stomped over to me, and stuck his heavy-duty motorcycle boots two inches in front of my chin. He jabbed his finger at me, and at the top of his lungs in that crowded room, bellowed "Apologize!"

Of course, I had little choice. But I don't remember anything about the rest of the dinner.

I guess my favorite moment with Stephen was late in 1998 when *Mix* editor Tom Kenny got him to agree to sit down with Tom and me for a freewheeling three-way conversation, which Tom would transcribe for a special "Audio 2000" supplement that the magazine was preparing. We made a date to meet at an AES conference, but then Stephen had a change of plans and didn't make it to the show. We tried to make other dates to get together in person, but eventually, as the deadline loomed, we had to settle on a conference call. It lasted a couple of hours, and Stephen and I were very surprised to find out, despite our extremely different writing styles, lifestyles, and attitudes towards firearms and government surveillance, that we had a lot in common. Both of our fathers were doctors, both of us thought that super-high sampling rates were a waste of bandwidth, and both of us were passionate about the communicative and transformative powers of music.

He brought his oversized, fearless, judgmental, but distinctly human personality to his writing.

I can write pretty gonzo now, too, and occasionally I do. I'm not afraid to be wrong, and occasionally I am. I think I learned how to do both of these from Stephen. He brought his oversized, fearless, judgmental, but distinctly human personality to his writing and made sure we knew that what he was telling us, whatever it was and however far out in left field it came from, *meant* something. Because he cared, we were going to care, too.

Thanks, Stephen, for showing us how it's done.